AF605975

Material Culture in Anglo-America

THE CAROLINA LOWCOUNTRY AND THE ATLANTIC WORLD
Sponsored by Program in the Carolina Lowcountry and the Atlantic World of the College of Charleston

Money, Trade, and Power
Edited by Jack P. Greene, Rosemary Brana-Shute, and Randy J. Sparks

The Impact of the Haitian Revolution in the Atlantic World
Edited by David P. Geggus

London Booksellers and American Customers
James Raven

Memory and Identity
Edited by Bertrand Van Ruymbeke and Randy J. Sparks

This Remote Part of the World
Bradford J. Wood

The Final Victims
James A. McMillin

The Atlantic Economy during the Seventeenth and Eighteenth Centuries
Edited by Peter A. Coclanis

From New Babylon to Eden
Bertrand Van Ruymbeke

Saints and Their Cults in the Atlantic World
Edited by Margaret Cormack

Who Shall Rule at Home?
Jonathan Mercantini

To Make This Land Our Own
Arlin C. Migliazzo

Votaries of Apollo
Nicholas Michael Butler

Fighting for Honor
T. J. Desch Obi

Paths to Freedom
Edited by Rosemary Brana-Shute and Randy J. Sparks

Material Culture in Anglo-America: Regional Identity and Urbanity in the Tidewater, Lowcountry, and Caribbean
Edited by David S. Shields

Material Culture in Anglo-America

Regional Identity and Urbanity in the Tidewater, Lowcountry, and Caribbean

Edited by David S. Shields

THE UNIVERSITY OF SOUTH CAROLINA PRESS

Published by the University of South Carolina Press
Columbia, South Carolina 29208

www.sc.edu/uscpress

Manufactured in the United States of America

18 17 16 15 14 13 12 11 10 09 10 9 8 7 6 5 4 3 2 1

Library of Congress Cataloging-in-Publication Data

Material culture in Anglo-America : regional identity and urbanity in the Tidewater, lowcountry, and Caribbean / edited by David S. Shields.

p. cm.

Includes bibliographical references and index.

ISBN 978-1-57003-852-5 (cloth : alk. paper)

1. Material culture—Virginia—Tidewater (Region)—History. 2. Material culture—South Carolina—Charleston Region—History. 3. Material culture—West Indies, British—History. 4. Regionalism—America—Case studies. 5. City and town life—Virginia—Tidewater (Region)—History. 6. City and town life—South Carolina—Charleston Region—History. 7. City and town life—West Indies, British—History. 8. Tidewater (Va. : Region)—Social conditions. 9. Charleston Region (S.C.)—Social conditions. 10. West Indies, British—Social conditions. I. Shields, David S.

F232.T54M385 2009

307.7609757'915—dc22

2009015501

This book was printed on Glatfelter Natures, a recycled paper with 30 percent postconsumer waste content.

Contents

Acknowledgments vii

Introduction 1
David S. Shields

PART ONE—MATERIALIZING REGIONAL IDENTITY

St. Augustine: The First Century, 1565–1665 15
Paul E. Hoffman

Building for Disaster: Hurricanes and the Built Environments in South Carolina and the British West Indies 29
Matthew Mulcahy

Christ Church, Savannah: Loopholes in Metropolitan Design on the Frontier 58
Carl R. Lounsbury

The Diversity of Countries: Anglican Churches in Virginia, South Carolina, and Jamaica 74
Louis P. Nelson

Colonial Castles: The Architecture of Social Control 102
Eric Klingelhofer

Rituals of Rulership: The Material Culture of West Indian Politics 115
Natalie Zacek

L'Hermitage on the Monocacy Battlefield, Frederick, Maryland 127
Paula Stoner Reed

A Dissenting Space: Meetinghouse and Location in Early Dorchester, South Carolina 155
Jeffrey H. Richards

Charlestown to Charleston: Urban and Plantation Connections in an Atlantic Setting 170
Roger H. Leech

PART TWO—LOCATING URBANITY

A Poetics of Urban Space 191
Bernard L. Herman

Building Charleston: The Expansion of an Eighteenth-Century British Atlantic Town 202
Emma Hart

Domestic Material Culture and Consumer Demand in the British Atlantic World: Colonial South Carolina, 1670–1770 221
R. C. Nash

The Archaeological Signature of Eighteenth-Century Charleston 267
Martha A. Zierden

Changing Our Habitation: Henry Laurens, Rattray Green, and the Revolutionary Movement in Charleston's Domestic Spaces 285
Benjamin L. Carp

Raphaelle Peale's *Still Life with Oranges:* Status, Ritual, and the Illusion of Mastery 310
Maurie D. McInnis

Urban Plantations in the National City: Slavery, Republican Ideology, and Conflict on the Streets of Early Washington 328
Laura Croghan Kamoie

Contributors 353
Index 355

Acknowledgments

The writing and research for the articles in this volume were partially supported by a 2002 Collaborative Research Award of twenty-four thousand dollars by the National Endowment for the Humanities. It also received support from the College of Charleston's Division of Humanities, for which I wish to thank Dean Sam Hines. The staff of the Program in the Carolina Lowcountry and the Atlantic World—Simon Lewis and Jane Aldrich in particular—were especially helpful. Emma Hart, Bernard L. Herman, Paul E. Hoffman, Carter L. Hudgins, Laura Croghan Kamoie, William Kelso, Eric Klingelhofer, Roger H. Leech, Carl R. Lounsbury, Maurie D. McInnis, Matthew Mulcahy, Dylan Peningroth, Jonathan Poston, Jeffrey H. Richards, Robert Blair St. George, Bruce Williams, Anne Yentsch, Natalie Zacek, Benjamin Carp, and Martha A. Zierden supplied a bracing conversation on the issues raised. For the preparation of the essays in this volume, I wish to thank particularly the critical assessments of Carter L. Hudgins and Robert Blair St. George. The patience of all the contributors too is highly commendable.

Introduction

David S. Shields

Do the buildings, furnishings, manufactured objects, and equipment produced in the Tidewater, the Carolina lowcountry, and the Caribbean possess a shared signature from the days when they came into being as distinct regions? Or did the built environment in these places simply refract the forms and functions of the larger transatlantic world in the seventeenth, eighteenth, and early nineteenth centuries?

Can region be found in material culture? This last question may sound odd to students of early American culture. So much of recent material-culture scholarship posits region as a delimiting feature of study that to question its pertinence—or its conceptual integrity—seems perverse. The roll call of reputable titles demonstrates that strength of region as a frame for conceiving the ambit of material to investigate: *Folk Housing in Middle Virginia, Everyday Architecture of the Mid-Atlantic, A Building History of Northern New England, Conversing in Signs: Poetics of Implication in Colonial New England Culture.*[1] Yet one puts down these books with further questions. How stable are regions over time? How integral is the material culture within a region? How diverse? How do regions defined by material practice fit with other registers of geographic organization, such as political states or zones of commercial activity? This last question, since it requests forms of understanding external to that provided by material-culture studies, requires that the findings of more than one discipline be applied to the examination of region. To this end the Program in the South Carolina Lowcountry and the Atlantic World of the College of Charleston[2] convened an interdisciplinary symposium of scholars from the fields of history, historical archaeology, anthropology, art history, philology, geography, literary studies, material culture, economic history, and social history in the spring of 2002 to explore the intersections of material history, cultural identity, and geography in three regions that are generally recognized as being distinct, yet possessed of broad affinities in political organization, commerce, social structure, and culture: the Tidewater, the lowcountry, and the Caribbean. Participants asked whether there existed material grounds for asserting the integrity and distinctness of these three regions.

It should be confessed at the outset that one advantage of the term "region" has been the slippage it permits in one's investigation.[3] If one studies a city, a colony, a state, or a nation, there are always political-diplomatic histories of boundaries, administration, and adjudication that must be comprehended if one is to know the place.[4] Yet when one's view does not coincide with the civic focus projected in histories of polities but ranges beyond the bounds or within them to examine zones interesting because they seem to display a distinct cultural geography, one can evade the tyranny that political narratives exercise over history. Sociology, anthropology, vernacular religion, foodways, commerce, and the arts and crafts of creating the material world emerge into greater visibility.

Inquiry into regional identity always proceeds from a current belief in the existence of both the region and the identity. One legacy of the linguistic turn of cultural history has been a new sensitivity to the multiplicity of identities that can attach to a place and to the ramified senses of region, inflected by history and colored by the onlooker's perspective. Maryland might be part of a historical South, but it is not part of the Bible Belt; it might be an important component of the Tidewater, but it also is an important component of geographer Jean Gottman's Boswash "Megalopolis," that vast metropolitan area that extends from Boston to the District of Columbia.[5] A further complication to the problem is that names for regions are not historically specific markers of the articulation of a cultural identity. Nor are the circumstances of the creation of names determinative of subsequent usage or anterior applicability. "Tidewater" for instance emerged in the 1800s and 1810s, during the great era of canal construction in the early republic, to designate those parts of Delaware, Maryland, and Virginia where tidal fluctuation influences water level; it first appeared in phrases such as "the tide water district." The lowcountry became low because of the distinction made between two types of rice cultivation: highland or dry cultivation and tidal, wet cultivation. In the 1830s and 1840s the term "lowcountry" came to designate the area of the coastal plain from Wilmington, North Carolina, to the wet rice lands and islands of Georgia. In current parlance "Tidewater" has nothing to do with canals or "lowcountry" with rice production. Nevertheless no one doubts that there is some common world and history behind the terms—and that the history extends back before the names came into common usage.

The anterior applicability of regional designations has a kind of brute logic to it. Something must exist before it knows itself to exist and names itself. More than that—the utility, longevity, and potency of a name resides in its ability to attract more significance to it, to overcome the mere circumstance of its production or the moment of its minting. It lives backward as well as forward. One thinks of "the South." The phrase first appears as a geographical designation indicating the theater of war in the American Revolution superintended by Gen. Nathanael Greene.[6] It emerges as a designator for a block of states with a common political interest in the ratification debates for the Constitution. It collects a cultural, particularly agricultural, dimension in the print culture of the 1820s to indicate cultivars and practices prevailing "at the south." In the wake of the nullification crisis and in writings of numbers of cultural commentators, particularly William Gilmore Simms, it became a political identity seeking ethnogenesis. When secession created the Confederacy, the new nation did not comprehend the South envisioned by Simms and others. Karl Marx indeed viewed the Civil War as a war of southern aggression in which the Confederacy sought to invade those regions—Kentucky, Maryland, Delaware, Missouri, and New Mexico—that it believed to be part of "the South," to constitute an imagined nation in which chattel slavery would prevail. In Reconstruction "the South" named the alienated domain within the American nation occupied by federal authorities. Afterward it became a place of roughly determinate shape haunted by history, typified by racial disharmony, and dominated by agriculture. The South's ramifications in twentieth century attest to its potency. That commentators could in 2000 at one and the same time proclaim the "death of the South" and "the nationalization of southern values" indicates the expansion of the term's semantic range to extraordinary vastness.

More interesting has been the backward extension of "the South" to name the place, culture, and life of a locale before the South's existence was proclaimed. No one misunderstood Richard Beale Davis in 1978, when he wrote *Intellectual Life in the Colonial South.*[7] Nor did they doubt the utility of the regional designation as a framework for Carl Bridenbaugh's 1952 *Myths and Realities: Societies of the Colonial South,* in which he made his pioneering discrimination between three subregional cultures: the Carolina lowcountry, the Chesapeake, and the southern backcountry.[8]

Since Bridenbaugh, history has recognized that there was a Tidewater (sometimes designated metonymically "the Chesapeake") and a lowcountry. Both were distinguished politically and culturally during the latter part of the eighteenth century from a backcountry. Divisions grew up between backcountry settlers and coastal planters. The Regulator revolts in the Carolinas—when backcountry farmers (yeomen herders and truck farmers with a penchant for evangelical religion) resorted to vigilante action to stop rural banditry and then threatened the coastal oligarchy, demanding the extension of civil protections and institutional life into the interior—were paralleled by a similar "buckskin" and cavalier division in Virginia politics and cultural life.[9] This story of the political articulation of these regions can be seen as the *doxa,* the received truth that explains regional identities of colonial interior and coast. Since 1970 the revisions to this political and social history have expanded the purview of inquiry beyond the bounds of the United States to recognize the imperial frame of the eighteenth century, so the politics and culture of the West Indies is now commingled with that of the "colonial South." There is an historical warrant for this conflation; the southern customs district administered by Whitehall throughout much of the eighteenth century extended from Pennsylvania to Barbados. Furthermore the cultural focus has expanded beyond the settler population to the cultures of other populations in the regions: the various native nations and Africans, whether slave or free. The interest in regional identity and social practice remains—witness Philip D. Morgan's *Slave Counterpoint: Black Culture in the Eighteenth-century Chesapeake and Lowcountry* (1998). The Caribbean has been added to the mix as a requisite locus of investigation for proper history. Yet questions remain. Is there a material dimension to the increasingly elaborate pictures of regional character? If so, when does it emerge and under what circumstances?

Bernard L. Herman has documented that travelers in Charleston and other early American cities noted in the built environment a distinct quality, what Herman calls "presence of place."[10] Does the significant material character of a city more resemble those of found in its region than other urban ports in the Atlantic trading world? Which dimensions of a city's material culture express what is local in a locality and which speak the larger language of empire, or international taste? Do patterns of consumption define regions as much as objects made of native materials? Or is the distinction found in cities? To what extent does urban material culture differ from rural? Do they speak different dialects, such as a city cosmopolitan dialect determined by nonlocal canons of taste and conceptions of use as opposed to a country, local dialect adapted to the conditions at hand? Or does the country penetrate the city? Does the rural landscape bespeak as international a template for material goods and uses as the city? Finally does the presence of place in various locales wax and wane over time? In order to take up this series of issues, the studies in this volume focus on two matters particularly: whether, and to what degree, were transatlantic templates of material form and function adapted to local conditions, materials, and employments (that is, to what extent can one see creolization of material culture in a region), and whether cities combine the cosmopolitan and the local in their material arrangement (to what extent can cities be deemed regional)?

It is generally understand that before regionalization of cultural practices can take place in new settled areas, a process of adaptation to local conditions—"creolization"—occurs. This collection therefore begins with a case study—outside the bounds, of Tidewater, lowcountry, and Caribbean—that enables us to concentrate on the nature and degree of settler accommodation to local material, indigenous cultural practices, and environment in the first area in North America settled by Europeans—Florida. Paul E. Hoffman, the premiere historian of Spanish "La Florida" and "Guale," reviews the first century of building at St.

Augustine, examining the ways in which the residents' organization of physical space mutated with their growing intimacy with native societies, albeit with an asymmetrical dominance of Spanish practices over native.

Certain features of the American environment were unprecedented in European experience. The prevalence of hurricanes in late summer and early autumn through the Caribbean and the southeastern mainland forced settlers to create new sorts of structures for protection and to adapt customary modes of construction in coastal areas to withstand storm winds that could intensify to 130 miles per hour. In "Building for Disaster," Matthew Mulcahy examines the most conspicuous instance of a regional sort of structure purpose-built for the lowcountry and the West Indies, the hurricane shelter. He also explores the extent to which these storms generally influenced styles of building, creating a range of creolian adaptations of European forms. Within the colonies, certain structures embodied the authority of metropolitan institutions: customhouses, courthouses, magazines, fortifications, and churches. These sorts of buildings existed in part to show the face of an authority that was not just here and now but radiated potency everywhere the empire claimed dominion. Carl R. Lounsbury, architectural historian at Colonial Williamsburg, and Louis P. Nelson, from the architecture school at the University of Virginia, explore church buildings as special cases of transatlantic forms that pursue the dual purpose of conveying the look of cosmopolitan style and evincing a local sense of fitness. Both Lounsbury's "Christ Church, Savannah: Loopholes in the Metropolitan Design on the Frontier" and Nelson's "'The Diversity of Countries': Anglican Churches in Virginia, South Carolina, and Jamaica" discover a building vernacular that diverges in marked ways from the metropolitan patterns available in architectural books. Eric Klingelhofer looks at another sort of importation into the building vocabulary of the New World, the fortified house or castle. The first settlement of America took place just after the rationale for constructing castles had evaporated in France and England, and by the mid–seventeenth century, even in Ireland. The form, however, enjoyed a brief, albeit spectacular, afterlife in the Americas. Klingelhofer examines English and French instances in the West Indies and the mainland, indicating how peculiar local political conditions—situations in which "political and military power was in the hands of a few wealthy landowners"—caused an adaptation of an old feudal form to American conditions.

Klingelhofer's castles appear in a transitional moment before the consolidation of executive control and legislative representation in the colonies. Certain of the colonies were more tractable to this organization. The West Indies, because of the insular nature of each island's society, became miniature theaters of imperial authority. Natalie Zacek's "Rituals of Rulership: The Material Culture of West Indian Politics" reminds us that the intra-imperial framework that governs much reflection on the nature and extent of creolization must be supplemented by an interimperial perspective. The styles of the metropole and of other portions of the empire mattered but so too did the style of imperial rivals. This was particularly the case in the Caribbean, where the mélange of Spanish, French, Dutch, and English jurisdictions, the perpetual trade rivalries, and periodic wars and privateering adventures (with their temporary alliances) gave rise to an intimate knowledge of the trappings of rival elites and the ceremonies of authority performed by competing powers. Zacek anatomizes the practices of the English in their various island settlements and finds the ritual objects and their deployments the most traditional feature of imperial material culture.

In these studies regional variation has been measured in terms of variation from metropolitan norms. Yet the transplantation of persons and building practices from colony to colony or region to region took place on a substantial scale during the seventeenth and eighteenth centuries. By contrast the anomalous building or settlement has a way of revealing the dominant local style. In Paula Stoner Reed's "L'Hermitage on the Monocacy Battlefield, Frederick, Maryland," we encounter an extraordinary instance of a colonial French-style building erected in the wake of the Haitian Revolution in the agricultural hill country that bounds Maryland's Tidewater. Its peculiarities of form took on a symbolic function for French refugees in the early republic, for whom the French style became an asylum. L'Hermitage reminds us that within every locale there is variety and that difference in material form can proclaim dissent or isolation for the prevailing *sensus communis.* "A Dissenting Space," Jeffrey H. Richards's literary archaeology of the New England Congregationalist enclave of Dorchester, South Carolina, dramatizes the scale and organization of religiously motivated internal migration within Anglo-America. "A Dissenting Space" poses how practices of spatial comportment translate from region to region. It is particularly interesting because the settlers attempted to re-create the favored form of civic organization (the town) in a Carolina landscape dominated by plantations, with few villages and one great colonial metropolis, Charleston.

Cities have always been special cases of study for scholars of the built environment. The second part of this collection treats the cities of the Tidewater, lowcountry, and West Indies. The intimate dependence of rural habitations on local materials and vernacular fabrication practices customary to the resident population fix the material culture to the biological range of certain trees, the incidence of certain types of clay and stone, and the history of local habitation. Urban settlements were inhabited by mobile populations with multifarious ethnic and cultural backgrounds. Roger H. Leech shows how cities collected things from far as well as near. The audience for the performance of manners and style was not restricted to the local populace. The traveling merchant, the temporary placeman, the military officer, and the churchman judged residences, equipages, costume, and china with eyes practiced in metropolitan taste. Yet the residents of America's towns and cities did not simply ape London modes or Parisian manners in a game of cultural adequacy. Most knew it was a game that could not be won. Rather the performance of style, or the demonstration of material competence, was foremost an expression of a localized civility. Indeed one can see over the course of the period examined in this volume a progressive condensation of material identity—material civic signatures. Kenneth Severens in *Charleston Antebellum Architecture and Civic Destiny* has provided a map of regional identity in urban architecture.[11] Bernard Herman in *Town House: Architecture and Material Life in the Early American City, 1780–1830*—particularly in his case history of the urban fabric of Lancaster, Pennsylvania—has explained how these regional identities didn't arise out of differences of function; a merchant's house performs roughly the same task of reputation building in Lancaster, Charleston, Portsmouth, or London. Rather their symbolic significance—written in the local inflection of ornamentation, spatial arrangement, and comportment—marks the merchant as one tied to the local populace, a trustworthy participant in the community of manners and values. Just as a Carolina candidate for a seat in the U.S. Congress makes sure his drawl is heard in the back row of the meeting room, so the aspiring actors in the urban cultures of Norfolk, Savannah, Charleston, Wilmington, Kingston, and Annapolis depended on their projecting their belonging to their community; a desideratum of an early American community was to materialize a *sensus communis,* a local style, so ready determination might be made of the extent to which someone subscribed to local identity.

Yet the process by which a city articulates a local or regional identity, while still claiming the worldly amenity of a city, is by no means simple. This is particularly true when the international character of cities, as Dell Upton has shown, transforms so markedly in terms of the arrangement of streetscape and the organization of interior space in civic structures. Nor can we see the creation of an aggregate civic style—a "presence of place"—in a city, something that can be reduced to the erection of a number of landmark buildings sponsored by a resident elite and performed by a handful of designers and skilled craftsmen. The whole fabric of a city—streets, yards, buildings, common spaces, markets, docks, and air—contributes to its ethos. In Tidewater, the lowcountry, and the Caribbean, most of this fabric was assembled by African and African American laborers, the most invisible of invisible hands. To complicate our understanding of how cities took on identity further, the vast majority of what was built, particularly the commonest structures, the plainest of vernacular erections—such as pale fences, back buildings, market stalls, troughs, and frame tenements—have been destroyed. Even substantial portions of the high style, elite structures in stone and brick have been lost through war, fire, development, and neglect. So the investigation of the material condition of cities in the eighteenth and early nineteenth centuries must make use of historical archaeology and archival investigation as well as analysis of the surviving material record.

Part 2 of this collection, "Locating Urbanity," begins with Bernard L. Herman's "A Poetics of Urban Space," an exercise in theory that connects the meaning making of scholarship with the object making of artisans and builders of historic urban centers. Herman's poetics gives voice to both the ambiguity and the lyricism of common objects extracted from urban excavations—the colonoware cooking vessels exhumed in various Charleston sites in recent years. Perhaps made by African slaves, these vessels bespeak cultural experience, commercial circumstance, and domestic function in a way that enables an onlooker to apprehend the richness and density of urban life. Herman's desire to capture the meaning of cities from a poetic induction from an object to a larger ethos counters the usual tendency in historical scholarship to visualize deductively, from a map of the whole and image of the corporate civic entity.

Historical archaeology and material culture studies share the task of conceiving an account of what was and what things meant in tension with a received story. Only the archaeology of nonliterate societies enables the material record to determine the history generated about it. So the findings of material-culture scholarship operates in a dialogue with other representations, both those penned by the literate inhabitants of a place during the time of study and subsequent accounts written by commentators and professional historians. In truth the dialogue is often one sided, for historians have sometimes manifested an indifference to the findings of historical archaeology and material-culture studies.

Herman posits his poetics as an alternative to the usual analytic approach of history. Yet there is something in the scale of cities that inclines economic and social historians to view them in aggregate. Charleston in particular has drawn the attention of historians of all schools because of its ascendancy at the end of the eighteenth century to a cultural splendor and its assumption of a civic pride unrivaled in the early republic. It was, in the words of a touring man of letters, "the ne plus ultra of worldly felicity" (J. Hector St. John de Crèvecoeur, *Letters from an American Farmer* [1782]). At the same time, it housed the most exquisite cultural contradiction, for its enslaved population lived in the most miserable material circumstances until the improvement campaigns of the 1840s and 1850s. How wealthy was this city? How did its concentration of cultural capital express itself in material terms—in expansion, rebuilding, civic improvement, furnishing, and dress? What ideological or extramaterial influences determined the character of material improvements? Emma Hart's "Building Charleston: The Expansion of an Eighteenth-Century British Atlantic Town" examines three moments requisite for expansion—"the purchase of land, the financing of its development with buildings, and the actual process of construction"—marshaling an array of archival information to determine who bought land, who financed the erection of buildings and to what ends, and finally the cost of building over time. In "Domestic Material Culture and Consumer Demand in the British Atlantic World: Colonial South Carolina, 1670–1770" R. C. Nash uses probate records, inventories, and other official accountings of possessions to determine what part of the population engaged in the transatlantic market for consumer goods, how much of a family's wealth was implicated in imported commodities at various wealth gradients in society. Nash documents historical change in consumption patterns, marked by a shift in who participated in the international market over time. Nash notes the difficulty of gauging wealth for two categories of expenditures: clothing and food. In "The Archaeological Signature of Eighteenth-Century Charleston," Martha A. Zierden, chief archaeologist of the Charleston Museum, provides concrete evidence on the latter. Her findings about the diet (derived from remains of food preparation and consumption) and tablewares for all classes of Charlestonians, provide important information about consumption unavailable in any written source.

Benjamin L. Carp in "Changing our Habitation" muses over the peculiar social, ideological, and stylistic disjunctures attending the Revolution as played out in a host of domestic settings in Charleston. Unlike the scenes of New England class warfare described by Robert St. George, in which artisans attacked the high-style houses they built for Tories,[12] both the patriot and loyalist leaders were invested in sumptuary gentility. The patriots feared the British would encourage slave uprisings, so it was the anti-English households that stood under threat. And the patriot city elite did not fear the urban masses so much as the upcountry yeomanry—the sons and daughters of the Regulators who had threatened Charleston a generation previously. So despite the changes in government and political rhetoric, an urban culture of material preeminence remained the style of the patriot leaders who controlled the city after the Revolution.

The nexus of republican politics, elite connoisseurship, and artistic expression is explored by Maurie D. McInnis in "Raphaelle Peale's *Still Life with Oranges:* Status, Ritual, and the Illusion of Mastery." As with Herman's essay, which explores Charleston by poetic induction from a colonoware vessel, an artifact of vernacular, low culture, McInnis explores Charleston by poetic induction from a painting, an object of high culture created for John A. Alston. In a virtuoso reading of the image, McInnis shows how it asserts an illusion of master over sumptuary excess. In the process it re-creates the bibulous, extravagant world of planter table hospitality, and the sorts of mechanisms of social control needed to enact it. The painting becomes one of an array of objects that reinforces a practice and image of bon-ton vivacity.

Having explored the political and material valences of post-Revolutionary Charleston, the chief metropolis of the lowcountry, the volume concludes by examining the chief metropolis of the Tidewater and the capital of the new republic, Washington, D.C. Urban geographers have for a generation recognized the way the plan of the District of Columbia emerged from a vocabulary of urban organization, as revealed in John W. Reps's landmark study, *Tidewater Towns*.[13] Laura Croghan Kamoie explores a new dimension of the city's debt to regional practices, documenting how many of the buildings constructed in Washington City were urban plantations, predicated in design upon a hierarchical organization of space and material function inscribing the slave system in brick, stone, and wood. Kamoie uses this material history to interrogate the republican symbolism deployed in the city's civic structures and in its design, and she enriches the deep sense of contradiction that surrounds the city. Is it northern or southern? It is southern. Is it republican or feudal? Not republican. In sum material culture is married to political and cultural history to exemplify a new sort of narrative understanding of the past.

One leaves off reading these essays assured that there was indeed a material component to the construction of Tidewater, the lowcountry, and the Caribbean, yet nothing so simple as a signature. Certain features of the built environment conveyed "presence of place," and those interested in regional or local branding emphasized these in their writings or in their material declarations of participation in a culture. (Having a joggling board on a Charleston piazza is a form of flag waving.) Yet other features belonged to a more general transatlantic language of styles and functions. The mixture of general lexicon and local dialect, universal function and local application, is perhaps the expected signature of colonial scenes of culture and provincial expressions in a world in which style-setting is determined by metropolitan arbiters. What ultimately engages attention are the quiddities, the specific things, the peculiar expressions that vivify life in locales, and how they speak and mean to those in the neighborhood. Then one encounters life, in all its concrete piquancies, in the material record.

Notes

1. Henry H. Glassie, *Folk Housing in Middle Virginia: A Structural Analysis* (Knoxville: University of Tennessee Press, 1975); Gabrielle M. Lanier and Bernard L. Herman, *Everyday Architecture of the Mid-Atlantic: Looking at Buildings and Landscapes* (Baltimore: Johns Hopkins University Press, 1997); James L. Garvin, *A Building History of Northern New England* (Boston: University Press of New England, 2002); Robert Blair St. George, *Conversing in Signs: Poetics of Implication in Colonial New England Culture* (Chapel Hill: University of North Carolina Press, 1998).

2. For the mission and history of CLAW see http://www.cofc.edu/atlanticworld/index.html.

3. Region is a category of interest to many academic disciplines. Material-culture studies and cultural history might benefit from examining a current sociological theorization in John Allen, Gill Court, Doreen Massey, Allan Cochrane, and Julie Charlesworth's

discussion of southeastern England, *Rethinking the Region* (London: Routledge, 1998). Geography taxonomizes realms, regions, and states. For the current conceptualization of region in the discipline, see H. J. DeBlij and Peter O. Muller's standard college textbook, *Concepts and Regions in Geography* (New York: John Wiley & Sons, 2004), 4–8.

4. One thinks of the political, ideological, and theological considerations that supplement the material-culture investigations in, for instance, Dell Upton's *Holy Things and Profane; Anglican Parish Churches in Colonial Virginia* (New Haven: Yale University Press, 1997), or Abbott Lowell Cummings's *The Framed Houses of Massachusetts Bay, 1625–1725* (Cambridge, Mass.: Belknap Press, 1998).

5. Jean Gottman, *Megalopolis: The Urbanized Northeastern Seaboard of the United States* (Cambridge, Mass.: MIT Press, 1964).

6. See my discussion of the history of the designation in "Literature of the Colonial South," *Resources in American Literary Study* 19, no. 2 (1993): 11–59.

7. Richard Beale Davis, *Intellectual Life in the Colonial South, 1585–1763*, 3 vols. (Knoxville: University of Tennessee Press, 1978). A more recent, and no less ambitious, synthesis of the region's intellectual history from 1810 to 1860, Michael O'Brien's award-winning *Conjectures of Order*, 2 vols. (Chapel Hill: University of North Carolina Press, 2004), presumes the integrity of the intellectual culture for that period immediately before and during the creation of the South's sectional identity within national politics.

8. Carl Bridenbaugh, *Myths and Realities Societies of the Colonial South* (Baton Rouge: Louisiana State University Press, 1952).

9. Marjoleine Kars, *Breaking Loose Together: The Regulator Rebellion in Pre-Revolutionary North Carolina* (Chapel Hill: University of North Carolina Press, 2002); George Lloyd Johnson Jr., *The Frontier in the Colonial South: South Carolina Backcountry, 1736–1800* (Westport, Conn.: Greenwood Press, 1997); Richard Maxwell Brown, *The South Carolina Regulators* (Cambridge, Mass.: Belknap of Harvard University Press, 1963).

10. Bernard L. Herman, *Town House: Architecture and Material Life in the Early American City, 1780–1830* (Chapel Hill: University of North Carolina Press, Omohundro Institute of Early American History and Culture, 2005), 2–7.

11. Kenneth Severens, *Charleston Antebellum Architecture and Civic Destiny* (Knoxville: University of Tennessee Press, 1988), 19–24.

12. St. George, "Attacking Houses," chap. 3 in *Conversing in Signs.*

13. John W. Reps, *Tidewater Towns: City Planning in Colonial Virginia and Maryland* (Charlottesville: University Press of Virginia for the Colonial Williamsburg Foundation, 1972).

Part One

Materializing Regional Identity

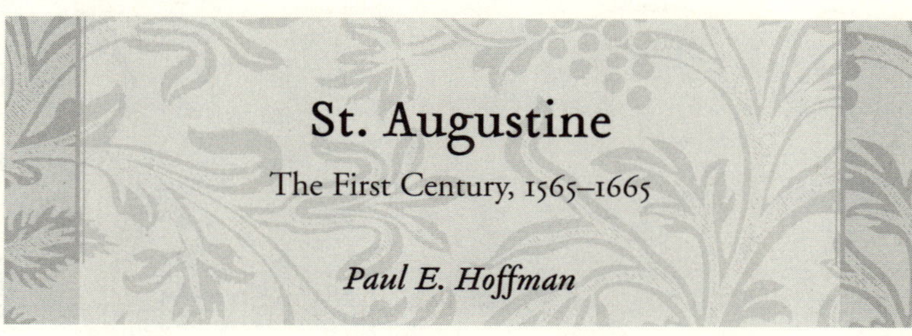

St. Augustine

The First Century, 1565–1665

Paul E. Hoffman

Spanish La Florida was never a staple colony and so presents a setting for addressing three questions: first to see if a creole hybridity existed in Spanish La Florida; second to see if urbanism operated as a cosmopolitan cultural force that helped retard the development of a creolized built environment; and third to see what legal, economic, religious, or social forces may have constrained the material expression of a purely local, perhaps "American" material culture. Of these questions, the last will receive only indirect attention.[1]

Webster defines "creole" from the original Portuguese as a person of European ancestry born outside of Europe who preserves some of her ancestral speech and culture. In south Louisiana and other parts of the area of the American African diaspora such people may also have African ancestry.[2] As used here, the term has its broad sense of persons and cultures with European ancestries but varying admixtures of other peoples and cultures, and in particular such hybrid peoples and cultures as are found in the Americas.

The material practices of the Spaniards in La Florida closely mapped their political claims, especially in St. Augustine.[3] A part of St. Augustine's social history involved the incorporation of Native American women as wives and of Indian men and women as laborers and domestic servants. The result is that St. Augustine has an archaeological record in which Spanish objects and ways of organizing physical space were socially dominant, while Indian ceramics and foodways were socially defined as secondary in importance even though they were actually numerically dominant in the material culture of the town.[4]

St. Augustine today may be in its third location. The first was Cacique Seloy's long house and a number of rectangular structures constructed with a west or east-of-north orientation on what are today the grounds of the Fountain of Youth property about a mile north of Castillo de San Marcos (see figure 1).[5] A second St. Augustine, or at least the second and third forts and associated

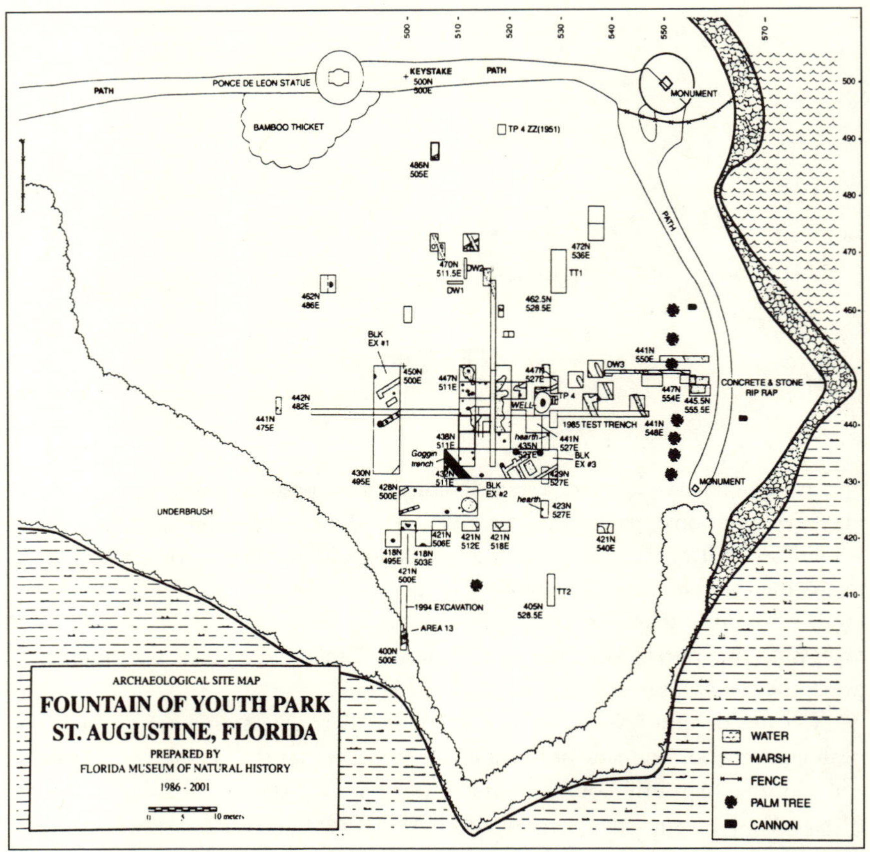

Fig. 1. Archaeological site map, Fountain of Youth Park, St. Augustine, Florida. From Jamie L. Anderson, "2001 Excavations at 8SJ31—The Fountain of Youth Park Site, 1565 Spanish Campsite," Florida Museum of Natural History, Gainesville, *Miscellaneous Reports in Archaeology*, no. 54 (2002): 17, fig. 5

barracks, was built on Anastasia Island circa 1566 and occupied until at least 1570.[6] The present town apparently was laid out circa 1572.

The Baptista Boazio engraving of Sir Francis Drake's raid of 1586 (see figure 2) rather schematically shows a town that consists of a core grid of six blocks that are twice as long, north-south, as they are deep, east-west. Three additional blocks south of that core are smaller, whether because the engraver ran out of space or because they were so in fact. A church ("O") is on the southeast corner of the cleared space north of the town, and the "town house" ("M")—almost certainly a fort—is on the western side of the same open area or plaza. Studies undertaken in the 1970s demonstrated that four small blocks that are south of the modern plaza once consisted of four lots (fifty by one hundred pies or forty-four by eighty-eight modern feet) of the exact dimensions ordered in 1563 and the 1572 Ordinances of Colonization for "peonia" or commoners' lots.[7] Post-1586 rebuilding of the town has obscured the two blocks to the north, but archaeology has shown evidence of the streets that would have defined them (see figure 3).[8] This core area is also where sixteenth-century ceramics are found.[9] Areas immediately adjacent to the six-block core also have sixteenth-century materials, more or less fitting the rest of the Boazio engraving.[10]

The fit of the plaza to the Ordinance of Colonization is more problematic. Boazio suggests that an informal plaza probably existed prior to the laying out of a formal plaza in 1598.[11] Both Boazio's open space and what is known of the 1598 plaza conform to the order that in a port town the plaza should open to the waterfront and have major civic buildings on its sides. Because of modern buildings archaeologists have not been able to examine the area between Artillery Lane and the modern plaza to determine if the three northern blocks of the original grid fell there (unlikely) or if Artillery Lane was the edge of the 1586 plaza. What

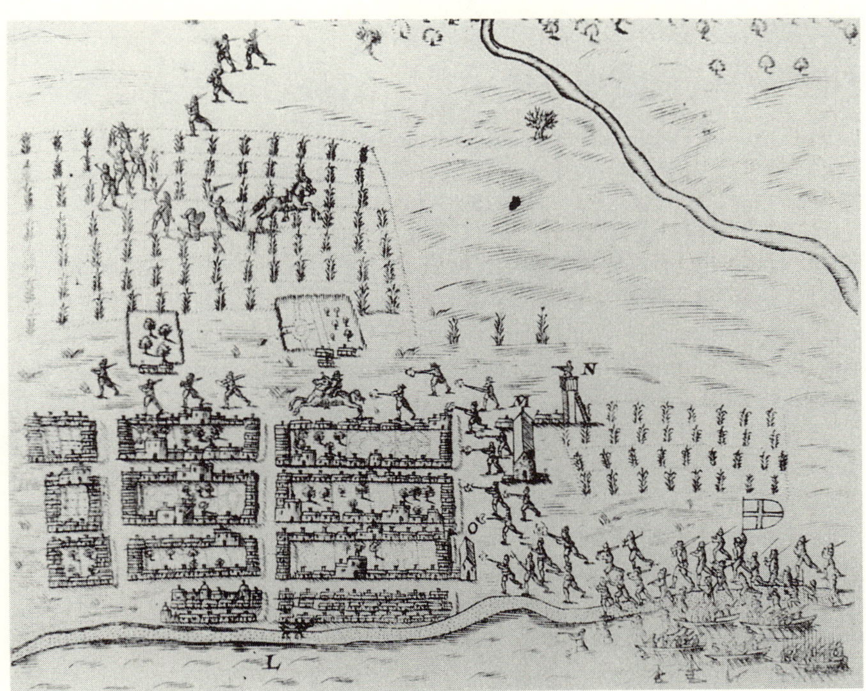

Fig. 2. The Boazio engraving of *Drake's Attack on St. Augustine,* 1586 (section). From Albert Manucy, "The Physical Setting of Sixteenth Century St. Augustine," *Florida Anthropologist* 38, nos. 1–2, part 1 (March–June 1985): 36, fig. 2

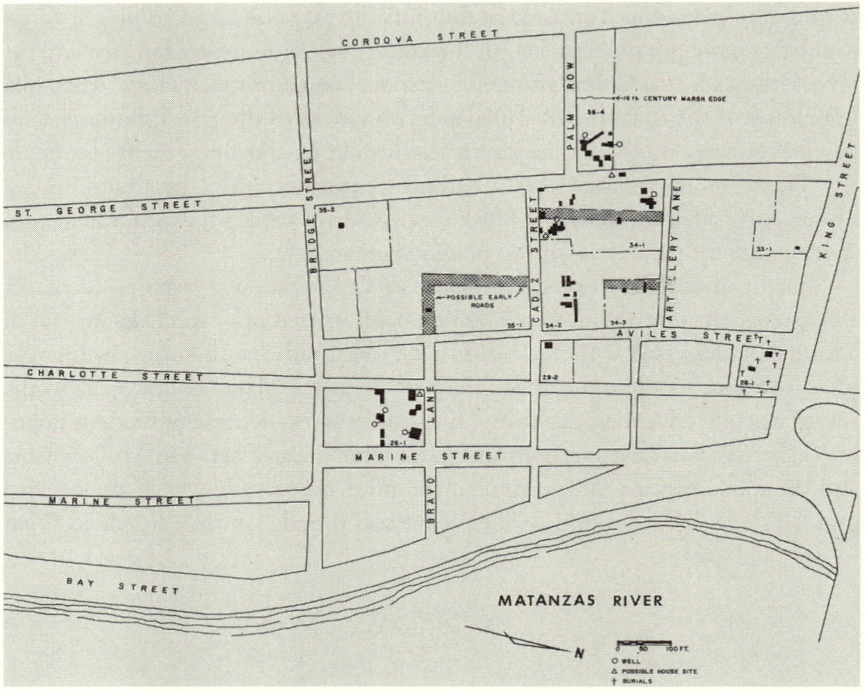

FIG. 3. Locations of excavations and features in the sixteenth-century settlement of St. Augustine, Florida. From Kathleen Deagan, "The Archaeology of Sixteenth-Century St. Augustine," *Florida Anthropologist* 38, nos. 1–2, part 1 (March–June 1985): 10, fig. 2

can be said is that the space between Artillery Lane and the north side of the current plaza would allow a water-front plaza of two hundred Spanish feet (pies), east-west, by three hundred Spanish feet, north-south, or some other combination of the 1:1:5 ratio decreed in 1563 but oriented with the long axis to the west (like the modern plaza).[12]

A partial map from circa 1595 shows that in the rebuilding after Drake burned the town, the 1586 plaza was invaded by structures seemingly placed at random except along the water's edge (see figure 4).[13] The creation of a formal plaza in 1598 undoubtedly eliminated some of that randomness, but the present street pattern (first mapped in 1737) shows that over the intervening centuries the residents of St. Augustine laid out additional streets and blocks without regard to the original grid, although they seem to have preserved the idea of the basic town lot and did preserve the general idea of a rectilinear street pattern.

That is, modern St. Augustine still shows the marks of the grid tradition of urban layout that was found throughout the Spanish American empire and that was ordered by the decrees of 1563 and 1572. The modification of that pattern after 1586 is a mark of the weakening of metropolitan influences, of the rise of creole Floridano dominance, and of adaptation to the local geography as well as other, presently unknown factors.[14] That adaptation likely was well advanced by 1665. In sum, a creole hybridity of sorts is evident in the street pattern of St. Augustine.

A final note on urban design: St. Augustine got its walls between 1708 and 1721, first across its northern approaches and then along its western side.[15] However, by then it had largely assumed the shape it retained for the rest of the colonial era.

As to the houses, Boazio's rendering, the 1595 description by Fray Andrés de San Miguel, the crude drawings on the map of the same year, and Kathleen Deagan's finding of daub and post molds provide such evidence as there is. In 1595 the city was newly rebuilt after Sir Francis Drake had burned it in 1586. The houses at that date were of rectangular European plan and framed in wood set

Fig. 4. A section of a c. 1595 map of San Agustin. Spain, Ministerio de Educacion, Cultura y Deporte, Archivo General de Indias, Sevilla, Mapas y Planos, Florida y Luisian, 3

into the ground or attached to wooden sleepers in trenches. Each house had a long side on the street, just as is common in all Spanish villages.[16] Deagan has shown that in the eighteenth century the north walls of houses had no openings against the winter's cold, while a loggia or arbor sheltered the south walls and their doors from the summer's heat. There were no chimneys; in the Andalusian manner, such winter heat as was wanted came from a charcoal brazier.[17] In design, then, houses in St. Augustine were pure southern Spanish except that ordinarily they did not have entrances directly from the street.

The poor with Andalusian origins (a majority of the Spanish population) probably used thatch to cover both the sides and roofs of their pole-framed structures until they could join persons with more means in the use of wattle-and-daub walls with thatch roofs. The wealthy, mostly of northern Spanish origins, used squared timbers for the house frames and vertical boards nailed to horizontal supports set between the framing beams, perhaps with wattle and daub between the beams to serve as insulation. According to Father San Miguel, all of the houses were built of boards, but the archaeological evidence of wattle and daub suggests that is not correct, or was not before Sir Francis Drake burned the town in 1586. It must be said that the archaeology is too chronologically imprecise to clarify if there was an evolution of building techniques. Such an evolution seems doubtful because in 1763, when Elixio de la Puente made his property map of the town, there were still wattle-and-daub and wooden structures as well as masonry ones that date after James Moore's destruction of the town in 1702. The use of "flat" roofs covered with lime-cement, documented for Santa Elena after 1576, is not known for St. Augustine. The church of circa 1595 was built in the same way as were the houses of the wealthy.[18]

The late Albert Manucy thought that many of the basic framing and thatching techniques used in the pre-1586 town(s) were probably Indian because that population was more familiar with the local materials.[19] If that is true, then the non-board-sheathed buildings were actually creole hybrid constructions incorporating European squared design, a mixture of European and native ideas about and techniques for framing, and Native American thatching and material selection (see figure 5). The use of wattle and daub could have come from Native Americans, Spaniards, or Africans because all three peoples used it (see figure 6). The board-sheathed structures were purely European in design and technique (see figure 7). Since they predominated until masonry construction began after 1702, they are another sign that the Spanish, urban, built environment showed a strong adherence to European norms even though creole constructions such as the wattle-and-daub houses were present as well.

So little is known about the placements of windows and other openings and the lengths of eves and existence or not of porches that no statement can be made

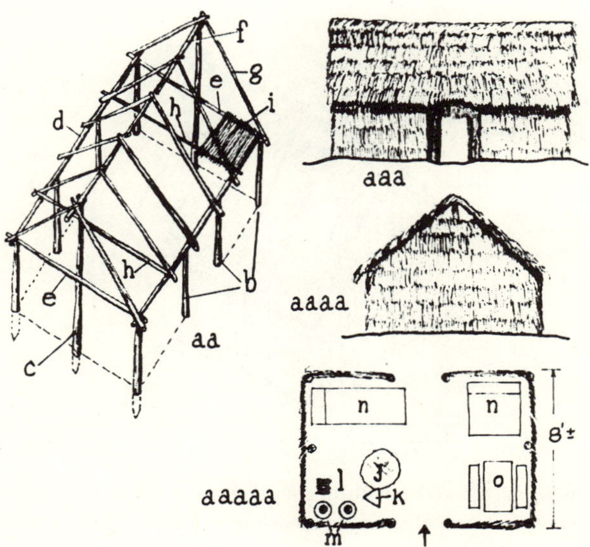

Fig. 5. House and plot plan for the home of Francisco González, drummer and town crier; aa: primary framing, b: wall posts, c: roof post, d: roof plate, e: tie beam, f: ridgepole, g: rafter, h: joist, i: loft floor (canes); aaa: eastern elevation; aaaa: southern elevation; aaaaa: floor plan, j: hearth, k: stool; l: fuel for hearth, m: food jars, n: bunks, o: table and benches. Courtesy of the St. Augustine Historical Society

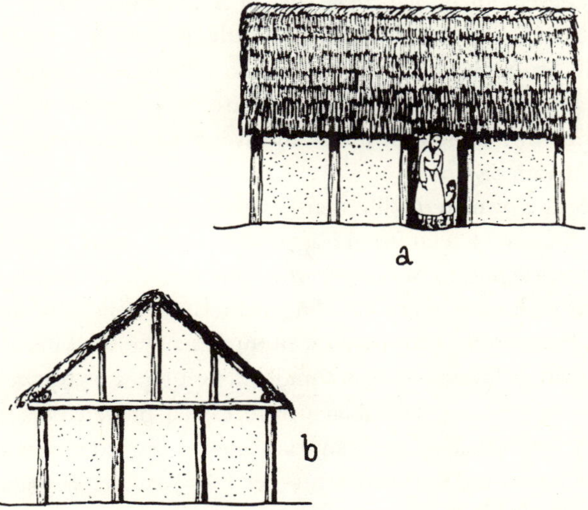

Fig. 6. Plot plan for the home of Juan Calvo, settler, farmer, and soldier; eastern (a) and southern (b) elevations of a 12 × 6 foot wattle-and-daub house. Courtesy of the St. Augustine Historical Society

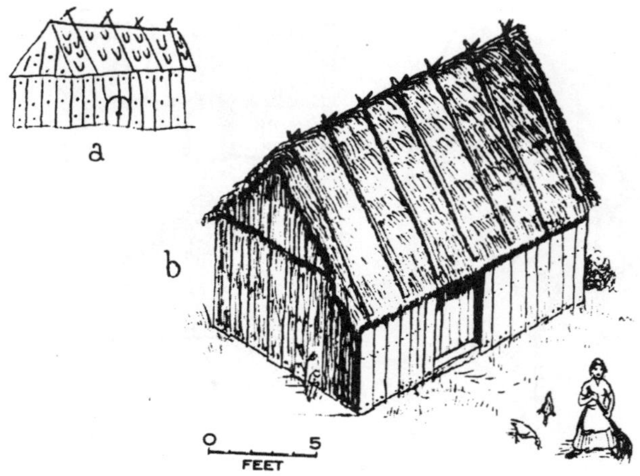

Fig. 7. A settler's house; a: map sketch with an arched entry that is not right for a board-walled house; b: an interpretation of the sketch showing a single-story house with vertical-board walls nailed to a timber frame, a palm-thatched gable roof, and pole hold-downs. Courtesy of the St. Augustine Historical Society

about a pre-1665 development of a creole style of architecture such as was appearing in the Caribbean. The late eighteenth- and early nineteenth-century buildings one sees today in St. Augustine in some cases do represent a Caribbean-derived creole style. Examples such as the Arrivas house fuse the Spanish one-story masonry tradition with Caribbean porch and wood construction ideas possibly having western African origins.[20]

The other feature of material life that has been extensively studied for early St. Augustine is the use of ceramics. Deagan and her students routinely classify all pot shards as belonging to Stanley South's "kitchen group" because they are mostly associated with trash pits (including abandoned wells) that also contain bones discarded from meals. Chinese export porcelain, eleven types of majolica, thirteen types of other European wares, and thirteen types of Native American wares constitute the ceramic assemblage from closed provenances of the five sixteenth-century sites that have been excavated.[21] Including unidentifiable shards, majolicas constitute 6.16 percent, other European wares make up 38.97 percent, and local aboriginal wares (four types) constitute 48.71 percent of sixteenth-century ceramics. The remaining 6.16 percent of the shards are non-local aboriginal wares (nine types) reflecting trade with the Guale and other, unidentifiable peoples. Among "other European wares," olive jar shards are the most numerous (81.55 percent; that is, 3,155 shards of 3,869) and rank second (at 31.78 percent) behind the St. Johns and San Marcos aboriginal shards in the overall assemblage. Clearly the residents of St. Augustine in the sixteenth century depended on imported olive jars for storage and locally made Native American wares for the majority of their other needs, especially for cooking.[22]

Deagan found that this predominance of Indian ceramics, especially with evidence of their use in cooking, "increased in intensity through time" from an average of 48.71 percent (54.87 percent if nonlocal Indian ceramics are included) in closed sixteenth-century provenances to 66 percent in those of the seventeenth century and 76 percent in those of the eighteenth-century.[23]

In another indication of the rise of a creole, hybrid material culture, Deagan found that four circa 1763 house sites chosen to reflect documented rising incomes and increasingly higher social status as measured by distance from Native American parentage[24] showed a decreasing percentage of Indian ceramics as wealth, with a rise in "Spanish" ethnicity and status (from 92.22 percent of all kitchen items to 47.9 percent) and a corresponding increase in majolicas (2.61 percent to 16.9 percent), Hispanic coarse earthenware, and glassware.[25] That is, the distinctively local or creole pattern of ceramic usage first evident in the late sixteenth century had continued and become a permanent part of the material culture of the town. "Spanishness," status, and wealth were publicly marked by more frequent use of majolicas and other ceramics of European types even as all social strata depended on Indian ceramics for day-to-day use in the kitchen.

The evidence of high usage of aboriginal ceramics, especially for cooking, is the material counterpart of the fragmentary documentary evidence for the formation of an increasingly mestizo, or creole, society in St. Augustine during the late sixteenth and early seventeenth centuries. Indian women were the wives of common soldiers in late sixteenth-century St. Augustine and constituted about 70 percent of the sixty or so wives in the town of the early seventeenth century. With time the percentage of Indian wives seems to have decreased as more of the married women were locally born of people best described as "Hispanic"—that is, creoles with some Indian ancestry but probably fewer Indian physical features as, over time, locally born women married new levies of Spanish soldiers sent to reinforce the garrison. However, Native American wives did not entirely disappear.[26]

Africans were present in the town from 1580 onward, but so little is known about them or most aspects of the local culture that no observations can be made about their influences on the material or any other aspect of the culture of St. Augustine in 1565–1665.[27] It seems likely that their main contribution was labor. Only with the advent of fugitive slaves from the Carolinas in the late seventeenth century did blacks become numerous enough to have a cultural impact, and even that is unknown.

Datable Sixteenth- to Early-Seventeenth-Century Ceramics (Non–Native American Types)

TYPE AND PLACE OF MANUFACTURE	FIRST DATE	LAST DATE
Majolicas		
Caparra blue (Spain)	1490	1600
Columbia plain (Spain)	1490	1650
Fig sprigs / San Juan polychrome (Mexico)	1590	1650
Ichtucknee blue on white (Spain)	1600	1650
Isabela polychrome (Spain)	1490	1580
Ligurian blue on blue (Italy)*	1550	1630
Mexico City white (Mexico)	1575	1650
San Luis blue on white (Mexico)	1575	1650
Seville blue on blue (Spain)*	1550	1630
Santo Domingo polychrome	?	?
Yayal blue on white (Spain)	1490	1625
Non-Hispanic Ware		
Brown Cologne stoneware	1530	1600
Chinese porcelain†	1550	?
Coarse Earthenwares		
Feldspar inlaid redware	1530	1600
Green Bacín / Green Lebrillo	1490	1600
Mexican red painted	1550	1750
Olive jars (early, to 1570; middle, 1560–1800)	1560	1800
Orange micaceous	1550	1650
Redware	1500	1750
Storage jar	1500	1800
Yucatán colonial earthenware	1570	1650

*Listed as Ichtucknee blue on blue in Kathleen Deagan, "The Archaeology of Sixteenth Century St. Augustine," *Florida Anthropologist* 38, nos. 1–2 (March–June 1985), 11, table 1, but here divided as indicated in Kathleen Deagan, *Artifacts of the Spanish Colonies of Florida and the Caribbean, 1500–1800* (Washington, D.C.: Smithsonian Institution Press, 1987), 63–64, 70.

†End date varies with type.

Source: Deagan, "Archaeology of St. Augustine," 11, table 1.

Regarding costume or clothing, because the accounting records of Spanish Florida seem to have disappeared for the years after 1617, little can be said about what sorts of clothing Spaniards used after that date. However, for 1565 to 1617 good records exist. They show various styles of European clothing in use among the Spaniards.[28] There is no documentary evidence that the Hispanic population adopted Indian styles or items of dress or modified the costume norms of the Spanish world to fit local conditions. Probably access to the markets of Mexico and Spain (via Havana and Mexico), social conservatism, and an intention to appear other than Indian account for this and most other retentions of Spanish material culture even when it was less functional than that of Native Americans.

In sum, wherever Spaniards were in La Florida during its first century, they used certain signs in the built environment and public displays of ceramics of European design, decoration, and clothing to mark their status and identity even as they were heavily dependent on Indian building techniques for their structures and on utilitarian wares for the actual preparation and storage of foods. That is, the degree of hybridity was limited. The Spaniards' village of St. Augustine likely provided enough cosmopolitan cultural force to keep them from a more extensive creolization of their material culture.

Answers to the three original questions can be posited. First, did a creole hybridity exist in La Florida? Yes, in limited ways. Second, did urbanism operate as a cosmopolitan force to retard the development of a creolized built environment? Again the answer appears to be yes, although the force of metropolitan laws clearly diminished after 1586. Third, what legal, economic, religious, or social factors constrained the material expression of a purely local, "American" material culture? On this issue the answer seems to be that such factors were at work, but their influence must be largely conjecture. The strength of Spanish village life evident in the built environment and an apparent preference for Spanish-style ceramics as individuals rose in status can, however, serve as proxies for the influence of these other factors. It can be shown that the presence of Indian women in St. Augustine helps to account for the predominance of Native American ceramics in cooking contexts and gave rise to a population and pattern of ceramic usage that was "creole" in the varying meanings that word came to have in areas where there were no Africans.

Notes

1. The question of cultural formation in Spanish La Florida is complicated because the Spanish frontier in La Florida was by definition an inclusive, incorporating frontier unlike the excluding Anglo-American frontier pioneered in Virginia in 1634. This meant that for the entire century under consideration, 1565–1665, perhaps 95 percent to two-thirds of the people in the colony were Native Americans, the percentage declining over time. For them, La Florida was defined as a relationship of a paramount people, the Spaniards and

their Hispanicized mestizo, African, and mulatto coculturalists, and subordinate but independent peoples: themselves. Thus the material culture of La Florida has two arenas, but only the Spanish one qualifies as "creole."

2. In a clear case of the use of material culture to mark political and social lines, within the mission villages the mission churches and rectories and even the kitchens of the friars followed European rectangular patterns, setting them apart in a visible symbolism of connection to the secular paramounts of the land. That visual symbolism was more important than the fact that many of the (early) churches were pole-framed wattle and daub construction with thatch roofs, following Native American building traditions (although there seem to have been pole-framed, thatched structures in Spain as well). The later, larger churches were probably timber framed and board sheathed in the Spanish manner. In the same way, Spanish ceramics (and later ceramics made locally but to Spanish patterns) seem to have been almost exclusively used by the resident friars, with Indian utilitarian wares numerically dominant on mission grounds as well as in the villages. See David Hurst Thomas, "The Archaeology of Mission Santa Catalina de Guale: Our First Fifteen Years," in *The Missions of La Florida,* ed. Bonnie G. McEwan (Gainesville: University Presses of Florida, 1993), 9, 12–19; and in *Florida Anthropologist* 44, nos. 2–4 (1991): 110–17. See also other essays in these volumes.

Yet by a twist, the friars' own custom of having housekeepers and female cooks became, with but little amplification, a means of identifying their high status *in Indian terms.* High-status Indian males had traditionally had more than one wife. Forbidding that, some friars appropriated the symbol by filling the rectories and their kitchens with serving, cooking, and cleaning women. At least that was the case with one "abusive" friar in the 1680s (Archivo General de Indias, Santo Domingo 226, no. 105, Lockey Collection, Library of Congress per microfilm at P. K. Yong Library of Florida History, University of Florida, Gainesville; Paul E. Hoffman, *Florida's Frontiers* [Bloomington: Indiana University Press, 2001], 165–66).

3. Kathleen Deagan, "The Archaeology of Sixteenth Century St. Augustine," *Florida Anthropologist* 38, nos. 1–2 (March–June 1985): 7–8, table 1 (11–12), showing 41.4 percent European ceramics and 50.7 percent aboriginal ceramics from five sixteenth-century sites (percent of total artifacts), 19, 29.

4. Jamie L. Anderson, *2001 Excavations at 8SJ31—The Fountain of Youth Park Site, 1565 Spanish Campsite* (Gainesville: Florida Museum of Natural History, Miscellaneous Reports in Archaeology, no. 54, [2002]), fig. 5 (p. 17), 69; courtesy of Dr. Kathleen Deagan.

5. Eugene Lyon, "The First Three Wooden Forts of Spanish St. Augustine, 1565–1571," unpub. manuscript on file at St. Augustine Research Foundation, Inc., Flagler College, St. Augustine, Fla., 1997, as noted in Gifford J. Waters, *1997 Excavations at the 8SJ34/ Nombre de Dios Site: Florida's First Spanish Fort* (Gainesville: Florida Museum of Natural History, [1998]), 4. See also Albert C. Manucy, *Sixteenth-Century St. Augustine: The People and Their Homes* (Gainesville: University Presses of Florida, 1997), 28–30.

6. "Ordinances for the governing of areas to be conquered in the Indies," Segovia, July 13, 1563, in *Colección de documentos inéditos relativos al descubrimiento, conquista y organización de las antiguas posesiones españoles de América y Oceania, sacadas de los archivos del reino y muy especialmente de Indias,* 42 vols. (Madrid: Real Academica de la Historia,

1864–84), 8:519–20; also in Dora Crouch, Daniel Garr, and Axe Mandingo, *Spanish City Planning in the New World* (Cambridge, Mass.: MIT Press, 1982).

7. Paul E. Hoffman and Eugene Lyon, "A Preliminary Report on the Layout of St. Augustine, Florida, ca. 1580" (January 1976, report filed with the St. Augustine Restoration Foundation, copy in collection of the author); Albert Manucy, "The Town Plan for St. Augustine 1580" (June 1977, report filed with St. Augustine Restoration Foundation, copy in collection of the author); Deagan, "Archaeology of St. Augustine," 10 (fig. 2), 13.

8. Kathleen Deagan, John Bostwick, and Dale Benton, "A Sub Surface Survey of St. Augustine City Environs 1976" (Tallahassee: Florida State University, 1976), figs. 4, 7, copy in collection of the author.

9. Of particular note are the three houses shown west of the first row of blocks south of the plaza. Excavations at "Palm Row," SA 36-4, have turned up sixteenth-century materials whose location corresponds to the structures shown. The De Leon site, SA 26-1, falls within the small southeastern small block in Boazio's nine-block grid. It too has sixteenth-century materials and post molds from an eighteen-by-twelve-foot wooden post building. See Deagan, "Archaeology of St. Augustine," 10 (fig. 2), 13.

10. Archivo General de Indias, Santo Domingo 224, Gonzalo Méndez Canzo to Crown, St. Augustine, February 23, 1598.

11. Hoffman and Lyon, "Preliminary Report," [4, 12, 18 (map)].

12. Archivo General de Indias [hereafter cited as AGI], Mapas y Planos, Florida y Luisiana 3.

13. AGI, Mapas y Planos, La Florida y La Luisiana, no. 40; Antonio de Arredondo, "Plan de la ciudad de Sn. Agustin de la Florida," Havana, May 15, 1737 (reproduced in Verne E. Chatelain, *The Defenses of Spanish Florida, 1565–1763* [Washington, D.C.: Carnegie Institution, 1941], map 10); Manucy, "Town Plan," 8–10.

14. Amy T. Bushnell, *The King's Coffer: Proprietors of the Spanish Florida Treasury, 1565–1702* (Gainesville: University Presses of Florida, 1981), traces the rise of the Menéndez Marqués family. Deagan, "Archaeology of St. Augustine," 13; and Kathleen Deagan, *Spanish St. Augustine: The Archaeology of a Colonial Creole Community* (New York: Academic Press, 1983), 247, note another spacial regularity: that wells are set twelve to fifteen meters (sometimes more) back from the street edge, reflecting a sort of "idealized Iberian spatial template" ("Archaeology of St. Augustine," 13).

15. Chatelain, *Defenses of Spanish Florida,* 84–85.

16. Boazio's rendering and excavations at SA-26-1 show this.

17. Deagan, *Spanish St. Augustine,* 109.

18. Manucy, *Sixteenth-Century St. Augustine,* 51 (San Miguel), 70, 77, 79, 85–88, 42–48 (drawings of probable houses); AGI, Mapas y Planos, Florida y Luisiana 3, St. Augustine, c. 1595; Deagan, "Archaeology of St. Augustine," 13, 16 (fig. 8); Deagan, *Spanish St. Augustine,* 26–27. Manucy, *Sixteenth-Century St. Augustine,* 113, argues without any evidence that "firepoof tabby must have become the preferred reconstruction material" after 1586.

19. Manucy, *Sixteenth-Century St. Augustine,* 52. On the other hand, the use of pole-framed, thatched structures was common in rural Andalucia, so that is an alternative source for construction techniques.

20. Jay Edwards, "Architectural Creolization: The Importance of Colonial Architecture," in *Architectural Anthropology,* ed. Mari-José Amerlinck (Westport, Conn.: Bergin & Garvey, 2001), 83–120; Jay Edwards, "In Praise of the Porch and Other African-American Contributions to America's Vernacular Architecture," in *Raised to the Trade, Creole Builders of New Orleans* (New Orleans: New Orleans Museum of Art, 2002). See also Peter Mark, "'Portuguese' Architecture and Luso-African Identity in Senegambia and Guinea, 1730–1890," *History in Africa* 23 (1996): 179–96.

21. Deagan, "Archaeology of St. Augustine," 11–12 (table 1). For the subsurface survey, findings of aboriginal St. Johns wares (to 1670), the Spanish majolicas Columbia plain (1500–1650), Ichtucknee blue on blue (1550–1640), Santo Domingo blue on white (1550–1630), orange micaceous ware (1550–1650), and Mexican redware (sixteenth century onward) were used to delimit the sixteenth-century part of town. Given the wide temporal spread of manufacturing for these wares, the dating is not certain.

22. Deagan, "Archaeology of St. Augustine," 19. The percentages may be biased by the large size of olive jars and aboriginal storage and cooking jars, all of which would break into more shards than smaller ceramic objects such as majolica plates and bowls.

23. Deagan, "Archaeology of St. Augustine," 19.

24. A Guale woman and a Mexican soldier, likely a mestizo (Maria de la Cruz site, 91–132 pesos annual income, SA-16-23); a criollo soldier (de Hita site, 264 pesos income, SA-7-4); a criollo officer (Ponce de León site, 480 pesos income, SA-36-4); and a Spanish official (Avero site, >590 pesos income, SA-7-5). See Deagan, *Spanish St. Augustine.*

25. Deagan, *Spanish St. Augustine,* 236–40, 242. She found that a statistical study showed that the sites are essentially the same except for the frequency of coarse earthenware and possibly majolicas but concluded that the generalization remains correct that high usage of Indian ceramics is characteristic of all social statuses in eighteenth-century St. Augustine and, as would seem obvious given cost factors, especially so for those who were poorer, that is, mestizo or Hispanicized Indian.

26. Hoffman, *Florida's Frontiers,* 54, 75–76 (forty-two of sixty wives were Indians or mestizos in 1607), 116, 141–42.

27. Ibid., 70. Four women came in 1580 with Doña María de Solís, wife of Governor Gutierre de Miranda. Thirty men and women (mostly men) arrived in 1583 to work on the fort; they had been in Havana working on that fort. Deagan thought that black slaves may have had a role in the production of colonoware during the eighteenth century (Kathleen Deagan, *Artifacts of the Spanish Colonies of Florida and the Caribbean, 1500–1800* [Washington, D.C.: Smithsonian Institution Press, 1987], 104).

28. Eugene Lyon, *Richer Than We Thought: The Material Culture of Sixteenth-Century St. Augustine,* a complete number of *El Escribano* 29 (1992), publishes several personal property inventories from 1566, lists of supplies sent from Spain in the 1570s, and other lists that include cloth and clothing prior to the 1580s. For gifts given to Indians and trade goods in 1611, see Hoffman, *Florida's Frontiers,* 102. We know that gifts were given after that, but we do not have any lists.

Building for Disaster

Hurricanes and the Built Environments in South Carolina and the British West Indies

Matthew Mulcahy

In his 1740 *New and Exact Account of Jamaica,* Charles Leslie warned readers and potential travelers to the island, "One is not to look for the Beauties of Architecture here." The island's public buildings "are neat, but not fine," Leslie wrote, while "the Gentlemens Houses are generally built low, of one Story." In Jamaica's towns there were "several Houses which are two Stories, but that Way of Building is disapproved of, because they seldom are known to stand the Shock of an Earthquake, or the Fury of a Storm."[1]

This essay explores the impact of hurricanes on architecture in Jamaica and the other colonies of the British Greater Caribbean—defined here as a region stretching from Barbados through South Carolina—during the seventeenth and eighteenth centuries. Historians of early America have long emphasized the importance of climate in shaping the architecture of the Greater Caribbean, particularly in the island colonies. Most have focused on colonists' responses to the tropical and semitropical heat of the region, highlighting the adoption of open floor plans and jalousie windows to facilitate the circulation of air, the development of piazzas and verandas to provide shade, and the elimination of unnecessary chimneys and fireplaces. In the region these accommodations contributed to the development of distinct creole house forms that represented a compromise between colonists' desire to replicate English cultural forms and the reality of the American climate. However, as Charles Leslie's brief comments suggest, climate involved more than temperature. Natural disasters, hurricanes in particular, also influenced architectural developments in the Greater Caribbean.[2]

The colonies of the Greater Caribbean shared a number of important social and economic characteristics, including large-scale plantation agriculture, extremely wealthy planter elites, and African slave majorities. They also shared experience with hurricanes; in the eyes of contemporaries, these colonies formed a well-defined hurricane zone.[3] Throughout the seventeenth and eighteenth centuries, hurricanes routinely leveled houses, churches, towns, and plantations, and the widespread devastation pushed colonists to rethink some of their basic ideas about the buildings they constructed. Beginning in the middle decades of the seventeenth century, many residents attempted to erect buildings they hoped would better withstand powerful storms. The most significant adaptations involved reducing the height of buildings and altering the materials used in construction. Some colonists also built specific structures—hurricane houses—to shelter themselves in the midst of a tempest. In addition, by literally sweeping away older buildings, hurricanes acted as a force of "creative destruction" and presented colonists with opportunities to rethink and redesign the layout of cities and plantations.[4]

These changes contributed to the emergence of a distinct built environment in the Greater Caribbean, one that routinely elicited commentary from observers such as Leslie. The impact of hurricanes, however, varied across the region. Architectural adaptations appeared most pronounced in the island colonies and were least visible in South Carolina. Indeed, despite several major storms in the eighteenth century, South Carolinians made relatively few accommodations to the threat from hurricanes, reflecting both different social and environmental conditions in the mainland colony and different perceptions of the relative danger from the storms. Even in the West Indies hurricanes did not completely transform building practices. Several factors—including experience with other disasters, immigration of new colonists who had no experience with hurricanes, and the desire among many to follow metropolitan fashions—at times mitigated the influence of hurricanes. Nevertheless, colonists could not ignore the frequent and widespread devastation wrought by hurricanes, particularly in the sugar islands, and over time experience with the storms helped shape a landscape that reflected, on the one hand, the basic mimetic desires of colonists to re-create the world they had left behind and, on the other hand, the realities of a new American environment that posed unique challenges to British notions of form and function.[5]

English colonists learned of the dangers posed by hurricanes to their dwellings almost immediately. Sir Thomas Warner and a small group of colonists established the first permanent settlement in the region on the island of St. Christopher (now called St. Kitts) in 1624. To claim title to the land and secure their possession, they erected a small fort and a few rudimentary shelters modeled after Carib Indian dwellings. John Smith wrote that colonists employed palmetto trees "to build Forts and houses, the leaves to cover them." Other accounts described early buildings in the Leeward Islands as "weak structures, which are sustain'd only by four or six forks planted in the ground, and instead of walls are encompass'd and palizado'd only with reeds, and cover'd with Palm or Plantane-leaves,

Sugar-canes, or some such material." These huts offered little resistance to hurricane-force winds. Smith reported that nine months after landing on St. Kitts, "upon the nineteenth of September came a Hericano and blew it [the new settlement] away." Less than two years after rebuilding their infant settlement, a second storm swept across the colony and again "blew downe all our houses." If these early shelters offered little protection against hurricanes, they did have the benefit of being rebuilt quickly. By the 1630s some colonists had learned enough to recognize that the collapse of dwellings posed their own dangers. John Taylor's account of a 1638 storm in the Leeward Islands stated that terrified colonists fled their houses and sought shelter in "holes, Caves, pits, Dens, and hollow places of the earth . . . which places are good harbours and defences against the Hurry-Cano."[6]

As soon as they could, colonists sought to replace these huts and to construct more substantial houses that better approximated the buildings they had left behind in England. The failure to develop a staple crop, and by extension an income that could pay for imported tools and materials, however, meant that colonial housing remained rudimentary for the first few decades of colonization. One Barbados planter named Thomas Verney wrote to England in 1639 that he was building "a sorry cottage" to house the servants he had purchased. Visitors described buildings in Barbados in 1643 as "mean, with things only for necessity." Most of these dwellings were likely either puncheon buildings constructed by driving posts directly into the ground and nailing boards across them or "hole-post" buildings that involved digging specific holes for the corner posts of the building and burying them at a set depth, which gave the structures a greater degree of uniformity. Wooden posts buried in the ground, however, rotted quickly, and some colonists replaced such dwellings with mortise-and-tenoned frame houses by employing horizontal sills laid across a foundation of wooden blocks or stones. Still, many visitors remained unimpressed by the dwellings they found in the region. George Ellwood reported to the Royal Society in 1672 that "ye buildings [on Nevis] are poore much like to a Hogstie in England."[7]

These basic, two- and three-room structures almost certainly remained the dominant house form in the region throughout the seventeenth and eighteenth centuries. As late as the mid–eighteenth century even some relatively prosperous pen farmers in Jamaica lived in three-room houses with mud-mortared walls. However, as planters and merchants began to amass more significant fortunes following the shift to sugar production in the mid–seventeenth century, they began to replace this "impermanent architecture" with larger, more substantial, and more ornate edifices. As they did, they looked to English designs and styles for inspiration. England underwent something of a revolution in house building during the seventeenth century, moving from "medieval modes of design" to a "Renaissance style." Important characteristics of this new style, most visible in urban areas and on gentry estates, included the increased use of brick and stone; greater symmetry in the placement of rooms, doors, and windows to create a classical appearance of balance and order; the incorporation of sash windows; a greater number of rooms; and increased height: three- and four-story buildings became common in towns and cities throughout England.[8]

Wealthy colonists incorporated many of these innovations into their own buildings beginning in the latter decades of the seventeenth century. In the major port cities, colonists constructed three and four-story structures modeled on English urban dwellings. Visiting Port Royal, Jamaica, in the 1680s, John Taylor found "600 well built brick houses, and many built with Timber; the houses are built four story high, covered with Tile, and glaised with Sash Windows." Taylor noted that in nearby Spanish Town, recently constructed brick buildings were "as lofty and butifull as our Buildings in London." Hans Sloane, another late seventeenth-century visitor to Jamaica, found that the colonists' houses were "for the most part Brick, and after the English manner." The governor of Barbados reported that streets of Bridgetown in the latter part of the seventeenth century exhibited many "very fair houses, some of brick, but most of stone." Other travelers noted that "the houses are well built in the English style." Large, multiple-story structures emerged in rural plantation areas as well. A French priest, Father Labat, visiting Barbados in 1700, found that the "houses on the plantations are much better built than those of the towns." Two extraordinary examples of grand seventeenth-century plantation houses still stand on the island, although they have been altered: Nicholas Abbey in St. Peter's Parish and Drax Hall in St. George's Parish. The former, with its curvilinear gables, reflects the Dutch influence in mid-seventeenth-century Barbados, while the latter, a double house with a multigabled roof, provides a vivid illustration of colonists' efforts to copy European designs and details in their dwellings.[9]

These two houses have withstood centuries of hurricanes, but most buildings in the region did not. Hurricanes routinely leveled the most substantial private dwellings and public buildings throughout the colonies. The 1681 storm in St. Kitts left Christopher Jeaffreson's dwelling "miserably torne, and flat with the ground." Following the 1712 hurricane in Jamaica, colonists faced "the most Melancholy and dismal Prospect, many houses in the Towns, as well as in the Plantations blown down, others uncovered, and none without some Damage." Seventeen people were crushed to death when the walls of a plantation house in the Scotland district of Barbados collapsed during the 1675 hurricane. The storm "levell'd with the Ground" houses throughout the island, and "the best Planters in the Island liv'd in Hutts."[10]

In addition to strong winds, floodwaters and storm surges, particularly in low-lying areas and in coastal port cities, regularly threatened structures. One account from Port Royal stated that during the 1722 hurricane, "Waters sapping the Foundations, gave continual and just Apprehensions of the Houses falling, as in effect half of them did, and buried their Inhabitants." Other accounts reported that dwellings in the town "were tumbling about the People's Ears, and burying many of them under the Ruins, so that they could neither go into the Streets, nor stay in their Houses with any Safety." A tempest in 1780 inundated the town of Savanna-la-Mar in western Jamaica with a "terrible swell of the sea, which, by afternoon, increased to such a degree, that it has not left the wreck of six houses on both the bay and Savanna and not less than 300 people of all colours were drowned or buried in the ruins." Hurricanes in South Carolina routinely flooded the streets of Charleston.[11]

Strong winds and storm surges damaged or destroyed all sorts of buildings in the colonies, but "English style" structures appeared especially vulnerable. Colonists in Jamaica discovered that the dwellings built by the Spanish prior to the English conquest in 1655 often withstood the worst storms while their own structures crumbled. An account of the 1722 hurricane in the *Weekly Jamaican Courant* found it "remarkable" that the houses built by the Spanish "suistain'd very little damage" during the storm, despite being among the oldest on the island. Edward Long, writing in 1774, noted that at least fifty preconquest buildings remained in Jamaica and that "their duration for so long a time in defiance of earthquakes and hurricanes, some of which, since the English settled here, have been so violent as to demolish several more modern buildings, is a demonstrative proof of the Spanish sagacity." He found the buildings "excellently well contrived" to guard against the "sudden concussion of earthquakes, [and] the impetuosity of hurricanes."[12]

Spanish houses were not the only structures that remained standing while the colonists' houses collapsed. One eighteenth-century visitor to French Guadeloupe reported to the Royal Society that he was shocked to find "the most solid buildings tumble down; whilst the villages of the little huts of the negroes stood unhurt." Charles de Rochefort noted that some colonists sought out "the little Huts built by Negroes" during the height of a storm. "It hath been found by experience, that these Huts, being round and having no place open but the door . . . are commonly spared when the highest houses are remov'd from one place to another, if not quite overthrown by the impetuous agitation of the winds raising this Tempest," he wrote. Charles Leslie likewise wrote that some Jamaican colonists "retire into the Huts of the Negroes, which are built exceeding low, and elude the Shocks of the Tempest." Slave houses, small outbuildings, and Spanish dwellings, of course, did not always stand up amidst a hurricane's fury, but the frequency of comments about them suggests that these "weak" structures may have survived as well as any other building in the colonies.[13]

Contemporaries offered several explanations for the surprising durability of these structures. Rochefort implied that the short, circular dwellings presented less surface area for the wind to strike; the winds deflected around them, whereas the square, flat-fronted houses colonists built acted as sails, catching the winds. Although Rochefort did not note it, the loose construction of the walls and the thatched roofs may have allowed the interior and exterior air pressures to equalize, whereas tighter walls acted as a barrier and eventually collapsed under pressure. Observers offered different explanations for the durability of Spanish structures. One seventeenth-century commentator in Jamaica suggested that Spanish houses "are but one storie height Becas of the Harrie Cane, for he doth many times com and giue them a vissit." Edward Long believed that the strength of Spanish houses reflected both their overall design and the materials employed in their construction. The houses had wooden posts, six to eight inches in diameter, buried in the ground at a depth of two to three feet. The Spanish colonists constructed these posts from the hardest available wood ("lignum vitae, brazilletto, or fustick"), which was then "well-seasoned and hardened in smoak." They stacked bricks between the posts and covered them with mortar. Wooden rafters, also "hardened in smoak," formed the roofs. Smoked canes were tied together with the bark of mangrove trees to cover the rafters. The whole was then covered first with mortar and then with pantiles, which made the roofs strong and thick. Such covering contrasted with the thin wooden shingles used on most English houses[14] (see figure 1).

Whatever the merits of such structures, English colonists had little desire to imitate Spanish or Carib forms and techniques as they set about building their settlements. The latter appeared too primitive, and English colonists viewed the former as either too small or too ugly. Writing in the 1680s, John Taylor compared Spanish houses in Jamaica unfavorably to barns and noted with disgust that the doors were so wide that "three Horsemen may ride in abreast." Long suggested that Spanish-style houses were "inconveniently small" and that many colonists preferred to erect "lofty houses after the models in the mother-country." English colonists let the Spanish buildings decay or converted them into stables and warehouses.[15]

Despite colonists' reservations about non-English structures, the widespread devastation wrought by hurricanes on Jamaica and elsewhere in the region forced many to rethink some of their basic ideas about buildings, and they slowly took steps to reduce their vulnerability to the storms. The most important and notable change reduced the height of structures from three and four stories to one and two stories. As early as the 1660s Rochefort wrote that in the English (and French) islands, "there are many very fair houses of Timber, Stone, and Brick, built after the same manner as those in their own Countries, save that for the most part they are but one or two Stories high at the most, that they may the more easily resist the winds, which sometimes blow in those parts with extraordinary violence." According to John Oldmixon, Barbadians who survived the

Fig. 1. View of a Spanish building. From Edward Long, *History of Jamaica* (London: T. Lowndes, 1774), 2:19–20, pl. 7. Courtesy of Thomas Cooper Library, University of South Carolina, Columbia

August 1675 hurricane "were afraid to run up their Houses to any Height" and instead "lower'd their Buildings" in the aftermath of the storm. The churchwardens in St. Michael's Parish decided one year after that storm to tear down the remains of the almshouse and to "build it up again one story high with as much conveniency and room as now it hath." The governor of the Leeward Islands reported to London in 1676 that in Charleston, Nevis, there were "good dwellings and storehouses, built with the country timber, not exceeding 60 feet long and 20 broad, story and a half, the 'Hurri-Canes' having taught the people to build low."[16]

The height of buildings continued to reflect the threat from hurricanes throughout the eighteenth century. An anonymous sailor traveling in the mid-eighteenth century wrote that St. John's, Antigua, contained "upwards of 500 houses pritty well built, tho low on acct. of the hurricanes." Janet Shaw, who arrived in Antigua following the 1772 hurricane, noted that many dwellings were "low and seem to crutch [ed. crouch] as if afraid of a second misfortune." John Luffman agreed, noting in 1786 that the houses "are for the most part low, on account of the hurricanes and earthquakes." A 1746 map provides some illustrations of Kingston houses from the period in which Leslie was writing. Although two stories, the houses are relatively short, especially compared to Taylor's description of earlier dwellings in Port Royal or some of the taller urban town houses being erected in other parts of British America during this period.

Changes to the height of buildings occurred fitfully over time, but by the middle of the eighteenth century the reduced height of dwellings had become a distinguishing feature of island architecture.[17]

Colonists also came to believe that low-profile roofs offered the best defense against hurricanes. One visitor to the Danish islands (which were culturally English) in the 1760s noted that "few houses have more than two stories and most of them are one-storied. Because of storms, roofs are low." Lower roofs usually meant hipped rather than gabled roofs, which colonists believed offered less resistance to the winds. Both roof forms were common in the colonies in the seventeenth and eighteenth centuries, but experience with hurricanes often pushed colonists to abandon gables in favor of hipped roofs. The 1780 hurricane crushed the "lofty gables" of William Senhouse's house on his Grove Estate in Barbados, and when Senhouse rebuilt the mansion house, he ordered "Hipping the roof in order to resist with more effect the force of any future Hurricane." Senhouse noted further that use of "gables have since [the hurricane] in a great measure been abolished in Barbadoes." Likewise, after the gable ends of the curing house collapsed on William FitzHerbert's Turners Hall plantation during the same storm, the overseer informed FitzHerbert that he was "flatting the roof of the Curing House." It is unclear if this resulted in a hipped roof or a truly flat one, but considering the importance of having some pitch to allow runoff, it seems likely that "flatting" meant some form of hipping. Roofs in the islands also exhibited relatively little ornamentation: domes or cupolas were rare, as were dormer windows because of their vulnerability during storms. One visitor to Barbados in the early nineteenth century wrote that "the houses, devoid of ornament, and without chimnies, conveyed the idea of barns."[18]

Beyond changing the height and roofs of buildings, some colonists altered the design and shape of their dwellings. In the aftermath of the 1780 storm, a chastened William Senhouse was determined to erect a building better suited to the vicissitudes of the West Indian climate. In addition to eliminating his gabled roof, he rebuilt "in a better stile and on a larger scale the windward wing of the Grove House, making the Eastern end of it circular." This contributed "no less to the strength than, at the same time, the beauty of the building," Senhouse wrote later in his memoirs. Other colonists sought to strengthen their houses by extending the galleries used to shade dwellings around the entire house. The Moravian missionary C. G. A. Oldendorp wrote that colonists in St. Croix did so to "give the buildings a bigger foundation and thereby make them more resistant to the winds of storms."[19]

Colonists rethought the materials they employed in constructing their edifices as well. Timber served as the primary building material throughout the region during the early seventeenth century. As the population grew and plantation agriculture expanded, colonists exhausted local supplies and increasingly relied on shipments of wood and other building materials from the mainland colonies. Timber remained important throughout the eighteenth century, but beginning in the 1660s many who could afford to do so turned to brick and stone for their buildings, in part because they believed that these materials could better withstand hurricanes. A Quaker traveler named George Welch reported that in Nevis the "houses comonly of late [1671] are built of Stone, and but one Story high, flatt at Top" because of the storms. The Reverend Robert Robertson in Nevis advocated the use of brick and stone following a 1733 hurricane, noting that "such Buildings wou'd prove a better Security against Storms than any we can make of Timber." A survivor of the 1772 hurricane on Antigua wrote that despite widespread damage to his plantation, "the new stone building, containing the Offices, stood it very well & was of great service." During that storm the governor of the Leeward Islands rushed his wife into a "low, strong, stone Building, near the principal Habitation, which being built of Wood, I thought insufficiently secure." Even those who could not afford to construct an entire house of brick or stone sometimes built one wall of brick and then used timber for the remaining walls, as happened on St. Christopher at the end of the seventeenth century.[20]

Brick and stone, however, did not prove a panacea for residents of several colonies that were faced with another natural hazard: earthquakes. All the colonies of the Greater Caribbean experienced earthquakes during the seventeenth and eighteenth centuries, but the threat, and the corresponding influence on architectural decisions, was most pronounced in the Leeward Islands and Jamaica. Hans Sloane wrote that earthquakes were so frequent in Jamaica that residents expected at least one a year. The island suffered perhaps the most devastating disaster in the region's history when the town of Port Royal sank into the sea during a 1692 earthquake. The Leeward Islands experienced a similar calamity in 1690 when an earthquake destroyed numerous buildings in Charleston, Nevis. An eighteenth-century minister on the island wrote that during his five-year stay, he experienced at least a dozen earthquakes, although they were all minor.[21]

Some residents in the Leeward Islands began to build with stone by the middle of the seventeenth century in response to the threat from hurricanes, but experience with earthquakes pushed them to rethink their decisions. A 1672 earthquake in Montserrat destroyed all the stone houses on the island but left the timber ones standing. The governor reported that colonists had previously constructed "some stone buildings, but the earthquakes having thrown them all down, they build with timber only except the boiling-houses for sugar, which in part must be built of stone." During the 1690 earthquake, "all the Houses in Charles Town that were made of Brick or Stone, dropt a sudden from the Top to the Bottom in perfect Ruins. Those that were made of Wood were no less violently shaken, but stood." The problem with brick and stone was their rigidity.

As one Nevis resident explained following the 1690 calamity, "the Rivetings of wooden Structures are far stronger, and are not so easily disjoynted as the Co-augmentations of Cement and Mortar." Many observers suggested that the presence of so many stone houses in the Leeward Islands contributed to the level of destruction wrought by the earthquake. Accounts of the Port Royal disaster likewise noted that "heavy buildings were everywhere destroyed." When a minor tremor struck Jamaica in 1688, Hans Sloane worried about the "Danger in being in an high Brick House" and tried to escape outside as quickly as possible.[22]

Colonists in the Leeward Islands and Jamaica thus faced an unenviable choice: they could build stone buildings that could (theoretically at least) better withstand hurricanes but would crumble during an earthquake, or they could risk building with timber and having the houses destroyed in a tempest. Individual colonists made their own decisions about which disasters posed the greatest risk as they set about constructing their dwellings. In his mid-eighteenth-century history of Jamaica, James Knight suggested that the Spanish viewed hurricanes as the greater threat and designed their buildings accordingly, implying that the English should as well. By contrast, one visitor to the region in the 1780s reported that "the dread of earthquakes . . . induce many people to build their houses very slight, and chiefly of wood." Robertson argued that stone was the best choice for structures in the Leeward Islands. He noted that some might object because of the threat from earthquakes, but he dismissed that idea, arguing that earthquakes resulted in relatively little damage, "whereas many a Life has been lost, and infinite other Damage done by the Fall of Houses in a Storm." Some colonists compromised by constructing dwellings with masonry or stone foundations or ground floors, on top of which they placed wooden frames.[23]

In addition colonists gradually learned to equip their houses with strong storm shutters, latches, hinges, and bolts to cover and secure windows and doors. Robertson wrote that "our Inhabitants wou'd do well to be constantly provided with strong wooden Bars, and to have Iron Hooks and Staples always ready fix'd at their Doors and Windows, into which to pin down those Bars on the Outside of the Houses." Bolting doors and windows before a storm provided greater security for the structures, according to Robertson, because once a door had been blown open and "the Wind enters, and fills the House, and whirls about within it, if the Doors and Windows on the opposite Side are not set open to give it instant Vent, the Roof is in Danger of being carry'd off at once." The South Carolina planter Henry Laurens likewise warned his estate manager Loveday, who had not experienced a hurricane, to "have Bars of strong Wood ready to fasten in all your Windows, keep every Article liable to Damage six inches off your Floors. and nothing so low as the common Surface of the Earth in the Cellars. these you must expect to be brim full, your House and Outhouses overflowed your fences blown down. __ prepare against the worst while the Weather is fair." One eighteenth-century traveler noted that when the signs of a hurricane appeared in the West Indies, "proper precautions are then taken to avoid the fury of the winds; the houses are propped, the windows and doors are barred up, and papers and other valuable moveables are secured in chests." Many colonists hoped that the combination of informed design, sound materials, and commonsense precautions would provide a degree of security against the storms, although they knew ultimately that such efforts offered only minimal protection.[24]

Hurricanes also influenced the construction of slave dwellings on some plantations, particularly at the end of the eighteenth century. Despite Rochefort's comments about circular slave buildings in the seventeenth century, most slave dwellings in the region were small rectangular huts with wattle-and-daub walls and thatched roofs. Slaves usually built their own houses and resisted planter interference. Planters, however, provided the materials used in the houses, and there is some evidence of increased planter intervention into their design by the end of the eighteenth century, in part due to experience with hurricanes. On the Codrington plantations in Barbados the estate's overseer managed the project of rebuilding slave houses following the 1780 hurricane. Another Barbadian planter, Philip Gibbes, offered several suggestions for the design of slave houses a few years after the storm: "No Negro House, not built of Brick or Stone, should be wider than ten Feet . . . Houses are weaker in proportion as they are wider, & less able to resist High winds." He also believed that "the Roofs of Negro Houses are all much too flat" and recommended that they "should be Hipped—not have gable ends." It is not known to what extent these suggestions were put into practice, but clearly hurricanes had become a factor some planters took into consideration on their plantations.[25]

Alterations to dwelling houses represented one response to the danger posed by hurricanes. Other colonists constructed special storm shelters, or "hurricane houses," into which they and their families could flee during a major storm. The earliest evidence of hurricane houses comes from the Leeward Islands. Following a French invasion of the islands in 1706, residents of Nevis and St. Christopher sought compensation from the British government for stolen and damaged property. As part of the process, they filed claims listing their specific losses. Many of the St. Christopher estates (the Nevis claims have been lost) noted damage to hurricane houses. These were long, rectangular, wooden structures—although few claims describe houses as "thatched and cain'd round," suggesting that sugarcane trash and leaves tied together formed the walls—that were built low to the ground. Significantly, some descriptions of hurricane houses mention "posts," indicating that these structures followed the older building pattern of sinking wooden posts into the ground.

On some estates the hurricane houses were almost as big as the main dwelling houses. Thomas Joseph had a three-room house measuring thirty-four feet by sixteen feet whose value he listed as £250, along with a "Hurry Cano house" measuring twenty-six feet by thirteen feet and valued at £12. These larger hurricane houses were valued at roughly £15–£30, but even smaller planters with little capital had storm shelters. John Abbot's estate totaled only £32, but he had a hurricane house worth £3. Another description of a hurricane house comes from the French islands at roughly the same period. According to Jean Barbot, when a hurricane threatened, planters "repair with their families and best moveables to their hurricane huts, each substantial planter having such a one near his plantation; being built low, on large stumps of trees deeply fix'd in the ground, and commonly not above seven foot high, of strong posts fasten'd to each other by cross pieces of timber, with ropes cast over the roof to secure it from flying away."[26]

Hurricane houses also appeared in Jamaica. Thomas Thistlewood wrote that during a September 1751 hurricane, "all the white people . . . all leave the great house and shelter in the storehouse and hurricane house." Thistlewood later bought his own pen on the island, which suffered great damage during major hurricanes in 1780 and 1781. As he set about rebuilding his house in the aftermath of the second tempest, Thistlewood ordered his slaves to construct a separate "stormhouse" for shelter lest another storm strike. His planning proved useful in 1784 when the third hurricane in four years swept across the island and Thistlewood and his slaves retreated into the shelter.[27]

During the early nineteenth century some planters in South Carolina began building "storm towers" in which slaves could seek shelter from a hurricane. The word "tower" is something of a misnomer for these brick structures, which were no more than twenty feet high. The buildings were circular, between twenty and thirty feet in diameter, and with walls nineteen inches thick (see figure 2). The floors were several feet off the ground to prevent their sinking into the loose soils of the coastal region. The towers provided important shelter for slaves working in the rice fields of the low-lying Santee delta. Use of the towers developed following the 1822 hurricane, when dozens of slaves lost their lives.[28]

Despite their appearance at different times and places throughout the region, the use of hurricanes houses does not appear to have been constant or widespread. The majority of the St. Christopher claims do not mention specific hurricane houses, although the number of them may be greater than first appears because the claims noted only damaged or lost property. There is no evidence of hurricane houses in Barbados during this period, and they appear to have fallen out of favor with planters in Nevis and St. Christopher by the mid–eighteenth century. Reverend Robertson noted in the aftermath of the 1733 hurricane that "Seventy or Eighty Years ago, our more provident Planters used to have what they

Fig. 2. Storm tower on the Santee delta. From David Doar, *Rice and Rice Planting in the South Carolina Low Country* (Charleston, S.C.: Charleston Museum, 1936), 23. Courtesy of Thomas Cooper Library, University of South Carolina, Columbia

call'd a Hurricane-House, to take Refuge in, in a Storm." The houses, he claimed, were "14 or 16 Feet square, and made of Stone and Lime from 3 to 4 Feet from the Ground to the Wall-plate, with Roofs as strong as cou'd be made of Hard-Wood." He wrote that he had seen the remains of such structures on the island and that they were still in use on French Martinique. He recommended that residents again start building them. Robertson claimed that constructing such a structure would cost no more than two hundred pounds, money well spent, he claimed, because a plantation equipped with a "Hurricane-Castle" would command a higher resale price. There is no evidence, however, that any local planters followed his advice.[29]

Why the use of hurricane shelters declined is unclear, but there are several possible explanations. Some planters, such as the ones Thistlewood described, may have used storehouses or other buildings as storm shelters since they were constructed along similar lines. Others may have had faith in the improvements they had made to their dwelling houses, believing that their shorter brick and stone houses offered the best protection from the storms. Regardless, the presence of hurricane houses or storm towers at various times in various colonies helped distinguish the plantation landscape of the Greater Caribbean during the seventeenth and eighteenth centuries, and South Carolina in the nineteenth century.

Hurricanes destroyed public buildings as well as private homes, and colonists also modified these structures to reduce their vulnerability to storms. Governor Jonathan Atkins reported that most of the churches on Barbados "were thrown down to the ground" or damaged during the 1675 hurricane. In Bridgetown the storm blew off the roof of the church, and the vestry ordered churchwardens to provide palmetto leaves to cover it. A report on churches in Jamaica in 1724 detailed the impact of a hurricane two years earlier. St. Andrews parish had "a very fine small Church before the Hurricane, but much shattered then, and not yet rebuilt." Clarendon Parish had "at the place called the Cross, one of the finest Churches in the Indies before the late hurricane," while the church at Vere was "much shattered in the storms of 1711 [*sic:* 1712], 1722." Even structures that managed to survive several storms over the course of the seventeenth and early eighteenth centuries eventually succumbed. St. George's in Barbados, initially built between 1637 and 1641, apparently lasted until 1780, when the "Great Hurricane" demolished it along with most of the other church buildings on the island.[30]

As colonial vestrymen surveyed the damage and envisioned the new structures that would rise from the ruins, they took precautions against hurricanes similar to those of individual property owners. Brick and stone universally replaced wood, with the hopes and prayers of parishioners against future devastation sometimes inscribed in the walls. "Erected from the Ruins of an unsparing Storm," reads the tablet above the door of St. George's, Barbados, completed in 1784. "Long may this Structure lift its vulnerable Head, unhurt by slow and creeping Hand of Time, or by the ruder and undistinguishing Assaults of Winds and Storms," it continued. Steeples, increasingly common in mainland urban areas, graced some churches in the islands, but they never appeared in great numbers. Instead, eighteenth-century West Indian churches often had short, squat, castellated towers, giving them a Gothic character. Many of the churches on Barbados rebuilt after the 1780 hurricane, including St. Lucy's, St. George's, and St. Michael's, provide good examples of this change. Likewise, the "elegant" brick St. Catherine's Church in Spanish Town, designed and built following the 1712 hurricane, had no tower or steeple during the eighteenth century. "As it is without a tower," Edward Long noted, "the congregation is summoned by a small bell hung in a wooden frame, which is erected in the church-yard."[31]

Some colonists may also have altered the design of their churches in response to the threat by hurricanes and other disasters. According to Charles Leslie, churches in Jamaica's towns were "generally in the Form of a Cross," and the development of these cruciform churches may have reflected colonists' increased experience with hurricanes and other disasters. "Cruciform churches, with their narrow roof spans, shorter wall spans, and twelve mutually-buttressing 90 degree corners," the architectural historian Louis Nelson writes, "may have seemed the more stable option than the longer linear plan or the broader auditory churches." Certainly, the threat from various calamities occupied a prominent place in the minds of Port Royal vestry officials. After having three churches fall in the space of the previous thirty years from the earthquake and two hurricanes, officials in

1725 erected a cruciform church with walls more than four feet thick, hoping such excess would provide added security and allow the church to survive the next calamity that seemed certain to strike the star-crossed city.[32]

In addition to churches, some government buildings gradually came to reflect the dangers posed by hurricanes. The best collection of surviving eighteenth-century official structures in the British islands is in Spanish Town, Jamaica, where the King's House, the assembly house, and colonial courts ring a central square. These are impressive buildings, incorporating numerous neoclassical elements and highlighting colonists' desire to mimic prevailing architectural trends in Britain. Jamaicans were immensely proud of their government buildings: Edward Long called the King's House "the noblest and best edifice of the kind, either in North-America, or any of the British Colonies in the West-Indies." However, even these buildings reflected the realities of the region's climate. They are short and long, with little roof ornamentation. (A small cupola briefly sat atop the assembly house roof, but it was quickly discarded because it was "too cumbersome." A cupola, however, was added to court buildings in the nineteenth century.) The assembly house included a long arcade across the front to provide shade against the tropical sun, and the gallery above was later covered for the same end. Both the King's House and the assembly building stand in stark contrast to the statehouses of Pennsylvania and Boston, with their tall towers, and to the governor's mansion in Virginia, with its multiple stories, dormer windows, and elaborate cupola. Colonists in Jamaica and elsewhere in the islands were anxious to proclaim themselves members of the British Empire, but by the eighteenth century hurricanes, along with other environmental forces, helped temper their efforts at cultural mimicry.[33]

The cumulative effect of various architectural adaptations to the threat from hurricanes helped create a distinct built landscape in the region, one that routinely elicited comments from both colonists and visitors. Hurricanes, however, did not completely transform building practices. As Edward Long and others observed, some colonists continued to construct dwellings modeled on metropolitan designs and "English styles." They did so for a variety of reasons. Some believed that the threat from storms had receded over the course of the seventeenth and eighteenth centuries or that the destruction of English-style houses was a fluke. John Oldmixon, for example, reported that by the early eighteenth century Barbados contained "many high Houses and some low ones." Colonists who "built immediately after the Great Storm in 1676 [*sic:* 1675]," Oldmixon explained, "were so apprehensive of another, that they lower'd their buildings; but those that have built since then, not having those Apprehensions, have rais'd their Houses to three and four Stories, and the Rooms are as lofty as in England." Despite the widespread devastation caused by the storm, Father Labat encountered numerous houses built in an "English style" on his visit in 1700. William Senhouse likewise suggested that the "toply houses" that became common in Barbados in the decades prior to the 1780 calamity reflected the belief among some that the threat from hurricanes had ceased.[34]

Some colonists clearly tempted fate, refusing to acknowledge the dangers posed by hurricanes. Others viewed the destruction from an individual storm as a once-in-a-lifetime event and simply rebuilt in familiar forms.[35] Indeed, the desire among colonists to re-create English cultural forms remained strong over the course of the eighteenth century, and aesthetics sometimes trumped safety. Janet Shaw found on her visit to Antigua a few years after the 1772 hurricane that for some houses, "by degrees they have come to the same standard as formerly." One Leeward Island resident believed that the continued presence of European designs and styles also reflected the ongoing immigration of new migrants to the colonies, many of whom had never experienced a storm, expressed skepticism of the dangers they posed, and found local adaptations unappealing. According to Robert Robertson, although the Leeward Islands experienced several minor storms in the period between the devastating hurricanes of 1707 and 1733, damage from them was slight, and many new immigrants failed to appreciate the threat from the storms. "Many of the present Inhabitants of our Leeward-Islands," Robertson wrote following the 1733 hurricane, "(especially of St. Christopher's) having settled here since the grand Storm in 1707, and suffer'd nothing very grievous from that Time by Storms, are too easily induc'd to study Ornament and Convenience in their Buildings, rather than Safety." All of these factors ensured that hurricanes did not suddenly and universally alter colonial building practices, but rather that change occurred over time and in response to specific calamities.[36]

The impact of hurricanes on architecture also varied across the region. Adaptations appeared most pronounced in the Leeward Islands and Jamaica and least so in South Carolina, where residents made few outward accommodations. Unlike travelers to the West Indies, visitors to South Carolina did not comment on the relationship between hurricanes and architecture, and no mainland equivalent of Charles Leslie emerged critiquing the lack of refinement in South Carolina buildings. Instead, visitors praised the Anglicized buildings of Charleston.

Colonists did not lack an appreciation of the power of hurricanes. Buildings in Charleston and the surrounding lowcountry suffered repeated damage from hurricanes over the course of the eighteenth century. One account written in the wake of the 1686 tempest noted that "the greatest part of our houses are blown down and still lie in their ruin." Many houses were "blown down & more damnified" in the 1700 tempest, and reports indicate that storms in 1713 and 1728 likewise damaged or destroyed numerous dwellings. The most spectacular damage occurred during two hurricanes in 1752, particularly the first on September 15. The storm flooded Charleston. Accounts indicate that the sea "rose upwards of

Ten feet above the high-water mark at spring-tides." The storm left large parts of the city in "ruins, many wooden houses were wrecked to pieces and washed away, and brick houses reduced to a heap of rubbish." The storm also damaged the surrounding plantation regions. Plantations on James Island and Kiawah Island flooded, and many houses were "beat down," while "the plantations between the Pon Pon and Santee River had their Negro houses and many of their out-houses blown down."[37]

Despite such experiences, South Carolinians followed metropolitan styles and designs more closely than did other colonists in the Greater Caribbean, and travelers and residents alike celebrated the "Englishness" of buildings in Charleston and the surrounding lowcountry. South Carolina's economic growth coincided with the emergence of Georgian design, and many of the dwellings in the capital city followed that fashion. Wealthy planters and merchants built large three- and four-story single and double houses that reminded visitors of English structures. As early as the 1720s one traveler commented on the "very fine" houses in Charleston, most "Glazed with Sash Window after the English Fashion." A British military officer visiting in the early 1760s wrote, "Many of the houses belonging to Individuals, are large and handsome, having all the conveniencies one sees at home."[38]

Public buildings also mirrored contemporary English designs more closely than their counterparts in the Indies did. Charleston's two major eighteenth-century church buildings, St. Philip's (1723) and St. Michael's (1761), both boasted fine, tall steeples. The former was begun in 1711, but the 1713 hurricane damaged the incomplete church. Construction was halted for a few years, and the disaster and delay allowed for the incorporation of new ideas about church building that were circulating in London at the time. When finished, St. Philip's struck one later visitor as a "grand church, resembling one of the new churches in London." St. Michael's likewise followed eighteenth-century English designs and boasted a tower and spire that rose over 165 feet. The statehouse and exchange in the city also closely followed English building styles. Indeed, the architectural historian Carl Lounsbury has concluded that, in general, "building in this city [Charleston] was more Anglicized, more substantial, and more embellished than in any other city in the entire South."[39]

South Carolinians did accommodate themselves to the region's climate. By the end of the eighteenth century colonists had incorporated piazzas on their dwellings to provide shade, although concerns about health as well as heat influenced such developments. Hurricanes also played a minor role in the increased use of brick in buildings during the eighteenth century. Colonists turned to brick in part because many believed it offered better security against both hurricanes and fires. The use of brick in Charleston increased following the 1740 fire, and Gov. James Glen suggested that such solid dwellings provided some security during the 1752 storms. After cataloging the deaths of numerous colonists in Charleston, Glen noted, "Numbers more must have perished had not our Houses been very Substantial, all those especially upon the Bay are so." In other parts of the city, "where the Houses were slight, and the Situation low," the storm caused greater damage and presented a "most surprising and shocking Scene." The devastation accompanying the storms encouraged even greater use of brick as residents rebuilt during the 1750s. According to a Rhode Island merchant who had visited the city in the 1740s and returned a decade after the hurricane, the city had doubled in size and "has increased with sumptuous brick houses in very great number. One cannot go anywhere where one does not see new buildings and large and small houses started, half-finished, and almost finished."[40]

The shift to brick, however, reflected influences besides the threat from storms, and little of the specific commentary linking hurricanes to building materials appears in West Indian accounts. Likewise, the issue of height, so common in descriptions of West Indian dwellings, is absent from discussions of the South Carolina landscape, and while hurricanes houses eventually appeared in the lowcountry, this was not until the early nineteenth century. Why hurricanes appeared to have had so little impact on South Carolina's architecture is not entirely clear. Hurricanes generated great concern among planters and merchants such as Henry Laurens and John Guerard, who feared the impact of storms on plantations and trade. Moreover, the storms worried Laurens enough that he warned his overseer to take precautionary steps to secure his house during the hurricane season. Such concerns, however, do not appear to have been so great as to alter general building practices in the colony.

Real and perceived differences between the lowcountry and island environments provide one explanation for Carolina colonists' willingness to mimic English styles more fully than their West Indian counterparts did. Carolina experienced fewer hurricanes than other parts of the region withstood, and more important, many contemporaries believed that the storms were not as strong or as damaging as those in the Caribbean. According to the naturalist Mark Catesby, Carolina represented the northern edge of the hurricane zone, and the storms "are much mitigated in their force by the time they reach Carolina." That perception, combined with a strong desire to mimic English culture, may have been enough to shape colonists' actions. Moreover, the climate of the colony was different from that of the West Indies. Despite the tropical summers, weather along the mainland coast was more variable than in the islands, and frosts and ice were not unknown during the winter months. Gov. James Glen believed that South Carolina's "Climate is various and uncertain, to such an extraordinary Degree, that I fear not to affirm, there are no people on Earth, who, I think, can suffer greater extremes of Heat and Cold." Having to accommodate themselves to the intense summer heat but also to the mild but occasionally cold winters meant maintaining certain functional items such as chimneys. As a result, colonists had more reason to look to English models and to follow them more closely than did their Caribbean counterparts. South Carolina shared many social and environmental characteristics with the West Indian colonies, including experience with hurricanes, but it is not a tropical island, and its buildings reflected that difference.[41]

The impact of hurricanes on architecture and building practices extended beyond damage to individual structures and the modifications colonists made in response. The destruction of numerous buildings at one time in colonial cities and on plantations presented opportunities to reimagine the layout of the built landscape in a broader sense, and many colonists embraced the occasion to transform and "improve" the physical spaces they occupied.

Some planters took advantage of the widespread destruction to alter the arrangement of buildings on their estates. William Senhouse, for example, disapproved of the common practice of allowing land surrounding the main dwelling houses on plantations to be "appropriated for the use of the Negroes, their houses &c &c.," which he believed formed "altogether a nuisance not at all to be tolerably borne." As Senhouse set about rebuilding following the 1780 hurricane, he ordered the quarters moved to what he called a "better situation where they were disposed in regular streets, every house in the centre of a piece of ground 20 yds. Square." In place of the slave houses, he planted a series of walks bordered by mahogany, coconut, and bamboo trees. As the bamboo walks grew, they formed an "impenetrable and most agreeable shade of about 200 yds. when taken all together." He claimed that the bamboo walks were the first of their kind in Barbados, and he took pride in his aesthetic achievement.[42]

A similar reorganization of space occurred on Turners Hall plantation following the same storm. The overseer, Richard Gill, undertook a systematic survey of buildings on the estate to determine whether they should be rebuilt in the same place and what functions they should serve. He informed the absentee owner William FitzHerbert that the boiling house and curing house should be rebuilt on their existing sites because the expense of moving them was too great. He consulted with a doctor about the position of the sick house, and both agreed "that tis on the best situation for that use." Gill altered the space inside that building, however. Previously it had served as hospital, jail, and cooper shop, but Gill moved the latter elsewhere, leaving just the "Sick House & Dungeon" in the new building, which he claimed was "now sufficiently large & very commodious & pleasant." Likewise he reorganized the still house and distillery, placing what had been separate operations and buildings ("with much waste room in the Distillery") under one roof.[43]

The reorganization of physical space in the wake of calamities also occurred in urban areas in the Greater Caribbean. Most cities in the region lacked formal plans and grew haphazardly in the years after their initial settlement. Disasters presented a chance to implement some form of urban planning. In the aftermath of the 1780 hurricane, local leaders in Savanna-la-Mar petitioned the Jamaican Assembly "to lay out the town anew, in a more regular manner." They hoped to move part of the town further inland so that "their lives and properties may be rendered more secure against perils of . . . nature" and to build the town on a "uniform and secure plan."[44]

In Charleston, South Carolina, repeated destruction from hurricanes and fires over the course of the eighteenth century contributed a great deal to the physical layout and development of the city. Charleston (actually the second incarnation of the city) developed on a peninsula between the Ashley and Cooper rivers. The city had a formal plan at its inception in 1680, but it also exhibited many medieval characteristics, including defensive walls and a moat. The city outgrew these boundaries during the eighteenth century and expanded somewhat randomly across the peninsula. Disasters provided officials with opportunities to order this otherwise unplanned growth and to improve existing parts of the city. A hurricane in 1700 destroyed most of the landing places along the Cooper River, and local officials ordered residents with property there to build up a retaining wall. The damage by a storm in 1713 contributed to the ultimate dismantling of the medieval walls that surrounded the city, although it took a few years for that to occur.[45]

The 1752 hurricanes played a particularly important role in shaping Charleston's physical layout and appearance in the second half of the eighteenth century. In the aftermath of the storms, officials ordered that many of the streams, creeks, and ponds that ran through the city be filled in to allow for more construction. Streets were widened and extended across the peninsula. South Carolina officials also took advantage of the hurricane's devastation to redesign and improve the city's defenses. Prior to the storm Gov. James Glen had complained that the city's forts had been constructed over time in a piecemeal and hasty fashion. If poor planning "has been formerly our Error," Glen stressed to the assembly in 1752, "let us not now persist in it." The hurricanes provided a powerful new incentive to think again about the design and layout of the city's defenses. The plans for the defenses sparked controversy between the governor and the assembly over the relative power and prerogatives of the different branches of government and delayed their implementation, but ultimately Charleston forts were reconstructed. The new fortifications that stretched around the city's southern point were four feet taller than the previous defenses. The higher wall not only strengthened Charleston militarily but also offered increased protection against the swelling sea that flooded the city during major storms.[46]

Nowhere is the relationship between disasters and urban planning more evident than in the establishment of Kingston, Jamaica, in the 1690s. Port Royal, a bustling trading center located on a thin slice of land jutting out into a large natural harbor on Jamaica's southern coast, served as the island's major port during the seventeenth century. As it grew, the city spread out along the peninsula in a haphazard fashion: the streets and alleys were narrow and followed no set patterns, and houses were clustered together tightly on small lots. The great earthquake in June 1692 sent much of the city plunging to the bottom of the harbor. In the aftermath of the disaster, local officials deemed Port Royal unsafe and ordered the development of a new city across the harbor. Unlike Port Royal, Kingston was a planned city. Streets followed a grid pattern, with a central square bordered by the church and other public buildings. All the main thoroughfares ran up from the harbor. Wide streets and relatively large building lots gave Kingston a feeling of openness and spaciousness compared to Port Royal.[47]

Kingston's urban plan likely reflected a number of different influences, including Spanish town planning ideas and William Penn's recent design for Philadelphia.[48] However, Kingston's layout also may have reflected the experience of the earthquake. Wide streets and large house lots offered greater protection against falling buildings, the cause of hundreds of deaths in the earthquake. Such planning ideas were common, if not always implemented, in the aftermath of earthquakes in Europe and Spanish America in the seventeenth and eighteenth centuries, and it seems possible that such ideas also influenced Jamaican officials anxious to avoid a similar tragedy in the future. Kingston's plan provided greater security from falling buildings during a hurricane and would help limit the major scourge of all early modern urban areas, fires.[49]

The dramatic destruction of Port Royal in 1692 and the subsequent planning of Kingston sometimes divert attention away from the fact that Port Royal did not disappear in the years following the earthquake. Residents complained that Kingston was sickly, and many wanted to rebuild on what they considered a better site for a port city. Port Royal gradually "increas'd in people who were invited to settle there by its Convenience for Trade," noted one eighteenth-century historian. Although "very short of its former Splendor," it soon contained "700 Houses and Warehouses." Port Royal's woes, however, continued. A major fire in 1703 burned the city to the ground, and in 1712 a hurricane swept along the southern coast, again damaging the city. Still, Port Royal hung on and, like a phoenix, continued to rise from its own dust and debris. Only after another major hurricane struck in 1722 did Port Royal finally cease to be a significant urban center and shipping point. The remaining buildings mostly housed military officers and troops stationed at Fort Charles. Thus, while Kingston owes its existence to the 1692 earthquake, Port Royal's demise as an important urban center must be located later in the eighteenth century, and hurricanes played some role in the process.[50]

Jamaica's physical and social landscape underwent numerous transformations between the period when John Taylor visited the island in the 1680s and when Charles Leslie recorded his impressions in the 1730s. By the time Leslie wrote, Port Royal no longer dominated the colony's social and economic life. The town remained, but only as a shadow of its former self, replaced in physical space and commercial importance by the new, formally planned city of Kingston across the harbor. Likewise, few seventeenth-century buildings remained on the island, other than those built by the Spanish. A series of hurricanes in 1712, 1722, and 1726, along with the great 1692 earthquake, leveled the dwellings, churches, warehouses, and other structures built by the early settlers. Not only had the old structures disappeared but so too had the old ways of building. Gone for the most part were the three- and four-story dwellings modeled after English buildings that had impressed Taylor. In their place were the shorter houses that Leslie found lacking in any real architectural grandeur but which appeared better suited to the disaster-prone environment.

In the half-century between Taylor's and Leslie's writings, colonists in Jamaica and elsewhere in the Greater Caribbean had learned to accommodate themselves to the physical environment in which they lived. Hurricanes were not the only force influencing buildings and designs; the tropical heat and humidity played perhaps an even greater role in the development of distinct architectural styles. Buildings in the region also reflected the mixture of various European and African cultures and the social hierarchies and relationships of the plantation society in which they were situated. Nevertheless, the widespread and repeated destruction by hurricanes helped alter colonists' notions about architectural form and function.[51]

The process of adaptation took time, and the rate and extent of change reflected a variety of factors, including accumulated experience with hurricanes, perceptions of the threat posed by the storms, the complex array of environmental forces facing colonists (including the presence of other disasters such as earthquakes), the continued migration of men and women from Europe who had to learn the hard lessons taught by nature on their own, and the continuing desire among many to replicate metropolitan forms and designs. Changes in the landscape thus were more pronounced at some points in time and in some places in the region than in others, but over the course of the seventeenth and eighteenth centuries, and throughout the region, colonists gradually took steps to accommodate their buildings to the presence of hurricanes. Their efforts offered only minimal protection against the fury of the storms, but they represented one part of the larger process of constructing colonial landscapes in which familiar English cultural forms were balanced against the realities of the American environment.

Notes

I am very grateful to Louis Nelson and Jack Breihan for reading an earlier version of this essay and offering numerous helpful suggestions.

1. Charles Leslie, *A New and Exact Account of Jamaica* (Edinburgh: Fleming, 1740), 30–31.

2. Richard Dunn, *Sugar and Slaves: The Rise of the Planter Class in the British West Indies, 1624–1713* (Chapel Hill: University of North Carolina Press, 1972), 287–99; A.C. Acworth, *Treasure in the Caribbean: A First Study of Georgian Buildings in the British West Indies* (London: Pleiades, 1949); Pamela Gosner, *Caribbean Georgian: The Great and Small Houses of the West Indies* (Washington, D.C.: Three Continents Press, 1982); David Buisseret, *Historic Architecture of the Caribbean* (London: Heinemann International Literature & Textbooks, 1980); Jay Edwards, "The Origins of Creole Architecture," *Winterthur Portfolio* 29 (Summer/Autumn 1994): 155–89; William Chapman, "Irreconcilable Differences: Urban Residences in the Danish West Indies, 1700–1900," *Winterthur Portfolio* 30 (Summer/Autumn 1995): 129–72; James Robertson, "Jamaican Architectures before Georgian," *Winterthur Portfolio* 36 (Spring/Summer 2001): 73–95; Carl Lounsbury, "The Dynamics of Architectural Design in Eighteenth-Century Charleston and the Lowcountry," in *Exploring Everyday Landscapes: Perspectives in Vernacular Architecture VII,* ed. Annmarie Adams and Sally McMurry (Knoxville: University of Tennessee Press, 1997), 58–72; Peter Coclanis, *Shadow of a Dream: Economic Life and Death in the South Carolina Lowcountry, 1670–1920* (New York: Oxford University Press, 1989), 3–11.

3. For contemporary ideas about hurricanes ending in the Carolinas, see Edward Randolph to the Lords Commissioners for Trade and Plantation, June 28, 1699, in A. S. Salley, ed., *Records of the British Public Record Office Relating to South Carolina* (Columbia: University of South Carolina Press, 1946), 4:95; Edmund Burke, *An Account of the European Settlements in America,* 6th edition (London: J Dodsley, 1777), 2:234–35; Mark Catesby, *The Natural History of Carolina, Florida, and the Bahama Islands* (London: Printed for the author, 1731–43), 11. For a discussion of the greater Caribbean, see Matthew Mulcahy, *Hurricanes and Society in the British Greater Caribbean, 1624–1783* (Baltimore: Johns Hopkins University Press, 2006).

4. Kevin Rozario, "What Comes Down Must Go Up: Why Disasters Have Been Good for American Capitalism," in *American Disasters,* ed. Steven Biel (New York: New York University Press, 2001), 72–102.

5. Jack Greene, "The Search for Identity: An Interpretation of the Meaning of Selected Patterns of Social Response in Eighteenth-Century America," in Greene, *Imperatives, Behaviors, and Identities: Essays in Early American Cultural History* (Charlottesville: University Press of Virginia, 1992), 143–73; Edward Brathwaite, *The Development of Creole Society in Jamaica, 1770–1820* (Oxford: Clarendon, 1971), xiii, 296.

6. Philip Barbour, ed., *The Complete Works of Captain John Smith, 1580–1632* (Chapel Hill: University of North Carolina Press for the Institute of Early American History and Culture, 1986), 3:233, 228–29; Charles de Rochefort, *The History of the Caribby-Islands,*

trans. John Davies (London, 1666), 177–78; John Taylor, *Newes and Strange Newes from St. Christophers of a tempestuous Spirit, which is called by the Indians a Hurry-Cano or whirlewind* (London, 1638), 8.

7. Carl Bridenbaugh and Roberta Bridenbaugh, *No Peace beyond the Line: The English in the Caribbean, 1624–1690* (New York: Oxford University Press, 1972), 37; "Some Observations on the Island of Barbados," 1667, *Calendar of State Papers, Colonial Series,* National Archives, Kew, Richmond, Surrey, U.K. (hereafter cited as *CSPC*), 528–29; Ellwood, quoted in Raymond Stearns, *Science in the British Colonies of America* (Urbana: University of Illinois Press, 1970), 229; Cary Carson, Norman F. Barka, William M. Kelso, Garry Wheeler Stone, and Dell Upton, "Impermanent Architecture in the Southern American Colonies," *Winterthur Portfolio* 16 (Summer/Autumn 1981), reprinted in *Material Life in America, 1600–1800,* ed. Robert Blair St. George (Boston: Northeastern University Press, 1988), 113–58. Robertson, "Jamaican Architectures," 73–95, has uncovered some sketch drawings of early houses on land surveys in Jamaica that resemble these early houses.

8. Douglas Hall, ed., "The Diary of a Westmoreland Planter: Thomas Thistlewood in the Vineyard," *Jamaica Journal* 21 (August/October 1988): 20–21; Dunn, *Sugar and Slaves,* 290–91; Richard Bushman, *The Refinement of America: Persons, Houses, Cities* (New York: Vintage, 1992), 100–117, quote on 103; Peter Borsay, *The English Urban Renaissance: Culture and Society in the Provincial Town, 1660–1770* (Oxford: Oxford University Press, 1989), 41–59.

9. John Taylor, "Multum in Parvo or Parvum in Multo: Taylor's Historie of His Life and Travels in America," 2:492, 509, Institute of Jamaica, Kingston; Hans Sloane, *A Voyage to the Islands Madeira, Barbadoes, Nieves, S. Christophers and Jamaica* (London, 1707), 1:xlvii; Governor Sir Jonathan Atkins to the Lords of Trade and Plantations, July 14, 1676, *CSPC,* 421; Neville Connell, ed., "Father Labat's Visit to Barbados in 1700," *Journal of the Barbados Museum and Historical Society* [hereafter cited as *JBMHS*] 24 (1957): 163, 171; Dunn, *Sugar and Slaves,* 292–93.

10. John Cordy Jeaffreson, ed., *A Young Squire of the Seventeenth Century: From the Papers of Christopher Jeaffreson* (London: Hurst & Blackett, 1878), 1:275–76; James Knight, "The Natural, Morall, and Political History of Jamaica," 1:198, additional manuscripts, 12418, British Museum; Griffith Hughes, *The Natural History of Barbados* (London: Printed for the author, 1750), 26; John Oldmixon, *British Empire in America* (London: John Nicholson, Benjamin Tooke, Richard Parker & Ralph Smith, 1708), 2:38.

11. J. Atkins, *A Voyage to Guinea, Brasil, and the West Indies* (London: Ward & Chandler, 1735), 239–40; Knight, "Natural, Morall, and Political History," 2:16; "Letter from the Inhabitants of Savanna-la-Mar to Gov. John Dalling," October 8, 1780, in John Fowler, *A General Account of the Calamities Occasioned by the Late Tremendous Hurricanes and Earthquakes in the West-India Islands* (London: J. Stockdale & W. Richardson, 1781), 7; David Ludlum, *Early American Hurricanes, 1492–1870* (Boston: American Meteorological Society, 1963), 41–51.

12. *Weekly Jamaican Courant,* September 12, 1722, Colonial Papers (hereafter Colo.) 137/14/175; Edward Long, *The History of Jamaica or a General Survey of the Ancient and*

Modern State of That Island with Reflections in Its Situation, Settlements, Inhabitants, Climate, Products, Commerce, Laws, and Government (London: T. Lowndes, 1774), 2:18–19.

13. Dr. Peyssonnel, "Observations upon the Currents of the Sea, at the Antisles of America," *Philosophical Transactions of the Royal Society* 49 (1756): 629; Rochefort, *History of the Caribby-Islands,* 145–46; Leslie, *New and Exact Account,* 43; Oldmixon, *British Empire in America,* 2:235. On slave housing, see Jerome Handler and Frederick Lange, *Plantation Slavery in Barbados: An Archaeological and Historical Investigation* (Cambridge, Mass.: Harvard University Press, 1978), 52–53; B. W. Higman, *Montpelier, Jamaica: A Plantation Community in Slavery and Freedom* (Kingston: University of the West Indies Press, 1998), 146–90.

14. Rochefort, *History of the Caribby-Islands,* 145–46; "Henry Whistler's Journal, March 1655," in *Narrative of General Venables,* ed. C. H. Firth (London: Longmans, Green, 1900), 168–69; Long, *History of Jamaica,* 2:19–20. Interestingly, Hans Sloane wrote in the 1680s that most of the remaining Spanish houses on the island were wooden, although he also emphasized the importance of grounding the wooden posts as a defense against earthquakes. See Sloane, *Voyage to the Islands,* 1:xliv; Andrew Gravette, *Architectural Heritage of the Caribbean: An A–Z of Historic Buildings* (Kingston: Marcus Wiener, 2000), 12; Ann Hodges, "Jamaican Traditional Building Materials and Techniques: Thatch," *Jamaica Journal* 19 (November/January 1986/87): 29.

15. Taylor, "Multum in Parvo," 2:509–10; Long, *History of Jamaica,* 2:19–20, 2:3. On the continuing influence of English aesthetics, see Dunn, *Sugar and Slaves,* 287–96.

16. Rochefort, *History of the Caribby-Islands,* 177; Oldmixon, *British Empire in America,* 2:38, 87; "Records of the Vestry of St. Michael," *JBMHS* 16 (November 1948 / February 1949): 59; "Answers to the Inquiries Sent to Colonel Stapleton, Governor of the Leeward Islands," November 22, 1676, *CSPC,* 499.

17. Anonymous, "A Voyage to North America and the West Indies, 1756–57," manuscript in Elsa Goveia Reading Room, the Library of the University of the West Indies, Mona, Jamaica; Evangeline Andrews and Charles Andrews, eds., *Journal of a Lady of Quality: Being the Narrative of a Journey from Scotland to the West Indies, North Carolina, and Portugal in the Years 1774–1776* (New Haven: Yale University Press, 1922), 88; Vere Langford Oliver, *The History of Antigua* (London: Mitchell & Hughes, 1894), 1:cxxix; Frank Cundall, *The Governors of Jamaica in the First Half of the Eighteenth Century* (London: West India Committee, 1937), unpaginated map; Dunn, *Sugar and Slaves,* 299.

18. C. G. A. Oldendorp, *A Caribbean Mission: History of the Evangelical Brethren on the Caribbean Islands of St. Thomas, St. Croix, and St. John* (1779), ed. Johan Jakob Bossard, 151, quoted in Chapman, "Irreconcilable Differences," 153–54; "Autobiographical Manuscript of William Senhouse," *JBMHS* 3 (November 1935): 13; *JBMHS* 2 (August 1935): 206; Richard Gill to William FitzHerbert, April 23, 1781, FitzHerbert Papers, M/E 20775, microfilm copy in the Barbados Archives, Black Rock, St. Michael's; George Pinckard, *Notes on the West Indies* (London: Longman, Hurst, Reese & Orme, 1806), 194. On roof ornamentation, see Gosner, *Caribbean Georgian,* 20–21; Gravette, *Architectural Heritage,* 112. A major finding of a 1990s study of hurricane damage in the United States was "the excellent performance of hip roofs compared to that of other types of roof systems, such

as gable types" (Michele Melarango, *Severe Storm Engineering for Structural Design* [Sydney: Gordon & Breach, 1996], 69–70).

19. "Autobiographical Manuscript of Senhouse"; Oldendorp, *Caribbean Mission,* quoted in Chapman, "Irreconcilable Differences," 153–54.

20. George Welch, "A Journal of my Voyage with ye Sundry passages thereof as I travel'd into divers parts of the West Indies, 1671," 80–81, manuscript, American Philosophical Society; Robert Robertson, *A Short Account of the Hurricane That Pass'd through the English Leeward Caribbee Islands* (London: Booksellers of London & Westminster, 1733), 18; D. Walsh to James Scott, September 18, 1772, repr. in Vere Langford Oliver, *Caribbeana: Being Miscellaneous Papers Relating to the History, Genealogy, Topography, and Antiquity of the British West Indies* (London: Mitchell, Hughes & Clarke, 1910), 2:322–23; Ralph Payne to Earl of Hillsborough, September 5, 1772, Colo. 152/52/103. On the use of stone and brick in one wall, see claim of William and Ralph Willet, Colo. 243/2, vol. 1, folio 42; claim of Mary King, Colo. 243/2, vol. 2, folio 432; Bridenbaugh and Bridenbaugh, *No Peace beyond the Line,* 370.

21. Sloane, *Voyage to the Islands,* 1:xliv; *An Account of the Late Dreadful Earthquake in the Island of Nevis, St. Christophers, &c.* (London, 1690); William Smith, *A Natural History of Nevis* (Cambridge: Bentham, 1745), 63.

22. *A Letter Sent from Barbados to a Friend in London . . . of the Great Earthquake at Montserrat* (London, 1672); "Answers to the Inquiries Sent to Colonel Stapleton," 500; *Account of the Late Dreadful Earthquake in the Island of Nevis;* Lt. Governor Stede to Lords of Trade and Plantation, April 23, 1690, *CSPC,* 249–50; Patrick Browne, *The Civil and Natural History of Jamaica* (London: Published for the author, 1756), 7; Sloane, *Voyage to the Islands,* 1:xliv.

23. Knight, "Natural, Morall, and Political History," 2:49; Benjamin Mosley, *A Treatise on Tropical Diseases; and on the Climate of the West Indies* (London, 1787), 38; Robertson, *Short Account of the Hurricane,* 18; Acworth, *Treasure in the Caribbean,* 8; Robertson, "Jamaican Architectures," 91–92.

24. Robertson, *Short Account of the Hurricane,* 18–19; Henry Laurens to John Loveday, June 21, 1777, *The Papers of Henry Laurens,* 16 vols. (Columbia: University of South Carolina Press, 1968–2002), 11:385; Peyssonnel, "Observations," 627; Smith, *Natural History of Nevis,* 240–42.

25. J. Harry Bennett, *Bondsmen and Bishops: Slavery and Apprenticeship on the Codrington Plantations of Barbados, 1710–1838* (Berkeley: University of California Press, 1958), 32; Philip Gibbes to Lord Penrhyn, 1788, FitzHerbert Papers, National Archives, U.K. M/E 20555 and 20777; Higman, *Montpelier,* 163–64; Handler and Lange, *Plantation Slavery,* 53, 95–97; Philip Morgan, *Slave Counterpoint: Black Culture in the Eighteenth-Century Chesapeake & Lowcountry* (Chapel Hill, 1998), 104–21.

26. Joseph, Colo. 243/2, vol. 2, folio 277; Abbot, Colo. 243/2, vol. 3, folio 646. On the "posts," see William Venton, Colo. 243/2, vol. 2, folio 422, and Mary King, Colo. 243/2, vol. 2, folio 432. See also Jean Barbot, *A Description of the Coasts of North and South Guinea,* reprinted in Awnsham Churchill, *Collection of Voyages and Travels,* 3d ed. (London, 1746), 5:578.

27. Thomas Thistlewood, diaries, Monson MSS, Lincolnshire Archives Office, Lincoln, England, U.K., September 11, 1751, July 30, 1784; Douglas Hall, *In Miserable Slavery: Thomas Thistlewood in Jamaica, 1750–86* (London: Macmillan, 1989), 20, 285.

28. Elias Bull, "Storm Towers of the Santee Delta," *South Carolina Historical Magazine* [hereafter *SCHM*] 81 (April 1980): 95–105; David Doar, *Rice and Rice Planting in the South Carolina Lowcountry* (Charleston: Charleston Museum, 1936), 23.

29. Robertson, *Short Account of the Hurricane,* 20–21. Bull, "Storm Towers of the Santee Delta," 95–105, suggests that the towers were common in South Carolina in the nineteenth century but that many were pulled down for their bricks after the regional rice industry collapsed at the end of the century. Richard Porcher of the Citadel suggested to me that he has seen no evidence of the towers anywhere but the Santee Delta (telephone conversation with author, November 2002).

30. Atkins to Lords of Trade and Plantation, July 14, 1676, *CSPC,* 425; "Records of the Vestry of St Michael, September, 1675," *JBMHS* 16 (November 1948/February 1949): 57; "State of the Church in Jamaica, 1724," in Oliver, *Caribbeana,* 3:343–45; *St Georges Parish Church* [pamphlet] (Bridgetown, Barbados, n.d.).

31. Long, *History of Jamaica,* 2:5. A wooden spire was added to the church in 1817. See Edward Crain, *Historic Architecture in the Caribbean Islands* (Gainesville: University Press of Florida, 1994), 183; Gravette, *Architectural Heritage,* 103–5, 227–89. On the rise of steeples on the mainland, see Bushman, *Refinement of America,* 170–80.

32. Leslie, *New and Exact Account,* 30; Louis Nelson, "Anglican Church Building and Local Context in Early Jamaica," in *Perspectives in Vernacular Architecture X* (Knoxville: University of Tennessee Press, 2006).

33. Long, *History of Jamaica,* 2:6–10; Acworth, *Treasure in the Caribbean,* 5–8.

34. Oldmixon, *British Empire in America,* 2:87; "Father Labat's Visit to Barbados," 163; "Autobiographical Manuscript of Senhouse" (August 1935): 206.

35. The force of inertia is a powerful one. On similar reactions in the aftermath of various calamities in Europe, see Stephen Tobriner, "Safety and Reconstruction of Noto after the Sicilian Earthquake of 1693—The Eighteenth-Century Context," in *Dreadful Visitations: Confronting Natural Catastrophe in the Age of Enlightenment,* ed. Alessa Johns (New York: Routledge, 1999), 49–77.

36. Andrews and Andrews, eds., *Journal of a Lady of Quality,* 88; Robertson, *Short Account of the Hurricane,* 13–14. On ongoing desire to replicate metropolitan forms, see Greene, "Search for Identity," 143–73.

37. "Paper to the Lords Proprietor, c 1686," reprinted in Ludlum, *Early American Hurricanes,* 41–42; account of 1700 storm, quoted in Jeanne Calhoun, *The Scourging Wrath of God: Early Hurricanes in Charleston, 1700–1804,* Charleston Museum Leaflets 29 (April 1983): 3; accounts of 1713 and 1728 in Ludlum, *Early American Hurricanes,* 43–44; *South Carolina Gazette* [hereafter cited as *SCG*], September 19, 1752; David Ramsay, *The History of South Carolina, from Its First Settlement in 1670 to the Year 1808,* 2 vols (Charleston: David Longworth, 1809), 2:179–82n.

38. Brian Enright, ed., "An Account of Charleston in 1725," *SCHM* 61 (January 1960): 15; "Journal of an Officer Who Traveled in America and the West Indies in 1764 and

1765," in Newton Mereness, ed., *Travels in the American Colonies* (New York: Macmillan, 1916), 398; Robert Weir, *Colonial South Carolina: A History* (Columbia: University of South Carolina Press, 1983), 238–64; Richard Waterhouse, *A New World Gentry: The Making of a Merchant and Planter Class in South Carolina, 1670–1770* (New York: Garland, 1989), 96–104; Lounsbury, "Dynamics of Architectural Design," 58–72.

39. Louis Nelson, "The Material World: Anglican Visual Culture in Colonial South Carolina" (Ph.D. diss., University of Delaware, 2001), 522–25, 162–91; Harley McKee, "St. Michael's Church, Charleston: Some Notes on Materials and Construction," *Journal of the Society of Architectural Historians* 23 (March 1964): 39–42; Carl Lounsbury, *From Statehouse to Courthouse: An Architectural History of South Carolina's Colonial Capitol and Charleston County Courthouse* (Columbia: University of South Carolina Press, 2001), 14–28.

40. John Crowley, *The Invention of Comfort: Sensibilities and Design in Early Modern Britain and Early America* (Baltimore: Johns Hopkins University Press, 2001), 230–59; Coclanis, *Shadow of a Dream,* 8–11, 186–87; James Glen to Secretary of State, September 19, 1752, Colo. 5/385/223–45; Thomas Tobias, ed., "Charleston in 1764," *SCHM* 67 (April 1966): 67–68.

41. On perceptions of weaker hurricanes, see Catesby, *Natural History of Carolina,* xi; Lionel Chalmers, *An Account of the Weather and Diseases of South Carolina,* 2 vols. (London: Edward & Charles Dilly, 1776), 1:23, 26; Glen quoted in Ted Steinberg, *Down to Earth: Nature's Role in American History* (New York: Oxford University Press, 2002), 71.

42. "Autobiographical Manuscript of Senhouse" (November 1935): 14.

43. Richard Gill to William FitzHerbert, April 23, 1781, FitzHerbert Papers, M/E 20775.

44. Vestry Minutes, Parish of Westmoreland, October 18, 1780, 2/7/1, Jamaica Archives, Spanish Town; Assembly minutes, November 25, 1780, in *Journals of the Assembly of Jamaica* (Kingston, 1802–4), 7:263.

45. Frederick Stevenson and Carl Feiss, "Charleston and Savannah," *Journal of the Society of Architectural Historians* 10 (December 1951): 4; "Description of a Hurricane in South Carolina, September 6, 1713," Papers of the Royal Society, American Philosophical Society, frames 7–9; Governor Johnson to Council of Trade and Plantations, January 12, 1720, *CSPC,* 300–301; Coclanis, *Shadow of a Dream,* 4, 179–80.

46. Ramsay, *History of South Carolina,* 2:179n; Harriott Horry Ravenel, *Charleston: The Place and Its People* (New York: Macmillan, 1906), 136; Terry Lipscomb, ed., *Journal of the Commons House of Assembly, 1751–52* (Columbia: University of South Carolina Press for the S.C. Department of Archives and History, 1983), 14:395; Jonathan Mercantini, "The Great Carolina Hurricane of 1752," *SCHM* 103 (October 2002): 351–65; Walter Fraser, *Charleston! Charleston! The History of a Southern City* (Columbia: University of South Carolina Press, 1989), 89.

47. Dunn, *Sugar and Slaves,* 296–99.

48. Ibid., 297.

49. Stephen Tobriner, "Earthquakes and Planning in the 17th and 18th Centuries," *Journal of Architectural Education* 33 (Summer 1980): 11–15; Charles Walker, "The Upper Classes and Their Upper Stories: Architecture and the Aftermath of the Lima Earthquake of 1746," *Hispanic American Historical Review* 83 (February 2003): 53–83.

50. Knight, "Natural, Morall, and Political History," 1:150, 2:14–16; *Weekly Jamaican Courant,* September 12, 1722, Colo. 137/14/175–76; Long, *History of Jamaica,* 2:143–48.

51. Bernard Herman, "The Embedded Landscapes of the Charleston Single House, 1780–1820," in *Exploring Everyday Landscapes: Perspectives in Vernacular Architecture V,* ed. Adams and McMurry (Knoxville: University of Tennessee Press, 1997), 41–57.

Christ Church, Savannah

Loopholes in Metropolitan Design on the Frontier

Carl R. Lounsbury

Scholars of early American architecture have traditionally sought to place colonial design within the broader context of European architectural history. They have traced the transfer of European design ideas to the American colonies, seeing late seventeenth-century artisan mannerism in the curvilinear gables of Bacon's Castle in Surry County, Virginia; Palladian influences in the chaste rectangular forms of mid-eighteenth-century gentry houses such as Drayton Hall outside of Charleston, South Carolina; and neoclassicism in the attenuated features and sinuous curves found in Benjamin Henry Latrobe's design for the Pennock house in Norfolk. From this perspective, the sources of these forms derived from the designs of great architects who defined their ages—Inigo Jones, Christopher Wren, Lord Burlington and his Palladian followers, Robert Adam, and William Chambers, for example—men who charted new directions in British architecture.[1]

Since there were no architects of such stature working in America—in fact the role played by an architect as a designer who conveyed his ideas through drawings was scarcely known here—academic ideas appeared in America through other sources. The colonies were filled with skilled craftsmen—carpenters, joiners, and brick makers who had trained in London or other English cities and immigrated to the New World with English-manufactured tools and an understanding of the latest fashions. Design ideas also traveled with colonists or Crown officials who had seen the works of English architects firsthand or knew the buildings of London and the provinces. In addition, the great variety of architectural books, published with increasing frequency in Britain from the early eighteenth century onward, made a lasting impact on American design in the late colonial period. They ranged from expensive portfolios such as *Vitruvius Britannicus,* which illustrated the best architectural commissions—mainly aristocratic houses—to cheaper and smaller builders' books that generally described methods

FIG. 1. Imaginary view of the new colony of Georgia with town and church in distance between rows of cultivated mulberry trees. From Benjamin Martyn, *Reasons for Establishing the Colony of Georgia* (London: Meadows, 1733). Courtesy of Library of Congress

of proportioning and the laying out of difficult elements such as stairs, arches, and roof frames and contained plates of display elements such as frontispieces, chimneypieces, and staircases. Although the influence of these books has often been overstated, they did provide a point of reference for a number of American clients seeking reassurance of their aesthetic sensibilities.

Craftsmen with English training and tools, clients with long memories of English buildings, and architectural books with showcase details provided the conduit for the transfer of ideas to the American colonies, but they were tempered by local influences. American architectural design was selective in nature. Colonists carefully chose those aspects of the metropolitan corpus that suited their own peculiar needs and desires. They sometimes transformed the manner in which a feature or detail was used or the way in which they were combined with other elements. Out of this selective blending came distinctive regional patterns that distinguish the early architecture of New England, the mid-Atlantic, the Chesapeake, and the Carolina lowcountry. To understand the colonial design process, it is necessary to consider the nature of those provincial filters (see figure 1).

The most direct link between English design and American building appeared in the drawings made by English architects for American projects. Measured drawings and specifications made explicit academic notions of plan, proportion, and classical detailing that were to be followed in the provinces. Needless to say, such colonial projects were extremely rare. However, the original design and construction of the first Anglican church in Savannah, Georgia, provides an unusual opportunity to observe the interplay between architectural intentions in the metropolis and the execution of those ideas on the periphery of empire. In this case local circumstances had a tremendous impact on the reception of outside sources. Individuals too played an important role in the shaping of the architectural character of the project. The cast included a warrior-idealist who became caught up in a war between two empires; an English craftsman raised to the status of an architect through aristocratic patronage; a cross-eyed, itinerant preacher whose gaze sparkled with holy zeal and mesmerized a generation of Americans; and an English gentleman of great perseverance but down on his luck who found little recompense in his travails as he tried to re-create one of the masterpieces of seventeenth-century church design on the banks of the Savannah River for his absentee masters (see figure 2).

In the early 1730s an unconventional combination of philanthropists and imperialists joined forces to persuade King George II to establish a colony in North America just south of the lowcountry plantations of South Carolina—an area where Spanish and English territorial ambitions clashed. They intended

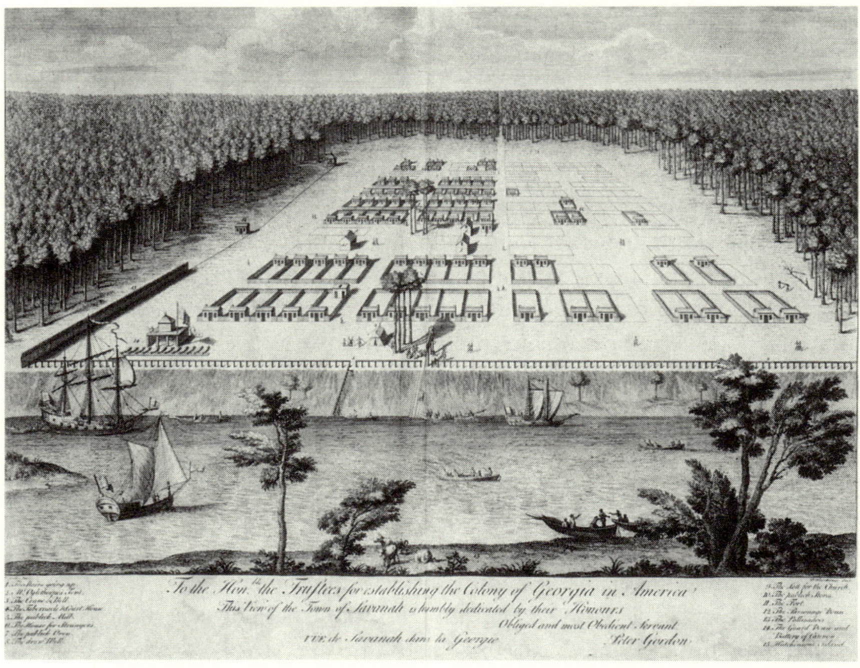

FIG. 2. View of Savannah, 1734; Peter Gordon, architect. Courtesy of Colonial Williamsburg Foundation, Williamsburg, Virginia

Georgia to be a buffer between South Carolina and Spanish Florida and a refuge for the poor and persecuted of England and the continent. The new colony of Georgia was governed during its first twenty years by a board of trustees composed of lords and gentlemen who had long-standing interests in American affairs. They included James Oglethorpe, a soldier who had taken to the cause of prison reform as a member of Parliament; Anthony Ashley Cooper, the fourth Earl of Shaftesbury; and John Percival, the Earl of Egmont, another prison reformer and patron and friend of William Byrd II of Westover.[2] The trustees carefully reviewed the affairs of the colony from their London boardroom, generating voluminous correspondence between them and their surrogates in Georgia. Nothing was too minute for the attention of this well-intentioned board, which sought to restrict the use of slave labor, limit land speculation, and prohibit the consumption of rum. At various times they ordered, cajoled, and implored their servants in Savannah to follow their advice for building houses, raising silk worms, and leading more productive lives. Yet, their effectiveness was limited since they could not control events or circumstances that transpired three thousand miles from their boardroom.

The initial plan to provide for the colonists' religious needs unraveled because of the tenuous threads that bound the trustees to their fledgling colony. Confrontation with the Spanish in the region had been simmering for a number of years and threatened to boil over into war, a crisis that would severely harm the philanthropic enterprise in its infancy. Concern for the spiritual as well as the physical welfare of the first settlers led the trustees to write in 1736 to General Oglethorpe in Savannah asking him to submit a plan for a brick church that would be built in "such a manner that it may on any sudden occasion serve for a Place of Defence; and that the Church Yard should be inclosed with a Palisade and a Ditch."[3] Three years after settlement, more than £750 had already been raised through subscriptions for the project and trust servants had been supplied with copies of the Bible, the Book of Common Prayer, and Richard Allestree's devotional guide *The Whole Duty of Man* from the company storehouse in Savannah.[4]

A year later, after no response from General Oglethorpe, who was busy erecting tabby-walled defenses on St. Simon's Island against Spanish incursions, the trustees decided to confer with London builders in order to obtain an estimate for constructing a substantial brick church "80 feet long, 40 feet broad in the clear, with a square tower 40 feet high, and 20 feet square from out to out. The walls to be 3 feet thick, 10 feet high, and 2 brick and half upwards, all to be render'd [that is, stuccoed on the outside] and white wash'd on the Inside. [There were to be] no windows from 10 feet high to the ground, but loop holes for muskets on occasion."[5] The size of the building suggests that the trustees were planning a structure that would accommodate the demands of a thriving urban population of several thousand inhabitants, as it was considerably larger than most Anglican churches erected in the southern colonies.[6]

The interior was to have a "pulpit, reading desk, communion rail and table, & no pews, but benches, as at Tunbridge."[7] The trustees later decided to amend the set of interior specifications to include a pew for the minister and one for the magistrates but remained adamant that the rest of the church would be filled by benches, which they believed would be "more capacious and less subject to Disputes for places" since pews were traditionally assigned by rank and status within a community.[8] Convinced that benches would "discourage Vanity and Pride of Distinction" that generally accompanied the designation of pew seats, they cited benches in the chapel of King Charles the Martyr in Tunbridge Wells, Kent, as well as in "some Country Churches in England" as felicitous precedents for this more indiscriminate form of seating.[9]

Even as England and Spain slid closer to war in 1738, the Georgia trustees nevertheless continued to make plans for building the Savannah church, which they estimated would cost as much as five hundred pounds.[10] They hired Henry Flitcroft, an architect employed by the royal board of works and a protégé of the third Earl of Burlington, to design a brick church according to their earlier specifications. Although not an architect of the first rank, Flitcroft was an important player in the promotion of Palladian design. In 1734 he completed St. Giles in the Fields in London, a building that derived from James Gibbs's earlier design of St. Martin-in-the-Fields about a mile or so to the south. Perhaps more relevant because of its relative modest scale was Flitcroft's 1737 design for St. Olave, Tooley Street, overlooking the south bank of the Thames in Southwark near London Bridge.[11] His friendship with several of the trustees, from whom he had obtained or was soon to obtain commissions for dwellings, plus his reputation gained from St. Giles and St. Olave probably made him an obvious choice for the Savannah church.[12] Unfortunately, none of his drawings for this commission are known to have survived. It is hard to imagine how he struggled to pare back his Palladian motifs to a few basic elements to fit the modest five-hundred-pound budget. One certainly wonders what Palladian loopholes may have looked like. Perhaps they were a smaller version of the circular windows that lit the second stage of the side aisles at St. Olave (see figure 3).

Flitcroft duly submitted to the trustees his plan for the brick church, which was approved at a meeting on May 17, 1738.[13] The trustees placed these drawings in the hands of Capt. John Thomas (or Tomas), an engineer who was about to embark for the colony in General Oglethorpe's fleet. They authorized the engineer "to make such Alterations in the plan as he may judge most necessary to answer the Intention of the Trustees," especially "if any small Alteration therein may make the said Building a Place of Refuge and Defence for the Inhabitants upon any surprise" since war with the Spanish seemed close at hand. They asked

FIG. 3. St. Olave, Tooley Street, London; Henry Flitcroft, architect. Author's collection

him to make an estimate of the expense of the church once he arrived in Savannah and return it to them.[14] Shipping out with Captain Thomas were supplies for the construction of the church, including several tons of stone for foundations and many bars of iron to be used in the fabrication of hardware. Stowed away in the holds of the transport ships were eighty-five tons of flint stones, five tons of "Dantzick stones" for the foundations, as well as seventy-seven bars of Swedish iron at thirty-two hundredweight, one hundred bars of Russian iron at fifty-four hundredweight, and "6 Faggots of steel" of four hundredweight, which were intended for hardware such as straps for roof trusses, hinges, and nails.[15] In addition, five hundred "deal boards" had been purchased and shipped along with the other items.[16]

Everything that could have been done in London to make the venture a success was done. Sufficient money for the church was in hand. The supply fleet that set sail for Georgia in early summer contained a skilled engineer carrying the plans devised by a prominent Palladian architect. Riding along in the ship's hulls were several essential manufactured materials necessary for the church's construction that would be hard to find in the colony. Captain Thomas had the power to retain as many of the trustees' laborers as were necessary.

Unfortunately, international events and personal tragedy disrupted their plans. General Oglethorpe returned to Georgia in September 1738 to strengthen the colony's defenses. Captain Thomas and his building materials arrived in Savannah with Oglethorpe's fleet, but there was little time for church building as he was sent to St. Simon's Island to help oversee the fabrication of fortifications. After nearly a year of work, mismanagement of the colony's supplies and the impending war put a halt to Oglethorpe's feverish preparations. Captain Thomas took advantage of this break in mid-August 1739 and left St. Simon's. He stopped briefly in Savannah before traveling on to Charleston, where he was to embark for England in a few weeks. While in Charleston in September 1739 he fell victim to smallpox, which was then raging in the city.[17] Apparently, Henry Flitcroft's church design disappeared with the engineer's death in Charleston. No effort was made by the trustees to recover the drawings or to request an additional set from the architect. A few weeks later Spain and England were at war.

After Captain Thomas's death and the realization that their fledgling colony could not sustain such an ambitious building in a time of war, the trustees scaled back their expectations and authorized the construction of a frame church. Savannah's population had decreased significantly in the early 1740s as many who chafed under the restrictive measures of the paternalistic board left the town and colony.[18] Under straitened circumstances, the trustees allotted the expenditure of three hundred pounds on the church and turned over the supervision of its construction to residents in Savannah. In 1741 they sent new instructions about the church, specifying that the frame was to stand on the imported flint-stone foundations and be stuccoed on the outside and plastered on the interior with local oyster-shell lime.[19]

Savannah, like many frontier towns, attracted adventurers, including two young clerics who did indeed make a name for themselves in later years: John Wesley and George Whitefield. The young and not-yet-famous John Wesley did himself little good the brief time he was in town. He started off on the right foot, providing regular worship services in the courthouse, a temporary log structure surrounded by piazzas on three sides.[20] However, his amorous pursuit of a storekeeper's daughter overstepped the bounds of propriety. After she spurned him and married another, he refused to serve her communion and was finally forced to bolt the city in the dead of night.[21]

The next minister to replace him, George Whitefield, would also become one of the most important clerics in eighteenth-century England and America. Whitefield used his position in Savannah to promote his own schemes, including the construction of the Bethesda orphans' asylum a few miles from town in 1740.[22] He spent much of his time employed by the colony's trustees traveling the breadth of the American colonies and stirring up the religious fervor that had begun to boil over in a movement known as the "Great Awakening." Early in his tenure in Savannah, Whitefield seemed to captivate "the People with his moving Discourse, which it was to be hoped would have a good Effect in reforming a great many loose Livers, who heard him gladly."[23] The consummate showman and forerunner of the televangelist of the present era, Whitefield reached the pocketbooks of thousands of colonists as he touched their hearts in a frenzy of preaching[24] (see figure 4).

As cash flowed into his orphanage, Whitefield pressed the trustees to turn over their money to him to supervise the construction of the Savannah church. He was able to get only £150 out of General Oglethorpe and threatened to extort more from the trustees by publishing his own account of their niggardly investment in church building—conveniently overlooking the earlier attempt to build Flitcroft's design. In January 1740 he averred that if no more money was forthcoming, he felt it his "duty to inform pious people in a Publick manner how little good has been done with their Charitable Contributions."[25] In March, Whitefield wrote to London asking yet again for the second £150 earmarked for the project in order to see the church begun. He promised that with this money in hand he would travel to Philadelphia to bring back craftsmen to "carry on the work."[26] The trustees held steadfastly to their money, and Whitefield soon found his interests drawn away from Savannah. Nothing was done over the next three

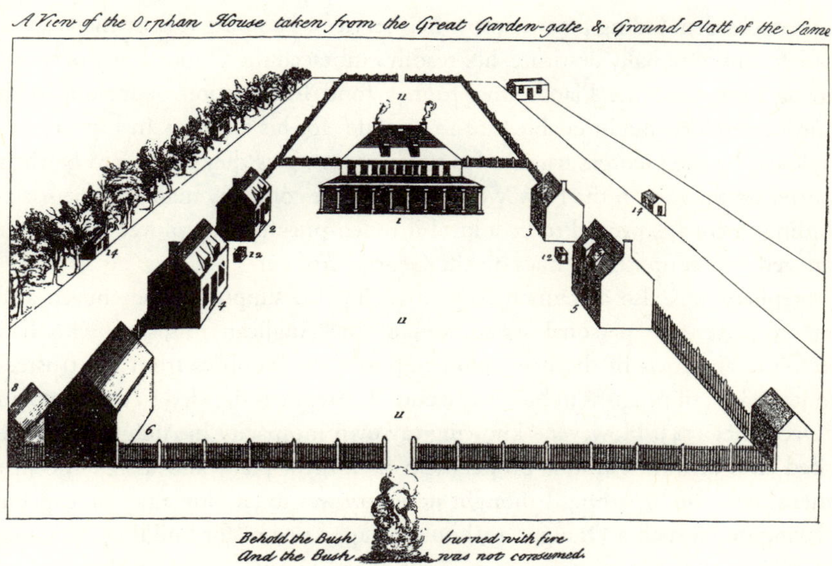

Fig. 4. Bethesda orphans' house, near Savannah, 1740. From George Whitefield, *An Account of Money Received and Disbursed for the Orphan-house in Georgia* (London: T. Cooper, 1741). Courtesy of Library of Congress

years as the trustees tried to recover the £150 that had been advanced to the itinerant evangelist.[27]

After the impasse with Whitefield, the trustees placed the responsibility for building the church on the resident governor William Stephens in May 1743.[28] If Savannah was a promising frontier for young men on the make, it was also a refuge for those hoping to turn their lives around. William Stephens was just such an individual, a man in his early seventies who was on a downward spiral at the end of a career that had a promising start. As a nephew recalled in his biography of his uncle, Stephens's education "was such as suited his Genius, which abhorred any Thing unmanly, therefore, not delighting much in Accomplishments of a softer Nature, such as Dancing, Drawing, etc., it was employed in the Classics, Fencing, Riding, and other manly Exercises."[29]

A graduate of King's College, Cambridge, who then enrolled in one of the temples of law in London, Stephens married well and entered Parliament to represent his family's interests in the Isle of Wight. Squeezed out of his seat by more powerful factions in the Tory Party in the early 1710s, Stephens became involved in overseeing timbering operations in Scotland. In the boom time of the 1720s, when easy money was to be had in schemes such as the "South Sea Bubble," investment in Scottish lumber seemed a good return. He later discovered that his benefactors had mismanaged the accounts, skimming off thousands of pounds for their own pockets. He was caught on the spot in northern Scotland by angry lumberjacks demanding payment for their services. Escaping this financial scam that left him personally destitute, he "readily embraced the Opportunity of transporting himself to the Plantations, from a fond Imagination of making such Improvements, as might enable him to provide" for his family.[30] In 1737 he was employed by the Georgia trustees "to write of things as they occur," to be their reporter on the spot in the New World.[31] A reliable company man of some social standing, Stephens proved to be a loyal if much-put-upon employee who never managed to recoup his fortunes on the Georgia frontier.

Stephens was also a staunch Anglican who had supported the church and despaired over the personal weaknesses of the Anglican ministers who had heretofore appeared in the new colony. Spurred by inquiries from the trustees about the lack of progress in building a church, Stephens decided to devise a plan in December 1743. However, "knowing my own incapacity in Architecture," he "dared not Venture without proper help to form a plan, and assign the just dimensions. The first thing I thought necessary was to employ a person capable of laying down such a Draught as should be approved of for building the same, and having seen several sketches of Peter Joubert (one of our Freeholders) in Engraving of various kinds, shewing his Ingenuity, (I wish I could say Diligence too), I resolved to try him."[32] Stephens's early education had marked him as a reluctant draftsman, so he was forced to choose someone who showed some sketching ability. Unfortunately, Peter Joubert was more noted for his idle and drunken ways, which a few years later led to his dismissal as the colony's schoolteacher.[33] Stephens had approached Joubert two months earlier with the idea but got nothing from him.

This unlikely partnership eventually produced a church design after a long conversation. They started the process by thinking about precedents from home, specifically a London church. They turned to a building designed by England's greatest early seventeenth-century architect. Stephens observed "that Covent Garden Church happening to be well known to both, I had recommended that to him as a Model in his Imagination to work by, as well for its being deemed a Curious piece of Inico Jones, as because the Work will come much Cheaper for being so very plain. Wherefore I apprehend the less we vary from it the better except in the difference necessary to observe in Relations to its Extension, and that admired Work the Roof, which surpasses all other skill here to imitate."[34]

As a former student at the temple and a member of Parliament, Stephens probably knew St. Paul's well from his time in London, but his memory may have been aided by a print of it that could have circulated in the Georgia colony. St. Paul's was built at the West End of Covent Garden, the first formal square developed in the early 1630s in London by the Earl of Bedford. Inigo Jones's simple design with deep projecting eaves came from a literal interpretation of the primitive Vitruvian Tuscan order described by Andrea Palladio. Though widely admired before the English civil war, it spawned few ecclesiastical imitators for nearly a century until the third Earl of Burlington, a Palladian enthusiast, restored its portico in 1727.[35] Alexander Pope gave Burlington's reputation a boost the following year in *The Dunciad*, a wildly popular poem that extolled the virtues of the man who "revived the true Taste of Architecture in this Kingdom."[36] By this time the fashion for the relatively chaste qualities of St. Paul's, with its simple forms, had displaced the more exuberant excesses of baroque design characteristic of the earlier works of Wren, Hawksmoor, and Vanbrugh. Derived from the precedents found in the works of Jones and Palladio, the Palladian-revival church design promoted by the earl and his circle of architects, including Henry Flitcroft, began to flourish throughout the kingdom by the 1730s. Even in the remote Lincolnshire wolds, the builder of St. Peter and St. Paul at Langton-by-Spilsby took his cue for his pedimented roof and pattern of fenestration from the metropolitan source at St. Paul's, Covent Garden[37] (see figure 5).

If the source of inspiration for William Stephens and his schoolmaster draftsman was well known and much admired, the reason for adopting and adapting its design derived purely from local circumstances. Joubert made a copy of their design, and Stephens shipped it off for the trustees' approval, which was slow in coming and filled with additional instructions. Needless to say, what rose on the banks of the Savannah River was not an incarnation of Jones's masterpiece but

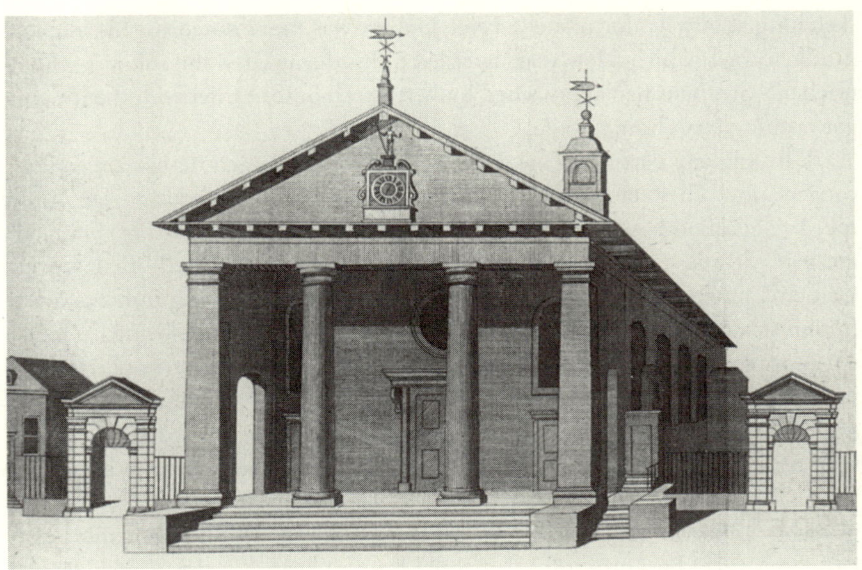

FIG. 5. St. Paul's, Covent Garden, London; Inigo Jones, architect. From William Maitland, *The History of London from Its Foundation to the Present Time* (London: T. Lowndes, G. Kearsly & S. Bladon, 1772). Courtesy of Colonial Williamsburg Foundation, Williamsburg, Virginia

rather a simple frame church standing on imported stone foundations. Work began in earnest on the building in March 1744 as carpenters and sawyers provided scantling and workmen burned lime and hauled materials, including Captain Thomas's flints, to the building site on trustee lot D on the southeast corner of Johnson Square.[38] On March 28 the Anglican rector Rev. Thomas Bosomworth conducted a cornerstone-laying ceremony for Christ Church with a sermon based on Psalm 122: "Let us go into the house of the LORD." Stephens noted that the service was "done with due decency" and was followed by "a small Collation provided for the principal Workmen . . . avoiding all excess in either etables or drink."[39] By mid-May the stone foundations had been completed three feet above ground level. As carpenters prepared the framing during the summer, Stephens began to worry that the project could not be completed for the three hundred pounds allotted by the trustees. In October the frame was completed, and workmen began preparations for closing it and covering the roof with cypress shingles. Shortly after this the money ran out, and work came to a standstill.[40]

Two years later, in September 1746, Stephens wrote to the trustees to remind them that the "Church unhappily stands a skeleton."[41] Their response the following spring expressed surprise; in their estimate, they had already expended more than four hundred pounds on a project that showed no sign of completion. In order to reduce costs, they recommended that instead of a stuccoed and plastered finish, the walls were to be enclosed with feather-edged weatherboards and covered with tar and sand, and the interior was to be sheathed with boards and painted since plasterwork, "unless very well done, will soon decay, and must be more expensive."[42] They also granted permission to the locals to spend more money to finish the project. With "new Life given Us for compleating the work," William Stephens and his committee decided after a long consultation with Savannah workmen to ignore these fresh instructions from London about walling materials. They were convinced, after a decade and a half of experience, that "no weatherboards will last above ten years, before the Heat of the Sun rends them" useless and that walls stuccoed with cement would last five times longer than weatherboards.[43]

With cash payments mounting to more than £522 over the following three years for labor and materials such as oil paint and crown glass for the sash windows, Stephens's group managed to finish the church according to their designs.[44] The exterior was stuccoed in imitation of stone in a manner similar to that used on the church erected farther up the Savannah River in Augusta at the same time. The outside of the Augusta church was described as "rough-cast with Lime and Gravil appearing like Stone, the inside Plaister'd white-wash'd, and arch'd." The interior of the church too may have been arranged in the same way as that of the Augusta church, with an entrance on each of the north and south long walls, and the pulpit, clerk's seat, and communion table arranged in a central row just east of the transverse aisle. On the opposite side of the aisle stood the pews for the principal officials. The Augusta church had a series of regular pews arranged along the outer walls as opposed to benches, as had been originally stipulated for the Savannah church.[45] In 1750, a dozen years after Flitcroft's initial drawings and following a number of false starts, design changes, the squandering of building funds, and long-distance wrangling over construction methods and materials, the trustees wrote to the Reverend Bartholomew Zouberbuhler, the man who had seen to it that Peter Joubert was fired from his post as schoolmaster because of his "Neglect and Drunkenness," that they were pleased "to hear that Divine Service is performed in the Church in Savannah."[46] Perhaps Joubert raised a glass of forbidden rum to toast the completion of his design (see figure 6).

Surprisingly, Christ Church survived for more than fifty years before it was replaced by a much larger structure after a fire destroyed much of Savannah in 1796. Long in coming, it outlasted trustee control of Georgia, whose charter reverted to the Crown in 1753. The church, like the history of the colony, diverged widely from initial intentions. Despite having a design produced by one of the leading Palladian architects of England, the trustees could do nothing

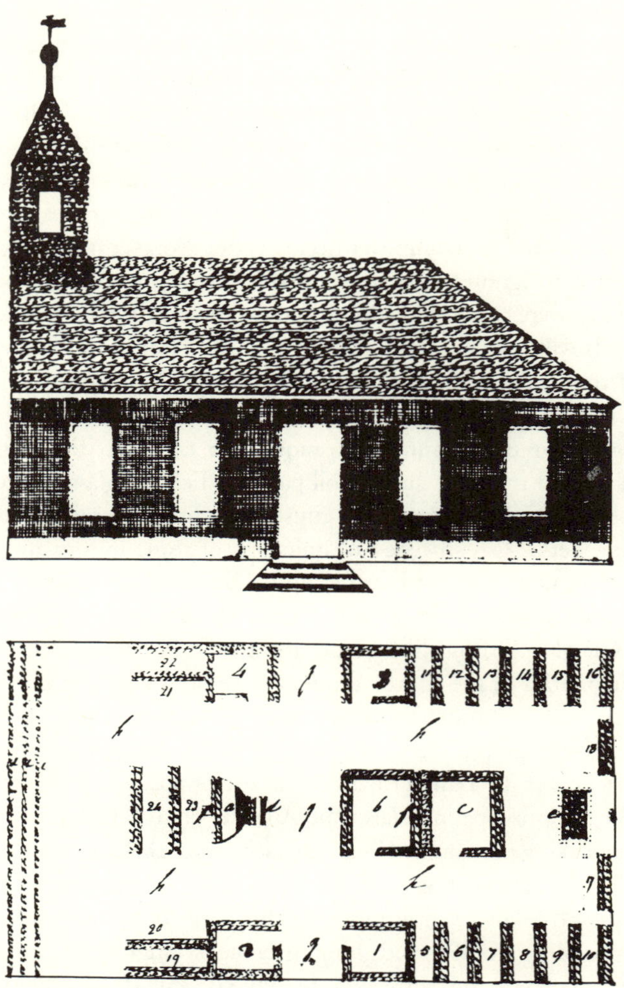

Fig. 6. Plan and elevation of St. Paul's, Augusta, Georgia, 1749. Courtesy of United Society for the Propagation of the Gospel, London, England

about the frailty of local conditions that prevented the execution of the plan as proposed. They even recognized the fact that Flitcroft's design would have to be modified to the economic and social circumstances of an infant colony uneasily poised on the border between two empires. Ambitious though it was, logistical impediments, the absence of a forceful and determined client in Savannah, and war defeated their best efforts. When building began in earnest in the 1740s, the experience of craftsmen with local materials and conditions transformed the church into something that was distinctly regional in character.

As the Savannah church episode underscores, few if any British academic design ideas transferred unaltered to the North American continent. Rather, there was an imaginative interplay between local practices and metropolitan ideas, producing variants that were recognizably Anglo-American in concept and in many small details but were distinctly regional in their overall form. The grammar of Georgia's early architecture may have been Georgian, but its syntax was peculiarly native due to the influence of local economic and social conditions, climate, topography, materials, technological capabilities, and craft skills. The long struggle to build the first Anglican Church in Savannah demonstrates how that process evolved. Architectural design in eighteenth-century America was not straightforward but is immeasurably more interesting because of the regional conditions that shaped it.

Notes

1. An influential standard treatment is John Summerson, *Architecture in Britain, 1530–1830,* 9th ed. (New Haven, Conn.: Yale University Press, 1993).

2. On the connection between William Byrd and John Percival, see Mark R. Wenger, ed., *The English Travels of Sir John Percival and William Byrd II: The Percival Diary of 1701* (Columbia: University of Missouri Press, 1989).

3. Kenneth Coleman and Milton Ready, eds., *The Colonial Records of the State of Georgia,* vol. 29, *Trustees' Letter Book, 1732–1738* (Athens: University of Georgia Press, 1985), 127.

4. Ibid.; *The Journal of Peter Gordon, 1732–1735* (Athens: University of Georgia Press, 1963), 38.

5. Robert G. McPherson, ed., *Journal of the Earl of Egmont: Abstract of the Trustees Proceedings for Establishing the Colony of Georgia, 1732–1738* (Athens: University of Georgia Press, 1962), 284.

6. Although St. Philip's Church in Charleston, which was finished in the early 1720s after more than a decade of work, contained more square feet (approximately sixty by seventy-five to eighty feet) as well as an impressive three-sided portico, the rural parish churches in South Carolina could not match the size of the Savannah design. Prince William, Sheldon, erected near Beaufort in the 1750s, measured forty-five by sixty-five feet. I am grateful to Louis Nelson for supplying the measurements of St. Philip's Church based on his study of its early history.

7. McPherson, ed., *Journal of the Earl of Egmont,* 284.

8. Trustees to General George Oglethorpe, June 11, 1740, Christ Church Parish Records, Georgia Historical Society, box 4, folder 89; transcript of Colonial Office 5/667, Public Record Office, London.

9. Kenneth Coleman, ed., *The Colonial Records of the State of Georgia,* vol. 30, *Trustees' Letter Book, 1738–1745* (Athens: University of Georgia Press, 1985), 132.

10. McPherson, ed., *Journal of the Earl of Egmont,* 285, 287.

11. I would like to thank Dr. Terry Friedman for drawing my attention to this Flitcroft design as well as reviewing an earlier draft of this essay (correspondence with author, November 10, 2000).

12. Henry Flitcroft designed No. 10, St. James's Square, London, in 1735–36 for Georgia trustee Sir William Heathcote, Bart. Between 1740 and 1744 the architect redesigned a number of rooms at Wimborne House in Dorset for the fourth earl of Shaftesbury. See Howard Colvin, *A Biographical Dictionary of British Architects 1600–1840,* 3d ed. (New Haven, Conn.: Yale University Press, 1995), 368–69. I would like to thank Howard Colvin for drawing attention to the connection between Flitcroft and his patrons who served as trustees of the Georgia colony (correspondence with author, December 8, 1991).

13. Allen Candler, ed., *The Colonial Records of the State of Georgia,* vol. 2, *The Minutes of the Common Council of the Trustees, 1732–1752* (Atlanta: Franklin Printing and Publishing Co., 1904), 243; McPherson, ed., *Journal of the Earl of Egmont,* 363–64.

14. Kenneth Coleman, ed., *The Colonial Records of the State of Georgia,* vol. 32, *Entry Books of Commissions, Powers, Instructions, Leases, Grants of Land, etc. by the Trustees, 1732–1738* (Athens: University of Georgia Press, 1989), 279.

15. Coleman and Ready, eds., *Trustees' Letter Book, 1732–1738,* 272.

16. McPherson, ed., *Journal of the Earl of Egmont,* 321; Allen Candler, ed., *The Colonial Records of the State of Georgia,* vol. 3, *The General Account of All Monies and Effects Receiving and Expended by the Trustees, 1732–1751* (Atlanta: Franklin Printing, 1905), 170.

17. William Stephens, *A Journal of the Proceedings in Georgia,* 2 vols. (London: W. Meadows, 1742; repr., Ann Arbor, Mich.: University Microfilms, 1966), 2:146.

18. Kenneth Coleman, *Colonial Georgia: A History* (New York: Charles Scribner's Sons, 1976), 53.

19. Coleman, ed., *Trustees' Letter Book, 1738–1745,* 228.

20. By the end of 1740 the building had fallen into disrepair and required significant shoring to prevent the decaying logs from sinking further. See William Stephens to Harman Verelst, December 31, 1740, Christ Church Parish Records, Georgia Historical Society, box 4, folder 97; transcript of Colonial Office 5/670, no. 240, Public Record Office, London; Clarence Ver Steeg, ed., *A True and Historical Narrative of the Colony of Georgia by Pat Tailfer and Others with Comments by the Earl of Egmont, 1741* (Athens: University of Georgia Press, 1960), 140.

21. Stephens, *Journal of the Proceedings in Georgia,* 1:45.

22. For a history, see Edward J. Cashin, *Beloved Bethesda: A History of George Whitefield's Home for Boys, 1740–2000* (Macon, Ga.: Mercer University Press, 2001).

23. Ibid., 222.

24. On Whitefield's uncanny ability to raise money from his audiences, see Leonard Labaree et al., eds., *The Autobiography of Benjamin Franklin* (New Haven, Conn.: Yale University Press, 1964), 177–79.

25. George Whitefield to Harman Verelst, Secretary to the Georgia Trustees, January 28, 1740, Letters from Georgia, box 51, folder 683, MH and DB Floyd Collection, Georgia Historical Society, Savannah.

26. Allen Candler, ed., *The Colonial Records of the State of Georgia* (Atlanta: Franklin-Turner, 1904–16), 22, pt. 2: 359.

27. On trying to trace the errant £150, see the letter from Benjamin Martyn to James Habersham, Whitefield's partner in the Orphanage House in Bethesda, May 10, 1743, in Coleman, ed., *Trustees' Letter Book, 1738–1745,* 272.

28. Ibid., 284–85.

29. Thomas Stephens, *The Castle-Builders; or, the History of William Stephens, of the Isle of Wight, Esq., lately deceased, a Political Novel* (London: printed for the author, 1759), 19.

30. Ibid., 91.

31. Ibid., 100.

32. William Stephens, *The Journal of William Stephens 1743–1745*, ed. Merton Coulter (Athens: University of Georgia Press, 1959), 50, December 14, 1743.

33. Merton Coulter and Albert B. Saye, eds., *A List of Early Settlers of Georgia* (Athens: University of Georgia Press, 1949), no. 740.

34. Stephens, *Journal of William Stephens*, 50–51, December 15, 1743.

35. Morris R. Brownell, *Alexander Pope & the Arts of Georgian England* (Oxford: Clarendon Press, 1978), 299.

36. In the third book of the *Dunciad*, Pope wrote of Lord Burlington: "You too proceed! Make falling Arts your care, / Erect new wonders, and the old repair, / Jones and Palladio to themselves restore, / And be whate'er Virtruius was before." See Pat Rogers, ed., *Alexander Pope: A Critical Edition of the Major Works* (Oxford: Oxford University Press, 1993), 511.

37. The interior of St. Peter and St. Paul was straightforward Georgian design, common to any part of the Anglo-American empire by the middle of the eighteenth century.

38. I would like to thank Caroline Warner of the Savannah College of Art and Design for providing this information.

39. Stephens, *Journal of William Stephens*, 77, 87.

40. Ibid., 103, 129–30,158–59.

41. Christ Church Parish Records, Georgia Historical Society, box 4, folder 98; transcript of Colonial Office 5/642, no. 22, Public Record Office, London.

42. Kenneth Coleman, ed., *The Colonial Records of the State of Georgia*, vol. 31, *Trustees' Letter Book, 1745–1752* (Athens: University of Georgia Press, 1986), 55.

43. Stephens and his committee contracted with workmen to finish the walls in August 1747 in the following manner: "To be watled betwixt the Studs with white Oak Watling, and filled up on each Side with a strong Plaister, that the Studs should be wholly covered at least three Quarters of an Inch, so that the Walls will be upwards of eight Inches thick; the Out Side to be covered with strong Cement, and neatly sett off in Imitation of Stone Work; the Inside when finished to be a clean plaistered White Wall" (Allen Candler, ed., *The Colonial Records of the State of Georgia*, vol. 6, *Proceedings of the President and Assistants, 1741–1754* [Atlanta: Franklin Printing Co., 1906], 188–89).

44. Candler, ed., *The General Account of All Monies and Effects Receiving and Expended by the Trustees, 1732–1751*, 317, 342, 355.

45. Description in Edward J. Cashin, ed., *Colonial Augusta: "Key of the Inian Countrey"* (Macon, Ga.: Mercer University Press, 1986), 112.

46. Coleman, ed., *Trustees' Letter Book, 1745–1752*, 216. The Reverend Zouberbuhler had replaced the Reverend Bosomworth as minister in Savannah in 1746.

The Diversity of Countries

Anglican Churches in Virginia, South Carolina, and Jamaica

Louis P. Nelson

> It is not necessary that traditions and ceremonies be in all places one, or utterly alike, for at all times they have been diverse, and may be changed according to the diversity of countries, times, and men's manners.

By including these words in the 1571 foundational document "The 39 Articles," the fathers of the Anglican Church understood that the visible church would take a multitude of forms as it was realized in a multitude of local circumstances. The founding fathers might not have realized, however, that the most formative local conditions that would shape the traditions of the local church would be not particularly religious but sociopolitical in nature. By the opening of the eighteenth century, the three regions under consideration in this book—the Chesapeake, the lowcountry, and the British Caribbean—had much in common. All three were founded in the seventeenth century and populated principally by the English. Each developed a highly profitable economy that depended on enslaved labor. In each the Church of England enjoyed establishment status that blurred the boundaries between church and state. That status opened public coffers for church construction and gave a certain political and social capital to membership in the church. Nonetheless, these three were distinct; the architecture of Anglicanism highlights far more the differences between these regions than their similarities.[1]

In a brief window of about eighteen months, three major Anglican congregations in Williamsburg, Virginia; Charleston, South Carolina; and Spanish Town, Jamaica, would begin designing churches that would eventually become the "mother churches" of Anglicanism in their respective colonies. The tall brick walls of Bruton Parish Church in Williamsburg (1711–15) rose on the plan of a narrow and elongated Latin cross (see figure 1). Nothing other than regular,

Fig. 1. Bruton Parish Church, Williamsburg, Virginia, 1711–15, with the 1750 addition to the east and the 1769 tower. Author's photograph

compass-headed sash windows and compass-headed double doors disturb the building's flat walls of rich Flemish bond masonry. Circular, or "bull's-eye," windows open through the otherwise plain northern and southern gable ends above the double doors. In the 1750s the church was lengthened to the east, and the simple western tower and spire were added in 1769.

Beginning in the same year, Anglicans in Charleston began designing a building that indulged in architectural refinements (see figure 2). St. Philip's (1711–23) was a large brick building that depended on rows of interior columns to support its great width. The body of the exterior alternated pilasters with huge, compass-headed windows. Three porticoes of monumental Tuscan columns, each carrying a pediment, fronted the western vestibule, one each facing north, west, and south. Above the vestibule rose an octagonal tower—again with pilasters—capped by a dome. The final product was often compared to the grand churches of seventeenth-century London. Sadly, it burned in 1834.

Like the new church in Williamsburg, St. Catherine's in Spanish Town (1712–14) would also have soaring brick walls rising on the plan of a Latin cross (see figure 3). The compass-headed windows of this church were filled with horizontal, vertical, and Y-shaped mullions, and like St. Philip's in Charleston, they alternated with pilasters along the building's exterior. A solid parapet of molded brickwork pierced by ornamental iron downspouts crowned the walls, and rusticated quoins defined the corners of the building and trimmed the door openings.

Fig. 2. St. Philip's Church, Charleston, South Carolina, 1711–23; burned in 1835. From *Gentleman's Magazine* (London), June 1753. Courtesy of Special Collections, Thomas Cooper Library, University of South Carolina, Coumbia

Fig. 3. St. Catherine's Parish Church, Spanish Town, Jamaica, 1712–14, as painted by Philip Wickstead in the early nineteenth century before the addition of the western tower and the Gothic revival chancel. From the Collections of the West India Committee, London

Similar to those of the structure in Williamsburg, circular windows lit the church through the gable ends. In 1817 a square tower with a wooden spire was erected at the western end, and in 1848 a large Gothic chancel replaced the eighteenth-century original.

The differences in these three near-contemporary colonial Anglican churches are telling evidence of the discrete sociopolitical circumstances in which each was designed and constructed. Architectural and cultural historians should look not for commonalities to link the Chesapeake, the lowcountry, and the Caribbean as components of a common cultural landscape but for differences that demonstrate the formation of local cultural conditions that materialized distinctive traditions.

Bruton Parish Church

In 1706 members of the vestry of Bruton Parish Church began to consider replacing their second church—an old and failing brick building erected in 1683—with their third. Hoping to spend no more than five hundred pounds, the vestry insisted that "a Church of ye same dimensions of ye old church will be large enough."[2] They would abandon their plan simply to replace the existing church when, in 1711, an eager Gov. Alexander Spotswood provided a ground plan for a cruciform church and public funds for the additional portions of their new building. Spotswood presented the vestry with a plat or draft of a church "whose length 75 foot, and breadth 28 foot in the clear, with two wings on each side, whose width is 22 foot."[3] The governor suggested that the vestry pay for the first fifty-three feet—not much more than they had already intended to build—and that he would finance the northern and southern wings. When the estimates for construction came in for more than the vestry had anticipated, Spotswood stepped in again, this time offering to provide the bricks at a rate lower than that estimated by the contractors.[4]

The church that Spotswood was so eager to see completed would differ from earlier Anglican churches in the colony in two important ways. First, Bruton Parish Church was erected according to a cruciform plan, the first example of that church plan in the colony (see figure 4). Older brick churches in Virginia—including the second Bruton Parish Church—were longitudinal structures with lengths at least twice their widths.[5] The 1680s Newport Parish Church in Isle of Wight County is a good example of this longitudinal plan (see figure 5). The principal entrance is through the western tower, and the clergy gained access through a smaller, southern chancel door, preserving an ancient English tradition. Close versions of this plan—in brick and frame, with and without the tower—appeared throughout the seventeenth-century Anglican world, including in rural parishes across England, in Barbados, and in Jamaica. Virginia was no exception.

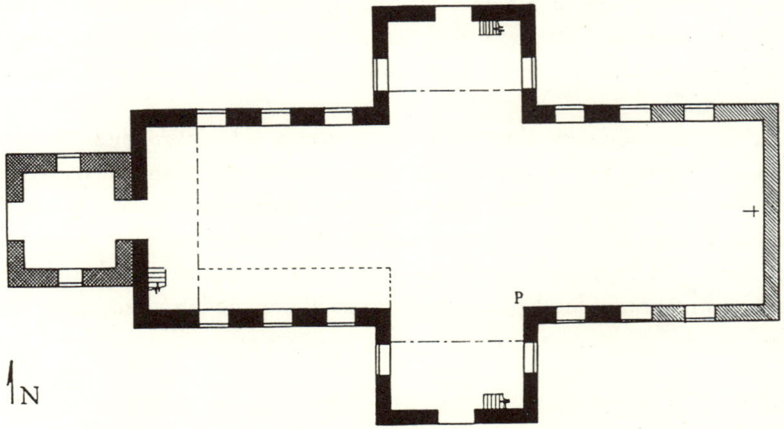

Fig. 4. Bruton Parish Church, Williamsburg, Virginia, 1711–15, with 1750 addition to the east and 1769 tower. Plan by Carl Lounsbury

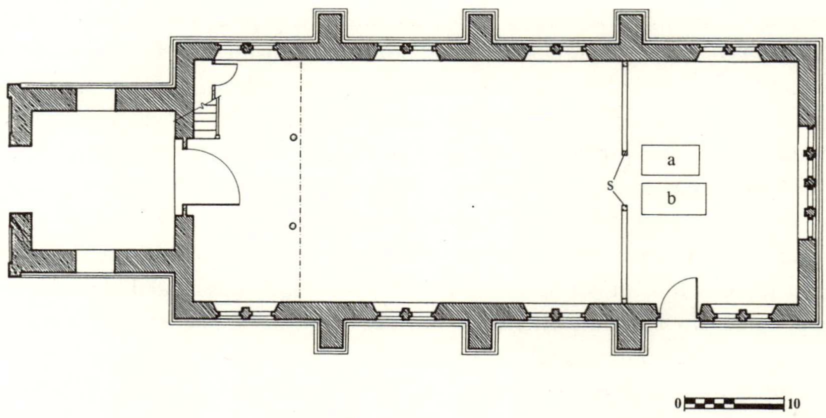

Fig. 5. Newport Parish Church, Isle of Wight County, Virginia, 1680s. Plan by Dell Upton

While Bruton Parish's cruciform plan appears to be an innovation suggested by the new governor, there is no evidence to suggest that Virginians understood this plan to symbolize the cross. Not once in the records do Virginians use the terms "cruciform" or "transept." In fact, the building is often discussed in terms implying that the northern and southern extensions are simply wings appended to a longitudinal body to accommodate additional seating. For example, Spotswood would write to the House of Burgesses in November 1712 stating, "Your address presented to me yesterday gives me occasion to let you know that I shall diminish the wings projected for the public use in the Parish Church of Bruton since I perceive you will be contented with less Room therein."[6]

For Spotswood and his Virginia audience, those northern and southern extensions were nothing more than symmetrical wings that provided additional space; they were not essential elements of a symbolic floor plan. There are at least two reasons why Spotswood's Virginia audience would not have conceived of the new church as cruciform. While Spotswood was familiar with cruciform-planned churches in their medieval inception in England, the vast majority of his audience was not. By the closing decades of the seventeenth century Virginia's resident population was native-born as a variety of other colonies—including South Carolina and Jamaica—became more popular immigration destinations. Contributing to this decline in immigration was the falling price of tobacco. Thus, by the opening decades of the eighteenth century Virginia's social hierarchy was in place.[7] The population was made up of the sons and grandsons of the elite cavaliers who had arrived in the middle decades of the seventeenth century.[8] The medieval cruciform-planned church was not part of their world.

Furthermore, the cruciform plan was almost entirely unknown in new church construction in post-Reformation England. With a small handful of exceptions, Anglicans in England almost never built on the cruciform plan. This is true because the vast majority of Anglicans, and especially those in Virginia, were Low Churchmen, Anglicans who had drunk deeply of the Reformation and rejected the liturgical forms, theology, and material trappings of their Catholic past. The cross was far too closely associated with "papism" to have been used by any English Protestants between the Reformation and the dawn of the nineteenth century.[9] A rare example of a seventeenth-century cruciform church is All Saints, Farley, in Wiltshire, from the 1690s (see figure 6). Yet, even here the northern wing serves as a private chapel and the southern wing as a vestry room, leaving the elongated nave to read as a traditional Anglican church. Again, the cruciform plan was a convenient answer to functional needs.

It comes as no surprise, then, that Bruton's vestry would refer to their new church as having wings and not transepts. The design of the new church departed from older Anglican churches in Virginia in a second important way: its adherence to an architectural language that favored symmetry and geometric proportions and eschewed extraneous ornament. The buttresses found along the walls of the earlier Bruton Church and along the sides of Newport Parish Church were eliminated. The new church also adopted an entirely different approach to fenestration than that evident in St. Peter's Parish Church, only ten years younger (see figure 7). At St. Peter's the windows were paired sash divided by a mullion and covered by a segmental arch, although the windows themselves remained rectangular. In the older church the windows were also arranged in ways that more clearly reflected the organization of the interior; two windows flanked the

Fig. 6. All Saints, Farley, Wiltshire, 1690. The principal entrance is through the western tower. The footprint is a cruciform plan—rare in seventeenth-century England—but the southern wing, visible in this image, is the vestry room, and the northern wing serves as a private chapel, so that the interior reads as a longitudinal nave. The smallest southern door opens directly into the chancel. Author's photograph

important southern chancel door, and the third simply floated in the midst of the wall. The curvilinear gable—partially obscured by the 1739–40 tower—provided a visual richness and ornament, while the English bond brickwork energized the wall plane with horizontal bands.

The builders of Bruton abandoned most of these features—including the southern chancel entrance—to adopt the symmetry and regularity that would become hallmarks of eighteenth-century Anglican churches in the colony. Compass-headed windows trimmed with rubbed-brick arches regularly opened through a plane of Flemish bond brickwork. Their precise sizes and regular spacing demonstrated a greater concern for the external order than was evident in earlier churches. This dependence on mathematical precision even extended to the proportions of the plan and elevation; Marcus Whiffen has demonstrated that the plan of the building was carefully driven by a geometry wedded to the golden section.[10] The vestry minutes do suggest that the church might have originally had ornamental gables comparable to those at St. Peter's. A 1742 entry indicates, however, that the "brick ornaments of the Gavel ends" were to be removed, further evidence that the church was striving to achieve a "neat and plain" appearance free from extraneous ornament.[11]

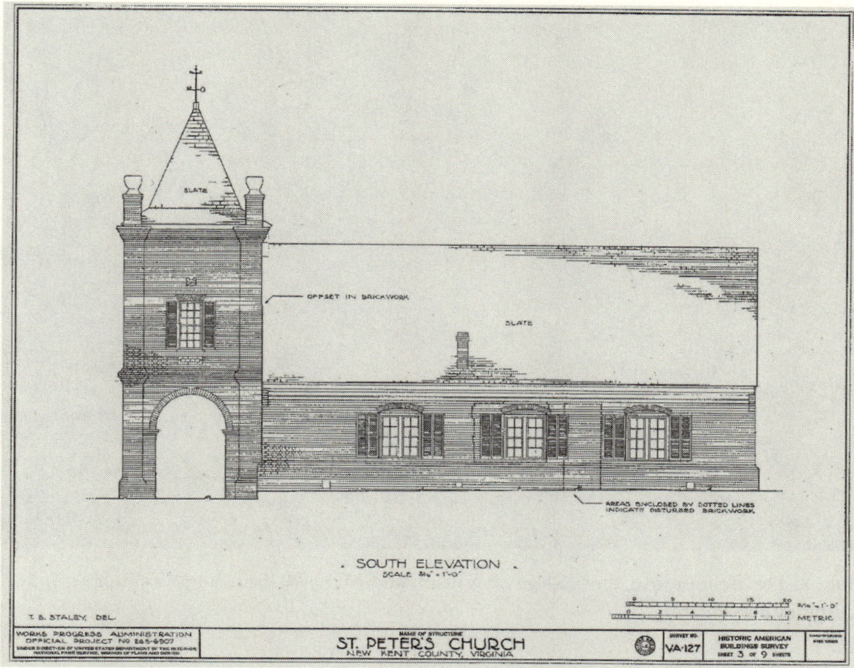

Fig. 7. St. Peter's Parish Church, New Kent County, Virginia, 1701–3, tower 1739–40. Courtesy of Library of Congress

The church that the Bruton vestry began to build in 1711 was quite different from earlier churches in the colony, but it found correspondence with the other public buildings rising in Williamsburg in the opening decades of the eighteenth century. In 1699 the capital of Virginia was moved from Jamestown to a remote site then called Middle Plantation, soon to become Williamsburg. The college building of William and Mary stood on the site before it became the colonial capital, but soon after 1699 a bevy of buildings would rise in the town: a capitol (1701–5); the Governor's Palace (1706–15); a powder magazine (1714–15); two flankers to the college, the Brafferton (circa 1723) (see figure 8) and the President's House (1732–34); and Bruton Parish Church. All these new buildings incorporated the new taste for mathematic regularity and the absence of extraneous ornament.

While historians might be inclined to chase after the origin of Spotswood's cruciform plan—he is attributed with the "beauty and conveniency" of the Governor's Palace—the greater import lies in the building's participation in the broader architectural shift that some refer to as "Georgianization."[12] The builders of Bruton made conscious architectural choices that integrated their church into

Fig. 8. The Brafferton at the College of William and Mary, Williamsburg, Virginia, c. 1723. Author's photograph

a larger architectural whole that was governed by a limited architectural vocabulary: geometrically and mathematically disposed plans and elevations and carefully proportioned sash windows trimmed with simple rubbed bricks and regularly positioned in walls of Flemish bond masonry, all finished with a plainness that eschewed extraneous ornament. Contemporary Virginians often used the phrase "neat and plain" to reflect these aesthetic choices.[13] As Dell Upton has shown, this limiting of the range of options in early eighteenth-century Virginia created "codes that depended on and at the same time reinforced the connections among small groups of people."[14]

By the early eighteenth century Virginia's elite—the famous "first families of Virginia" who largely arrived in the middle decades of the seventeenth century—had become well entrenched, and they utilized the "neat and plain" architecture of the church, the state, and their homes as a way of asserting and maintaining their sociopolitical status. It is in this context that the fairly widespread adoption of the cruciform plan in eighteenth-century Virginia should be understood. The use of this plan was certainly no sign that Virginia's Anglicans were High Churchmen, for history tells us otherwise. The adoption of the cruciform plan by later builders—Robert "King" Carter's Christ Church, Lancaster, is an excellent example—was a way for other Virginia elites to associate themselves with an architectural vocabulary of established political authority begun in Williamsburg and perpetuated throughout the colonial period (see figures 9 and 10).[15]

Fig. 9. Christ Church, Lancaster County, Virginia, 1732–35. Author's photograph

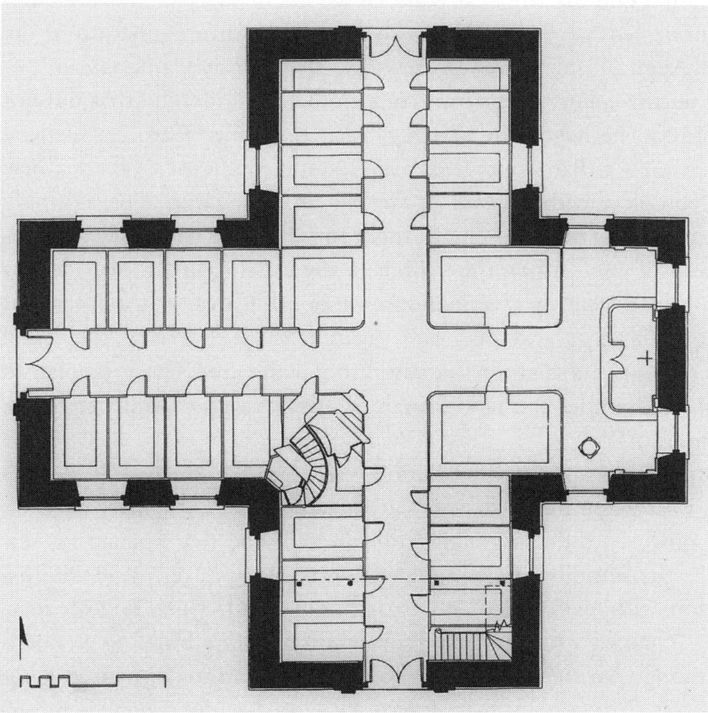

Fig. 10. Christ Church, Lancaster County, Virginia, 1732–35. Plan by Carl R. Lounsbury

However, that specific architectural code would apply only to Virginia. Just a few hundred miles southward, South Carolinians would erect Anglican churches that responded to an entirely different social and historical context.

St. Philip's, Charleston

Upon his arrival in South Carolina in 1708, the Reverend Gideon Johnston informed the bishop of London that the colony was comprised of people "from Bermudas, Jamaica, Barbadoes, Montserat, Antego, Nevis," among a handful of other locales.[16] As Johnston began to take stock of his surroundings, he noted the heavy preponderance of Caribbean immigrants in South Carolina. This preponderance would have appeared even more so to a new Anglican minister since the vast majority of those Caribbean immigrants were Anglican. Given that approximately 54 percent of all white immigrants who entered the colony between 1670 and 1690 were from Barbados alone, Johnston's notion that South Carolina conceived of itself as the offspring of the Caribbean was well founded. Historians of South Carolina have made much of the colony's Barbadian roots.[17] The emphasis on this Barbadian connection has birthed a mythology that South Carolina's colonial architecture owes much of its character to that of the Caribbean.[18]

Historians often cite the Anglican Church as one of those institutions that most closely connected South Carolina with Barbados. An examination of the architecture of Anglicanism indicates, however, that South Carolina's unique context would set the colony on its own course of cultural identity that did not reflect its Caribbean heritage. On March 1, 1711, the South Carolina General Assembly passed an act that empowered Charleston's Anglicans to erect a new brick church "complete with a tower or steeple" in their city.[19] The assembly appointed a minister and five prominent Anglican merchants to oversee the construction. Instead of conforming the church to the existing urban plan, as was the case with all the dissenting meetinghouses in South Carolina, the Anglicans chose to disrupt the city's grid plan and position their church as the visual terminus of the major north-south avenue through the city. The 1739 plan of Charleston, which includes the new church, illustrates well the impact of the new site (see figure 11).

In a dramatic scheme informed by baroque city planning, the new St. Philip's in Charleston visually dominated the city's urban landscape. The church as it was begun in 1711, however, differed greatly from the building that opened for services in 1723. In the summer of 1713 Gideon Johnston, minister to St. Philip's, sailed to London with the specific intent of raising funds from English merchants. He was "charged with procuring subscriptions for ye building a church in his parish among ye merchants trading to that place, without which it is not possible to finish it."[20] In a letter from the clergy carried by Johnson, the ministers informed the bishop of London, "They are now building a large brick

Church at Charles Town 100 foot long in the clear and 45 broad."[21] These dimensions suggest that the new church followed the proportions of traditional seventeenth-century longitudinal Anglican churches. Reverend Johnston departed for London with the specific intention of establishing connections with London—an increasingly powerful and cosmopolitan community—merchants, and he carried with him the plans for a large but typical Anglican church.

While in London, Johnston received the news that a hurricane had extensively damaged the unroofed shell of the new church in Charleston. Undaunted, Johnston desired to make "a second effect, and design, please God to prevent a like accident, to carry it to its former height, I hope people will be so charitable to assist me in so good a design."[22] After spending another year in London with the knowledge that his church in Charleston stood as a ruined shell, the clergyman almost certainly had taken stock of the extensive church-building programs then under way in London. Johnston had been resident in London during two of the most formative years for eighteenth-century Anglican church design.

Christopher Wren, the architect of fifty-one Anglican churches in London after the great fire of 1666, was still alive, and London's steady growth necessitated more churches in the suburbs of the city.[23] In 1711 Queen Anne passed an act to build fifty new churches, appointing a body of commissioners to undertake the task. Having met, these commissioners agreed on a basic formula for the next wave of church buildings after Wren's reconstruction of the city in the 1680s and

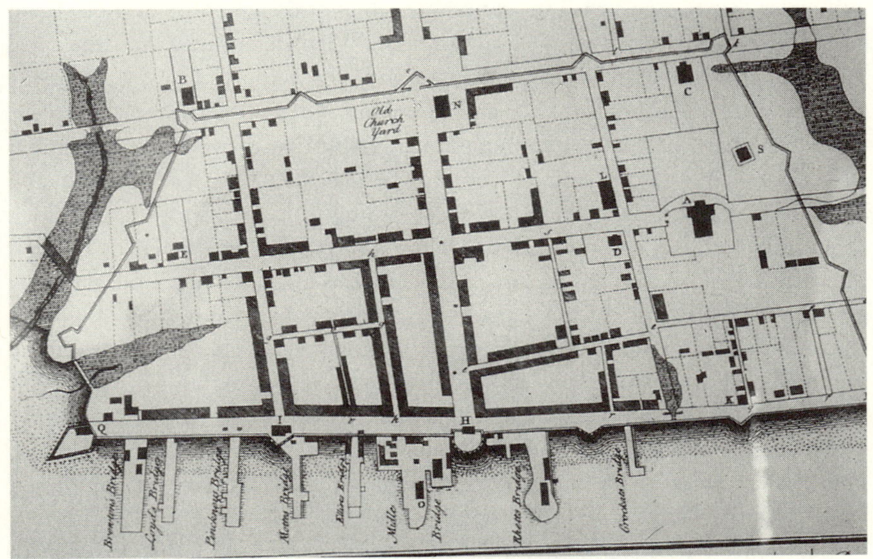

Fig. 11. Detail from *Ichnography of Charles Town at High Water, 1739*. St. Philip's is marked "A" and stands as the visual terminus of Church Street. Courtesy of Library of Congress

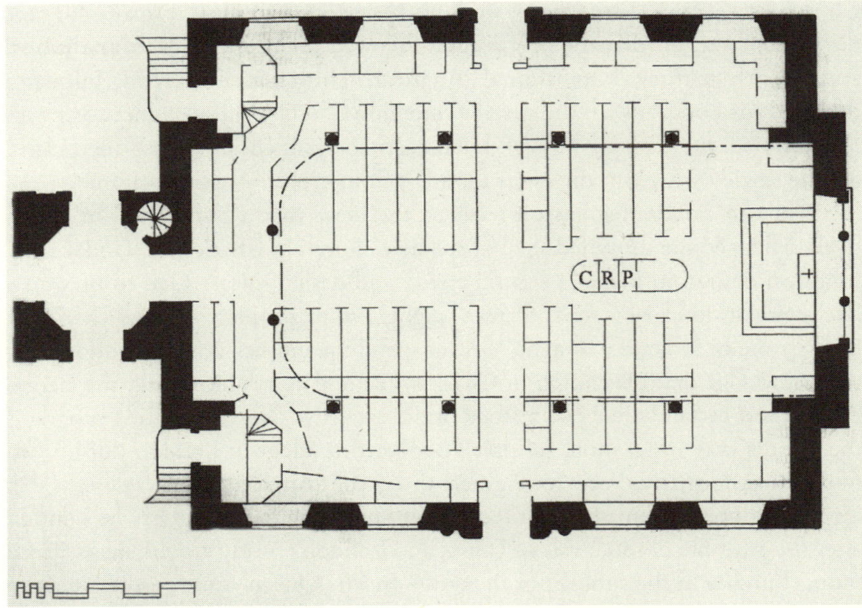

FIG. 12. St. James, Piccadilly, London, designed by Christopher Wren, 1684. Plan by Carl R. Lounsbury

1690s.[24] At the request of the new commissioners, Wren codified those planning principles that had governed his church design after the great fire of 1666. From his extensive experience with church design, Wren determined that the ideal Anglican church would be designed as an auditory, with "50 feet distant before the Preacher, 30 feet on each side, and 20 behind the pulpit." He went on to say, "By what I have said, it may be thought reasonable that the new Church should be at least 60 Feet broad, and 90 feet long, besides the Chancel at one End, and the Belfry and Portico at the other."[25] According to these principles, the older, longitudinal model was outmoded. Of the many churches erected in London after the fire, Wren selected St. James, Piccadilly, as his most successful, probably because it was one of the few erected as an entirely freestanding building—an unusual condition for Wren's churches and one that generally appeared on cramped and awkward urban lots (see figure 12). St. James, built in 1684, conforms to Wren's ideal of a compact rectangle, measuring approximately seventy-five by eighty-five feet, with doors centrally located on the northern, southern, and western sides of the building. Although Wren's ideas were not published until 1750, their impact was tremendous decades earlier.[26]

Adopting Wren's planning principles, the commissioners for the second wave set down rules in July 1712 that should govern the design of the new churches. As realized in St. Anne's, Limehouse, they agreed that since these churches were in the less developed suburbs, they should be freestanding on their sites and apart from the dense urban fabric; they should be erected of stone as a fire preventative; there should be a large space at the western end of each building for parish business in addition to "handsome porticos"; and each should have a steeple.[27] Before Johnston had departed London, the walls of the first of these new churches, St. Alphege's, Greenwich, had been completed, and five others had been begun. The close connections between the offices of the church commissioners and those of the bishop of London meant that the new churches must have been a regular topic of conversation during Johnston's two-year stay. When Johnston returned to Charleston in 1715, he brought with him a whole new set of ideas about how to build city churches. He was probably not displeased to learn that upon his arrival "Nothing has been done to our new Church since its being blown down by the Hurricane."[28]

Abandoning the earlier walls, the commissioners set out in 1715 to build a church that would in 1774 be described as "a grand church, resembling one of the new Churches in London."[29] That association was no mistake. Abandoning the one-hundred-foot by forty-five-foot ruined shell, the Charleston builders began a new church with an auditory nave approximately seventy-five feet long by sixty feet wide with a substantial vestibule—a place for parish business—to the west (see figure 13). The London church commissioners' "rules" included the statement that "there be handsome Porticoes at the West end of each Church where

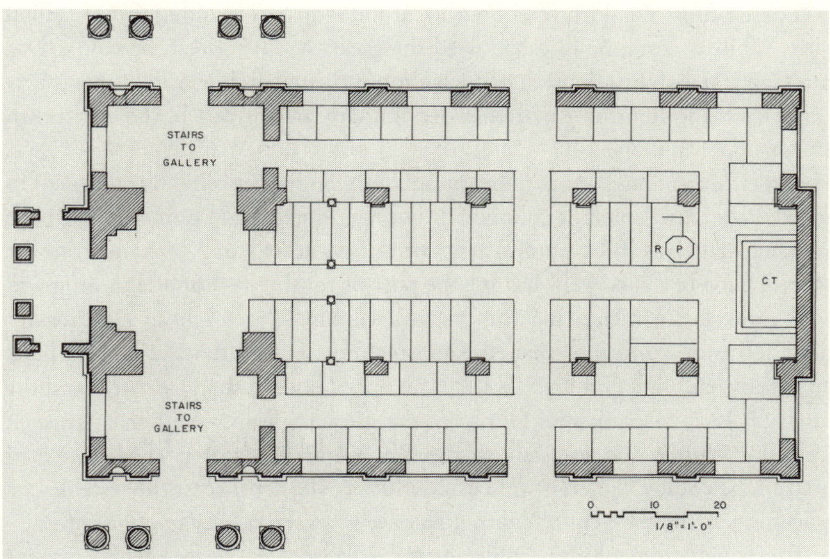

Fig. 13. St. Philip's Church, Charleston, South Carolina, 1711–23. Reconstructed floor plan by the author

the scite will admit of the same." Accordingly, St. Philip's had not one but three monumental porticoes at the west end—one over each of the three entrances into the vestibule. Furthermore, the entire brick exterior of the church was covered in stucco and scored to look like stone, in further emulation of the new churches in London, since no stone was available in the swampy conditions of the low-country.

The effect was successful, for one English visitor to the city in 1765, confused by the mask of stucco, described St. Philip's along with St. Michael's as "Large Stone Buildings with Portico's with large pillars and steeples."[30] The builders of St. Philip's and their mercantile financiers were clearly intending to keep pace with their counterparts in London. The whole impact of this design, completed and opened for services by 1723, was spectacular. With the church's three grand porticoes, extraordinarily large nave, and steeple covered with a dome, it is no wonder that most visitors to eighteenth-century Charleston commented on the building and its likeness to the new churches in London. St. Philip's church commissioners, who were mostly merchants, had successfully completed a church that linked them with the growing cosmopolitanism of London's mercantile community.

While it is tempting to interpret the new church as a manifestation of South Carolina's magnificent wealth, this drive by Charleston's merchants to establish material connections with London occurred in the early 1710s, before rice began to produce the extraordinary returns of the second quarter of the eighteenth century. These profits would propel South Carolina far past Virginia in per capital wealth. While it certainly foreshadowed the great wealth soon to be enjoyed by South Carolinians, the adoption of such a monumental architectural form is better understood in light of the intense denominational conflict of the eighteenth century's opening years.

In an effort to draw a sustainable population, South Carolina was founded in 1670 as a religiously tolerant colony without any established church. In 1703 the emergence of a powerful Church Party, comprised heavily of Anglicans from the Caribbean, made a successful bid for the post of royal governor after a long and heated contest. Characterizing the political climate, the Anglican commissary Gideon Johnston confirmed that "the debates and contests, that are on foot here, are not between High and Low Churchmen; but between the Dissenters and the Church."[31] In 1704 Nathaniel Johnston, the new Anglican governor, attempted to pass the Church Act to establish the Church of England as the established church in the colony. When it was passed in 1706, the act successfully established Anglicanism as the state church with direct access to the colony's public coffers.[32] Not surprisingly, the colony's Anglicans moved just a few years later to cement their political authority within that still-contested landscape by availing themselves of those public coffers to erect an Anglican church that announced their

FIG. 14. St. Stephen's Parish Church, St. Stephens, South Carolina, 1762–67. In this view the church's classical pilasters and ornamental gable are visible. Author's photograph

political authority to dissenters at home and to merchants abroad. On its new commanding site and in an architectural form of grandeur and monumentality, St. Philip's declared the establishment of Anglicanism as the state church in ways that nothing else could.

Just as local builders in Virginia looked to their urban church as a model, so too did those in South Carolina. Although only a few other churches had porticoes, the auditory proportions and classical architectural elements that characterized St. Philip's would determine the basic footprint of a vast majority of churches in the colony through the rest of the eighteenth century (see figure 14). With their broad naves and varied applications of classical detailing, Anglican churches in South Carolina differed from the more plain and elongated or cruciform churches of eighteenth-century Virginia. So too they would differ from Anglican churches in Jamaica, which returned to the cruciform plan but for different reasons.

St. Catherine's, Spanish Town

Jamaica's settlement pattern was not dissimilar to that of South Carolina. Ten years after the English occupation of Jamaica in 1655, Sir Thomas Modyford, a successful Barbadian planter who had persuaded eight hundred others to follow him from Barbados to Jamaica, was elected governor of the young colony, establishing the largest island in the English Caribbean as decidedly Barbadian. In

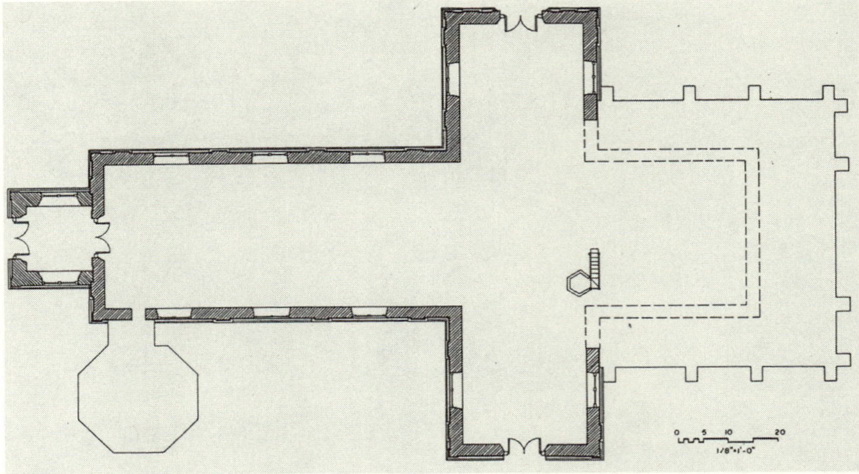

FIG. 15. St. Catherine's Parish Church, Spanish Town, Jamaica, 1712–24, with the 1817 tower, the 1848 chancel, and the 1930 octagonal vestry room. Plan by the author

fact, over half of Jamaica's seventeenth-century population had emigrated from the older Caribbean colony.[33] Those emigrants brought with them a sugar-planting culture that transplanted nicely to Jamaica and realized a stable economy more quickly than in South Carolina. In fact, Jamaica was significantly more profitable than either Virginia or South Carolina, a fact that resulted in a far greater black-to-white ratio—eleven to one by the American Revolution—than existed in any of the mainland colonies. In addition to the constant threat of insurrection, white Jamaicans were throughout the seventeenth century under assault by the Maroons, escaped slaves who lived in large numbers in the island's interior. As a result, Jamaica would have a high rate of absenteeism; overseers governed plantations while the masters and their families returned home—which for most Jamaicans meant England.

It comes as no surprise that the same longitudinal church plan seen throughout the British Empire appeared also in seventeenth-century Jamaica. However, in the early eighteenth century Anglicans in Jamaica also began to fashion an architecture of Anglicanism specific to their immediate circumstances. In 1712 a disastrous hurricane destroyed the refitted Spanish Catholic chapel that Anglicans in Jamaica's capital city of Spanish Town had been using since the English occupation of the island in 1655. Within two years members of the vestry had completed a new Anglican church that materialized their notion of appropriate Anglican architecture in the newly established capital of Spanish Town. St. Catherine's was one of three early eighteenth-century churches that established the cruciform plan as the new model for Anglican churches in early eighteenth-century Jamaica (see figure 15).[34] Following this precedent, almost five of every six churches newly built on Jamaica in the eighteenth century were cruciform.[35]

The preponderance of this plan on Jamaica is remarkable; nowhere else in the eighteenth-century Anglican world is it found in such abundance.[36] What makes the cruciform churches in Jamaica different from those in Virginia is their consistency. Virginia had a significant percentage of cruciform churches mixed in with longitudinal-planned and T-shaped churches. This was not the case in Jamaica, where the cruciform church was far and above the most common choice. The regular critique of the state of the church in eighteenth-century Jamaica as dismal does not suggest that the cruciform plan was adopted to house large congregations.[37] This consistency was a product of the extreme nature of Jamaica's racial and economic profile at the time. By the early eighteenth century Jamaica was an increasingly agricultural colony subdivided into large plantations, governed increasingly by absentee ownership, and marked by the largest population of enslaved Africans and a greater disproportion of blacks to whites than any other British colony.[38] By the 1710s blacks outnumbered whites by eight to one.[39] The number of Africans on the island more than doubled between 1700 and 1750 and increased by a factor of five by the end of the century.[40] This ratio had sharp implications for race relations; after the 1670s slave riots became increasingly common, resulting in greater racial instability in Jamaica than in Britain's other plantation colonies.

This economic and concomitant racial shift had distinct implications for the physical nature of the Jamaican landscape. Writing soon after his arrival in Jamaica in the opening years of the nineteenth century, Matthew Lewis complained that "the houses are absolutely transparent; the walls are nothing but windows-and all the doors stand wide open. No servants are in waiting to announce arrivals; visitors, negroes, cats, dogs, poultry, all walk in and out . . . your rooms, without the slightest ceremony."[41] Life in Jamaica was not the cosmopolitan experience Lewis had known in London. By comparison Jamaica was raw, savage, uncivilized, and disorderly. Another Englishman noted that the seemingly innumerable slaves in Jamaica were summoned to their labors not by European bells but "by the sound of a Conche-shell."[42] He went on to note that thatched huts on this tropical island made "every Plantation look like a little African city."

The heat and humidity, the dense and lush vegetation, and the exotic flowers and birds were a far cry from England; as a result, an increasing percentage of Jamaican landowners began returning to England and turning over management of their estates to attorneys. By the later eighteenth century the rate of absenteeism was sufficiently high for one observer to assert that in Jamaica slaves had far greater liberties than did those in Britain's other plantation colonies.[43] The sounds, smells, and sights of Jamaica more closely approximated those of Africa than England. In the midst of that landscape stood hulking brick cruciform churches that were decidedly English in their appearance.

The cruciform plan was closely associated with England among local gentry who were regularly absenting themselves from Jamaica to return to England for extended stays. In this way the cruciform plan served as a familiar cultural marker and reinforced their authority in an alien and highly contested landscape. Just as eighteenth-century cartographers used the common symbol of a simplified building surmounted by a cross as a way of marking the place of the Anglican church in a landscape, so too did Jamaica's Anglicans imprint the landscape with one of the most overt signs of their Englishness—the cruciform Anglican church.

There is also some evidence to suggest that Jamaica's Anglicans were not as Low Church as those who populated the mainland colonies. Unlike Virginia and especially South Carolina, Jamaica was not characterized by religious plurality. Although the principle port city of Port Royal had small communities of Jews, Anabaptists, Catholics, Presbyterians, and Quakers in the late seventeenth century, these groups were never much of a threat to the establishment status of the Church of England.[44] Small congregations of Quakers in Kingston and Spanish Town and a band of Moravians that settled in St. Elizabeth's Parish in the 1750s were the only other congregations of Protestants on the island in the eighteenth century. One Jamaican chronicler indicated that the intolerance that marked the Catholic regent James II's reign in England seems to have been readily accepted in Jamaica: "The character of this religion was perfectly well supported by the spirit [of persecution] which was let loose against all non-conformists."[45]

In a radical departure from the iconoclasm that characterized most of the mainland colonies, Anglicans in Spanish Town erected two large statues to Moses and Aaron in their chancel. Although Anglicans in at least one Virginia church had paintings of Moses and Aaron flanking the Ten Commandments, there is no evidence for freestanding statues in the mainland colonies.[46] By the opening years of the eighteenth century Anglicans in Jamaica seem to have been less rigidly anti-Catholic than those on the mainland, and they experienced little of the dissenting critique that characterized Anglicanism in Virginia after the 1730s and in South Carolina from the outset. Thus, the cross might have been a more theologically comfortable symbol in Jamaica than it was for Anglicans on the mainland.

The cruciform plan also functioned in clear ways in Jamaica; the very form and fittings of the church reinforced social segregation. The multiple arms of St. Catherine's separated the occupants of one arm from the other two, and the farther one sat from the heart of the building, the lower one's position on the social scale. In St. Catherine's Church, for example, the governor's cushioned pew, which does not survive but sat near the crossing, was raised above the rest and was constructed of the best mahogany, had detailing that matched the pulpit, and was covered by a canopy. Conversely, at the rear of the church, benches reserved for common soldiers were located at the far end under the organ loft. If there was any correspondence between Jamaica and other colonies, slaves who attended service stood or sat in the aisles, and those who did not congregated outside, often disrupting the services.[47]

The building's ornamental program also reinforced elite authority. A molded water table that turns down at the doors supports the bases of engaged pilasters that rise to each side of the door over a plane of glazed-header Flemish bond. Rubbed bricks compose the quoins that surround the door. The pilasters support a molded cornice, which carries an attic complete with a niche (see figures 16 and 17). The brickwork of the highly ornamented northern elevation served as an elaborated stage for the arrival and departure of the elite.

Sunday service was one of the two primary opportunities for elite self-presentation. According to one mid-eighteenth-century observer, "The common Dress here is none of the most becoming: The Heat makes many cloaths intolerable, and therefore the Men generally wear only Thread stockings, Linen Drawers and Vest, a Handkerchief tied round their Head and a Hat above. Wigs are never used but on Sunday, or in Court-time; and then Gentlemen appear very gay in silk Coats, and Vests trimmed with Silver."[48] Among the most refined

FIG. 16. Detail of the northern-wing water table with a base of pilaster and quoins, St. Catherine's Parish Church, Spanish Town, Jamaica. Author's photograph

Fig. 17. Detail of the attic parapet with iron downspouts. St. Catherine's Church, Spanish Town, Jamaica. Author's photograph

Fig. 18. Detail of face, western entrance, St. Catherine's Church, Spanish Town, Jamaica. Author's photograph

FIG. 19. St. James, Montego Bay, Jamaica, 1775–82. Author's photograph

ornamental brickwork on the island, this door and its elaborate frame served as an appropriately dramatic proscenium for the church-going elite.

At the other end of the social spectrum, the turbaned head of an African ornaments the keystone of the western door, suggesting the probability that that door, which accessed those seats farthest removed from the points of authority on the interior, was intended for use by the lowest ranks of free society (see figure 18). This same hierarchical arrangement of ornament of various elevations appears on other Anglican churches on the island and suggests that on Jamaica individual elevations were intended for use by specific social classes. In its form, scale, and ornament, the new church in Spanish Town reinforced the authority of the English elite in a landscape that was decidedly un-English in appearance.[49]

Although the specifics of details, proportions, and scale would change depending on the relative wealth of the parish, Anglicans in Jamaica throughout the rest of the eighteenth century would adopt the cruciform plan for church design, demonstrating an extraordinary consistency in the material world of Anglicanism in Jamaica. Built in the emergent mercantile center of Montego Bay, the parish church of St. James, with its gleaming white stone, corner quoins, high parapet, and predictable cruciform plan, found a middle road between a building material that participated in the cosmopolitan expectations of eighteenth-century English merchants and the plan that squarely located the church in Jamaica (see figures 19 and 20).

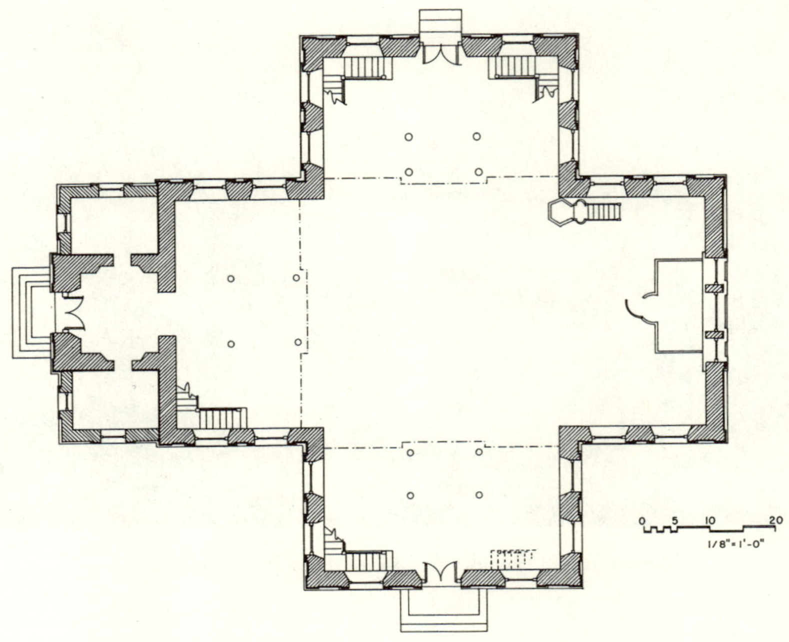

Fig. 20. St. James, Montego Bay, Jamaica, 1775–82. Plan by the author

Conclusion

Although the earliest generations of both South Carolina and Jamaica settlers found their roots in Barbados, their descendants' eighteenth-century churches participated in a process of cultural self-definition that was driven by local circumstances. The material evidence does not sustain the regular argument that South Carolinians and Jamaicans understood themselves to be extensions of Barbadian culture. Images of Barbados's seventeenth-century churches suggest that Jamaicans and Carolinians were not looking to the older Caribbean island. St. Michael's church, erected in the 1670s in Bridgetown, Barbados, had a steeply pitched roof, a long narrow nave, and crenellations along each of the long elevations—features alien to typical church design in both Jamaica and Carolina (see figure 21).

As early as the second decade of the eighteenth century, local conditions far outweighed any Caribbean cultural consistency in the formation of these material landscapes. While Jamaica's Anglicans were building churches that imposed English order and authority over a non-English landscape from their permanent homes in England and South Carolinians were building churches that recalled and rivaled cosmopolitan models as a way of cementing their place in a landscape

FIG. 21. St. Michael's, Bridgetown, Barbados, 1670s. Detail from Samuel Copen, *Prospect of Bridgetown in Barbados,* engraving (London, 1695). Author's photograph

of contested local politics and in a transatlantic economic market, Virginians were designing neat and plain churches that reified the church as an agent of a stable elite culture. In each case the architectural language of Anglicanism was specific to immediate circumstances. Where curvilinear gables were an integral part of Anglican architecture in South Carolina, they were absent in eighteenth-century Virginia and Jamaica; rusticated quoins that appear in both South Carolina and Jamaica are absent from Virginia's "neat and plain" churches. The imposing cruciform plan that appears consistently throughout Jamaica was among a variety of options in Virginia and appeared in only two instances in South Carolina. These distinct traditions suggest that architecture was a powerful tool enlisted by local Anglicans to negotiate local political conditions. This study of three comparable colonial contexts demonstrates this political function of the architecture of the established church. In this way the study of the material culture of the "diversity of countries" enriches our understanding of the complexities of the colonial experience.

Notes

1. This examination of the regional characteristics of Anglican churches depends on the work in this area already begun by Carl Lounsbury in "Anglican Church Design in

the Chesapeake Colonies: English Inheritance and Regional Interpretations," *Perspectives in Vernacular Architecture* (Knoxville: University of Tennessee Press, 2003), 22–38. The most comprehensive discussions of eighteenth-century Anglican churches appear in Nigel Yates, *Buildings, Faith, and Worship: The Liturgical Arrangement of Anglican Churches, 1600–1900* (Oxford: Oxford University Press, 1991; repr., 2000); G. W. O. Addleshaw and Frederick Etchells, *The Architectural Setting of Anglican Worship* (London: Faber and Faber, 1948); and Marcus Whiffen, *Stuart and Georgian Churches* (London: Batsford, 1947). For comprehensive discussions of eighteenth-century Anglican churches in the colonies, see Dell Upton, *Holy Things and Profane: Anglican Parish Churches in Colonial Virginia* (Boston: Architectural History Foundation, 1986); Donald Friary, "The Architecture of the Anglican Church in the Northern American Colonies: A Study of Religious, Social, and Cultural Expression" (Ph.D. diss., University of Pennsylvania, 1971); Louis P. Nelson, "The Material Word: Anglican Visual Culture in Colonial South Carolina" (Ph.D. diss., University of Delaware, 2000), which includes catalogs of all the colonial Anglican churches in South Carolina and Jamaica. The Anglican churches of eighteenth-century Jamaica are published only in the early twentieth-century narrative by Frank Cundall, *Historic Jamaica* (London: West India Committee, 1915), and more recently by L. Emile Martin, *Jamaica's Churches: Part of Our Heritage* (Montego Bay: Unlimited Exposures, 1995). Martin's book includes useful photographs but abounds in inaccurate information. The traditional view of Anglicanism in Virginia appears in Rhys Isaac, *The Transformation of Virginia, 1740–1790* (Chapel Hill: University of North Carolina Press, 1982). John K. Nelson has recently reassessed Anglicanism in Virginia in *A Blessed Company: Parishes, Parsons, and Parishioners in Anglican Virginia, 1690–1776* (Chapel Hill: University of North Carolina Press, 2001). For Anglicanism in South Carolina, see Charles Bolton, *Southern Anglicanism: The Church of England in Colonial South Carolina* (Westport, Conn.: Greenwood, 1982). The only extensive discussion of Anglicanism in Jamaica is R. A. Minter, *Episcopacy without Episcopate: The Church of England in Jamaica before 1824* (Worcester: Self-publishing Association, 1990). A brief discussion of the Anglican Church appears in Brathwaite, *Development of Creole Society*, 20–25. A good introduction to the Anglican Church in the Caribbean is chap. 7, "Sugar, Slavery, and the Planters' Church (1655–1823)," in Arthur Charles Dayfoot, *The Shaping of the West Indian Church, 1492–1962* (Barbados: Press, University of the West Indies, 1999).

2. Rev. W. A. R. Goodwin, *Historical Sketch of Bruton Church, Williamsburg, Virginia* (Petersburg, Va.: Franklin Press, 1903), 32.

3. Ibid., 33.

4. Ibid., 34.

5. For the traditional Anglican plan, see Yates, *Buildings, Faith, and Worship*, 68–76. The observation on the persistence of the longitudinal plan in Virginia is made by Carl Lounsbury in "Anglican Church Design in the Chesapeake Colonies."

6. Reprinted in Marcus Whiffen, *The Public Buildings of Williamsburg: Colonial Capital of Virginia* (Williamsburg, Va.: Colonial Williamsburg Foundation, 1958), 79.

7. Jack P. Greene, *The Pursuits of Happiness: The Social Development of Early Modern British Colonies and the Formation of American Culture* (Chapel Hill: University of North Carolina Press, 1988), 82.

8. David Fischer, *Albion's Seed: Four British Folkways in America* (Oxford: Oxford University Press, 1989), 212.

9. Upton makes this point in *Holy Things and Profane,* 118–19. On the adoption of the cross in nineteenth-century America, see Ryan Smith, "The Cross: Church Symbol and Contest in Nineteenth-Century America," *Church History* 70, no. 4 (December 2001): 705–34.

10. Whiffen, *Public Buildings,* 80–82.

11. Goodwin, *Bruton Church,* 36.

12. Quote cited in Whiffen, *Public Buildings,* 93. On Georgianization in Virginia, see Henry Glassie, *Folk Housing in Middle Virginia: A Structural Analysis of Historic Artifacts* (Knoxville: University of Tennessee Press, 1975).

13. Carl R. Lounsbury, *An Illustrated Dictionary of Early Southern Architecture and Landscape* (Oxford: Oxford University Press, 1994), 240, 277.

14. See Dell Upton, "The Power of Things: Recent Studies in American Vernacular Architecture," in Thomas Schlereth, *Material Culture: A Research Guide* (Lawrence: University Press of Kansas, 1985), 57–78. Dell demonstrates this in *Holy Things and Profane.*

15. Of the thirty-eight extant colonial Anglican churches in Virginia, all are "Georgian," but only eight are cruciform. They are Bruton Church, Williamsburg, built in 1711–15; Elizabeth City Parish Church, Hampton, begun in 1728; Lower Church in St. Stephen's Parish in King and Queen County, built in 1730–34; Christ Church, Lancaster, built in 1732–35; North Farnham Parish, Richmond County, begun in 1734; Elizabeth River Parish Church, Norfolk, begun in 1739; Abingdon Church, built in 1751–55; Aquia Church, built in 1754–57; and St. Paul's Parish Church, King George County, begun in 1766.

16. Gideon Johnston to Secretary, September 20, 1708, Society for the Propagation of the Gospel [hereafter cited as SPG], 1702–37, series A, vol. 4, no. 311.

17. See Dunn, *Sugar and Slaves;* Jack P. Greene, "Colonial South Carolina and the Caribbean Connection," in Greene, *Imperatives, Behaviors, and Identities,* 87–112; Eugene Sirmans, *Colonial South Carolina: A Political History, 1663–1763* (Chapel Hill: University of North Carolina Press, 1966); Richard Dunn, "The English Sugar Islands and the Founding of South Carolina," *SCHM* 72 (April 1971): 81–93; Richard Waterhouse, "England, the Caribbean, and the Settlement of Carolina," *Journal of American Studies* 9 (December 1975): 259–81; Warren Alleyne and Henry Fraser, *The Barbados-Carolina Connection* (London: Macmillan Caribbean, 1988).

18. Locally produced histories of early South Carolina abound with this mythology. St. James Goose Creek Parish Church, a small, pink stucco church with bold quoins and a pronounced classical door surround built in the second decade of the eighteenth century, survives as one of the most often cited material referents to South Carolina's Caribbean connection. For discussions of the church, see Lounsbury, "Dynamics of Architectural Design," 58–74; Samuel Guillard Stoney, *Plantations of the Carolina Lowcountry* (Charleston: Carolina Art Association, 1938), 50–51; chap. 11, "St. James' Church, Goose Creek," in Michael J. Heitzler, *Historic Goose Creek, South Carolina, 1670–1980* (Easley, S.C.: Southern Historical Press, 1983), 177–201.

19. Repr. in Frederick Dalcho, *An Historical Account of the Protestant Episcopal Church in South Carolina* (Charleston, 1820; repr., Charleston: Diocese of South Carolina 1970), 454.

20. "Mr. Johnston's reasons for staying so long from his Cure at Charles Town, June 1714," SPG, series A, vol. 9, no. 72.

21. "A True Copy of the Clergy of South Carolina's Instructions to Mr. Johnston Charles Town, March 4, 1712/13," Bodleian Library, Oxford.

22. Gideon Johnston, November 19, 1714, SPG, series A, vol. 9, no. 27.

23. The best source for Wren's city churches is Kerry Downes, *The Architecture of Wren* (New York: Universe Books, 1982). See also Linda Soo's section on Wren's 1714 letter to the London church commissioners in *Wren's "Tracts" on Architecture and Other Useful Writings* (Cambridge: Cambridge University Press, 1998).

24. For a complete list of the commissioners' "Rules for the Fifty New Churches," see appendix 4 in Pierre de la Ruffiniere du Prey, *Hawksmoor's London Churches: Architecture and Theology* (Chicago: University of Chicago Press, 2000), 143–44. The other five churches include St. Paul's, Depford (1712–30); St. George's, Hanover Square (1712–24); St. Anne's, Limehouse (1712–24); St. John's, Westminster (1714–28); and St. Mary le Strand (1714–17).

25. Christopher Wren, *Parantalia* (London, 1750), 318.

26. See Howard Colvin, "Fifty New Churches," *Architectural Review* 107 (1950): 189–96.

27. The rules of the commissioners are reprinted as appendix 4 in du Prey, *Hawksmoor's London Churches,* 143–44.

28. Gideon Johnson, December 19, 1715, SPG, series B, vol. 4, no. 37.

29. John Gillies, *Memoirs of the Life of the Reverend George Whitefield* (New York: Hodge and Shober, 1774), 47.

30. Pelatiah Webster, Monday, May 27, 1765, "A Journal of a Voyage from Philadelphia to Charlestown in South Carolina begun May 15, 1765," South Carolina Historical Society [hereafter cited as SCHS], Charleston.

31. Gideon Johnston, September 20, 1708, SPG, series A, vol. 4, no. 311.

32. For more on the political conflict, see Sirmans, *Colonial South Carolina,* esp. chap. 5, "The Renascence of Factions, 1700–1712," 75–102; and Bolton, *Southern Anglicanism,* 16–36.

33. See Dunn, "English Sugar Islands," 153. The material landscape of Barbados, which might at first appear to be a more logical choice for comparison, has been almost entirely decimated by the regular barrage of hurricanes that buffet the island. Occupied as an English colony in 1628, Barbados was by 1652 divided into eleven parishes; most had churches by the close of the seventeenth century. Only two eighteenth-century churches, both from the end of the century, still stand on the island.

34. For a longer discussion of the physical characteristics of Jamaica's Anglican churches, see Louis Nelson, "Building 'Cross-wise': Reconstructing Jamaica's Eighteenth-Century Anglican Churches," *Jamaica Historical Review* (Spring 2003): 11–39, 70–76.

35. This statistic is taken from the churches for which some information about the plan survives. Cruciform churches erected in eighteenth-century Jamaica include St. Andrew's Parish Church (1692–1705), Kingston Parish Church (1701–3), St. Catherine's Parish Church (1712–14), Clarendon Parish Church (1722–40), Westmoreland Parish Church (before 1722), Port Royal Parish Church (1725), St. Thomas-in-the-East Parish Church (c. 1750), St. Anne's Parish Church (1765), St. James Parish Church (1774), St. George's

Parish Church (before 1802), and Portland Parish Church (before 1804). Those that were not include Hanover Parish Church (before 1774) and Trelawney Parish Church in Falmouth (1796).

36. For example Dell Upton's work in Virginia suggests that of the thirty-three colonial churches in that colony for which the plan is known, only nine were cruciform. See Upton, *Holy Things and Profane.*

37. Brathwaite, *Development of Creole Society,* 25, notes that in the late eighteenth century the Church of England in Jamaica was ineffective largely because there was only one Anglican minister to every fifteen hundred white inhabitants and to every fifteen thousand to eighteen thousand total inhabitants. Others who have noted the feeble condition of the Church of England are Lowell Joseph Ragatz, *The Old Plantation System in the British Caribbean* (London: Bryan Edwards, 1953), 13–15; and A. Caldecott, *The Church in the West Indies* (London, 1898), 49, 55. For other primary commentary, see J. Stewart, *View of the Past and Present State of the Island of Jamaica, with remarks on the moral and physical condition of the slaves and on the abolition of slavery in the colonies* (Edinburgh, 1823), 45–47.

38. See Douglas Hall, "Absentee-Proprietorship in the British West Indies to about 1850," *Jamaican Historical Review* 4 (1964): 15–35. On increasing absenteeism, see also Long, *History of Jamaica,* 2:386. Trevor Burnard and Kenneth Morgan, "The Dynamics of the Slave Market and Slave Purchasing Patterns in Jamaica, 1655–1788," *William and Mary Quarterly* 58 (January 2001): 205, states decisively that "Jamaica had the largest demand for slaves of any British colony in the Americas."

39. Dunn, *Sugar and Slaves,* 164–65.

40. Burnard and Morgan, "Dynamics of the Slave Market," 205–6.

41. Matthew Gregory Lewis, Sunday, January 28, 1816, *Journal of a West Indian proprietor kept during a residence in the island of Jamaica* (London: John Murray, 1834), 149.

42. Oldmixon, *British Empire in America,* II:120.

43. Long, *History of Jamaica,* 2:389.

44. David J. Buisseret, "Port Royal, 1655–1725," *Jamaican Historical Review* 6, nos. 1, 2 (1988): 25.

45. Long, *History of Jamaica,* 2:234.

46. 1722, FPC, 18:228. See also Upton, *Holy Things and Profane,* 120.

47. St. Catherine's vestry minutes, March 1, 1761, November 6, 1762, May 15, 1764, October 15, 1768; Long, *History of Jamaica,* 2:5.

48. Charles Leslie, *A New History of Jamaica from the Earliest Accounts to the Taking of Porto Bello: Thirteen Letters from a Gentleman to His Friend* (London, 1740), 34. For an excellent discussion of elite self-presentation, see the collection of essays edited by George Marcus, *Elites* (Albuquerque: University of New Mexico Press, 1983).

49. This argument is presented in far greater detail in Louis Nelson, "Anglican Church-Building and Local Context in Early Jamaica" in *Perspectives in Vernacular Architecture X,* ed. Alison Hoagland and Kenneth Breisch (Knoxville: University of Tennessee Press, 2003), 63–8.

Colonial Castles

The Architecture of Social Control

Eric Klingelhofer

European overseas expansion began in Africa with the Portuguese conquest of Cueta, Morocco, in 1415. Later in the fifteenth century the Portuguese reached Central Africa and established a trading post at El Mina, Ghana, while Columbus took Castilians to the New World, settling at La Navidad in Haiti. Early on, Iberian authorities erected *castellos* or *castillos* in what J. H. Parry called "the overseas tradition of conquest."[1] Not just the Castilian and Portuguese *reconquista* of the Iberian Peninsula but also Italian-Aragonese territorial holdings in the post-Crusader Aegean used castles until they were replaced by Renaissance artillery fortification. This explanation accounts for the presence of castles in Iberian colonies of the 1400s and 1500s, but it does not explain the castles that appear in English and French colonies of the later 1600s is of interest. This essay examines the case for these structures, the existence of which has been eclipsed by the follies of the Gothic revival, the baronial homes of industrial tycoons, and even the Citadel in Charleston, South Carolina.

By the 1500s feudalism was dead. There was no place for castles in Renaissance warfare, which Sir John Hale and Geoffrey Parker considered to have undergone a revolutionary professionalism.[2] Yet languages, like institutions, are conservative: a military function for even new structures called "castles" could survive Hale's revolution. In England, Henry VIII spent enormous sums to create a system of imaginative coastal artillery defenses, which he called not forts but castles. His French contemporary, Francis I, alarmed by the near loss of the great port of Marseilles in 1527, built an artillery fort to defend the harbor. Like his English rival, he referred to it as a castle: "Chateau d'If" would later become the setting for Dumas's *Count of Monte Cristo.*

These centuries witnessed the end of feudalism per se but not the end of aristocracy nor the kind of behavior associated with the medieval past that Ben Jonson and Cervantes parodied. For at least fifty years spanning the turn of the

FIG. 1. Sherborne Castle, Dorset. The upper story is a Jacobean addition. Author's photograph

seventeenth century, England underwent a revival of castle building, essentially castellated country houses called neomedieval and mock castles by scholars such as Mark Girouard.[3] The term "Spenserian" more precisely assigns the impetus to the Elizabethan court and to its archetypal statement, Edmund Spenser's *Faerie Queene.* The architectural style was started early in her reign by Robert Dudley, Elizabeth's great favorite, at Kenilworth Castle and was vigorously continued by a later favorite, Walter Ralegh, at his country home, Sherbourne Castle (see figure 1). The name of a residence was ordinarily retained when remodeling or new erections took place on the site of an existing castle, as at Lulworth Castle (see figure 2). Where a great house was erected de novo, it received an appropriate noncastle name, usually "hall" or "manor," but others appear: "place," "court," or even "park." In keeping with the chivalric ideal and the accompanying aristocratic status of the builder, these country houses had a strong military appearance, but their defenses were of little real use against an organized military force. The Crown preferred England's leading families to look out through glass windows, not gun loops—or cannon embrasures.

More sober, perhaps, and certainly more militarily effective were the fortified residences built by the colonizing English in the contemporary "plantation period" of Tudor and Stuart Ireland. Typically constructed on newly expropriated estates, they often incorporated a medieval tower-house castle keep in the

Fig. 2. Lulworth Castle, Dorset. The corner towers appear medieval, but the doorway is classical in style. Photograph by Roger H. Leech

Fig. 3. Carrick-on-Suir, County Waterford. A medieval tower house protected the Tudor-style mansion erected by Elizabeth's cousin, the Earl of Ormond. Author's photograph

FIG. 4. Durrus Court, County Cork. The heavy machicolation contrasts with fine chimney stacks. Author's photograph

new building (see figure 3).[4] These structures became the seats of new English lordships and were usually called "castles" after their predecessors or "manors" when new to the site. With a variety of plan types, these multistoried masonry residences embodied such defensive elements as crenellation, machicolation, corner towers, gun loops or pistol holes, and splayed or battered wall bases (see figure 4).[5]

Given the dominance of castellation in Tudor-Stuart Ireland, it is surprising to hear not of castles but of "forts" in the contemporary colonial ventures into the New World. The documents speak of palisades, demilunes, sconces, and redoubts but not of castles. We find angled bulwarks of Italian origin and round bulwarks favored by the English. Whether Italian or English, however, these are artillery emplacements and not castles. The seventeenth-century settlements in the Amazon and Guiana have no reference to castles, nor do the early records of Virginia, Maryland, and the Caribbean Islands. Bermuda has one reference: the King's Castle. According to John Smith, Governor Richard More built this fortification in 1612, and Governor Nathaniel Butler added a stone house for its captain and *corps du guard* in 1621.[6] The Smith drawing (see figure 5) shows it to be similar to other Bermuda forts, stone-built with heavy artillery, so it seems that the term "castle" applied not to a traditional role as a defended residence but to its function as the center of military operations on a strategic island base.

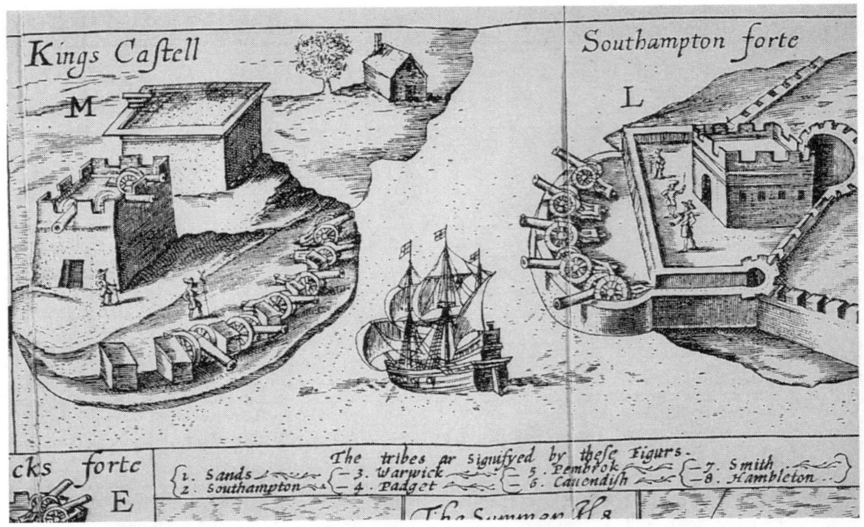

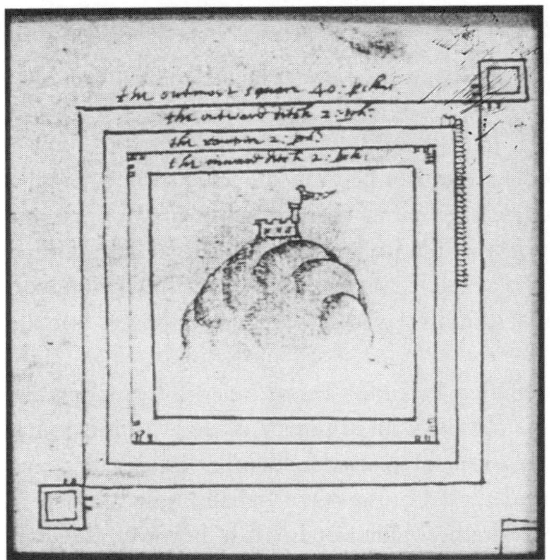

FIG. 5. (*above*) Capt. John Smith's illustration of fortifications on Bermuda. From Capt. John Smith, *The Generall Historie of Virginia, New England, and the Summer Isles* (London: Michael Sparkes, 1624)

FIG. 6. John Winthrop II's drawing of defenses for Massachusetts. From *The Journal of John Winthrop, 1630–1649* (Cambridge, Mass.: Harvard University Press, 1996). Courtesy of Harvard University Press

Castle Island in Boston Harbor, like the one in Bermuda, controlled the ship channel and would have been the key fortification for the early colony, though little is known of its seventeenth-century defenses. A schematic drawing in Gov. John Winthrop's journal (see figure 6), begun at the colony's founding in 1630, depicts plans for square defenses of ditch and palisaded bank, which could possibly be for Castle Island.[7] Although the signal tower at the top of a central hill has a certain charm, there is nothing about these defenses that resembles a castle.

FIG. 7. Bacon's Castle, Virginia, with the porch tower in front and the stair tower in rear. Author's photograph

In Virginia, Bacon's Castle is the commonwealth's finest surviving seventeenth-century country house (see figure 7). Built in 1665, this handsome cross-plan brick structure, with porch and stair towers, is not in the tradition of fortified residences, despite its name. That was later attached to the building because of its role in Nathaniel Bacon's armed revolt of 1676. The term "castle" rarely appears in the American colonies; more common are other typical English names for the homes of local gentry: "manors" and "halls." Lacking integral defensive features, these structures are manor houses rather than castles, Spenserian or otherwise. A Caribbean example is Drax Hall in Barbados, which was owned by the wealthy and influential William Drax, whose stature ensured him a share of public authority but whose home was undefended.

The Bermuda, Massachusetts, Virginia, and Barbados examples show that, despite the terminology, early colonial settlements lacked castles and European-style fortified houses. Why was that? First of all, these colonies were created and directed by companies, groups of businessmen and investors who cared more for effective rule and immediate returns than seigneurial ideals and chivalric romanticism. In addition, of course, these colonies were founded over a century after the Iberian empires began, and European cultures had changed during that time.

Yet there were castles and fortified houses in the later seventeenth-century American colonies. Fortified plantation houses constructed in an American

FIG. 8. Stokes Hall, Jamaica. The center of the structure is lost, but the four corner blocks still stand. Courtesy of Heinemann

vernacular appeared in the Tidewater and the lowcountry areas of North America. Examples are the post-built "Cliffes Site" excavated by Fraser Neiman at Stratford Hall on the Potomac and the tabby-walled Wormsley Manor outside Savannah, excavated by William Kelso.[8] Seventeenth-century castle-houses in the European tradition do not appear in North America, but they can be found in the Caribbean.

Outside Ireland, the castle-house is most common in Jamaica, conquered from Spain in 1655. Spanish efforts to retake the island and the presence of hostile Maroon communities of ex-slaves made domestic security a greater concern for the planters on Jamaica than for those, for example, on Barbados. There were no less than six named castles in colonial Jamaica.[9] Most typical was the H-plan, such as that used for Stokes Hall, a rectangular house core with four corner towers and loopholes, which could have been transplanted intact from Ireland (see figure 8). Colbeck Castle stands in the center of a rectangular walled enclosure, with strong outbuildings at the corners (see figure 9). David Buisseret thought Colbeck an enigma but noted that local historians claimed it was built around 1700 as a campsite for the local regiment of militia.[10] Great landowning planters

FIG. 9. Colbeck Castle, Jamaica. The four corner blocks or towers of the residence are matched by four L-shaped structures in the courtyard corners. Courtesy of Heinemann

commanded militia units, and their houses, like those of "plantation-period" Ireland, served as bases for security forces.

The reason for the castellated building style and the choice of the name "castle" must lie in the intended role of these houses as structures both public and private: a political and social architecture. More than symbolic, they are part of a group of early colonial houses named as castles, manors, courts, or halls in recognition of the public authority based there. Owners held political office, playing a judicial role as justices of the peace, and they certainly commanded militias that were expected to supply their own arms and munitions, a point that needs further study. These large country houses of the seventeenth century, especially those with a sizable hall or meeting room, mark the re-creation in the New World of the English squirarchy, a development that began architecturally at midcentury. The establishment of a permanent gentry class, despite the inroads made by death and the attractions of the home country, dictated changes in architecture and nomenclature, at least for one or two generations. Once the colonies had "caught up" in this and in the artisan mannerist style, they followed the evolution of English country houses toward a newer style, Georgian formalism.

A similar development no doubt took place among the Dutch landowning patroons and their estates along the Hudson Valley.[11] The more dangerous western Caribbean, though, called for more overtly defensive features. On Curaçao, Brievengat great house blends Dutch and Caribbean architectural elements in the residence, but its raised terrace enclosure has a pair of what surely look like flanker bases with gun-proof splays (see figure 10).[12]

FIG. 10. Brievengat, Curaçao. The curves of the "Dutch" gable contrast with the massive bases of the towers flanking the terrace in front. Courtesy of Heinemann

English gentlemen and Dutch businessmen had a sense of class identity and public authority, which led them to specific forms of social architecture. It is to the French colonies of Louis XIV, however, that one must turn for true grandeur. France's experience in the New World was superficially similar to England's: failed sixteenth-century enterprises, then seventeenth-century permanent holdings in North America, followed soon by others in the West Indies. In actuality, English and French colonization are comparable only in the islands, where both nations early adopted the plantation system, first tobacco with indentured workers and then sugar with slave labor. These island settlements proved hard to defend from competing colonial nations or the kind of plundering raids that had first brought the northern European nations to the West Indies.

The first French governor-general of the West Indies, the chevalier de Poincy, held authority over all French islands but ruled more directly on St. Christopher (St. Kitts) in the Leewards and on St. Croix in the Virgins. In the mid–seventeenth century each island was commanded by a chateau, a French castle or fortified country house. By the end of the century both buildings were destroyed; that on St. Kitts was brought down by the great earthquake of April 1690, and that on St. Croix by decay after Louis XIV ordered the colonists removed to Haiti in 1695.

The greater structure was on St. Kitts, at what became known as Estate de la Fontaine for the stream descending the mountain behind it. Begun in 1640, the chateau was considered the finest residence in the New World, and de Poincy proudly sent a drawing of it to France for publication (see figure 11). The chateau was described as nearly square, of four stories, and furnished with handsome wood floors and large windows.[13] A flat roof was used for entertainment; from its parapet de Poincy hung French royal pennants and flags he captured in battle. The chateau stood within a double enclosure, beyond which lay the "Angola village" of agricultural workers. The outer yard contained the estate storehouses, workshops, and lodgings for industrial and domestic servants. The inner courtyard was terraced by a battered masonry wall mounting several cannons. Behind the chateau a formal walled garden lay on higher ground. Standing on the site today are the defensive wall, the garden enclosure, and the ruins of outbuildings.

In 1659 the Chevalier du Bois, de Poincy's lieutenant on St. Croix, erected a more modest structure that nonetheless also contained defensive elements. A French print shows an elevated, two-story great house with square, pennant-bearing end towers that project forward from the front corners (see figure 12).[14] Another pair of pennants was set at the ends of the hipped roof, an unlikely

Fig. 11. Chateau de Poincy, St. Christopher (St. Kitts). This illustration from Rochefort's *Histoire naturel et morale des Iles Antilles* (Rotterdam: Arnout Leers, 1665) depicts a residence in the style of Louis XIII with formal gardens and fortified surroundings with slave quarters outside.

Fig. 12. Chateau du Bois, St. Croix. This illustration from Jean-Baptiste du Tertre's *Histoire générale des Antilles habitées par les François* (Paris: Jacques Langlois, 1667–71) shows the residence, outbuildings, and formal gardens but does not indicate the walls that connected buildings to create courts and work yards.

location suggesting that an engraving error removed evidence of matching towers at the rear corners. A formal garden was connected to the house by a tree-lined avenue. The sides of the chateau and the scattered outbuildings seem to have been further protected by two curious round towers—clearly not windmills. Warehouses line the front of the yard, hinting at a site not far from the beach. Field investigation has disproved its identification with "Judith's Fancy," a working sugar plantation until fairly recently. Nothing survives of the French chateau, and its site has not yet been located. Yet the seventeenth-century drawing of the two chateaus cannot be dismissed as fanciful. Outside interest is unwelcome to owners of the St. Kiss site, but the extent of the drawing's accuracy, one hopes can be determined by archaeological investigation in the not too distant future.

In conclusion, chateaus and castle-houses, unlike the *castillos* of Iberian empires, first appeared in the northern European colonies in the middle of the seventeenth century, just when defended houses were no longer built in Ireland. Castles were erected under special conditions of colonization and unusual local circumstances, where political and military power was in the hands of a few wealthy landowners—or where those who held such power could soon join the ranks of the magnates. Neither fully private nor entirely public, castles—and the halls and manors that were theoretically subordinate—were built as architecture of social control. Members of colonial societies recognized and presumably accepted these structures not just as symbols of status and authority but also for their very real strengths (essentially as strongholds) in resisting opposition. That, of course, is why castles were created in the first place.

By the eighteenth century, though, colonial castles were obsolete. Public and private spheres became more firmly drawn, and the ideal of aristocratic independence yielded to one of civic participation. New country houses embodied the rational architecture of men who had learned to balance private commercial fortunes against the public power of the developing state.[15] More effective imperial control over colonies and new fashions flowing from capital cities hastened the end of colonial castles. Wealth and power had changed their forms of display and means of security. The need for castles—and the propriety of their construction—no longer existed.

Notes

1. J. H. Parry, *The Spanish Seaborne Empire* (London: Hutchinson, 1966; repr., New York: Knopf, 1971), 27–37. Paul E. Hoffman, *The Spanish Crown and the Defense of the Caribbean, 1535–1585* (Baton Rouge, La., 1980), and personal communication suggest that the later use in the New World of the term "castillo" instead of the more typical "fortaleza" was due to antiquarianism.

2. J. R. Hale, *Renaissance War Studies* (London: Hambleton Press, 1983); Geoffrey Parker, *The Military Revolution: Military Innovation and the Rise of the West, 1500–1800* (Cambridge: Cambridge University Press, 1988).

3. See Mark Girouard, *Robert Smythson and the Architecture of the Elizabethan Era* (London: Barnes, 1966), 159–72, with "Spenserian buildings" on 171. M. W. Thompson, *The Decline of the Castle* (Cambridge: Cambridge University Press, 1987), 125–35, presents several examples of chivalric revival architecture.

4. Harold G. Leask, *Irish Castles and Castellated Houses* (Dundalk, U.K.: Dundalgan, 1951).

5. Eric Klingelhofer, "Vernacular Architecture of the Munster Colony" (paper presented at the 111th Annual Meeting of the American Historical Association, Atlanta, 1996); Eric Klingelhofer, "*Castles Built with Air:* Spenserian Architecture in Ireland," in *Military Studies in Medieval Europe, Papers of the 'Medieval Europe Brugge 1997' Conference,* vol. 11, ed. Guy de Boe and Frans Verhaeghe (Zellik, Belgium, 1997), 149–54. See also Eric Klingelhofer, "The Castle of the *Faerie Queene,*" *Archaeology* (March/April 1999): 48–52.

6. A. G. Bradley, ed., *Travels and Works of Captain John Smith,* part 2 (Edinburgh: John Grant, 1910), 644, 678.

7. John Winthrop, *The Journal of John Winthrop 1630–1649,* ed. Richard S. Dunn et al. (Cambridge, Mass.: Harvard University Press, 1996), 732, 734, 735. The editors believe that John Winthrop II drew the fortification before sailing to Massachusetts.

8. Fraser Neiman, *The "Manner House" before Stratford* (Stratford, Va., 1980); William Kelso, *Captain Jones's Wormslow* (Athens: University of Georgia Press, 1979).

9. T. A. L. Concannon, "The Great Houses of Jamaica," in *Ian Fleming Introduces Jamaica,* ed. Morris Cargill (Kingston, Jamaica: Deutsch, 1965), 117–26; list of great houses, 125–26.

10. See Buisseret, *Historic Architecture,* 14, 15.

11. Helen Reynolds, *Dutch Houses on the Hudson before 1776* (New York: Classic Textbooks, 1929); Montgomery Schuyler, *The Patroons and Lords of Manors of the Hudson* (New York, 1932); S. G. Nissenson, *The Patroon's Domain* (New York, 1937).

12. Buisseret, *Historic Architecture,* 11, 12.

13. Cesar de Rochefort, *Historie Naturelle et Morale des Iles Antille* (Lyons, 1667), 51–54.

14. *Jean Baptiste du Tertre on the French in St. Croix and the Virgin Islands,* trans. Aimery Caron and Arnold R. Highfield, College of the Virgin Islands, occasional paper no. 4 (N.p., 1978); J. B. du Tertre, *Histoire general des Antilles* (Paris, 1667–71; repr., Fort-de-France, Martinique, 1973). See also Florence Lewisohn, *Diverse Information on the Romantic History of St. Croix* (Christiansted, St Croix: Saint Croix Landmarks Society, 1964), 5–7; material drawn from Johannes Brondsted, ed., *Vore Gamle Tropekolonier,* vol. 2 (Copenhagen, 1952).

15. Matthew Johnson, *An Archaeology of Capitalism* (Oxford: Blackwell, 1996), esp. 152–54. My comments on crop-based colonial/commercial capitalism supplement rather than challenge Johnson's focus on English rural capitalism causing the postmedieval aristocracy to shift their seats of authority from castles to country houses.

Rituals of Rulership

The Material Culture of West Indian Politics

Natalie Zacek

In the course of his extensive travels throughout the West Indies in the 1880s, the English historian James Anthony Froude compared the towns of the English islands unfavorably with those he had seen in the Spanish colonies. In Froude's rhapsodic description, Havana was "a city of palaces, a city of streets and plazas, of colonnades, and towers, and churches and monasteries. . . . The Spaniards built as they built in Castile; built with the same material, the white limestone which they found in the New World as in the Old. The palaces of the nobles in Havana, the residence of the governor, the convents, the cathedral, are a reproduction of Burgos or Valladolid, as if by some Aladdin's lamp a Castilian city had been taken up and set down again unaltered on the shore of the Caribbean Sea."[1] Froude unflatteringly compared the urban centers of the English islands to the splendors that to him typified the Spanish colonizing impulse; he claimed that "we English have built in these islands as if we were but passing visitors, wanting only tenements to be occupied for a time. . . . Kingston [Jamaica] is the best of our West Indian towns, and Kingston has not one fine building in it."[2]

Admittedly, by the time Froude made his visit to the English islands, they were a century past the apex of their prosperity, the foundations of their wealth shattered by the effects of imperial reorganization and slave emancipation. Cuba, on the other hand, had arisen as the world's preeminent producer of cane sugar in response to the decline of the English sugar islands and to the transformation of the colony of Saint Domingue into the black republic of Haiti. At the close of the nineteenth century, Cuba had just reached the peak of its prosperity. However, the difference between the urban landscape of Havana and those of Kingston; Bridgetown, Barbados; St. John's, Antigua; and other English West Indian towns had existed for the preceding two centuries, at a time in which the English islands were the most valuable possessions in Europe's wealthiest and most powerful empire. In the period between the Restoration and the American

Revolution, nearly every traveler to or colonial official arriving in the English islands depicted the cities and towns as being crude, unattractive, and even decrepit; as Barry Higman has written, "they heaped scorn on these ugly sinks of death and disease . . . however briefly a visitor stayed in an island, there was always time to bestow a curse on its town."[3] At the beginning of the nineteenth century, the missionary Thomas Coke admitted that a few of the English towns had some positive aspects, but he was generally appalled by "the asylum of filth and low dissipation which disgrace[s] most British West India towns."[4]

An unnamed visitor to St. John's, the capital of Antigua, in 1713 described the town as a small settlement in which "the houses are mostly built of wood, without any glass windows, ye Streets are not pav'd, which makes ye Town very foul in wet weather, and obliges ye people to put on boots to cross ye streets. Their Church is of a piece with ye houses being all of wood, and without glass windows, they have but one Small Bell, ye chief ornament within is a few handsome Pews, and two or three marble Tomb-Stones."[5] Half a century later few improvements had been implemented; the streets of St. John's remained unpaved, and "all the good living is amongst the planters in the country."[6] By the end of the eighteenth century the town could boast a courthouse, a jail, and a customhouse, but even on the brink of emancipation a visitor opined that, although St. John's might rank with the Danish West Indian towns of Christiansted and St. Croix, it was no match for the cities of the Spanish and, to a lesser extent, the French islands.[7] Charlestown, the capital of Nevis, appeared to be not merely unattractive but also unhealthy; the physician James Rymer, a visitor of the 1770s, was astounded that a colony that annually produced six to seven thousand hogsheads of sugar would have as its principal entrepôt a town "composed of wooden houses and huts . . . surrounded by marshy ground, and stagnant water," rendering its "vulgar and illiterate" inhabitants vulnerable to the deadly tertian fever.[8]

The English town of Basseterre, St. Kitts, was not much more impressive to its visitors. The unpaved, sandy streets were too narrow to accommodate carriages and coated pedestrians with mud and dust; the buildings' "uniformity in design or capacity seldom extend[ed] beyond half a dozen buildings in succession, without being interrupted by ill-considered wooden tenements, or small square hovels of one or two rooms, that might be compared to bird-cages, jammed in between so many larger packages. . . . Here and there a well finished building . . . meets the eye . . . but the general aspect of the place denotes poverty and depression of trade . . . metropolitan signs of a populous and affluent community are equally obsolete."[9] These few "well finished buildings" were mostly souvenirs of the French occupation of the town; inhabiting Basseterre from the beginnings of European settlement in the 1620s until the signing of the Peace of Utrecht, they had built themselves attractive, substantial brick houses and had erected "a great church, a Court of Justice or Maison de Ville, a hospital with doctors, apothecaries, and chirurgeons, and a great chateau for the governor, with wonderful gardens."[10]

In 1690 an earthquake had demolished many of these "piles of Brick and Stone," including "the *Jesuites* Colledge," but the town remained imposing enough to dazzle the English when they took control of it in 1713, so superior did it seem to their former capital at Old Road Town.[11] The marine engineer Jacques Bellin, who sailed through the Antilles in the 1750s, claimed that even after four decades the English, who preferred to live in dispersed plantations, had done little to put their own stamp on the old French capital; even the old French Jesuit College had been rebuilt in its original form and, under the name of St. George's, come "into the Hands of the English Protestants."[12]

It might seem logical to interpret these observations as indications that the English planters lacked either the desire or the ability to pursue a luxurious style of life. However, such was clearly not the case, as many of the same commentators who lamented the seemingly arrested urban development of the English colonies simultaneously remarked on the lavish houses, furnishings, and clothing of these planters. Froude, upon visiting a house erected by "the most splendid of the old Barbadian merchant princes," was sufficiently impressed by the sight of "the drawing-room, a magnificent saloon . . . filled with rare and curious things . . . selected with the finest taste" that he admitted "there had been fine culture in the West Indies when all these treasures were collected."[13] The unidentified compiler of *A Complete System of Geography* was struck by the tendency of the English to settle in a scattered manner, unlike the apparently communalist French, but remarked that the English planters of St. Kitts lived in "very fine houses, of cedar, and adorn'd with Walks and Groves of Oranges and Lemon."[14]

Seventeenth- and eighteenth-century visitors to the Caribbean, particularly the Leeward Islands, remarked on the splendid objects purchased and displayed by the English planters. George Rutherford, an Antiguan physician of the late eighteenth century, owned a sideboard valued at £23, twelve silver spoons, a silver fruit stand, a knife case containing twenty-one knives and twenty-two forks, and no fewer than 110 gallons of casked rum, all of which accoutrement reflected the islands' ethos of lavish hospitality.[15] John Panton, a member of St. Kitts's ruling council during the War of the Spanish Succession, owned costly imported walnut and cedar furnishings, an elbow chair, a spinet, and a Turkey leather chair.[16] In 1722 the furnishings of the widow Mary Pinney's house in Nevis were valued at £512 and included a damask bedstead, a black japanned tea table, an oak escritoire, and three silver tankards.[17]

English West Indians were similarly renowned for the lavishness of their dress. In a 1711 number of the *Spectator,* Richard Steele fixed in the metropolitan eye the image of "the gay West Indian . . . in a Summer-Island suit . . . who appeared in all the colours which can affect an eye that could not distinguish between being fine and tawdry."[18] Throughout the eighteenth century an over-fondness for gaudy dress emerged as a major component of the stereotype of the English planter as an individual who was "amazing fond of costly, tinsel frippery," to the extent that the bankrupt West Indian was reported to have "dress[ed] away [his] fortune."[19] Metropolitan observers believed that West Indian men were "too much addicted to expensive . . . dress and equipage," which caused them to "plunge deeper in debt and distress [until] . . . they leave at their decease their whole fortune to be torn piecemeal"; such was the cost of maintaining a "peacock wardrobe" for men and women alike.[20]

Even those participants in white West Indian society, such as Scottish-born overseers, who lacked the financial resources necessary to offer lavish hospitality and dress in the height of fashion felt culturally obligated to adopt a style of life that imitated, albeit in stylized and unconsciously parodic fashion, that of their wealthy employers. The nineteenth-century Antiguan writer Mrs. Amelia Flannigan described such aspirant grandees as members of a "mushroom gentry": their evening suits "bore ample marks of time"; their dinner guests "indulged in such luxuries as fowls' necks and odd ends of pudding, washed down by a single glass of wine"; and they traversed the island in "a rattling, shaking, tumble-down carriage, drawn by a pair of spavined horses, and further graced by a shoeless coachman."[21] The desire to live in a luxurious manner and to impress others with one's wealth and style was sufficiently powerful that it encouraged English West Indians to consume to the outer limits of their financial resources and of metropolitan conceptions of good taste.

If many of the planters of the English islands possessed the means, taste, and ability to acquire luxurious goods and erect lavish houses in which to display them, why did they apparently have so little interest in making their towns attractive and orderly? More importantly, what does the paucity of urban development, and in particular the lack of impressive public architecture, imply about the philosophy and practice of colonial government in the English West Indies? What sort of social or cultural logic might explain or even mandate this disjuncture between private luxury and public parsimony?

Many scholars of the English Caribbean, including Richard Dunn, Orlando Patterson, Margaret Rouse-Jones, Alan Karras, and Andrew O'Shaughnessy, have described white West Indians as "short-termers" who looked to Britain as their natural home and thus were reluctant to make any significant investment in the development of a local infrastructure.[22] They point out that these colonies' governors had an extremely difficult time convincing their subjects to finance the construction of crucial defense features, such as jails and fortifications, let alone to erect courthouses, government houses, or other civic buildings. However, if one wishes to make the counterclaim that a significant percentage of white West Indians did conceive of the islands as a permanent home rather than as a temporary stopping place, it is necessary to examine the reasons why the locals were so reluctant to invest in the creation and deployment of local structures of administration.

In examining this apparent reluctance to support the material elements of political life, it is important to recall that white West Indians already labored under a heavy burden of taxation, particularly in the Leeward Islands, which had managed to purchase their independence from Barbadian control in 1670 only by accepting a tax in perpetuity of 4.5 percent on all exports.[23] Moreover, the planters were quite aware of the long list of disasters, both natural and man-made, with which their islands had been afflicted in living memory: fires, floods, earthquakes, volcanic eruptions, and raids by rival European powers. What was the point of investing in urban development if its results were constantly confronted with the threat of imminent destruction?[24] In addition to these practical objections, many West Indian planters retained a "country" as opposed to a "court" ideology, fearing anything that could be seen as "big government" and viewing the erection of substantial government buildings as leading to the creation of a carceral landscape that was as threatening to individual and communal liberty as the prospect of a standing army.[25]

Despite these "country" leanings, however, the planters were at the same time deeply mimetic of what they saw as aristocratic values, which emphasized private hospitality and sociability rather than the development of a significant public sphere.[26] Consciously or unconsciously they worked to adopt what they imagined to be a rural aristocrat's lifestyle, a way of living to which their financial and social position had not entitled them in Britain. Through adoption of the mentality and accoutrement that characterized landed gentility, West Indian planters, many of whom had little or no experience of metropolitan life, could sustain "the foundation myth that English overseas colonies were transplanted fragments of English people and their institutions" and could employ such an ideology and style of life as "an important signifier or the contemporary, ruralist distillate of national life."[27] The ideal of the country estate was crucial to the formation of a planter self-image, as a symbol of tradition and hierarchy that denied the twin realities of slavery and the protoindustrial nature of plantation production. Richard Sheridan has claimed that "prior to the age of steam power, limited companies, and free labour, the unit of production in the West Indies was the family-owned plantation, buttressed by the ancient institutions of primogeniture and entail . . . the relationship between master and slave was not unlike that of the patriarchal family system."[28] However, as Sidney W. Mintz has argued, the organization and operation of large-scale sugar plantations were in actuality "precocious cases of industrialization," a highly undesirable image that planters sought to occlude behind the image of agrarian gentility.[29]

Taking these constraints under consideration, how might a governor express or exercise his authority? The possession of a private fortune, which allowed one to dress and entertain lavishly, was a prerequisite. The governorship of the Leeward Islands was the lowest-paid of all such positions in the first British Empire, but nonetheless it was essential that the post holder maintain an appearance of affluence by renting or purchasing a commodious residence, dressing with formality and style, and offering lavish and open hospitality.[30] Eighteenth-century English commentators and modern historians have converged to ridicule the flashy style in which West Indian planters and, particularly, their wives and daughters dressed, seeing them as gaudy in their tastes and naive in their belief that the possession of fine clothes indicated the wealth and reputability of their wearers. However, it is important to bear in mind that in societies such as those of the Leewards, in which even those who owned vast plantations and hundreds of slaves were constantly dependent on the extension of credit in both the islands and the metropole, the maintenance of a luxurious lifestyle served as evidence of one's solvency and thus one's suitability for the extension of loans or credit.[31] A governor who possessed a substantial private income could be relied on to cut the right sort of figure among the local planters; at least as importantly, he would not need to resort to cheating or embezzling from public funds, "grinding and fleecing" his subjects in order to support himself. His wealth would render him independent, in the sense that he would be his own man and need rely on no one else for financial support. This "independency" was a central tenet of early modern British and colonial British American political philosophy, which limited electoral participation to those who possessed sufficient land or income to rank among each polity's independent men.

Additionally a rich governor could serve as a source of patronage, spreading his wealth among those he favored. This would increase his influence, thus increasing the power and prestige of his government, and also yield tangible benefits to at least some of his subjects, which encouraged their loyalty. The governor, after all, served as the representative of the monarch, and appearing either penurious or parsimonious would reflect as badly on him as it would on a king or queen. As an example, we can look to George Thomas, who governed the Leewards in the 1750s and was "respected, not beloved." Although he was deemed sensible and honest by his subjects, he was not a truly popular or effective leader, at least in part because he was "considered as parsimonious, and not living equal to his rank. . . . to be popular, a man must not only keep an hospitable table, but be the jolly companion."[32]

To gain the public's respect, the governor had to engage in rituals that allowed local planters to construct and conceive of themselves as loyal, public-spirited

Englishmen and as members of a landed gentry. Because no official governor's mansion existed in the Leewards until the end of the eighteenth century, it was essential that the governor rent or purchase a lavish residence in which he could live and entertain in the style appropriate to his rank. As local assemblies were reluctant to vote the governor additional funds for house rent, the issue of accommodation served as yet another reason for a successful governor to have a private income. The dispersed nature of settlement in the Leeward colonies required that the governor not merely remain within his residence but also be mobile and master public spaces throughout his territory. For this reason, Daniel Parke, governor of the Leewards from 1706 to 1710, who lacked a significant income of his own, attempted to force the assembly of Antigua to purchase a sloop for his use, which would allow him to travel between the four Leewards in order to carry out his administrative responsibilities. The assembly was extremely unwilling to buy such a vessel for Parke, being not only resentful of the additional expense but also wary of setting such a precedent. This seemingly trivial disagreement contributed significantly to the breakdown of relations between Parke and his subjects, which led eventually to his murder by an outraged mob. The results in this case bear witness to the importance of personal wealth for a West Indian governor.

Similarly it was important that the governor have a supply of horses and slave attendants, in order that he might progress around his jurisdiction with ease and in style. At the beginning of the eighteenth century, the French missionary Father Jean-Baptiste Labat described the travels of Leeward governor Christopher Codrington the younger: "The General mounted his horse a quarter of an hour after we left the table, where we sat for nearly three hours according to the English custom. Two trumpeters rode in front of him, and he was accompanied by eight persons who appeared to be his servants, as only his chaplain and M. Hamilton, his Major-General, sat at table with us. Nine or ten negroes ran in front of the trumpeters. . . . I felt sorry for a small negro about 15 years old who was being taught to be a runner. He . . . was made to take off . . . [his] garments and run naked in front of everyone. He was followed by a negro with a whip which was applied every time he came within range."[33] In this instance we can see the governor's progress as a performance emphasizing excess and waste, represented by the ostentatious use of slaves in a nonproductive capacity, comparable to their frequent appearances in the portraits of aristocratic women in early modern England.[34] The gratuitous use of the whip to spur on the naked slave runner served to show observers that Codrington was willing to tolerate and even encourage the use of brutality, an important attribute in a society that had to contend with the constant threats of warfare and slave revolt.

As the Leewards attained ever higher levels of prosperity, and as a result emerged as among the most lucrative colonial possessions within the first British

Empire, stylized social rituals evolved. These rituals facilitated societal cohesion and substituted for public buildings and urban development in instilling in local planters a sense of their position within the imperial system. Most prominent among these was the annual governor's ball, which allowed local elites to display themselves, to see and to be seen, and emerged as a marriage mart in which eligible young women were paraded before prospective husbands, both islanders and visitors from the metropole. The clergyman and poet William Shervington depicted a ball of the 1740s as "that pleasing night / When late th'assembled charmers shone so bright . . . Cecilia's sons th'harmonious lyre attune / And blazing lights recal[l] the absent noon."[35] Such an event might yield matrimonial success for the host as well as for his guests. For a governor, a wife was desirable for her assistance at social and ceremonial events and also as an ornament who would augment her husband's prestige through deployment of elegant manners and lavish clothing. To marry an eligible young woman of the islands and make her "the Governor's lady" provided tangible and intangible benefits for both the governor and the lady.[36]

Other rituals that evolved were less opulent than the governor's ball but were still crucial in encouraging the plantocracy to construct themselves as loyal members of the extended family of Britons. Upon the accession of a new monarch, the governor would lead the members of the island's council and assembly and other prominent local men in drawing up ceremonial proclamations in praiseful acknowledgment of the new king or queen's authority. The most important element of this event was the ritual of signing one's name to the proclamation, which served as each individual's promise of loyal service to the monarch, encouraging the signer to figure himself as both a highly placed member of his community and a participant in imperial governance. The reigning monarch's birthday was similarly an opportunity for personal display of fealty. The elite gathered in order to drink "bumpers" in honor of His or Her Majesty, accompanied by "a splendid entertainment for the governor and the gentry" at which on at least one occasion "above Two Hundred Pieces of Cannon [were] fir[e]d among the afternoon rejoicings," followed by a great ball. These celebrations were so absorbing to the plantocracy that slaves came to see them as ideal moments to assert themselves. The planned Antigua slave rebellion of 1736, for example, was to have taken place on October 11, at which time most planters would have been at the St. John's "great house" of Christopher Dunbar attending a ball in honor of George II.[37]

Material objects specifically associated with administrative power, in addition to lavish personal effects and opulent displays of hospitality, were deployed by English West Indian governors as sources and symbols of their authority. A mace was commonly carried by the governor at official events; along with the royal seal, it served as a signifier, even a fetish, of authority. Whereas the mace was a permanent element of each colony's regalia and was passed from one governor to the next, the seal was created, destroyed, and re-created in connection with each administration. When a governor took office, the privy council issued a newly produced seal and dispatched it to the islands for his exclusive use. When that governor left office, he was expected to break the seal into several pieces, preventing its unauthorized use should it fall into others' hands, and return it to the privy council, thus bringing symbolic closure to his administration.

Among the many charges that Daniel Parke's subjects leveled against him, one of the most serious was that, rather than returning his late predecessor's broken seal to the privy council, he had ordered it melted down and fashioned into a tankard for his own use. Parke's opponents produced no evidence in support of their claim, and Parke defended himself by claiming that the pieces of the seal had been stored temporarily in a desk, which had inadvertently been removed from his rented house before he had the chance to send it on to London. Despite the absence of corroborating evidence and the plausibility of Parke's explanation, the allegation was met with rage and horror by his subjects. To retain government property and deploy it for unauthorized personal use was a grave offense against the body politic and an act that in the public imagination symbolized Parke's disregard for the force of law and his contempt toward those over whom he held authority. As Capt. John Blackwell had noted in the early years of William Penn's "holy experiment," objects such as seals were more than props or decorations; they "signifye[d] much, and [have] at all times been counted sacred."[38]

In conclusion, it is important to bear in mind the small physical size of these plantation societies. Each of the Leeward Island colonies covered fewer than fifty square miles of territory, and none could boast of a white population greater than a few thousand residents at any point in the eighteenth century. These colonies were, in Joanne Freeman's phrase, "small-scale, localized political realm[s] [that] magnified" colonial British American culture's pervading concern with reputation and honor as the basis of individual position and societal harmony.[39] They were also marked by a "hierarchical pattern of officeholding . . . [in which] the most prestigious and powerful positions—councillor, assemblyman, judge, and commander of a militia regiment—were reserved for the colonists of the highest economic and social standing."[40] In a situation where all forms of authority are personal and hierarchical, rather than institutional, it falls to individuals to assume the roles and responsibilities that in more highly articulated societies are associated with the public sphere. Such individuals can strengthen their positions through deployment and control of objects and rituals that facilitate their attainment and maintenance of power. Eighteenth-century West Indian governors were well advised to heed the "old saying in London, That the city is not so much Governd by the Wisdome of the Maior, as the Capparisens of his horse, [and] The Cap of maintenance & sword carried by him that bears it."[41]

Notes

Versions of this essay have been presented at the College of Charleston, the University of Aberdeen, and the University of St. Andrews. I am grateful to audiences at these seminars for their comments and suggestions, and to R. C. Nash, Jeffrey Webb, and Stewart King for their careful readings.

1. James Anthony Froude, *The English in the West Indies, or The Bow of Ulysses* (London: Longmans, Green, and Co., 1888), 256.

2. Ibid.

3. Barry Higman, "Urban Slavery in the British Caribbean," in Elizabeth M. Thomas Hope, *Perspectives on Caribbean Regional Identity* (Liverpool: Centre for Latin American Studies, University of Liverpool, 1984), 1.

4. Thomas Coke, *A History of the West Indies, Containing the Natural, Civil, and Ecclesiastical History of Each Island,* 3 vols. (Liverpool: Nuttall, Fisher, and Dixon, 1808), 2:416.

5. "Voyage to Guinea, Antego, Bay of Campeachy, Cuba, Barbadoes, &c.," 1713–23, British Library Additional Manuscripts 39946.

6. Edward Thompson, *Sailor's Letters,* 2 vols. (London, 1766), 2:11.

7. Paul C. Cloyd, *Historic Architecture: Design Guidelines for a Historic District, St. John's Antigua* (Privately printed, 1984), 54; *The West India Sketch Book,* 2 vols. (London: Whittaker & Co., 1834), 2:158. Although the government and the Catholic Church provided some support for the development of infrastructure in the French colonies, recurring natural disasters discouraged substantial investment; in Saint Domingue, Port-au-Prince, described by Moreau de Saint-Mery as a "vast Tatar camp," was shattered by an earthquake in 1771, and Cap Français was burned in the 1690s and again in the 1750s. My thanks to Stewart King for this last point.

8. James Rymer, *A Description of the Island of Nevis; with an Account of Its Principal Diseases* (London: T. Evans, 1775), 3, 23.

9. *West India Sketch Book,* 2:2–3; Maria Riddell, *Voyages to the Madeira and Leeward Caribbean Isles, with Sketches of the Natural History of These Islands* (Edinburgh: Peter Hill, 1792), 26.

10. *Recueil de divers voyages faits en Afrique et en l'Amerique* (Paris: Louis Billaine, 1674), 51.

11. Everett C. Wilkie, "'Une Bibliotheque Bien Fournie': The Earliest Known Caribbean Library," *Libraries and Culture* 25 (1990): 178.

12. Jacques Bellin, *Description geographique des Isles Antilles possedees par les Anglois* (Paris: Didot, 1758), 108; *A Complete System of Geography,* 2 vols. (London, 1747), 2:724; Kathleen D. Manchester, *Historic Heritage of St. Kitts, Nevis, and Anguilla* (Privately published, 1971), 26.

13. Froude, *English,* 104, 106.

14. *Complete System,* 2:724.

15. Public Record Office, London, C.O.108/245.

16. Margaret Deanne Rouse-Jones, "St. Kitts, 1713–1763: A Study of the Development of a Plantation Colony" (Ph.D. diss., Johns Hopkins University, 1977), 14.

17. Nevis Assembly Minutes, March 30, 1722, cited in Richard Pares, *A West-India Fortune* (London: Longmans, Green, and Co., 1950), 336–39.

18. Quoted in N. Darnell Davis, *The* Spectator*'s Essays Relating to the West Indies* (Demerara: Argosy Press, 1885), 9.

19. Erin Skye Mackie, "Cultural Cross-Dressing: The Colorful Case of the Caribbean Creole," in *The Clothes That Wear Us: Essays on Dressing and Transgressing in Eighteenth-Century Culture,* ed. Jessica Munns and Penny Richards (Newark: University of Delaware Press, 1999), 259–60.

20. Long, *History of Jamaica,* quoted in Wylie Sypher, "The West Indian as a 'Character' in the Eighteenth Century," *North Carolina Studies in Philology* 1 (1939): 506–7.

21. Amelia Flannigan, *Antigua and the Antiguans,* 2 vols. (London: Saunders and Ottley, 1844), 2:195.

22. See Dunn, *Sugar and Slaves;* Orlando Patterson, *The Sociology of Slavery: An Analysis of the Origins, Development and Structure of Negro Slave Society in Jamaica* (London: MacGibbon & Kee, 1967); Rouse-Jones, "St. Kitts"; Alan Karras, *Sojourners in the Sun: Scottish Migrants in Jamaica and the Chesapeake, 1740–1800* (Ithaca, N.Y.: Cornell University Press, 1992); Andrew O'Shaughnessy, *An Empire Divided: The American Revolution and the British Caribbean* (Philadelphia: University of Pennsylvania Press, 2000).

23. Dunn, *Sugar and Slaves,* 123–24.

24. The Leewards suffered severely from natural disasters in the seventeenth and eighteenth centuries. St. Kitts experienced four earthquakes in the period between 1668 and 1690. In the last of these, "the earth opened nine feet [deep] in many places and buried solid timber sugar mills . . . it threw down . . . all other stone buildings." Antigua endured six earthquakes between 1690 and 1766, the first, and most destructive, of which "laid some buildings in rubbish" and damaged Gov. Christopher Codrington's property to the tune of two thousand pounds. See G. R. Robson, "An Earthquake Catalogue for the Eastern Caribbean, 1530–1960," *Bulletin of the Seismological Society of America* 54 (1964): 789–90.

25. On the carceral landscape, see Michel Foucault, *Discipline and Punish: The Birth of the Prison,* trans. Alan Sheridan (New York: Vintage Books, 1979), esp. 293–308.

26. Cynthia A. Kierner, "Hospitality, Sociability, and Gender in the Southern Colonies," *Journal of Southern History* 62 (1996): 449–80.

27. Michael Craton, "Property and Propriety: Land Tenure and Slave Property in the Creation of a British West Indian Plantocracy, 1612–1740," in *Concepts of Property in the Seventeenth and Eighteenth Centuries,* ed. Susan Staves and John Brewer (New York: Routledge, 1994), 498; Paul Gilroy, *The Black Atlantic: Modernity and Double Consciousness* (Cambridge, Mass.: Harvard University Press, 1993).

28. Richard Sheridan, "The Rise of a Colonial Gentry: A Case Study of Antigua, 1730–1775," *Economic History Review* 13 (1960): 344.

29. Sidney W. Mintz, *Sweetness and Power: The Place of Sugar in Modern History* (New York: Viking, 1985), 59.

30. The Nevis house rented by Governor Hart in 1722 contained lavish furnishings of oak, cedar, and walnut, with silk upholstery and hangings, as well as a silver table service and a vast store of fine linens; the rent came to one hundred pounds per year. See Pares, *West-India Fortune,* 336–39.

31. See Mackie, "Cultural Cross-Dressing"; Toby L. Ditz, "Shipwrecked: Imperiled Masculinity and the Representation of Business Failures amongst Philadelphia's Eighteenth-Century Merchants," *Journal of American History* 81 (1994): 51–80.

32. Thomas Hulton, "Account of Travels" (Codex Eng. 74, John Carter Brown Library, Brown University), 68–69.

33. Father Jean-Baptiste Labat, *The Memoirs of Pere Labat, 1693–1705* (London: Frank Cass, 1970), 214–15.

34. See Kim F. Hall, *Things of Darkness: Economies of Race and Gender in Early Modern England* (Ithaca, N.Y.: Cornell University Press, 1995), chap. 5; Rebecca Earle, "Consumption and Excess in Spanish America" (paper presented at the Seminar in Latin American Cultural Studies, University of Manchester, Manchester, U.K., February 2003); Cathe Mizell-Nelson, "Angel or She-Devil: White Creole Women's Performance of Waste in Eighteenth-Century Literature" (unpub. manuscript in author's possession).

35. W. S. A. B., *The Antigonian and Boston Beauties* (Boston: D. Fowle, 1790), 3–4.

36. See, for example, Laetitia Pilkington, *Memoirs* (London: George Routledge and Sons, 1928), 354.

37. David Barry Gaspar, *Bondmen and Rebels: A Study of Master-Slave Relations in Antigua* (Baltimore: Johns Hopkins University Press, 1985), 3–4.

38. Quoted in Jeffrey B. Webb, "Reasonable Distinction: The Formation of an American Status Discipline in the Pennsylvania Hinterland, 1682–1740," 2 vols. (Ph.D. diss., University of Chicago, 2001), 2:291.

39. Joanne Freeman, "Dueling as Politics," *William and Mary Quarterly* 53 (1996): 296.

40. Richard S. Dunn, "The Barbados Census of 1680," *William and Mary Quarterly* 26 (1969): 18.

41. Webb, "Reasonable Distinction," 2:291.

L'Hermitage on the Monocacy Battlefield, Frederick, Maryland

Paula Stoner Reed

A structure seemingly out of place exists on the Monocacy National Battlefield grounds in Frederick County, Maryland. In the midst of a countryside dotted with material remains of historic German and English settlement, a distinctive stone, hip-roofed, French-looking barn can be found on the field made famous by an 1864 Civil War engagement. The barn, moreover, is part of a farm complex with a fascinating history that stretches from France to Haiti to Maryland (see figure 1). This plantation is distinctive within the context of farms and plantations in mid-Maryland, where the norm was a hybrid of English and German traditions. The Frenchmen here seem to have been viewed as part of an alien culture misunderstood by the locals, and they fostered the notion of separateness in part through their buildings, which appear quite different from those of the surrounding culture.

The Vincendieres were planters near St. Marc in western Saint Domingue (Haiti). Etienne Bellumeau de la Vincendiere's plantation produced coffee and was in the area of Grands-Cahos. His wife's family through her mother, Marie-Francoise Sterlin de Magnan, had a plantation on the Plaine de l'Artibonite that produced indigo, and Payen Boisneuf had a plantation in the vicinity of St. Marc that produced sugar. All of these plantations were in the western section of Saint Domingue.[1] When a slave rebellion erupted in the French colony of Saint Domingue in the 1790s, these families along with thousands of other refugees fled. The slaves, who by the late eighteenth century greatly outnumbered the planters and tradesmen, revolted beginning in 1791, and by 1804 they had successfully established the republic of Haiti. The revolt spawned brutal violence inflicted on both sides. While homeless French refugees found asylum in numerous havens throughout the Atlantic and gulf coasts after 1791, some of the Vincendiere family came to Maryland in 1793. Baltimore was a major harbor for

FIG. 1. West view of l'Hermitage. Author's photograph

Frenchmen fleeing both the French Revolution and the Saint Domingue slave uprising. Frederick County, about forty miles west of Baltimore, was the most populous jurisdiction in the state at the time, according to 1790 census records, and also was among the most prosperous. However, Victoire Vincendiere and her mother, Magnan, may have fled first to Charleston, South Carolina, and migrated from there to Baltimore and Frederick, Maryland, in late 1793, possibly through a prior arrangement with a neighbor, the merchant-planter James Marshall.

The connection between Frederick and Baltimore, Maryland, and Saint Domingue may spring from the export of Maryland and Pennsylvania flour to Saint Domingue and other islands in the West Indies. Through the late eighteenth and early nineteenth centuries wheat continued to be in great demand throughout the Caribbean, and "Baltimore became known as the 'granary of the West Indies.' Vessels traveling between Baltimore and the West Indies were able to make the voyage a day faster than ships sailing from other eastern grain ports. Baltimore wheat withstood quick spoilage. For decades, merchants and traders in the Caribbean regarded 'Baltimore flour' as among the best in the world."[2] Frederick County, where first James Marshall and then the Vincendieres settled, and adjacent Washington County were the leading wheat- and flour-producing counties in Maryland. By the last decade of the eighteenth century Frederick County had as many as eighty grist mills and three to four hundred stills producing marketable finished goods, flour, and whiskey.[3] The mills in the mid-Maryland wheat belt had an annual value of more than $1.5 million.[4] "By 1810 Maryland had become the third-largest flour-producing state in the nation behind Pennsylvania and Virginia."[5] Flour and grain products funneled from mid-Maryland to Baltimore and from there to the West Indies, other North American ports, or overseas.

The head of the family, Etienne Bellumeau de la Vincendiere, did not join his wife and children in Maryland. Instead he established residence in Charleston, South Carolina, and remained there for the rest of his life. He stated in his will, written in 1802 in Charleston, that he resided at the plantation at "les grands Cahos" [Les Grands Cahots—"the Big Ups and Downs"[6]] in Saint Domingue from June 23, 1747, until December 31, 1792, "when in order to avoid being murdered by the assassins armed by the Civil Commissioners Polverel and Sonthonax against all the planters of the said Island of St. Domingo, I shipped myself by furlow from the Municipality of St. Marc's recorded in that of the petite riviere my parish for North America where I arrived, in this City of Charleston, the first of February one thousand seven hundred and ninety three, on the brig Governor Pinkney[,] Captain Dardillier."[7] He remained in Charleston until his death in 1802, living with his brother Henri in a house on King Street belonging to a French physician, Vincent le Seigneur. There is no credible record that Etienne Bellemeau Delavincendiere ever appeared in Maryland or shared in the family's property and wealth there. He left his small estate to his brother Henri and Vincent le Seigneur. As for his property in Saint Domingue, "situated at the grands Cahos and also my store at plassac St. Yéronimos [*sic*] parish petite riviere district of St. Marc on said Island, they belong by right half to my Wife, our property being in common and the other half to the children issued of our marriage. My executor, hereinafter named will find in my large chest a file of papers sealed which are the only ones to be sent to my Wife by the way she herself will chuse, and to her he will forward beforehand a certificate of my decease with the French consuls Visa, she will find in said file of papers a copy of the present Testament."[8] This was the only reference in Etienne's will to his wife and children living in Maryland.

Aboard the ship *Carolina,* Etienne's daughter Victoire arrived in Baltimore on October 25, 1793, just days after her seventeenth birthday.[9] With her, although possibly traveling on other vessels and arriving separately, were her mother, Magnan; her older brother, Etienne; her older sister, Pauline Dugas, who was married; and her younger sisters Emerentienne and four-year-old Adelaide. The baby Helene was born in Maryland on September 4, 1794.[10] Also traveling with the family was Payen Boisneuf, a cousin of Magnan Delavincendiere, who would remain with the family until his death in 1815. Current research suggests that Victoire traveled from Saint Domingue to Charleston first and from there to Baltimore. The party apparently then proceeded directly to Frederick County, about forty miles west of Baltimore. The family's "Declaration of Negroes," filed by

Fig. 2. Front (east) elevation of the main house. The left portion is the wing constructed c. 1794. The taller right section took on its present appearance about 1820. Author's photograph

Victoire, her mother, and her brother on December 24, 1793, stated that they were by that time residents of Frederick Town.[11] Just south of the town they established the Hermitage on land purchased in 1791 by a local merchant, James Marshall. The teenaged Victoire Vincendiere emerged as the leader of the family.

By 1798 Victoire had purchased over 740 acres, part of which land the family was already occupying as the Hermitage. Multiple housing units on the property, census records, and written documents indicate that the Vincendieres, with the help of James Marshall, a neighbor, merchant, and landowner, operated an asylum for other refugees from Saint Domingue. The plantation's buildings were constructed about 1794. Victoire later modified the main house in the 1820s. The farm complex today has an amazingly high level of historical and architectural integrity and is the only known intact French-Caribbean plantation complex in Maryland, according to the Maryland Historical Trust.

The story of the Vincendiere family and the other Caribbean refugees who resided with them begins to unfold through examination of the plantation's remaining buildings and historical records. The buildings, two houses and a barn, are the above-ground material remains of the French refugee occupation (see figures 2–5). The buildings are very different from typical farmsteads in central Maryland. They seem to blend what may be a particular combination of French and West Indian influence with materials and techniques common to the

Fig. 3. A digitally altered photograph of the front of l'Hermitage suggesting its overall form after 1794, with shed-roofed extension, based on architectural evidence in the building. Author's photograph

Fig. 4. North view of the main house. To the right is the c. 1794 main section. Behind it is the c. 1820 addition. Wooden sections to the left include an eighteenth-century one-story log kitchen, at the extreme left, and later frame infill dating from the third quarter of the nineteenth century. Author's photograph

Fig. 5. A digitally altered photograph of the east elevation of the house as it may have generally appeared in the late eighteenth century. Author's photograph

Fig. 6. The secondary house, east view of the west elevation. A one-story, east-facing stone dwelling, predating the Vincendiere occupation, was enlarged with a west-facing second story of log construction with two separate chambers, each with a door opening onto a gallery porch. The porch is no longer there. The doors are partially covered with later siding. Author's photograph

FIG. 7. French-style, hip-roofed stone crop barn, c. 1794, northeast view. Author's photograph

mid-Maryland region, such as the use of log and stone construction, and vernacular manifestations of current architectural styles.[12]

In the late eighteenth century in mid-Maryland the most frequently used structural component was log, followed by stone or brick, depending on local geology, soils, and availability, and then timber frame. Most houses were gable-roofed with chimneys inside the end walls. The U.S. direct tax records for 1798 for neighboring counties in Pennsylvania where such documentation survives reveal that approximately 90 percent of the buildings assessed were log structures. Barns were either small log crib structures or, more prevalently in the nineteenth century, larger buildings often described in contemporary documents as "Swisser" barns, which are common to the region (see figure 6). Each of these barns has a ramp at the back to give access to the upper threshing floor and a forebay at the front, which may either project outward from or be partially enclosed by extensions of the foundation wall. These barns were designed to accommodate grain farming, which dominated central Maryland's agriculture from the last quarter of the eighteenth century through most of the nineteenth century. The term "Swisser" leaves little doubt as to the cultural origins of these structures.

The barn on the Hermitage is not a Swisser like the others in central Maryland. Rather, it is unique to the region with its hipped roof and absence of a forebay and animal shelter at the ground level (see figure 7). It looks French, not

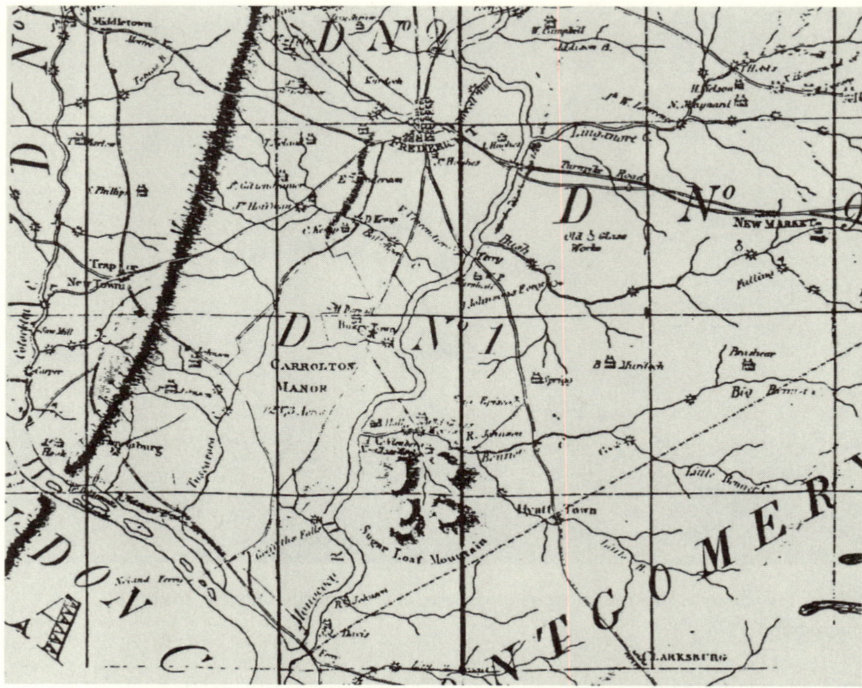

FIG. 8. A section of Charles Varlé's 1808 map of Frederick and Washington counties. L'Hermitage appears, with the symbol for a plantation dwelling with "V" for Vincendiere's name, just south of Frederick on the Monocacy River. James Marshall's plantation is just across the river.

German or English. The main house, which also originally had a hipped roof, is unlike the English and German dwellings of central Maryland. The Hermitage represents a different culture and a different architectural repertoire from other farmsteads and plantations in the area. A look at cultural distribution interpreted from the 1790 census explains why the Hermitage differs so vastly from the norm. According to those tabulations, Frederick County's white population numbered 26,937. Of those (according to surnames of heads of families), 5,137 (20 percent) were of German descent. The vast majority, 19,525, were labeled as "English and Welsh." The French population was counted as 265 in 1790. Estimates vary as to the relative percentages of the various ethnic groups represented in Frederick County and Frederick Town by 1790. A literal reading of the 1790 U.S. population census using names of heads of household to judge ethnicity estimated that approximately 73 percent of county residents were of English descent and 20 percent were of German ancestry.[13] However, anglicized names are likely to have skewed that percentage spread to some degree. Analysis of Frederick County voting rolls and court records has led some researchers to estimate

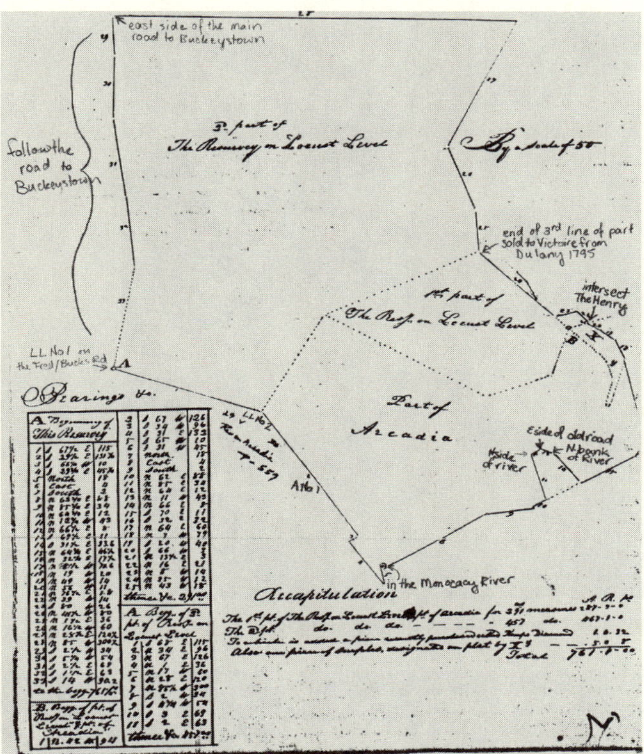

FIG. 9. An 1835 plat of the Hermitage, showing the Marshall tract made up of Arcadia and Locust Level, and the Dulaney tract, from Locust Level. The buildings were constructed on the Locust Level section of the Marshall tract, according to the 1798 tax assessment for Frederick County. From Frederick County Survey Record, vol. THO1, p. 512

as much as 60–70 percent of Frederick County residents in 1790 to be of German descent.[14] The actual number likely lies somewhere in between at approximately 40–50 percent German, with the remaining percentages representing English, Scots-Irish (generally combined), Welsh, French, and others.

Julian Ursyn Niemcewicz, a Polish traveler who recorded his impressions of America in 1797–99, spent several days in the Frederick area in June 1798. He made these observations: "There is nothing more fertile than this land. They rarely manure it; it never lies fallow, nonetheless it continually produces all sorts of grain. The fields groan under the weight of Indian corn, wheat, rye, etc. The meadows are covered with clover, the orchards filled with fruit, and the forests are full of the most beautiful oak trees." He also commented on the German population of Frederick: "The inhabitants are largely of German descent, with the exception of perhaps 20 families in town and the environs. [This is probably an exaggeration, given the census numbers.] They preserve to a large extent the

FIG. 10. A 1935 aerial view of the Hermitage complex

FIG. 11. Detail from *Carte de L'Isle St. Domingue dressée pour l'ouvrage de M.L.E. Moreau de St. Méry . . . par L. Sonis,* 1796. The Vincendiere property was on the Artibonite River near St. Marc. Courtesy of Geography and Map Division, Library of Congress, Washington, D.C.

Fig. 12. Portrait of Adelaide Vincendiere, age seven, artist unknown. Courtesy of Paul Foster, Southport, North Carolina

customs and the language, especially among themselves. . . . Though even the oldest inhabitant was born in America, nevertheless, by dress and way of life it is easy to recognize them as Germans and even place them as Germans of the 16th century. Old women, with coifs tied under their chins, wear on top of them large white hats without crowns like huge flat plates. The men have long, wide linen trousers. They are hard working, industrious, neat, clean and extraordinarily diligent."[15]

Agricultural prosperity made Frederick County an attractive place to settle and was perhaps what drew the Vincendieres and other refugees to the region. James Marshall, who became something of a benefactor to the Vincendiere family, was a merchant, and it is possible that Marshall and the Vincendieres had a previous business relationship in Saint Domingue. Into this environment the French-West Indian planter Vincendiere family arrived (without Victoire's father, Etienne, and her uncle Henri, who were in Charleston, South Carolina) and developed the Hermitage, most likely with substantial help from Marshall. They may have begun growing grain as did their neighbors. Records from the nearby Bloomsbury Mill for 1807 show that Victoire contracted for hauling, storage, and sale of wheat.[16] However, they may also have grown tobacco, which was still being produced in central Maryland.

The "asylum" at the Hermitage began almost as soon as the Vincendieres arrived. Marshall, a native of Scotland, had developed a landholding of nearly 2,000 acres along the Monocacy River (see figure 8). Most of this land he acquired in 1759 and 1765.[17] He also operated a ferry crossing of the Monocacy River on the road from Georgetown to Frederick, which passed in front of the Hermitage (see figure 9). On April 15, 1791, Marshall bought 86 additional acres, part of the tract called Locust Level, from Daniel Dulaney, a Maryland speculator who owned many thousands of acres throughout the state. This piece was on the west side of the Monocacy River and adjoined Arcadia, an 881-acre tract, which Marshall acquired in 1765. On Arcadia, land assembled by Marshall, the Vincendieres established the Hermitage (see figure 10).

Evidence that the Vincendieres, having fled from Saint Domingue, almost immediately harbored other refugees and constructed new buildings comes from architectural evaluation of the buildings and from contemporary documents (see figure 11). One of the refugees residing with the Vincendieres was Pierre Laberon. He arrived in Frederick in July 1794 and took up residence at the Hermitage. Born in 1731 in France, Laberon became ill and died in January 1795. He wrote his will in French at the Hermitage on December 23, 1794. At the end of the document he specified, "Done in Chambre S*ud* du Pavillon *Est* [south chamber of the east wing—pavillon may be a building or extension of a building] of the Hermitage estate near Fredericktown in Frederick County, State of Maryland, North America."[18] This simple concluding statement made by an ailing sixty-three-year-old man reveals that the Vincendieres, with whom he was living, were occupying the Hermitage estate and calling it that within a year of their arrival in

FIG. 13. South room of the c. 1794 main section, first floor, mantelpiece detail. Author's photograph

Fig. 14. South chamber of the 1794 main section (second floor). Author's photograph

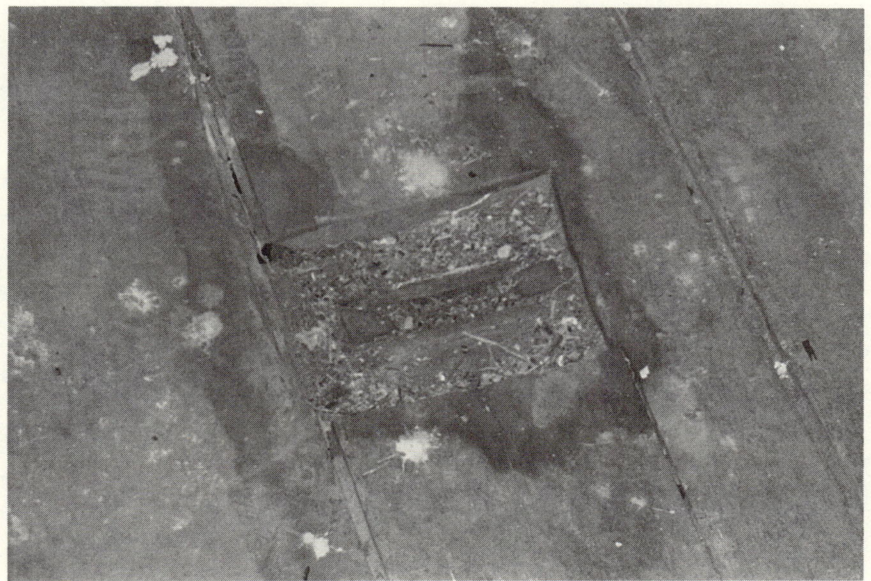

Fig. 15. Attic floor, main section, c. 1794, showing remnant of post cut off at floor level. This and another vertical post would have supported the original hipped roof over this section. Author's photograph

Fig. 16. Wall of former shed-roofed section over the north rooms, with brickwork extending the width and raising the height. Author's photograph

Fig. 17. View of northwest formerly exterior corner of the c. 1794 hip-roofed east wing, with cornice molding and added shed-roofed extension to the right. Brickwork supported the raised gable roof added in the 1820s. Author's photograph

Fig. 18. Drip course on chimney where it originally extended above the former shed roof. It is now within the expanded attic space. Author's photograph

Fig. 19. Cellar under the main block, c. 1794 section, showing chimney base and closely spaced joists. Author's photograph

Fig. 20. Evidence of corner shelving or a cupboard in the southwest corner of the chamber, second floor room in the c. 1794 main section. Author's photograph

Frederick. They had made substantial improvements to the property, constructing the "east pavillon." At this point they did not yet own the property; it still belonged to James Marshall.

Esther Winder Polk Lowe, who married Adelaide Vincendiere's son, Maryland governor Enoch Louis Lowe, wrote an account of her life for her children (see figure 12). In this memoir, written in 1913, she recalls the Vincendieres' story of their flight from Saint Domingue and their life at the Hermitage:

> They were refugees from San Domingo. Aunt Victoire told me that her uncle was one of the victims of the insurrection, having been shot by a native whilst seated at the dinner table. . . . Your grandmother was Adelaide said to have been beautiful and accomplished. . . . Aunt Victoire was 16 years old—a charming young girl who gave up an engagement of marriage with a young nobleman to remain with her mother and devote her life to the education of her brothers and sisters. . . . The Hermitage, their home was bought by the family and there they lived until the changes of time and conditions made it necessary to leave and move into the town.

FIG. 21. Stuccoed surface on north wall of 1794 main section on right, where it is abutted by the later shed-roofed addition on left. The exterior stuccoed surface beneath the present interior plaster indicates that the main block stood alone for a time before the shed extension was added. Author's photograph

> I have been told that their home was beautiful and an asylum for many penniless exiles from France and San Domingo.[19]

Mrs. Lowe's memoir also tells the story of a friend of Victoire, a fellow refugee who was wandering through the South with her two granddaughters. When Victoire found out about their homeless condition, she sent for them, and the three came to live at the Hermitage, where the two granddaughters grew to adulthood. The memoir corroborates census records and the will of Pierre Laberon, which indicate that the Hermitage was indeed a place of refuge for French planters displaced by the slave revolt.

The 1800 U.S. census listed Victoire as head of a household with six men, twelve women, and ninety slaves. The eighteen men and women listed in this census far exceeded the number of Vincendiere family members and certainly must have included homeless refugees. In the 1810 census she is listed with one man, six women, and ninety slaves. The 1820 census shows her with six men, five women, two foreigners not naturalized, and fifty-two slaves. These records suggest that the Vincendiere household was fluid with people coming and going.

The ninety slaves enumerated in the census made Victoire one of the largest slaveholders in Frederick County and indeed in the state of Maryland. While slavery was not pervasive in Frederick County, the 1790 census revealed that 15.5 percent of Frederick County residents owned slaves. Most of the slave owners had fewer than six; only one owner had more than one hundred.[20]

The memoir of Mrs. Lowe, which characterizes Victoire as "charming," even angelic, may not be entirely accurate. In Frederick County court dockets of criminal trials for 1797, Victoire was named as a defendant along with Payen Boisneuf for "abusing and ill treating her slave, Jenny." Victoire was also charged with assault against "Rosina" Cecille. The case was struck off, but Victoire paid $272 in attorney's, clerk's, and sheriff's fees. Boisneuf was found guilty for "excessively, cruelly and unmercifully beating etc. of his slave Negro Shadrack." Witnesses for the defense included Mrs. Vincendiere, Miss Vincendiere, Miss Rosona, Mr. Hispaniol, and Mr. James Marshall, interpreter. Boisneuf was also found guilty of "not sufficiently clothing and feeding his negroes etc." In both of these cases there was a long list of witnesses for the state of Maryland, plaintiff. Boisneuf had eight separate indictments for abusing his slaves. The slaves, according to census records, actually belonged to Victoire, who at that time in 1797 was only twenty years old.[21]

FIG. 22. Attic floor framing, c. 1794 main section. The diagonal brace or strut supported the hip rafter. The bricks above the floor system were added when the hipped roof was converted to a gabled roof in the 1820s. Author's photograph

FIG. 23. Attic floor framing for the shed-roofed addition, showing tapered joists to support the shed roof. Boards have been attached to the joists to create a level support for the present flooring. Brickwork above the joists was added to create the north gable in the 1820s. Author's photograph

FIG. 24. Nails in east surface of chimney, which rises through the shed-roofed addition. The nails held flashing in place above the original roof line. Author's photograph

FIG. 25. Corbeled drip course at the original top of the chimney through the shed-roofed addition. The chimney was extended in height when the high gabled roof was added. Author's photograph

To put these court cases in a larger context, the late 1790s was a time of strong anti-French sentiment in the United States. The XYZ Affair involving the French foreign minister Tallyrand's attempt to bribe American commissioners occurred in 1797. In the summer of 1798 Congress passed the Naturalization Act, extending to fourteen years the period of residency required for U.S. citizenship. Congress also passed the Alien Act that summer, authorizing the president of the United States to expel aliens he deemed dangerous to the United States. These acts were pointed at the large population of French refugees living at the time in the United States, which was on the verge of war with France. Thus the current situation with foreign affairs may have influenced the action toward this colorful and perhaps haughty group of French refugees residing in Frederick County, Maryland.

The buildings of the Hermitage as tangible records of the French plantation and asylum amplify the documentary history of this place. Immediately, or nearly so, the Vincendieres set to work constructing a hip-roofed stuccoed stone manor house, a log and stone secondary dwelling with several living units, and a large hip-roofed stone crop barn. These are the buildings that survive today. The complex also would have included quarters for the ninety slaves Victoire owned and various support buildings. Archaeological investigation indicates that the

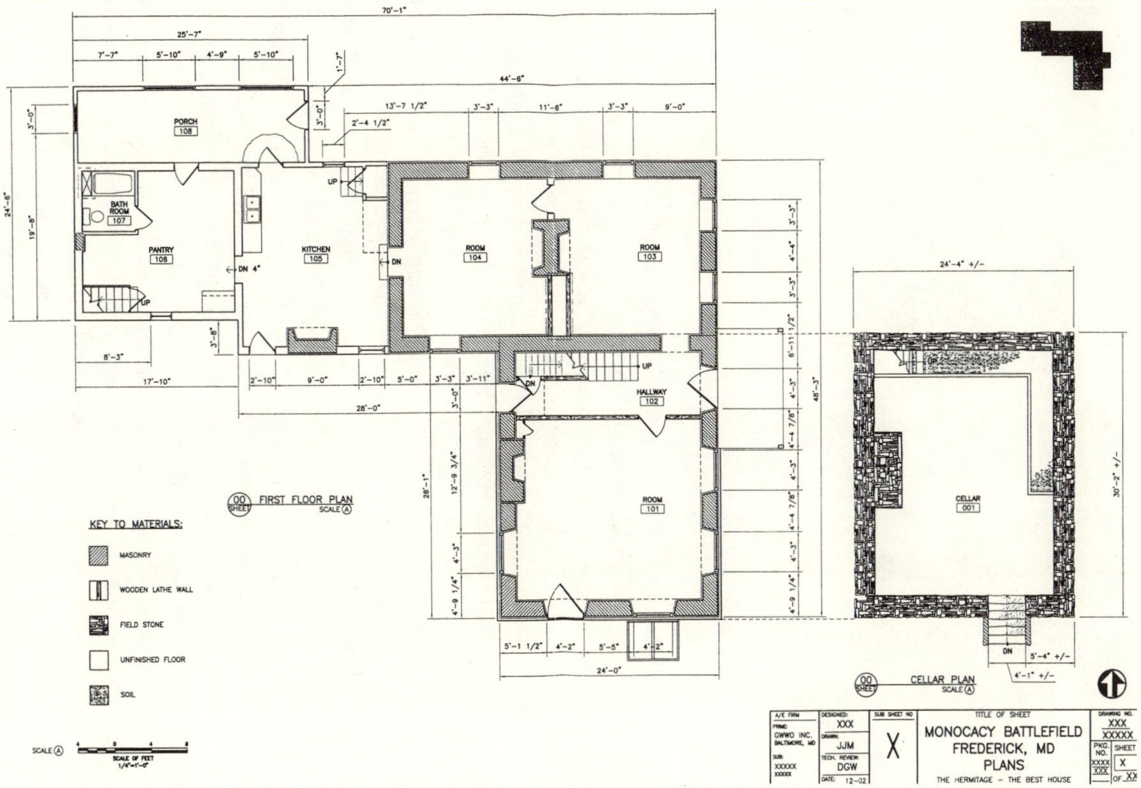

FIG. 26. First floor and cellar plans. Courtesy of Grieves, Worrall, Wright & O'Hatnick, Inc., Baltimore, Maryland

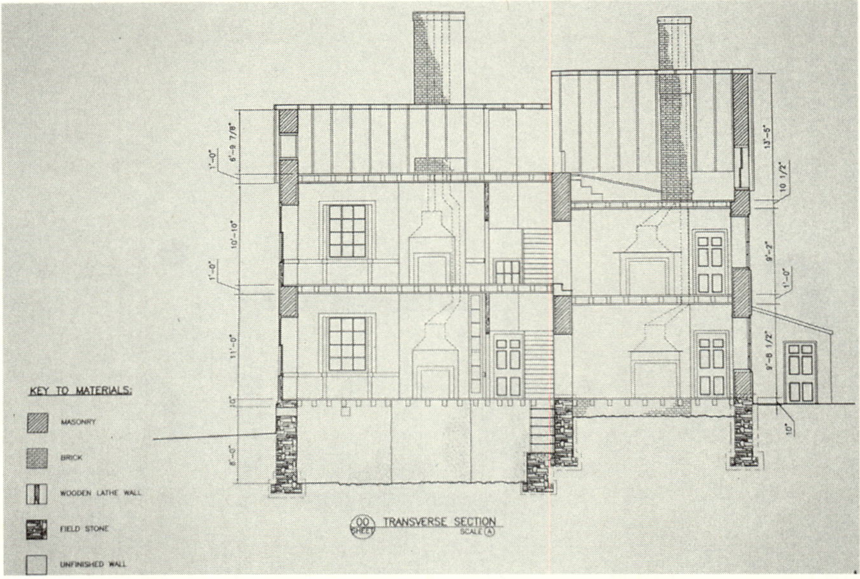

FIG. 27. Section through the house, west view from front. Courtesy of Grieves, Worrall, Wright & O'Hatnick, Inc., Baltimore, Maryland

slave village was in front of the main house, between it and the road to Georgetown (approximating today's Maryland Route 355). By their ambitious construction project, the Vincendieres, led by Victoire, made a statement that they were intending to stay in Frederick County and were establishing a presence on a grand scale. They transformed a leasehold near a mid-eighteenth-century river crossing site into a substantial and distinctive 748-acre plantation. Although Madam Magnan Vincendiere lived in France on and off either in her husband's house or in a place of her own, she was a Saint Domingue native, and she probably had a hand in planning the design of the buildings constructed on their Maryland plantation. Likewise, her cousin Payan Boisneuf, who was a national assemblyman, was a friend of Tallyrand and Citizen Genet, and went to Philadelphia to visit these dignitaries, was born in Saint Domingue in 1738. Boisneuf made his home with the Vincendieres from at least 1797 until his death in 1815. Thus, with these cultural roots, the Hermitage buildings resemble plantation houses and barns of the Caribbean and to some extent farmsteads of France.[22]

The Polish traveler Niemcewicz's descriptions may be suspect because he repeats gossip told to him by the German stage driver with whom he sat on the trip up the Georgetown road into Frederick, but he recorded his view of the Hermitage: "Four miles from the town we forded the river [Monocacy]. On its banks one can see a row of wooden houses and one stone house with the upper stories

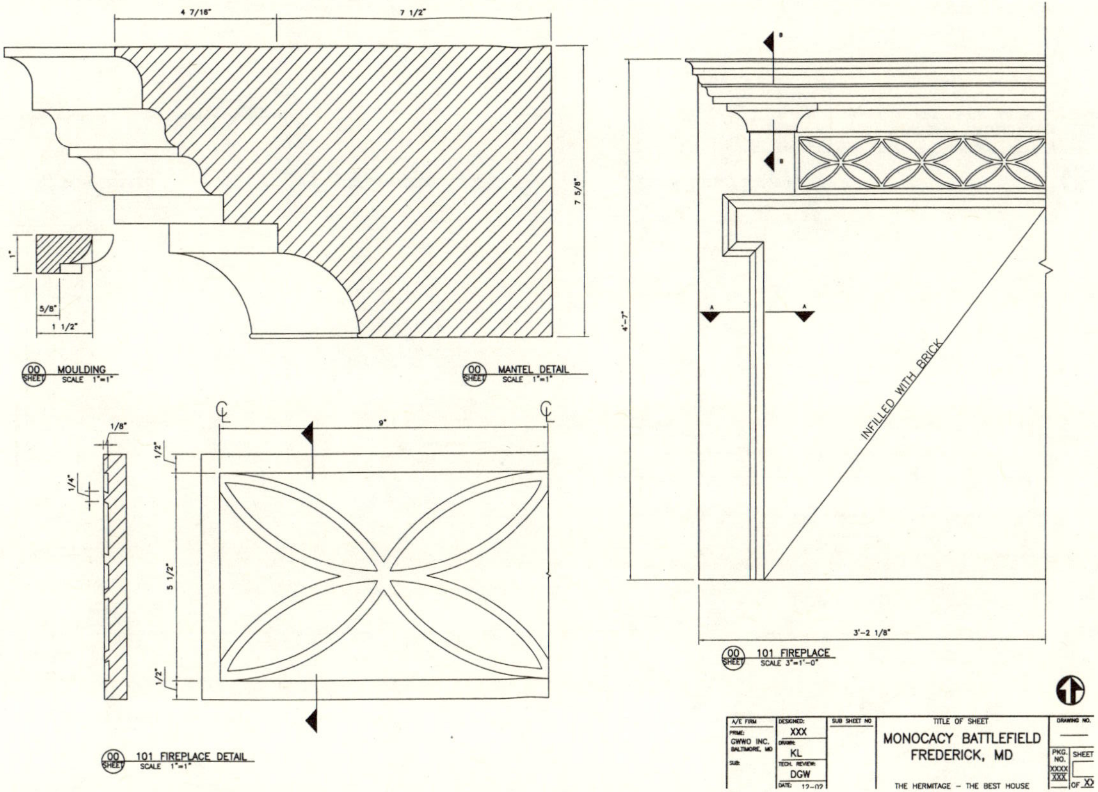

MOULDING
SCALE 1"=1"

MANTEL DETAIL
SCALE 1"=1"

FIREPLACE DETAIL
SCALE 1"=1"

FIREPLACE
SCALE 3"=1'-0"

INFILLED WITH BRICK

MONOCACY BATTLEFIELD
FREDERICK, MD
THE HERMITAGE – THE BEST HOUSE

FIG. 28. Detail, fireplace mantel and molding, main section, first-floor parlor, c. 1794 section. Courtesy of Grieves, Worrall, Wright & O'Hatnick, Inc., Baltimore, Maryland

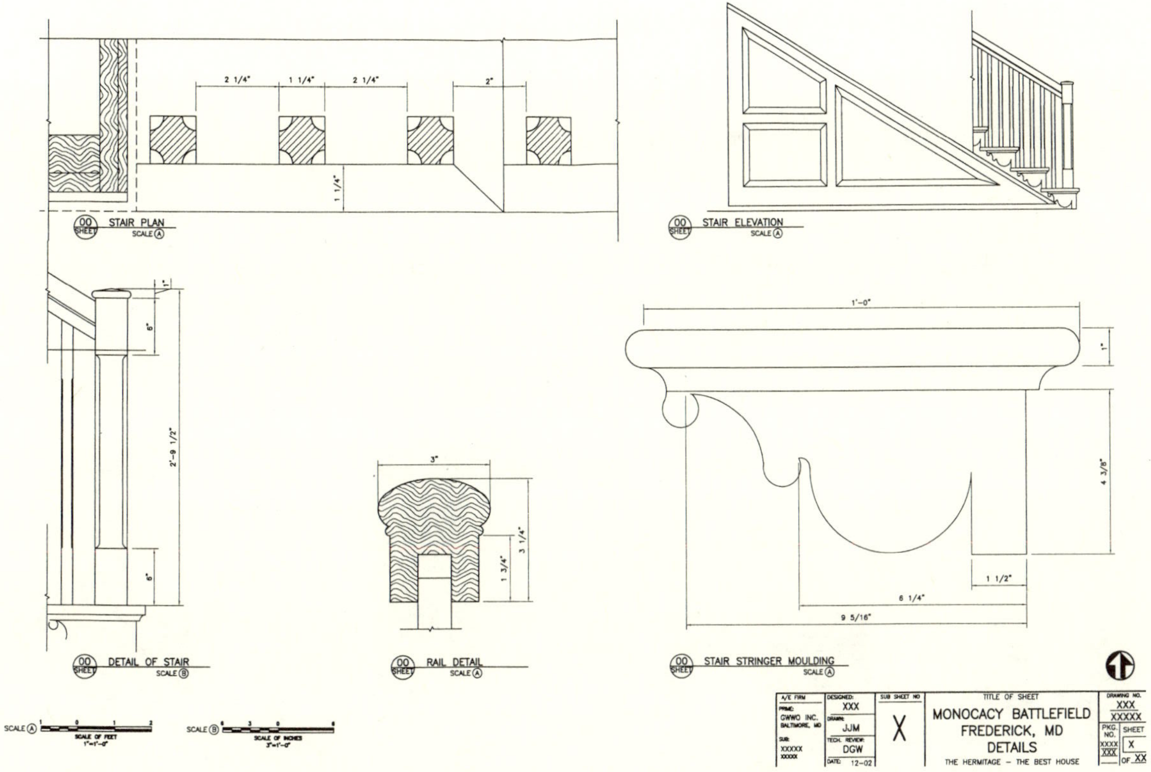

STAIR PLAN
SCALE (A)

2 1/4" 1 1/4" 2 1/4" 2" 1 1/4"

STAIR ELEVATION
SCALE (A)

DETAIL OF STAIR
SCALE (B)

1" 6" 2'-9 1/2" 6"

RAIL DETAIL
SCALE (A)

3" 1 3/4" 3 1/4"

STAIR STRINGER MOULDING
SCALE (A)

1'-0" 1" 4 3/8" 1 1/2" 6 1/4" 9 5/16"

SCALE (A) SCALE OF FEET 1"=1'-0"

SCALE (B) SCALE OF INCHES 3"=1'-0"

A/E FIRM	DESIGNED: XXX	SUB SHEET NO	TITLE OF SHEET	DRAWING NO. XXX XXXXX
PRIME: GWWO INC. BALTIMORE, MD	DRAWN: JJM	X	MONOCACY BATTLEFIELD FREDERICK, MD DETAILS	PKG. NO. XXXX XXX / SHEET X
SUB: XXXXX XXXXX	TECH. REVIEW: DGW		THE HERMITAGE – THE BEST HOUSE	OF XX
	DATE: 12-02			

FIG. 29. Detail, main staircase, c. 1794 main section. Courtesy of Grieves, Worrall, Wright & O'Hatnick, Inc., Baltimore, Maryland

painted white [probably the stone secondary house with the log second story]. This is the residence of a Frenchman called Payant [Payen Boisneuf], who left San Domingo with a substantial sum, and with it bought two or three thousand acres of land and a few hundred Negroes whom he treats with the greatest tyranny. One can see on the home farm instruments of torture, stocks, whips, etc."[23] Actually, Boisneuf's assets were in Saint Domingue and thus not available to him in the United States. He also did not purchase thousands of acres as Niemcewicz stated. In 1796 he bought 280 acres, which he lost in a sheriff's sale in 1799 to pay his debts. He was listed among Maryland's insolvent debtors.[24]

The twenty-four-by-thirty-foot main block of the Hermitage as constructed about 1794 was a formal, two-story stuccoed stone and brick building struck to look like ashlar block, with a hipped roof and rooms with eleven-foot high ceilings. It had a formal stair and entrance passage and only one large room on each floor. Unusually large and abundant windows (five per room) provided plenty of light and air. To the south of the entrance and stair hall in the main block is a formal room, clearly intended to be a parlor. Four large windows brighten it, and a fifth was converted to a door in the early twentieth century. The windows are large with splayed jambs and are set above recessed dadoes. The placement of the fireplace in this room is unusual in central Maryland, being set in the back wall rather than the more regionally typical end wall. The mantelpiece retains its original black paint and is in its design a transition between the Georgian and Federal styles, with a crossetted architrave and delicate oval swags carved onto the frieze below the mantel shelf (see figure 13). There are other similar mantels in the region, but the firebox is unusually shallow. The large window openings are also unusual among eighteenth-century houses of central Maryland (see figure 14). The room directly above the parlor at the second story has the same layout, although it is appointed more simply. Evidence remains in the walls of this chamber of built-in corner shelves above the chair rail in the southeast and southwest corners (see figure 15).

Traces of the original construction appear most clearly in the attic. The 1794 east wing retains remnants of two vertical posts, which once supported its hipped roof (see figure 16). Notches in each corner of the attic floor mark the location of hip rafters, which extended from the plate to the roof ridge at the top of the vertical posts. (see figure 17). Under the attic floorboards the joist system runs east-west with diagonal beams/struts running from each corner and intersecting the joists. In the 1820s the original hipped roofing system was removed and replaced with the current gabled roof (see figures 18 and 19).

A two-story, shed-roofed extension was added, probably shortly after construction, to the north wall of the circa 1794 main block. The shed-roofed section provided four more rooms, two per story (see figures 20 and 21). Later, in the 1820s when Victoire Vincendiere remodeled the house, the shed-roofed north section, along with the hip-roofed main block, was changed to its present gabled form. In the attic the original shed-roofed form of the north addition is clearly readable. Beneath the attic floorboards the joists are tapered at their ends to accommodate the shed roof (see figures 22 and 23); the shed roof's outline is visible on the brick chimney just above the attic floor; the original corbel at the top of the chimney is visible where the chimney was extended in height when the shed roof was raised to a high gable; and part of the top of the original west wall of the shed-roofed section remains in the attic. A large section of brick infill was added in the 1820s to support the high gable added over the north wing. The original north wall of the 1794 section, exposed in the attic of the north wing, shows a remnant of eaves boxing and cornice and the plate along the north wall (see figures 24 and 25).

When Laberon used the term "east pavillon" in his will, it certainly implied that the chamber where he wrote this document was a portion of something else. He likely referred to the easternmost building in the complex, the "secondary house." This is a log and stone multiple-unit dwelling with dimensions of approximately eighteen by thirty-six feet (see figure 26). When Victoire Vincendiere and members of her family occupied the property in 1793 or 1794, they immediately began to construct the main house and the secondary house. The second story had two separate rooms or chambers, each with an entrance onto an elevated gallery or porch (see figure 27). A 1924 photograph shows part of this building with a small shed-roofed entrance porch sheltering the south door. This building apparently housed refugees in need of a place to live. The new log structure was clearly oriented to the big house with doors opening to face it and presented a symmetrical facade toward the main house. The place had a fair amount of refinement, stylish moldings matching those in the big house, and plastered wall surfaces (see figure 28). An enclosed stair allowed separate access from each of the upper-level rooms to the lower level hall (kitchen) and also to the attic above (see figure 29).

One of the most unusual features of this extraordinary complex is the hip-roofed stone barn set well behind the other buildings on the farm. It looks nothing like the barns that are common to the region, which typically had a ramp or bank at the back and a cantilevered forebay. The Hermitage barn has no ramp, no forebay, and no upper threshing floor. It is a rectangular structure with its broad sides facing east and west. The front and rear stone walls are interrupted by wide openings that extend from the ground fully to the roof. These openings are centrally located in the east and west walls to allow wagons to pass through the building for loading or unloading. The upper portions of these open areas are currently filled in with vertical board siding. In the north-end wall there is a window with a segmentally arched top. Seams in the stone indicate that this north-end opening was once a door and was later partially enclosed. The walls are constructed of narrow, flat courses of local stone with leveling courses at regular intervals. The barn rests on a slightly raised flat area.

Victoire made extensive alterations to the main house at the Hermitage in the 1820s. The hip-roofed east wing, constructed in 1794, was restructured into a gable-roofed building to blend with the new reconstructed and expanded north section. This portion of the house was raised to two full stories with a broad gabled roof span. New neoclassical interior appointments were made to bring the house up to date. These alterations date from shortly before Victoire and her sister Adelaide moved to Frederick Town and possibly were done to accommodate another sister, Emerentienne Corbaley, and her husband, who may have been living at the Hermitage. These were the last major alterations made to the buildings. After the Vincendieres left, the Hermitage was never again owner occupied. The plantation appears today much as it did when the Vincendieres left in the early 1820s.

Thus the story of the Vincendieres' arrival in Frederick County and their transformation of an English-influenced leasehold property into an impressive plantation that is markedly different from others in mid-Maryland begins to unfold. Perhaps in time information will come to light about this family's homesteads in western Haiti and in Bressuire, France, and how similar or dissimilar the Hermitage is to other French–West Indian buildings from the late eighteenth century outside of Maryland.[25]

Notes

1. État Détaillé Des Liquidations, Paris, 1834, Special Collections, University of New Orleans, New Orleans, La.

2. Glenn O. Phillips, "Maryland and the Caribbean, 1634–1984: Some Highlights," *Maryland Historical Magazine* (Fall 1988): 203, citing Suzanne E. Greene, *Baltimore, an Illustrated History* (Woodland Hills, Calif.: Windsor Publications, 1980), 14, 32; Paul C. E. Clemens, *The Atlantic Economy and Colonial Maryland's Eastern Shore: From Tobacco to Grain* (Ithaca, N.Y.: Cornell University Press, 1980), 177–179.

3. T. J. C. Williams, *History of Frederick County, Maryland* (1910; repr., Baltimore: Regional Publishing, 1967), 267.

4. J. S. Van Ness, "Economic Development, Social and Cultural Changes, 1800–1850," in *Maryland: A History, 1632–1974*, ed. R. Walsh and W. C. Fox (Baltimore: Maryland Historical Society, 1974), 175.

5. Susan Winter Frye, "Evolution of Mill Settlement Patterns in the Antietam Drainage," typescript, College of William and Mary, 1984, 45.

6. Translation by Jacques Petit, Buc, France, June 2002.

7. Will of Etienne Bellumeau Delavincendiere, January 28, 1802, Charleston County, S.C., probate records, 28:323. The copy of the will in the Courthouse of Charleston County is a typed translation and transcription and may contain inaccuracies of spelling and meaning.

8. Ibid.

9. Cahiers du Centre de Genealogie et D'histoire des Iles D'Amerique, Bellumeau de la Vincendiere genealogy; Victoire Vincendiere is listed as born October 3, 1776 (courtesy of Jacques Petit).

10. Frederick County, Md., land records, Liber WR12, folio 292, November 4, 1794. Victoire requested that the following be recorded, extracted from the Register of Baptisms of the Roman Catholic Church in Frederick Town: "Baptised Helen Victorie the daughter of Etienne Bellumeau De La Vincendiere and Marguerite Elizabeth Pauline Magnan his wife inhabitants of St. Domingo's French part residing in this Town the child was born on the fourth of September last."

11. "Declaration of Negroes," Liber WR11, folio 755, Frederick County, Md., land records.

12. Architectural evaluation of the buildings shows them to be distinctive among farms and plantations, more similar to French traditions than the English/German-derived architecture typical of central Maryland. Architectural evidence also is consistent with construction in the last decade of the eighteenth century, with modifications in the 1820s.

13. *A Century of Population Growth from the First Census of the United States to the Twelfth, 1790–1900* (Baltimore, Md.: Genealogical Publishing Co., 1970), 272.

14. Millard Milburn Rice, *New Facts and Old Families* (Baltimore: Genealogical Publishing Co. 1984), 28, citing Elizabeth Kessel, "Germans in the Making of Frederick County."

15. Julian Ursyn Niemcewicz, *Under Their Vine and Fig Tree: Travels through America in 1797–1799, 1805 with Some Further Account of Life in New Jersey* (Elizabeth, N.J.: Grassman Publishing, 1965), 112.

16. Bloomsbury Mills record book, 1807, Maryland Historical Society collection, Baltimore, Md.

17. Frederick County, Md., land records, F:654.

18. Frederick County, Md., wills, Liber G.M.3, folio 27; translated from the original French by Dr. David A. Wallace.

19. Autobiography of Mrs. Enoch Lewis Lowe, written March 14, 1913, Brooklyn, N.Y., Lowe Family papers, MS 1949, Maryland Historical Society, Baltimore.

20. *Century of Population Growth,* 289.

21. Frederick County, Md., court minutes, March 1797, 65, 91, 97; Frederick County, Md., criminal trials dockets, November term, 1797.

22. See Crain, *Historic Architecture.*

23. Niemcewicz, *Under Their Vine,* 111.

24. Frederick County, Md., land records, WR 19/56.

25. Much of the historical context in this chapter was derived from an article by Paula S. Reed, "L'Hermitage: A French Plantation in Frederick County," which appeared in *Maryland Historical Magazine* (Spring 2002): 61–78. Portions also appear in "The Hermitage on the Monocacy," *Catoctin History* (Fall 2002).

A Dissenting Space

Meetinghouse and Location in Early Dorchester, South Carolina

Jeffrey H. Richards

Just off the Dorchester road in the county of that name in lowcountry South Carolina, on a rise that appears to be the highest point in the immediate area, is the gated cemetery of the Summerville Presbyterian Church. At the center of the property, on the peak of the rise, is a pile of old brick, with a fractional portion of one wall standing, surrounded by gravestones from the twentieth century (see figure 1). The cemetery, following years of (romantic?) neglect, is now well tended and in use; but the old bricks appear rather odd in their current surroundings, as if someone forgot to clean up an otherwise tidy site. This modern rubble constitutes the material remains of White Meeting, a Congregational church building first erected more than three centuries before but now, despite a discreet sign at the entrance of the cemetery and its location on a moderately busy two-lane road, a virtually forgotten piece of local lore, out of the way and out of sight for most county residents. Unexplored by archaeologists and long abandoned by its builders and their descendants, this brick pile is the visible sign, and essentially the only one remaining, of a once-thriving dissenting religious community. One wonders why it is *there* at all.[1]

The reason for a meetinghouse to be built somewhere in the lowcountry might be traced back indefinitely, but one moment of origin occurred on December 20, 1695, when a small group of individuals from the Congregational church in Dorchester, Massachusetts, arrived by ship in Charleston, South Carolina, to search for a place of settlement in that colony and to establish a new site for Congregational worship. By mid-January 1696 the group, led by the Reverend Joseph Lord, had identified two adjoining plots of land on the Ashley River, about twenty miles from the seaport but still relatively remote in that early year of South Carolina colonization. They visited the site, made an agreement for the land, worshipped there, and then returned in February to Massachusetts to

FIG. 1. Ruins of the Congregational Church at Dorchester, called White Meeting, as they appeared in 2002. Author's photograph

begin preparations for the move. By early 1697 families began to occupy tracts of land that they acquired by lottery on a site with a total of 4,050 acres. One small portion of the land, along the Ashley and just above the river's confluence with Booshoo or Bosho-ee Creek, was laid out as a town, with small lots, a marketplace, a nearby mill site, and a wharf area. Unlike what has been taken as the usual New England pattern of placing a church in the town center with the square before it, the settlers of Dorchester, as the village became known, chose to distinguish the area with small lots and streets as a place of trade but to build their house of worship in one of the outer ranges, near where the minister, Lord, had his property of first 50 and then 100 acres (see figure 2). This location, on which the ruins of the original church remain, served the community during its half-century of occupation of the site until, feeling the need for more land and a healthier climate, the Congregationalists began moving en masse to Liberty County, Georgia, starting in 1752.[2]

Populated thereafter largely by white Anglicans, or at least those accepting of Anglican hegemony, and their more numerous African slaves, Dorchester survived as a distinct town until the ravages of the Revolution sent it into a steep decline. By 1800 most residents of the town center had moved elsewhere, either to plantation homes, to nearby Summerville (which was not in as low an elevation), or to more distant locations. By the mid–nineteenth century Dorchester was a colorful ruin visited by Charlestonians in their carriages for picnics but essentially defunct as a place of settlement. The Congregational meetinghouse, irregularly used after the departure of its original occupants, was repaired in 1794, pressed into service for periods during the early nineteenth century, and then functionally abandoned; it remained standing until 1886, when it was fatally damaged by the earthquake of that year. Except as a relic in the countryside, the building ceased to have spatial meaning once the families of the original congregants had departed.

Today Dorchester survives still as a picnic spot, a state historic site where one may spend a quiet hour strolling the grounds and watching the alligators swim up the river. A few signs of the old town survive: a tabby fort from the Seven Years' War, some grave markers, and the tower of the Anglican church that occupied the town center beginning in 1719. Although the town was created by Congregationalists, there is essentially nothing visible to the naked eye that would indicate their presence. Indeed, it is the Anglican church tower that stands out as

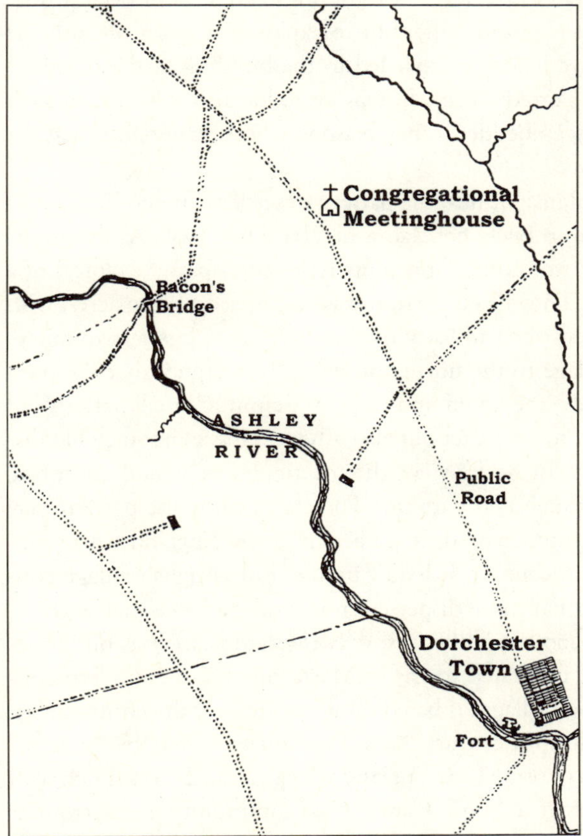

FIG. 2. Map showing location of White Meeting relative to trading town of Dorchester. The Anglican church, built in 1719, was within the grid at lower right, which in this rendering is not precisely to scale. Map by Karen Vaughan and Jeffrey H. Richards, based on maps by Henry A. M. Smith, *Historical Writings*, 3 vols. (Spartanburg, S.C.: Reprint Co., 1988), 2:2, 3:203

the defining marker, one built for missionaries from the Society for the Propagation of the Gospel (SPG) in Foreign Parts. For several years archaeologists at the historic site have been conducting digs at the location of the Dorchester Free School, but that facility was not built until the late 1750s, a time after the majority of Congregationalists had moved away. In addition, while Presbyterians and other dissenters moved to the area, eventually acquiring the land on which the cemetery now sits, the particular culture created by the Congregationalists departed with the migrants in the relocation of 1752–56. A question worth exploring is why these dissenters from the established church, coming from a Congregational majority area and used to the town centrality of a meetinghouse, would build a church in what appears to have been a peripheral position.

In one important sense this question has already been answered. In a recent essay the archaeologist Monica Beck has examined the two dominant religious communities of Dorchester, dissenting and established, and concluded that for the former, "The seemingly peripheral location of the Meeting House . . . was in fact 'central' to the dispersed planter community and located on a prominent land feature adjacent to a major roadway."[3] I want not to argue with Beck, whose conclusion makes eminent practical sense, but to explore the edges of both the literal site and the figurative landscape that led to the building of the meetinghouse two miles from the plotted village. In reasons to locate a structure of such symbolic import are often embedded other reasons whose materiality may be both tantalizing and elusive.

Because the most useful insight into the pattern of settlement and location of the meetinghouse comes from Beck, her claims deserve a first look. As she points out, the village area and surrounding farm plots represent a pattern typical of a "New England township." The village portion was comprised of fifty acres, with the remaining four thousand acres in forty-five- to fifty-acre plots in two ranges moving away from the village to the north and west. Beck argues that the preference of residence outside the town indicates a "seminucleated pattern" of settlement, that is, having a town center but also other centers in a somewhat dispersed form of community. In Beck's view, the meetinghouse would constitute another center in the seminucleated pattern.[4] Therefore, while the pattern may differ from what has been understood as traditional New England town construction in the seventeenth century, it is not unlike some English village construction in which a somewhat more dispersed model of residence was used.

Further, as Joseph S. Wood hypothesizes, drawing on his analysis of villages created on the outskirts of nucleated towns in Massachusetts, the modern conception of the New England "village" is based more on nineteenth-century developments than what seventeenth-century New Englanders meant by "village." Indeed, Wood's description of some New England villages accords very much with the construction of Dorchester in South Carolina—a community that surrounds a meetinghouse in a dispersed model of habitation, one that does not depend on a nucleated town center for its identity.[5] As the Anglican missionary Francis Varnod observed three decades after the construction of the dissenter house of worship, it "lies in a very Convenient Place to resort to, and as it were in the Center of the Parish."[6] For Beck, the location of the meetinghouse indicates additionally an adaptation to the prevailing agriculture and settlement in a colony where there were few real "towns" of any significant population density: "It appears that the nucleated village was never the center of the Dissenter community. They apparently established a village to facilitate trade, while emulating their neighbors who capitalized on the possibilities of plantation agriculture. The location of their meeting house and their residences supports this."[7]

Although there is some suggestion that the first meetinghouse was built of wood, it appears to have been replaced relatively early by a square brick structure about thirty by thirty feet in dimension and with two stories (see figure 3). The common image of New England Congregational churches is that of elongated structures with a steeple at the entrance end and the pulpit in the rear of the rectangle; but in fact a number of early meetinghouses were built on a square pattern, without tower-style steeples. The Second Meetinghouse in Hingham, Massachusetts, completed in 1684, is one of many New England Congregational churches that began life on the square, with a steeply pitched roof (see figure 4).[8] How much the Dorchester builders were influenced by local construction practices in South Carolina is hard to say. There was an independent meetinghouse in Charleston also inspired by New England migrants and models; in any event, the apparent simplicity of structure and solidity of construction allowed the church to stand even with long periods when it was not used, for nearly two centuries.[9]

Of equal importance, the square represents an architecture of more egalitarian character than the medieval nave does, with its head at the front and parishioners stretched out far to the rear; it is a more community-centered architecture, keeping everyone in nearly equal sight, with the minister sometimes sharing his pulpit space in a row with seated parishioners. Thus whatever practical architectural issues the Dorchester Congregationalists faced in raising their brick meetinghouse in 1700, they chose a plan that gave maximum visibility to all those seated within its walls. By the same token, the square also creates a symbolic shape for the community's total tract. Although in real terms the land from Booshoo Creek to William Norman's land upriver (beyond—that is, northwest of—Bacon's Bridge in figure 2) is longer that way than the connecting sides moving away from the river, the idea of a square persists, in which people look inward from the four walls not only to the minister but also to each other and symbolically at the meetinghouse itself, rather than down a long nave of land whose residents at the end they cannot see. Having a square meetinghouse more central to

FIG. 3. Congregational meetinghouse at Dorchester, as it appeared in 1875. Illustration from *Harper's New Monthly Magazine,* December 1875

FIG. 4. Second Meetinghouse ("Old Ship"), Hingham, Massachusetts, built 1681–84 by Joseph Stockbridge of Scituate, Massachusetts. Photograph by Robert Blair St. George

the larger square of the land creates an echo effect that might bind the community closer together.

The known papers of the founding minister, Joseph Lord, reveal relatively little directly about the community's concept of itself and its understanding of the significance of the meetinghouse location.[10] Lord's publications all appeared after his return to New England in 1717, and most have to do with Cape Cod church controversies into which Lord entered after his becoming minister at Chatham. His first book, however, published in 1719, was in fact written largely in 1702 while he was in Dorchester. It is a tightly argued rebuttal to the Anabaptist notion of adult emersion and a strident defense of infant sprinkling. Baptists appeared early in lowcountry South Carolina, and during a period when Lord had returned to Massachusetts to get married, a preacher of that persuasion attempted to make inroads on the Congregationalists. Rather than worry about the established church, whose presence in Proprietary South Carolina was still rather tentative in the 1690s, Lord was much more concerned about threats to his community from other dissenters.

One wonders, therefore, about the location of the meetinghouse as a defensive posture. To be sure, the English colonists in South Carolina feared Spanish invasion, and building away from the river's edge might serve to protect them in case of river-borne attack. Was it also imagined that building outside of town but in the midst of farmers whose primary loyalty was to the church would also protect the congregation against theological encroachment? Lord clearly felt that he needed to be present and that he had to put quill to paper, but perhaps such threats had been anticipated in the original construction.[11] In any event, if conscious, the strategy seems to have worked. Despite the continuing presence of Baptists in the area and Anglican missionaries from 1719 on, the Congregationalists had significant group cohesion, even building a second meetinghouse, Beach Hill, in the 1730s to accommodate church members in a more remote part of the settlement.

Besides his treatise on baptism, Lord also wrote letters from his home at Dorchester, located near the meetinghouse. Ten letters to a member of the Royal Society survive; they are all narrowly though intelligently focused on matters of natural history, written in a tiny script that fills nearly every space of the no doubt valuable sheets of paper, with not a word about the community or things religious.[12] An earlier letter written to his father-in-law within a few months of his return from Massachusetts in 1698 shows his concern with plants and seeds brought from home, including herbs, berry bushes, and apple seedlings.[13] Although these letters, indicating Lord's botanical and zoological interests, seem peripheral to the location question, they may not be entirely. In many ways Lord's living well away from town gave him opportunities for botanizing that he might not have had in a market area with streets on a grid. Lord was in fact a significant early natural historian in colonial America whose specimens and observations made their way into publications by Royal Society members in London.[14] He must have brought with him from Massachusetts a knowledge of plants and a scientist's curiosity, particularly about discovering medicinal herbs, that would make proximity to nature—the woods—an ideal location for his other community role, that of physician. Lord was an exceptionally astute amateur botanizer, and lacking easy access to the European medicines of his day, he sought to use local plants for meeting the needs of a community often prone to lowcountry diseases, including malaria. Living where he did, next to the meetinghouse, he could serve his patients from a central location, just as he served congregants. Might Lord's personal interests and dual function amidst his flock have played a part in deciding the meetinghouse location?[15]

As Beck notes, the most overtly revealing contemporary document of the founding of Dorchester is the journal kept by the church elder William Pratt.[16] Pratt describes the first voyage from Massachusetts, meetings with various people to negotiate for a site, and the founders' favorable impression on Lady Rebecca Axtell, who would help them secure the Ashley River land. One thing he omits, however, is any word about the building of the meetinghouse. Curiously, Pratt recorded the following when he met with some of his South Carolina hosts who were trying to interest the Massachusetts visitors in a site near Willtown, then New London, South Carolina: "we keept sumthing secrit from others which was greatly for our benifit."[17]

To some degree the Dorchester Congregationalists have kept a great deal secret about their lives in Dorchester. We know from Pratt that on March 23, 1697, they drew lots for sites in what Pratt identifies as "the trading town," four lots of which were reserved for use by the church. Yet we also know that the majority of original settlers, including the minister, did not reside in town but lived on their farms in the larger acreage outside the plotted town center. From settlement patterns, ownership records, and comments by Pratt and Lord, we can see that Dorchester proper had one distinct function: it was the location for trade.[18] A map of the town made in 1742 by Samuel Stevens shows names or symbols on only 46 of the 116 town lots, each a quarter-acre in size (see figure 5).[19] Of the twenty-five or twenty-six surnames on the map, five can be positively identified as Congregationalist, nine as Anglican, and the rest with religious affiliation unknown.[20] In a 1728 census of all families in St. George's Parish compiled by Francis Varnod, the SPG missionary in Dorchester, fifty-two families are listed as "Dissenter," although some might have been Baptist or Quaker.[21] This suggests that only about 10 percent and certainly no more than 20 percent of Congregational households held land in the town proper. Indeed, the SPG missionary claimed that in the village, where his church was, there were only six families total in 1728.[22] How many lots were built on by midcentury is not clear;

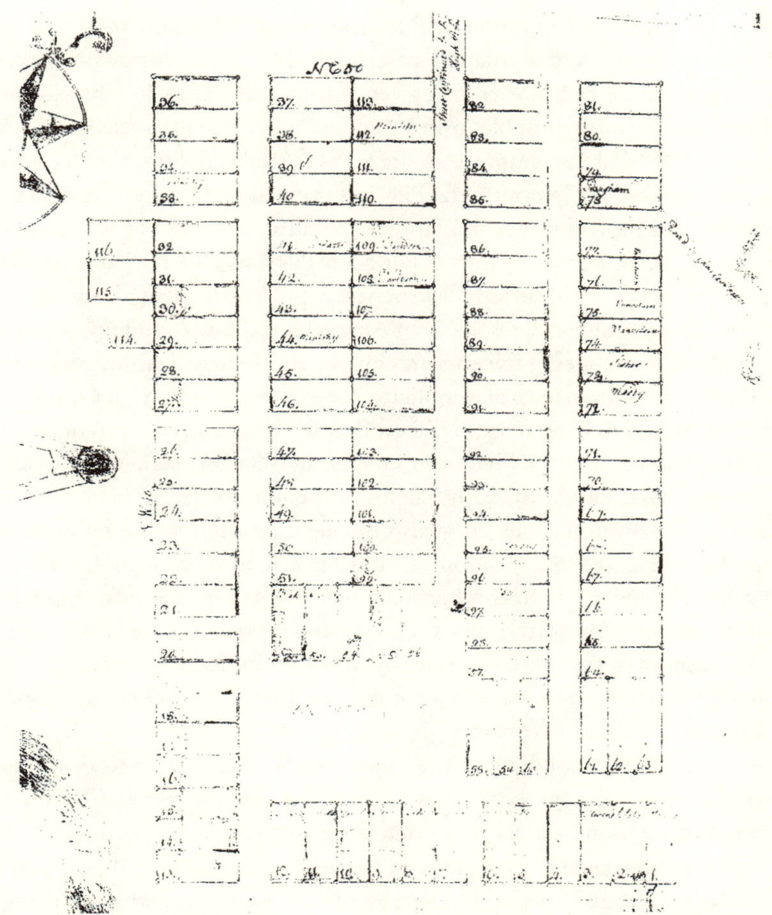

Fig. 5. Map of Dorchester town by Samuel Stevens, 1742, showing ownership of individual lots. Map reprinted from Daniel Bell, *Old Dorchester State Park Visitor's Guide* (Columbia: South Carolina Department of Parks, Recreation and Tourism, 1995), 11

during and after the Revolution visitors noted the air of prosperity the town must have had before hostilities affected Dorchester.[23] Regardless, it seems apparent that however many people lived in town–and the largest contemporary estimate of houses there is forty in 1780[24]—in whatever manner of habitation, few residents of the town proper either in 1698 or 1750 would have considered themselves part of the Congregational "community."[25]

The history of Massachusetts Bay indicates that Puritans were not averse to trade; whatever desires to worship freely may have motivated the original migrants in 1630, they made a point of working and trading and obtaining wealth based on trade. Samuel Sewall, a friend to Joseph Lord, is one example of a devout New England Congregationalist who also developed a significant personal fortune through transatlantic enterprise. The Separatists who preceded them to Massachusetts, however, had given considerable effort to achieving communitarian goals through public ownership and an essentially socialist economy that they hoped would preempt the desire for personal gain. Still, after a few years of experimentation in Plymouth, the Pilgrims decided to allow private ownership of property and individual accumulation of wealth as a necessary concession to the fallen nature of human beings.[26] For both Pilgrims and Puritans, the desire for common ideals amid an ethic of personal prosperity created tensions that never could be satisfactorily resolved. In American Calvinist ideology, recourse is often made to the model of the ancient church, an idealized institution in which pure faith and maintenance of simplicity overcome the natural corruptions to which flesh is heir.[27] Even when William Bradford was forced to recognize that utopia was not possible in Plymouth colony, he, like his somewhat wealthier Puritan neighbors, sought to claim a significant commitment of members of the community to community-based goals of general prosperity and righteousness. Because Massachusetts as a location was unforgiving to those who did not wrest a living from it, the desire to conduct such business as kept them from privation was strong enough to motivate most citizens to engage with the world in a full range of business activities. Consequently, the establishment of a place of trade in Dorchester, South Carolina, was a natural outgrowth of practices developed in New England over three generations.

Nevertheless, the building of the church two miles from the town center marks a significant distance between secular and sacred, one that at the same time preserves a distinction between work and trade. Although the topography along the river befits the general term given to the area, "lowcountry," the church was built on higher ground, near the public road to Charleston and away from the river. As Jules David Prown remarks, objects in material culture, "artifacts," have to be interpreted in terms of the meaning assigned to them by the general society, often in metaphors for values or ideas held by the community in which the object has a place.[28] Insofar as the metaphor could match reality, the White Meeting was converted by its location to the equivalent of a place on Pisgah, from which one might see Canaan or perhaps that city on a hill, from Matthew 5:14 and on which John Winthrop famously discoursed in 1630.[29] In other words, the meetinghouse had its own distinct space, one in public sight, on the road, but not compromised by competition with other structures or spaces with rival symbolic import. It was a place from which to see the glory and to be seen by God and the general eye of humankind.

At the same time, trade could *not* be witnessed, although labor or its products in the actual growing and harvesting of crops could. The Dorchester residents were almost exclusively farmers whose productions would be traded for goods or gold. Therefore, one reason for the church's location could have been to separate trade and faith; if trade were the necessary activity humans in their corruption must practice, the church represented that place where corruptions may be laid aside or overcome or not allowed to interfere with one's relationship to God. Although the Anglicans had no qualms about acquiring lots in town and building their church right in front of the market square, the dissenters, whose minister's father-in-law was the last governor of the Plymouth colony, found separation a better way.

When these New England husbandmen moved to South Carolina, they realized quickly that they could not simply replicate the crops and agricultural methods they used in the rocky soil of a northern climate. Part of the ultimate problem for Dorchester was that the local agriculture was plantation based; this required large tracts of land, much larger than the relatively small plots they were first allotted in fifty-acre parcels. This shift from small farm to plantation meant a certain amount of dispersal to the locations of occupation. The population center would have been closer to where the church was built than in town, to which people would go infrequently—on market day or to ship or purchase goods from vessels coming upriver from Charleston or vendors. In 1723 Dorchester was named by the government as a place where semiannual public fairs would be held, four-day events designed to stimulate trade and at the same time provide entertainment, and where twice-weekly markets were allowable.[30] For the time during the Congregational settlement, however, and especially in the first two decades, Dorchester may not have been large enough to accommodate what might be called a thriving trade.[31] Therefore, with relatively few goods and services available on a frequent basis until after 1730 and because there was no school in the village until 1760, the town center may not have been envisioned as a necessary daily destination for the residents of the community.

Another factor occasioned by the community's having to adopt new modes of agriculture was the source of labor. Although slavery was practiced in Massachusetts, freeholders would have been unlikely to have more than one or two, if any, slaves. In South Carolina the situation was far different. As Peter Wood has shown, the latter colony had a majority of slaves by the first decade of the eighteenth century.[32] In certain lowcountry locations, however, such as St. Andrew's and then (after 1718) St. George's Parish, slaves were the vast majority of the population, outnumbering whites in some locales from two to one to four to one. This meant that the white Massachusetts yeomen suddenly found themselves owners of multiple slaves. True, the Congregationalists as a rule did not own slaves in the numbers that Anglican plantation owners, with their larger landholdings, did. Using Varnod's 1728 census data, we find that forty-two of the fifty-two dissenting households owned slaves, many with just one but others in varying amounts up to the 61 each owned by Elizabeth Diston and Susanna

Baker.[33] With those two large-scale slaveholders included, the average household among the dissenters in 1728 owned 6.8 slaves, with ten households owning none at all. Although the average without the two largest slave owners drops significantly, the fact remains that 355 slaves were recorded as owned by dissenting families, many more than were owned by an equivalent population in New England.

To be sure, the practice of slave ownership on this scale meant that the faithful had to be engaged in the process of purchasing human beings with some frequency, most likely in town. One advantage of having the church outside of the market in this particular area was that sales of Africans, or the place of sale, would not be observed from the meetinghouse windows, even though the occupants of the boxes would have had to engage in the trade in order to use the local plantation methods. It is hard to know the effect the rapid change to larger-scale slave ownership had on the religious beliefs or scruples of Dorchester Congregationalists. Although it is clear that they adapted and that their moving to larger plantation lands in Georgia indicated they accepted using slave labor, the whites who originally settled in 1697 would have had little prior exposure to such practices (unlike the many Barbadians who settled in South Carolina in the 1670s and 1680s, including in neighboring Goose Creek). Whether the original settlers chose to place the meetinghouse away from town for reasons of the slave trade cannot be known with certainty, but the location would have preserved consciences from a close self-perusal on the biblical lawfulness of their enterprise.

The location of the Congregational meetinghouse in Dorchester seems at once materially explicable and symbolically mysterious. On the one hand, we might see the peripheral site, following Joseph Wood's analysis of seventeenth-century New England villages, as reflecting a more dispersed or, as Monica Beck suggests, seminucleated settlement pattern familiar to New Englanders, with the church in the midst of a population but not placed at the town center. On the other hand, South Carolina looked little like Massachusetts; the climate, flora, and predominant mode of agriculture all differed substantially from those the Dorchester settlers knew. Perhaps the builders thought the swampy lands along the Ashley to be unhealthy; perhaps they worried about flooding and the resulting collective cost of repair of the meetinghouse; or possibly they considered other local advice in situating their house of worship for strictly practical reasons. They may have been led by more positive concerns, such as the symbolic value of the square or their minister's desire to botanize, or negative ones, such as fear of encroachment by a rival religious sect. Even with material factors, they brought with them an English Puritan perspective filtered through two or three generations of New English experience. They were conscious enough of creating a community to have removed to Georgia almost entirely as a body more than fifty years later.

The meetinghouse would have had primary importance to a group of people sent originally by a church to establish a Congregational colony in the South. While they would not have feared trade in itself, they may have feared, based on their observation of the more built-up towns of Massachusetts, that trade could serve as a diversion from faith and compromise the spiritual lives of the Congregational community. Maybe, too, they worried about the effects of flesh-peddling, lawful though it was in the colonies, on their original identities as small farmers or on their attempt to form a coherent, unified society based on ethnicity. Whatever the reasons, Elder Pratt's thoughts still haunt: "they" kept something secret in 1696 that has lasted over three hundred years, even as the ruin of their meetinghouse teases us with its extant foundation and broken bricks.

Notes

1. My researches into the Dorchester meetinghouse and community have been aided by several people whom I wish to acknowledge: Monica Beck, former staff archaeologist at the Dorchester historic site; Daniel Bell, historian with the South Carolina parks service; Ashley Chapman, park manager at Dorchester; Rusty Clark, staff archaeologist at Dorchester; and Bill Wright of the Summerville Presbyterian Church, Summerville, S.C. In addition, I would like to thank Karen Vaughan, digital services coordinator at the Old Dominion University library, and Robert Blair St. George, Department of History, University of Pennsylvania, for their kind assistance with illustrations.

2. Information on early Dorchester is largely from Henry A. M. Smith, "The Town of Dorchester, in South Carolina—A Sketch of Its History," *South Carolina Genealogical and Historical Magazine* 6, no. 2 (1905): 62–95; and Daniel Bell, *Old Dorchester State Park Visitor's Guide* (Columbia: South Carolina Department of Parks, Recreation and Tourism, 1995).

3. Monica L. Beck, "Anglicans and Dissenters in the Colonial Village of Dorchester," in *Another's Country: Archeological and Historical Perspectives on Cultural Interactions in the Southern Colonies,* ed. J. W. Joseph and Martha Zierden, foreword by Julia A. King (Tuscaloosa: University of Alabama Press, 2002), 177.

4. Ibid., 168.

5. Joseph S. Wood, "Village and Community in Early Colonial New England," in *Material Life in America,* ed. St. George, 159–69.

6. Francis Varnod to SPG, April 3, 1728, in SPG Letter Books, series A, 1702–37, vol. 21, p. 80. By "parish" he means St. George's, or as it was often called, St. George Dorchester, an area that before 1719 was part of St. Andrew's Parish.

7. Beck, "Anglicans and Dissenters," 168.

8. Illustration in Robert J. Dinkin, "Seating the Meetinghouse in Early Massachusetts," in *Material Life in America,* ed. St. George, 408. The seating plans for other period churches reproduced by Dinkin show how widespread the square floor plan was.

9. Although the 1886 earthquake effectively destroyed the building, some walls remained at least partially intact until Hurricane Hugo struck the area in 1989 (information from Bill Wright).

10. The only reliable account of Lord's life is Clifford K. Shipton, *Sibley's Harvard Graduates,* vol. 4 (Cambridge, Mass.: Harvard University Press, 1933), 101–6.

11. Joseph Lord, *Reason Why, Not Anabaptist Plunging but Infant-Believer's Baptism . . .* (Boston: Kneeland, 1719). In two prefaces, dated 1702 and 1712, both during his Dorchester period, Lord explains something of the history of his book's composition. This writing of a 170-page treatise suggests that Lord had the intellectual capability and inclination to enter the wider world of Protestant argumentative discourse with the kind of essay that his mentors in Cambridge and Boston were writing at the time; but the fact that he waited seventeen years to put his document into print indicates that the distance from a printing press—there would be none in South Carolina until the early 1730s—made it extraordinarily difficult from the position of his frontier meetinghouse to participate in print culture. Lord first mentions the rival preacher in the letter to Thomas Hinckley cited below in note 13.

12. These letters to James Petiver along with drafts of Petiver's letters to Lord survive in the Hans Sloane Papers in the British Library: 4063.132, 155; 4064.4, 69, 148, 150, 155, 192, 233, 258.

13. Thomas Hinckley et al., "The Hinckley Papers: Being Letters and Papers of Thomas Hinckley, Governor of the Colony of New Plymouth, 1676–1699," Massachusetts Historical Society *Collections* 35 (1861): 304–6.

14. See Jeffrey H. Richards, "Robin or Fieldfare? Joseph Lord and the Origins of Natural History Writing in Colonial America" (paper presented at the Modern Language Association conference, New Orleans, La., December 2001); "Joseph Lord, the Herbals, and Materia Medica in the Lowcountry Frontier" (paper presented at the Omohundro Institute of Early American History and Culture special conference on natural history, New York, March 2002). The best published account of Lord's natural history career is Stearns, *Science in the British Colonies,* 297–305.

15. The only other Lord letter of which I am aware that discourses directly on human life in Dorchester is one to Samuel Sewall in New England from March 25, 1706. There, in addition to valuable commentary on local Indian tribes, he largely expresses his gratitude that war with the Spanish has not directly affected them. See Joseph Lord to Samuel Sewall, *New England Historical and Genealogical Register* 13 (1859): 299–300.

16. William Pratt, "Journal of Elder William Pratt, 1695–1701," in *Narratives of Early Carolina, 1650–1708,* ed. Alexander S. Salley Jr. (New York: Barnes and Noble, 1911), 194–200.

17. Ibid., 196.

18. Ibid., 199. The archaeological record of the trading area or market in Dorchester is relatively scant, although timbers of the original wharf can still be seen on the Ashley at low tide. However, Ashley Chapman is conducting the first comprehensive archaeological survey of that area of the town and may have much more to show than was available in 2002.

19. Map reproduced in Bell, *Old Dorchester State Park,* 11.

20. Beck, "Anglicans and Dissenters," 170.

21. Frank J. Klingberg, *An Appraisal of the Negro in Colonial South Carolina* (Washington, D.C.: Associated Publishers, 1941), 58–60.

22. SPG Letterbook, cited in Beck, "Anglicans and Dissenters," 174.

23. Bell, *Old Dorchester State Park,* 10, 12, 22.

24. This estimate is by Lt. Anthony Allaire of the British army in April 1780, cited in Bell, *Old Dorchester State Park,* 10.

25. The matter of congregational population numbers is somewhat confusing; see, for instance, somewhat differing numbers from these in Beck, *Anglicans and Dissenters,* 168; and D. Ray Sigmon, "Dorchester, St. George's Parish, South Carolina: The Rise and Decline of a Colonial Frontier Village" (M.A. thesis, University of South Carolina, 1992). One estimate of the town's population that is surely in error is that of John Oldmixon, *The History of the British Empire in America* (1708), when he claims that Dorchester has 350 souls; see Salley, ed., *Narratives of Early Carolina,* 366.

26. See William Bradford, *Of Plymouth Plantation 1620–1647,* introduction by Francis Murphy (New York: Modern Library, 1981), 132–34.

27. On this aspect of Puritanism, see especially Theodore Dwight Bozeman, *To Live Ancient Lives: The Primitivist Dimension in Puritanism* (Chapel Hill: University of North Carolina Press, 1988).

28. Jules David Prown, "The Truth of Material Culture: History or Fiction?" (1993), repr. in *American Artifacts: Essays in Material Culture,* ed. Jules David Prown and Kenneth Haltman (East Lansing: Michigan State University Press, 2000), 11–27.

29. John Winthrop, "A Model of Christian Charity," in *Winthrop Papers,* vol. 2 (Boston: Massachusetts Historical Society, 1931), esp. 295.

30. Bell, *Old Dorchester State Park,* 8–9.

31. If one might infer from his letters to James Petiver, Joseph Lord appears to have gone to Charleston about once a year, possibly to meet with other dissenting ministers and to purchase goods that simply did not come to Dorchester in sufficient quantities to be easily obtainable.

32. Peter H. Wood, *Black Majority: Negroes in Colonial South Carolina from 1678 through the Stono Rebellion* (New York: Knopf, 1974).

33. Klingberg, *Appraisal of the Negro,* 59–60.

Charlestown to Charleston

Urban and Plantation Connections in an Atlantic Setting

Roger H. Leech

In the material world of seventeenth-century Tidewater, Virginia, and the Caribbean many echoes of the architecture of urban and rural England were to be found. Settlers from southeast England would have found one such echo in later seventeenth-century Jamestown, Virginia, in the row of houses recorded by twentieth-century archaeologists as "Structure 17." These four houses now read as a solitary transplant to a North American context of an urban house form familiar to townspeople in the cities, towns, and ports of southeast England from at least the late sixteenth century.[1] Citizens of the Dutch world or from southwest England would have found similar echoes in the "single houses" of Charleston, South Carolina. Urban houses of similar plan and set similarly to their Charleston counterparts in relation to the tenement plots as a whole were to be found in late seventeenth-century New York, formerly New Amsterdam, and in Topsham, the port for Exeter in south Devon, England (see figures 1–3).[2]

In the rural plantation landscapes of the Caribbean and mainland North America there were similar echoes of England and Europe. "To know one's own": the thoughts embedded in the setting out of the geometric linear field systems of early seventeenth-century Nevis (see figure 4) or late seventeenth-century South Carolina were equally familiar as explanation and justification to the Dutch and English surveyors responsible for laying out the newly enclosed fields of the Cambridgeshire and south Lincolnshire fenlands.[3]

Other elements of the new and emerging English world of the North American Atlantic littoral and Caribbean were less familiar. One that has preoccupied late twentieth-century architectural historians and archaeologists was the technique of anchoring timber houses in the ground, using a form of construction largely abandoned in England, France, and the Low Countries in the late twelfth

Fig. 1. Drawing of Dutch houses in New York City by Pierre Eugene du Simitiere, c. 1769. The three houses, one dated 1689, are set at right angles to the street with open tenement plots between each house. Courtesy of Library Company of Philadelphia, Pennsylvania

and early thirteenth centuries.[4] Such buildings were to be found not only in seventeenth-century Virginia and Maryland, as is well known, but also on the English islands of the Caribbean. In seventeenth-century Charlestown, then and now the largest town on the island of Nevis, buildings constructed in this way stood against the main street and close to the waterfront probably devastated by earthquake and tidal wave in 1690; their plan was revealed by excavations in 2000 (see figure 5). Such houses, of earth-fast construction and as built in Virginia and Maryland in the seventeenth century, were not necessarily impermanent or seen by contemporaries as impermanent.[5]

On Nevis one such structure is the Hermitage, a plantation house. Excavations and earlier observations have shown that this building was of earth-fast construction. The posts were left unfinished and as tree trunks below ground level; above ground level they are neatly chamfered with lamb's tongue stops and morticed and tenoned into the wall plates with double pegged joints. This house consisted initially of an open hall with a single cross wing, both of which still stand (see figure 6). The finish of the house above ground is entirely of English inspiration, but anchoring the posts in post holes in the ground may have owed more to combating the hurricane and knowledge of the Spanish and Native American worlds than to almost entirely and long-forgotten methods of construction once employed in medieval England.

Earth-fast houses were certainly widely built in seventeenth-century Virginia, Maryland, and the English Caribbean. Such houses may also have been cheaper

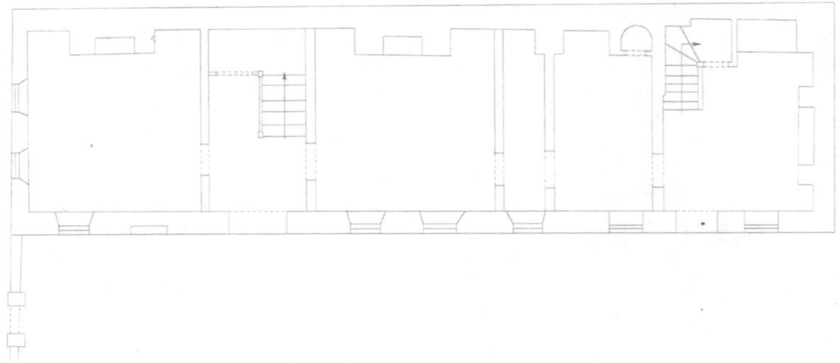

Fig. 2. Plan of no. 34 The Strand. Plan after John Thorp, 1995

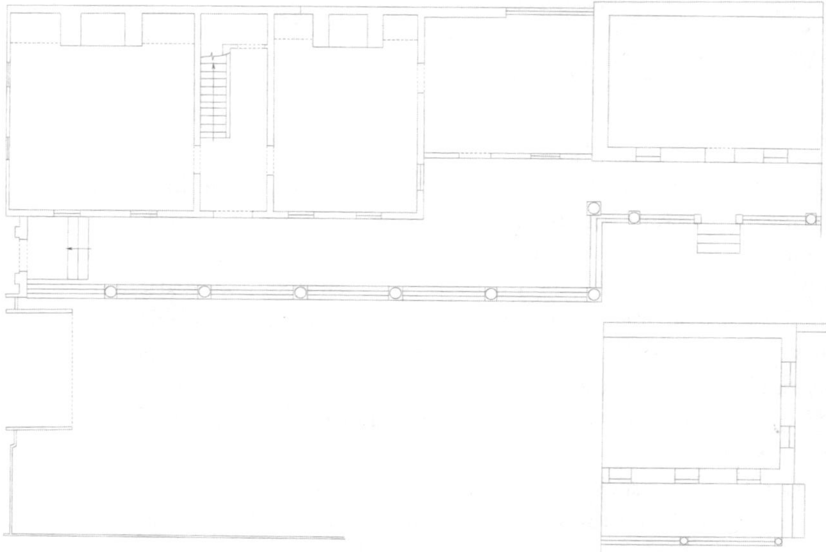

Fig. 3. Plan of no. 4 Orange Street, Charleston. After Louis Nelson, Bernard Herman, and Steven Bauer, 1994, *Vernacular Architecture Forum Handbook*

to construct than masonry houses of similar proportions. Looking at the long "great rebuilding" in the southern colonies, Cary Carson and his coauthors have argued that the mere fact that a house now "stood on continuous sills or was made entirely of brick had little social significance; its real value was something an appraiser or a tax assessor could put a figure on, a monetary value."[6] To establish convincingly, though, that such houses were less expensive to construct perhaps needs further research, and whether building in brick in the seventeenth century was entirely without social significance can be questioned. Investigation into the English context for the masonry houses of seventeenth-century Virginia and the English Caribbean can be instructional.

Recent research, notably by David Brown and Dwayne Pickett, has provided a new overview of the extent to which houses of masonry construction were built in Virginia during the seventeenth century. Bacon's Castle is the one well-known surviving brick house from seventeenth-century Virginia, but as many as twenty-four have been recorded through archaeological investigations.[7] Research by Julia King and Edward Chaney has similarly extended our understanding of the masonry tradition in the seventeenth-century Chesapeake, focusing on Mattapany, the plantation house of Charles Calvert, the third Lord Baltimore, and linking the construction of this house to the social and economic status and ambitions of its owner.[8] St. Nicholas Abbey on Barbados has often been claimed as the best preserved stone house from the seventeenth-century English Caribbean. Recent research by Ed Chappell, Willie Graham, Carl Lounsbury, and others has provided a much extended catalog of masonry houses on the island known to survive from the seventeenth century. My own research has been focused on two of these houses, Alleynedale Hall and St. Nicholas Abbey.[9]

FIG. 4. Geometric rectilinear land divisions on Nevis, southeast part of the island. Courtesy of the United States Air Force

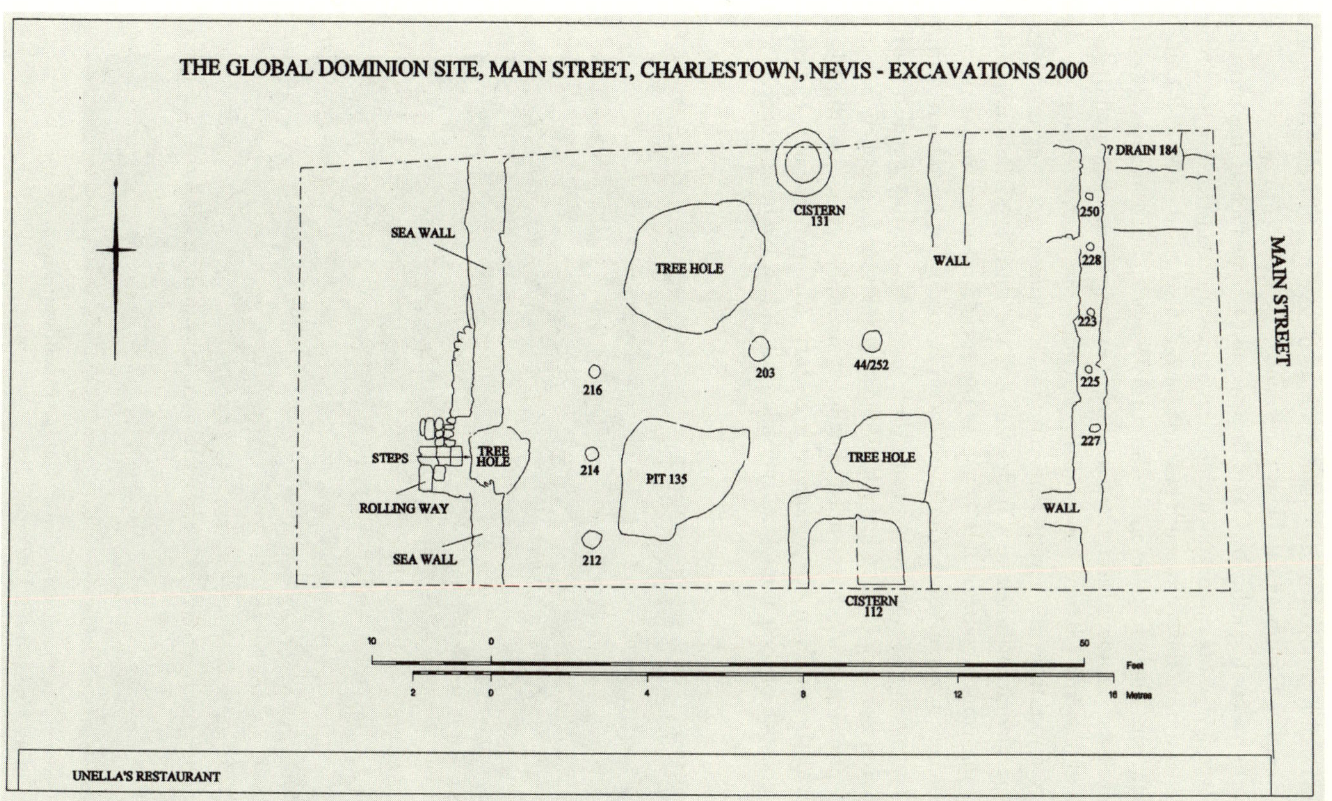

Fig. 5. Charlestown, Nevis, plan of excavations, 2000. Author's drawing

FIG. 6. The Hermitage, Nevis: the open hall looking west. Author's photograph

The increase in domestic brick architecture in Virginia and the Tidewater during the second half of the seventeenth century has been linked to its use by a colonial elite. Brown has seen "the connection between masonry architecture and political office holders as unmistakeable"; "brick and stone architecture during the 17th century in Virginia may have symbolized power and the unity of the political elite."[10] Pickett has argued that this same elite used brick architecture as a means of enforcing social distinctions, by marking the owners of brick houses as those who controlled the landscape and other people.[11] King and Chaney have argued that "in a landscape dominated by earth-fast buildings, Mattapany surely represented the wealth and power of the governor in a striking fashion."[12] I propose that the context of these masonry houses, and those of the English Caribbean, was more complex and must be sought also in contemporary seventeenth-century urban England.

"Artisan mannerism" is the name coined by John Summerson for an architectural style that emerged in England in the first half of the seventeenth century, a style strongly mannerist in character and used for building until the last quarter of the century by masons and carpenters centered predominantly in and around London. Features characteristic of the style included the use of gables with curved sides, with flat tops carrying pediments, with pilasters rising through two floors, and with exaggerated classical forms and the extensive use of molded brick.[13]

Fig. 7. Samuel Fortrey's house at Kew, 1631. Courtesy of Nicholas Cooper

Summerson's term originated in his own preoccupation with the mannerist style as worked in the hands of London artisan masons; but it was a style utilized for the benefit of London's elite. A term such as "London baroque" might be more appropriate, but this would need to be argued at greater length than is possible here.[14]

As previous scholars have recognized, Bacon's Castle was built in the artisan mannerist style, characterized here by the use of curved gables, molded brickwork, and window architraves with exaggerated lugs.[15] In a discussion of the excavated evidence for the long-demolished John Page house, now within Williamsburg, the brickwork that adorned this structure was judged to be "typical of the Artisan Mannerist movement."[16]

The use of the artisan mannerist style was urban based. Many of the houses built in this style were constructed for clients with London connections or were built within close proximity to London. The "Dutch House" at Kew was built circa 1631 for Samuel Fortrey, a merchant in the city of London (see figure 7).[17] "Kew Palace" is as much a misnomer for this house as "Bacon's Castle" is for Arthur Allen's brick house in Surry County, Virginia. Even closer to London and possibly by the same architect was the Fairfax house on Putney High Street, built in the 1630s for a London baker, Henry White (see figure 8).[18] Swakeleys in Middlesex was built in brick and stone circa 1638 for Sir Edmund Wright, a merchant originally from Cheshire but by 1640 sufficiently entrenched in the city of

FIG. 8. Henry White's house at Putney, built c. 1630, later known as the Fairfax House. British Library 05092, used with permission of English Heritage, National Monuments Record

London to become its lord mayor.[19] On Croom's Hill at Greenwich the Presbytery was one of several suburban houses built circa 1630, looking north over the Thames and east across the road in front of the houses to the royal park. Its probable first owner, Dr. Robert Mason, chancellor to the Diocese of Winchester, would have been firmly enmeshed in London business.[20]

Much farther from London at Hamworthy in Dorset, a house now known as "The Old Rectory" was probably built by an architect closely familiar with Fortrey's house beside the River Thames at Kew.[21] The key to understanding the context of this house, built in a London style but close to the south coast of England, is its location. Hamworthy is immediately across the water from Poole, an important port trading from the early seventeenth century onward with North America and then with Newfoundland in particular. The house at Hamworthy would have been but a ten or twenty minutes' row from the Poole waterfront. Mercantile connections are most likely to have brought Fortrey's architect and his client to Poole. London connections similarly brought John Juxon's architect to Aldbourne Place in West Sussex. John Juxon, brother to the archbishop who tended Charles I on the scaffold, retained Aldbourne Place as his country residence before his death in 1655 as a citizen of the parish of St. Benett in London.[22]

FIG. 9. Alderman Hooke's house at Ashley, Bristol. Courtesy of Bristol City Library, England

Maintaining this duality of residence, thinking of oneself as a citizen but wishing also to maintain a country house, was a characteristic of urban elite mentality by the seventeenth century, though not all citizens were so inclined. On Sunday, July 14, 1667, following a weekend visit to Epsom and the Surrey countryside, Samuel Pepys noted: "My resolution is never to keep a country-house, but to keep a coach, and with my wife on the Saturday to go sometimes for a day to this place, and then quit to another place; and there is more variety and as little charge, and no trouble, as there is in a country-house."[23] Pepys's comments can also be taken to imply that other citizens might have considered purchasing country residences for weekend use as far as Epsom—some sixteen miles from the center of the city of London. Certainly by the 1660s, an increasing number of citizens possessed suburban or country houses that were secondary to or complemented residences in the city.

Forty Hall at Enfield was built in 1629 for Sir Nicholas Rainton, a city merchant and later lord mayor. Swakeleys near Uxbridge was built for another lord mayor in 1638.[24] Both these houses would have been accessible by coach and road from London, much as Pepys traveled to Epsom in 1667. The greatest number of such houses probably lay east and west of the city close to the River Thames and were accessed most easily by water. Samuel Fortrey is likely to have traveled upstream to his house at Kew, built in 1631, by river on the incoming tide. On the opposite bank, now in Brentford, was Boston Manor, built circa 1623, also possibly a country retreat.[25] Closer to London, Putney was a favorite location for the suburban residences of London citizens such as the baker Henry White.[26] Downstream from the city were the houses built on Croom's Hill at Greenwich, at least two of which were visited by Pepys. From the city these were all accessed most easily by river.

Sir William Hooker, a citizen of London, sheriff, and to become lord mayor in 1673, entertained Pepys at dinner in his out-of-town house on Croom's Hill in December 1665; he kept "the poorest mean dirty table in a dirty house . . . a plain

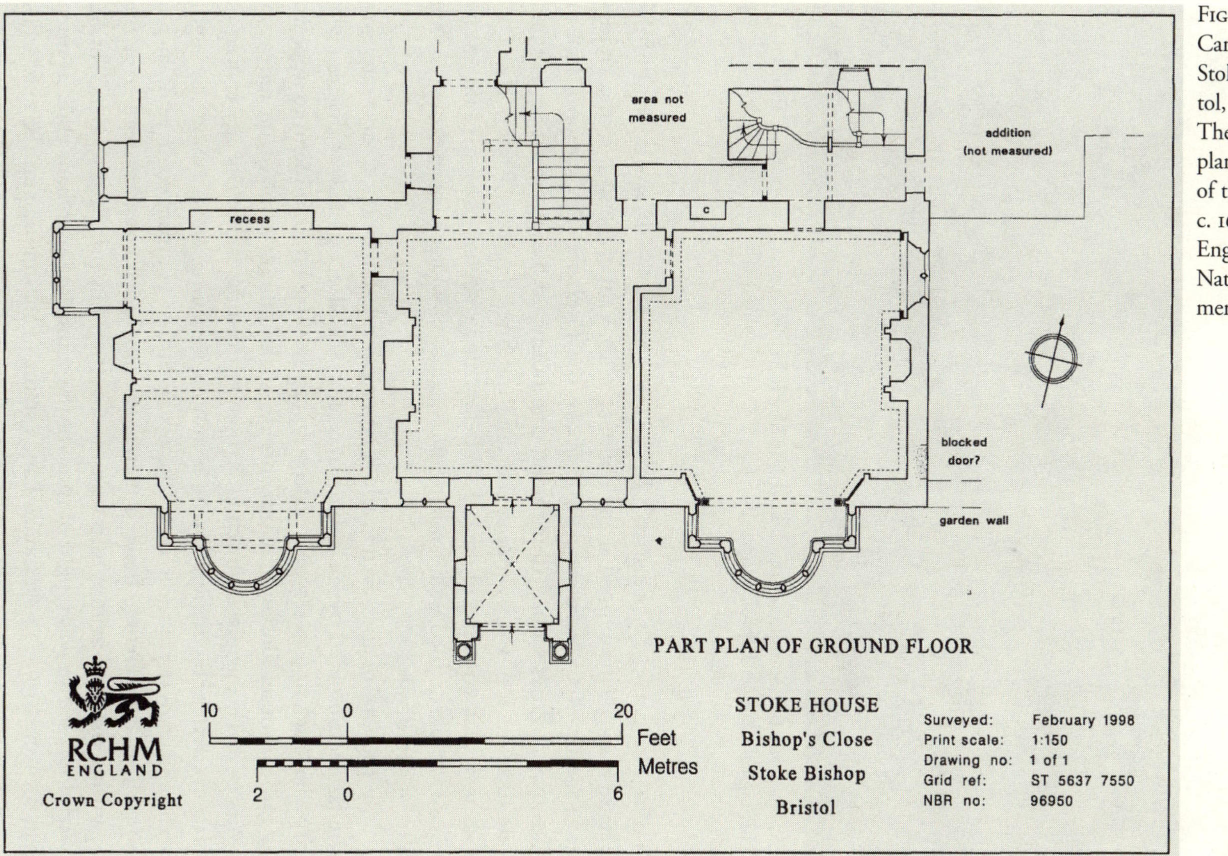

Fig. 10. Sir Robert Cann's house at Stoke Bishop, Bristol, now Trinity Theological College, plan of ground floor of the part built c. 1669. Courtesy of English Heritage, National Monuments Record

Fig. 11. Stoke Bishop house, Bristol, as painted by J. M. W. Turner. Courtesy of Trinity Theological College, Bristol, England

ordinary silly man . . . but rich." In the same month—this was the end of the plague year—Pepys supped at the house of Mark Cuttle, registrar to the Prerogative Court of Canterbury, a little above the Presbytery on Croom's Hill at Greenwich. Pepys wrote: "dined nobly and neatly; with a very pretty house and fine turret at top, with winding stair and the finest prospect I know about all Greenwich, save the top of the hill."[27] Below the Presbytery, Croom's Hill was by circa 1700 likely lined with similar houses, some of which survive though much altered and divided.

By the end of the seventeenth century Bristol, England's second city, was similarly surrounded by the suburban, country, and occasional residences of its city elite. Such houses served a variety of purposes: for entertainment; to impress; as garden houses alongside allotments or smallholdings; as places of retreat in times of plague; as places for childbirth away from the unhealthy city center; as places of retreat for tranquillity on a summer's evening or for a Saturday night and Sunday away from the city. One of the earliest glimpses we have of such a house is that of George Lane, a merchant who had become a member of the Spanish Company in 1605 and who died in 1613. His principal residence in St. Werburgh's Parish was typical of those of the ruling and merchant elite, its open hall furnished so as to symbolize Lane's status in the militia and the city.[28] His

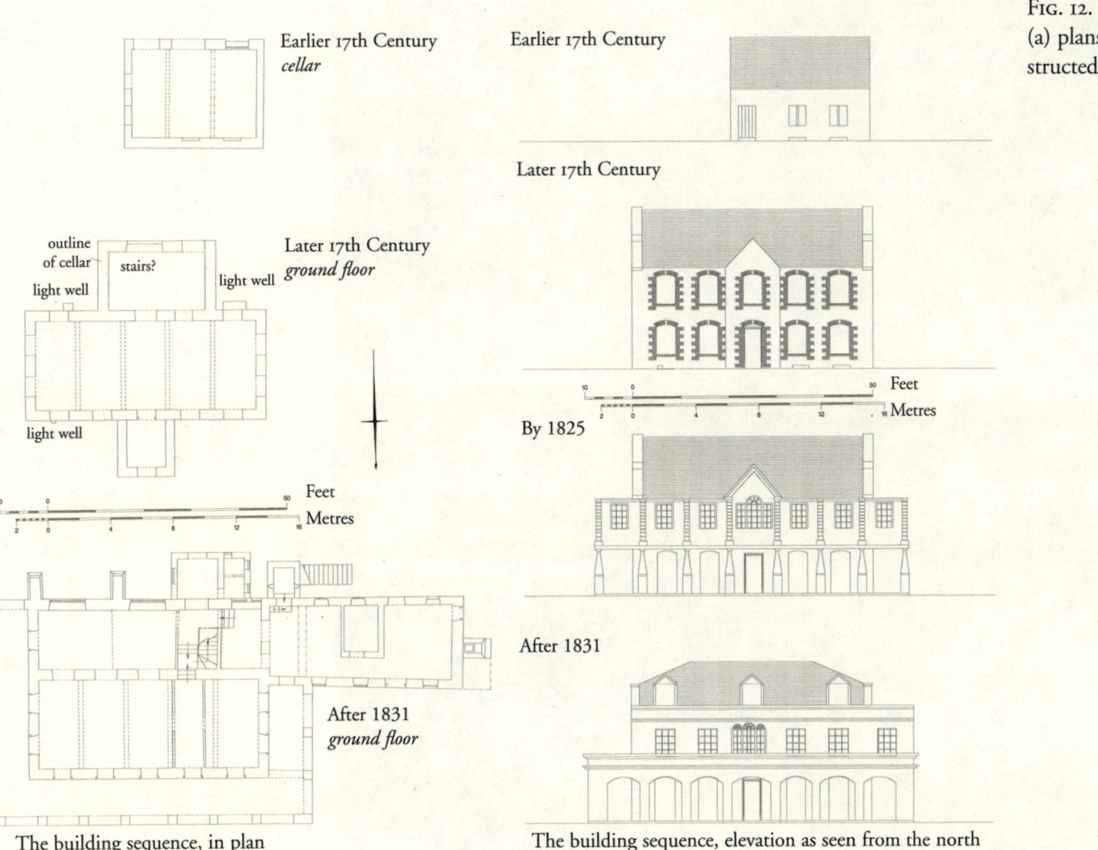

Fig. 12. Alleynedale Hall, Barbados: (a) plans of ground floor; (b) reconstructed elevations. Author's image

Fig. 13. Spencer-Pierce-Little house, Newburyport, Massachusetts. Photograph by Mary Beaudry

suburban house, described in the inventory of his possessions as the "house att the hill," served both as a retreat from the city and as a working farm or smallholding.[29]

Farther from the center of Bristol were more such country retreats. At Ashley was Alderman Hooke's house, now demolished (see figure 9). At Stoke Bishop the merchant Robert Cann possessed a small lodge by the early 1660s, supplementing this in 1669 with an altogether grander residence. The restricted amount of service accommodation contrasted with the amount of space given to an impressive entry and stairs. The plan of Cann's house was similar to that of Bacon's Castle and the John Page house, the so-called cross plan (see figure 10). Cann's house was an occasional residence built to impress the occasional visitor; his principal residence was in the center of the city.[30]

Robert Cann, the builder of the Stoke Bishop house, was the son of William Cann and Margaret Yeamans. Margaret was the sister of John Yeamans, who in the 1660s and early 1670s was briefly the owner of St. Nicholas Abbey on Barbados and who was to play a major role in the foundation of South Carolina. It was the superficial resemblance of St. Nicholas Abbey to the Stoke Bishop house, as painted by J. M. W. Turner (see figure 11), that occasioned the author's research on Barbados—"superficial" because a survey has shown that the gables of St. Nicholas Abbey are not original to the seventeenth-century roof and are probably of the mid–eighteenth century or later. The archaeology and form of the seventeenth-century house is largely hidden by render and plaster. The survey of a second seventeenth-century masonry house on Barbados, Alleynedale Hall, has shown how much might remain hidden in a house such as St. Nicholas Abbey.[31]

The plantation house at Alleynedale, two miles from Speightstown in the north part of Barbados, was rebuilt in the later seventeenth century. The masonry walls of the new house were of coral limestone, with brick quoins to the windows and doorways and with curved gables in the artisan mannerist tradition. Traces of red paint on the coral limestone indicate that it was intended to make the house as a whole appear to be of brick. Almost all of the ground floor was given over to one large room, in which the main and most of the subsidiary ceiling beams still survive. From a later drawing and from the survey data, it can be argued that the house was approximately of a cross plan, with a projecting porch on the north and wider projecting stairs on the south (see figure 12). The plan of Alleynedale, seemingly given over to entertainment, and its proximity to Speightstown, "Little Bristol" in the seventeenth century, indicate that this was possibly a residence secondary to the main concerns of its owner—who may have lived for the most part elsewhere, perhaps in Speightstown.

The research undertaken by Brown and Pickett has highlighted that in the seventeenth-century English settlement of Virginia, masonry structures were first built within Jamestown. By the 1680s a greater number of masonry houses were located around Jamestown, with a distinct concentration of such houses in Middle Plantation, upon which Williamsburg was later built as the new colonial capital.[32] Brown and Pickett have seen construction in masonry as a means by which the colony's elite enforced social distinction. Masonry and especially brick houses, and the plans utilized for these houses, marked the elite as a separate and not easily approached group. However, building in masonry might also have been a conscious or subconscious element of the urban mind-set. Discussing the evolution of the Rich Neck plantation, Philip Levy has argued that many of Virginia's elite "were acutely aware of changing trends and styles in the era's increasingly trendy metropole," namely London, and that "these elites were particularly attuned to the life and values of England's towns in general."[33]

Building in the artisan mannerist style was certainly a development rooted in the building practices of the city of London. Building a smallish or sometimes not so modest house in the country for occasional use, to impress visitors, and for a variety of other purposes was similarly part of the culture of merchant life in larger cities such as London and Bristol. As merchants and/or holders of political office, the greater number of the first owners of these houses would have spent at least some of their working days in Jamestown. In considering the reasons why in the mid- to late seventeenth century Virginia's elite increasingly constructed masonry houses, it may be necessary to reexamine the daily lives of merchants, plantation owners, and other members of the colony's political elite. Such examination could uncover, for example, to what extent the brick houses on the slopes and ridges of Middle Plantation above Jamestown were occupied by their owners intermittently—though it has to be said that some of these owners, for instance of Rich Neck, certainly wished to be buried there. Examination could also uncover to what extent the new brick house of the merchant Arthur Allen was a distant echo of the house of Samuel Fortrey, a merchant of London.

That such suggestions are not entirely implausible might be reinforced by looking northward to the Massachusetts Bay Colony. The one masonry house surviving from the seventeenth century in Massachusetts is the Spencer-Pierce-Little house south of Newburyport, now thought to have been built in the 1690s, with its brick porch set firmly in the artisan mannerist tradition (see figure 13). The most likely candidate as builder of the house is Daniel Pierce, a wealthy merchant who also owned a house on the main waterfront street of the town. Nancy Curtis has argued that "to build a large stone house resembling a manor would seem the ideal manifestation of Pierce's worldly status."[34] Anne Grady, though, has concluded that "Pierce, in residing at the Waterside, became the first of a number of owners of the Spencer-Pierce-Little House to have a primary residence near the centre of trade on the Merrimack River."[35] By drawing on the context of contemporary English cities such as London and Bristol, it can be proposed that to own a suburban or country residence for occasional use was part of contemporary merchant culture and served a variety of ends. Daniel Pierce's country house, large though it was by contemporary standards for Massachusetts, was first built as a residence for occasional use. Daniel Pierce and the builder of later seventeenth-century Alleynedale in Barbados embraced the established English mercantile tradition of living in part in the countryside and perhaps for the most part within the nearby town or city.

The land of Virginia leaves us with a paradox that will take time to resolve. On the one hand, there is the scant urbanity of seventeenth-century Jamestown, St. Mary's City, and other towns.[36] On the other hand, there is the much more evident urbanity of a merchant-planter elite constructing within the hinterlands of these places masonry buildings in a style and to plans grounded within the English city and its suburban surroundings. Urban and plantation connections in an Atlantic setting, ambiguities and possibilities, will be a profitable area for further research and enquiry.

Notes

For advice in the preparation of this paper, I am especially indebted to Mary Beaudry, Marley Brown III, Anne Grady, Willie Graham, Peter Guillery, Julia King, Eric Klingelhofer, Carl Lounsbury, Gary Stanton, and Angus Winchester. For help in the identification of source material, I am also most grateful to Ian Leith and Veronica Smith of English Heritage, and Guy and Marion Walker of Aldbourne Place, West Sussex.

1. Roger H. Leech, "The Prospect from Rugman's Row: The Row House in Late Sixteenth- and Early Seventeenth-Century London," *Archaeological Journal* 153 (1996): 218–24.

2. Roderic H. Blackburn, "Dutch Domestic Architecture in the Hudson Valley," *Tijdschrift van de Koninklijke Nederlandse Oudeheidkindige Bond* 84 (June 1985): 156; John Thorp, "Town Houses of the Late Seventeenth and Early Eighteenth Centuries," in *Devon Building: An Introduction to Local Building Traditions,* 2d ed., ed. Peter Beacham (Tiverton, U.K.: Devon Books, 1995), 122–23.

3. For "to know one's own" and the intellectual context of early modern agrarian improvement, see Andrew McRae, *God Speed the Plough* (Cambridge: Cambridge University Press, 1996), 169–97. For late seventeenth-century North Carolina, see Sirmans, *Colonial South Carolina,* end map. For the Dutch surveyors, see Kees Zandvliet, *Mapping for Money: Maps, Plans and Topographic Paintings and Their Role in Dutch Overseas Expansion during the 16th and 17th Centuries* (Amsterdam: Batavian Lion International, 1998), 164–209.

4. Carson et al., "Impermanent Architecture," 135–96.

5. Roger H. Leech, "Impermanent Architecture in the English Colonies of the Eastern Caribbean: New Contexts for Architectural Innovation in the Early Modern Atlantic World," *Perspectives in Vernacular Architecture,* forthcoming.

6. Carson et al., "Impermanent Architecture," 178.

7. David A. Brown, "Domestic Masonry Architecture in 17th-Century Virginia," *Northeast Historical Archaeology* 27 (1998): 85–120; Dwayne W. Pickett, "The John Page House Site: An Example of the Increase in Domestic Brick Architecture in Seventeenth-Century Tidewater Virginia" (M.A. thesis, College of William and Mary, 1996).

8. Julia A. King and Edward E. Chaney, "Lord Baltimore and the Meaning of Brick Architecture in Seventeenth-Century Maryland," in *Old and New Worlds: Historical / Post Medieval Archaeology Papers,* ed. Geoff Egan and Ronald L. Michael (Oxford: Oxbow Books, 1999), 51–60.

9. Roger H. Leech, "Alleynedale Hall, Barbados—A Plantation House of the Seventeenth Century," *Journal of the Barbados Museum & Historical Society* 48 (2002): 123–41.

10. Brown, "Domestic Masonry," 89, 103.

11. Pickett, "John Page House," 75.

12. King and Chaney, "Lord Baltimore," 57.

13. See the chap. "Artisan Mannerism" in John Summerson, *Architecture in Britain, 1530–1830* (London: Penguin, 1953), 97–105.

14. Nicholas Cooper has argued that the term "remains accurate and acute"; see Nicholas Cooper, *Houses of the Gentry 1480–1680* (New Haven, Conn., and London: Yale University Press, 1999), 173, endnote 65.

15. Summerson, *Architecture in Britain,* 100.

16. John Metz, Jennifer Jones, Dwayne Pickett, and David Muraca, *"Upon the Palisado" and Other Stories of Place from Bruton Heights* (Williamsburg, Va.: Colonial Williamsburg Research Publications, 1998), 56.

17. John Charlton, *Kew Palace* (London: Department of the Environment, 1983).

18. Dorian Gerhold, *Putney Past* (London: Historical Publications, 1994), 24–25.

19. Summerson, *Architecture in Britain,* 100.

20. Beryl Platts, "The Oldest Road in London? Crooms Hill, Greenwich-1," *Country Life* (November 1966): 1262.

21. Royal Commission on Historical Monuments (England), *An Inventory of Historical Monuments in the County of Dorset, Volume Two South-East, Part 2* (London: Her Majesty's Stationary Office, 1970), 238.

22. Cooper, *Houses of the Gentry,* 178.

23. Samuel Pepys, *The Diary of Samuel Pepys,* vol. 8: 1667, ed. R. Latham and W. Matthews (London: Bell, 1974), 339.

24. Cooper, *Houses of the Gentry,* 154.

25. Ibid.

26. Gerhold, *Putney Past,* 25.

27. Pepys, *Diary,* 171.

28. Roger H. Leech, "The Symbolic Hall: Historical Context and Merchant Culture in the Early Modern City," *Vernacular Architecture* 30 (2000): 1–10.

29. Roger H. Leech, *The St Michael's Hill Precinct of the University of Bristol: The Topography of Medieval and Early Modern Bristol, Part 2* (Bristol: Bristol Record Society, 2000), 52:22–26.

30. For the houses of Hooke and Cann, see Roger H. Leech, "The Garden House: Merchant Culture and Identity in the Early Modern City," in *Archaeologies of the British,* ed. Susan Lawrence (London: Routledge, 2003).

31. For St. Nicholas Abbey and Alleynedale Hall, see Leech, "Alleynedale Hall."

32. For a map of masonry structures in later seventeenth-century Virginia, see Brown, "Domestic Masonry," 91, fig.7.

33. Philip Levy, "A Planter's Urbanity" (paper presented to the 32d Annual Meeting of the Council for Northeast Historical Archaeology, Montreal, Quebec), cited in Brown, "Domestic Masonry," 108.

34. Nancy Curtis, "Spencer-Pierce-Little Farm: Piecing the Puzzle," in *Society for the Preservation of New England Antiquities Annual Report 1990* (Boston: Society for the Preservation of New England Antiquities, 1990), 6.

35. Anne A. Grady, *Spencer-Pierce-Little House Historic Structures Report* (Boston: for the Society for the Preservation of New England Antiquities, 1988; rev. ed., 1992).

36. For the scant urbanity of seventeenth-century Jamestown, see Kathleen Bragdon, Edward Chappell, and William Graham, "A Scant Urbanity, Jamestown in the 17th Century," in *The Archaeology of 17th Century Virginia,* Special Publication No. 30 of the Archaeological Society of Virginia, ed. Theodore R. Reinhart and Dennis J. Progue (Richmond, Va.: Dietz Press, 1992), 223–49.

Part Two

Locating Urbanity

A Poetics of Urban Space

Bernard L. Herman

Charles Olson, author of the *Maximus Poems,* commented in a letter to the editor of the *Gloucester Daily Times* on the sense of place and loss that defined the poetical topography of this New England seaport town: "What bastard man today does not know, or his fellows who sell to him abuse in and for him, is the created conditions of his own nature. One of these certainly is topography, that is that the shape of things on earth, of his own tools and constructions, the paths he and animals made and the roads which followed on and after those earlier means of his own movement, have, like the air and odors of spring and fall, or the difference of light and color when Winter's air is cold, and like food, and love-making, and children, and a place he lives in, much to do with how alive he himself or her personally is."[1] Olson's letter, like his *Maximus Poems,* describes a world where the past not only infuses the present but also communicates an aesthetic presence of being in the world. The nature and poetics of that presence are at once spatial and experiential.

A poem is an artifact. "Poetry," avers Edward Hirsch, "is a soul-making activity, and the reader in part authors that activity by responding to the form of the poem, its way of shaping itself." Hirsch continues, "I have an idea that a certain kind of exemplary poem teaches you how to read it. It carries its own encoded instructions, enacting its subject, pointing to its own operation. It enacts what it is about—a made thing that indicates the nature of its own making." He elaborates, "Poems communicate before they are understood and the structure operates on, or inside, the reader even as the words infiltrate the consciousness." "The form is the shape of the poem's understanding," Hirsch concludes, "its way of being in the world, and it is the form that structures our experience." Urban space, it seems, is a poem.[2]

The idea of a poetics of urban space originates in reaction to critical conventions and methodologies that dominate the study of material culture. We tend, for example, to look to science, and by definition methodological objectivity, for our explanatory approaches as if the rigor of typology, morphology, or other organizing schemes will domesticate the expressive licentiousness of everyday life. A poetics of material culture, and in this discussion a poetics of urban space, looks of necessity to explanatory strategies that privilege ambiguity over certainty. This poetics resides in the play between language and performance and the instabilities of meaning. It possesses two key attributes: ambiguity and lyricism.

Ambiguity addresses two problems in reading material culture. First, because we are so text dependent in such literal ways, we tend to distrust the voice of the object due to its inexactness. The artifact simply does not state what meanings it superintends; rather it lends itself to acts of inscription that invite us to write significances onto its surfaces. As critical graffiti, acts of interpretation have the capacity to "tag" territory and to realize a kind of substitution where our interpretations overwrite and mask the nature of the things we study. The connotative quality of objects, their semiotic ambiguity, is what makes their ability to convey sense and significance at once situational, provisional, and performative. In essence, we carry meaning to the world of things; our acts of interpretation are constant and slippery.[3] Ambiguity admits that there are multiple, simultaneous, often conflicted constructions of meaning. Basically, what things mean depends on the perceptions of audience and actors in shared contexts.[4] Ambiguity holds the capacity to admit and reconcile difference in a single critical gesture.

Lyricism functions in a poetics of urban space by incorporating subjectivity, sensuousness, and cadence.[5] Lyricism speaks to the fact that any understanding of urban space is at some fundamental level physical and personal. Striving to write and speak about urban space is how we begin to construct and communicate an order of things that we know through subjective experience. Most useful in the notion of lyricism in this application is its implication of an aesthetics of experience. The use of aesthetics here departs from what constitutes a philosophy of the beautiful and concentrates instead on the idea that aesthetics are a vital aspect in the practice of everyday life.[6] Aesthetic process is located in the worlds of act and expression that describe the balances (and imbalances) between people and the worlds they make, inhabit, communicate, and render symbolically coherent. Aesthetics are not intrinsic to the physical appearance of objects but are grounded instead in the circumstances of individual and group expression and reception. This directs us to questions of cadence or measure.

Lyricism as an aestheticized form of writing depends on the measured use of language. Urban space, however, is lyric in the sense that it is what might be thought of as "projective." Projection, in a theory of the poetics of urban space, finds its origins in Charles Olson's formulation of projective verse, an approach that privileges voice over text. It is literally the shout in the street, the breathed word performed.[7] Performance, however, is spatial in its execution and cinematic in the sense that it is an unfolding of visible action. What is lyric ceases to be fossilized in written word and is energized through performance of place. Olson's projective verse is also linked to his formulation of proprioception—that is, the sense by which the body locates and understands itself in space: "the data of depth sensibility / the 'body' of us as object which spontaneously or of its own order produces experience of."[8] What is projective depends on the physical and experiential insinuation of the poetic self into the very fabric of the landscape. Thus, Olson begins his *Maximus Poems,* celebrating the history and persona of his Massachusetts seaport home, with the invitation "I, Maximus of Gloucester, to You" and quickly moves into a breathlike representation of place:

> the thing you're after
> may lie around the bend
> of the nest (second, time slain, the bird! The bird!
>
> And there! (strong) thrust, the mast! Flight
> (of the bird
> O kylix, o
> Antony of Padua
> sweep low, o bless
>
> the roofs, the old ones
> on whose ridge-poles the gulls sit, from which they depart,
> And the flake-racks
>
> Of my city.[9]

Ambiguity and lyricism in a poetics of urban space embrace the idea of "affecting presence," the emotional response to the material world. Affecting "objects and happenings in any given culture are accepted by those native to that culture as being purposefully concerned with potency, emotions, values, and states of being or experience—all, in a clear sense, *powers.*"[10] Three key attributes define affect: it is about feeling; it is presentation or enactment; and it is material, either as artifact or recorded event. A core idea lurking within the concept of affect recognizes that aesthetic and critical thought is not necessarily objective thought.[11] Although the intended use of the concept of affect tends to privilege the ascription of purpose and intent, we can enlarge the idea to comprehend a concept of tradition as the cultural process of making situational, strategic, and continuing sense of the world around us.[12] Tradition enables us to read purpose and intent into objects as well as out of them. Tradition is performative, rendering sense and enacting sense two aspects of the same process. As with ambiguity and lyricism, affect and tradition invite a quality of sensuousness into a poetics of urban space.

Interpretations of Charleston's eighteenth-century urban landscape set a poetics of urban space in operation. The constellation of historical evidence that informs our understanding of the Charleston cityscape is diverse. In addition to the architectural record of buildings and streets, our efforts are fueled by documentary evidence such as land surveys, probate records, trial transcripts, and all the grist that historians grind. Add to this the archaeological record, the evidence of ceramics, glass, metal, bone, and earth. What is revealed in this mass of information is the suggestion of relationships that enable us to move beyond conventional, object-bound interpretations of complex behaviors. Habit makes us think of space in limited ways: the plan of the city, the market square and exchange, the house and its rooms. A poetics of urban space, however, argues that urban space is contained in the ambiguous and lyrical relationships between the people and objects that populate the city. Urban space is defined by performance; its myriad artifacts hint at a diversity of possibilities and consequences. Where do we begin? It depends a great deal on where we wish to go, but as a rule the places that we understand the least are those that map the greatest interpretive opportunities.[13] Let us begin with the colonoware—coarse-bodied, low-fired earthenware associated with both African American and Native American potting traditions—excavated from Charleston archaeological sites.

In a city and countryside defined in the eighteenth and early nineteenth centuries by its extraordinary consumption of refined body earthenware, European and Asian porcelains, and decoratively etched glassware, colonoware stands out for its associations with coastal Carolina's African American and Native American peoples.[14] Colonoware is a hand-molded earthenware ranging from gray to tan in color. Although early scholarship first assigned colonoware production to Native Americans who traded the vessels to European settlers from Maryland to Georgia, more recent work, especially that of archaeologists, places many of these wares in a West African craft tradition imported into the American colonies by enslaved Africans.[15] Brian Crane extends the origins of the colonoware tradition into Caribbean contexts but focuses, like most archaeologists, on the predominantly African American associations—in terms of both production and use—that describe the colonoware tradition.[16] Archaeologists also speculate that colonoware pots were important to the preparation of certain African American foods, concoction of herbal medicines, and practice of religious rituals.[17]

Historical archaeologists working in South Carolina recognize two, sometimes three, categories of colonoware.[18] "Yaughan" describes colonoware that is typically thick bodied with a dull surface ranging in color from burnt browns to deep irregular grays. Yaughan vessels include a variety of globular shaped pots that appear to have served a variety of storage and cooking functions. "Lesesne Lustered" designates an intermediate category in which the vessels tend to be slightly more delicate with burnished surfaces in a color range that includes darker browns and tans as well as the grays of Yaughan colonoware. The differences between Yaughan and Lesesne Lustered and the third category of "River Burnished" colonoware are more pronounced. River Burnished comprises a category of colonoware ceramics that is fired to a greater hardness, thinner walled, highly buffed, and occasionally decorated. River Burnished ware also represents the category of colonoware that most often appropriates European vessel forms into its own distinctive tradition. These wares represent a ceramic tradition that may have the closest ties with Catawba Native American ware produced in the Carolina backcountry, carried to Charleston, and sold or bartered to city residents—both black and white.

The only seeming certainties about the colonoware archaeologically recovered from Charleston sites begin with the observation that colonoware forms on average 5 percent of the ceramic assemblages recovered from city archaeological sites.[19] The height of colonoware production appears to date from the late eighteenth through the early nineteenth centuries. Archaeologists observe that although colonoware was most likely produced away from Charleston's urban environment, it still constituted lowcountry products.[20] The conclusion shared by archaeologists is that colonoware with its strong African and African American associations flourished in a landscape ostensibly dominated by the political, economic, and social culture of white plantation owners. Not only did the production and use of colonoware thrive in an environment ambivalent and even hostile to the maintenance of African traditions, but so too did its exchange in city and plantation marketplaces.

What, then, is the motive and market for colonoware, and how does it define urban space? Two interpretations suggest themselves, both of which are equally viable and both of which compromise an asserted cultural authority ascribed to genteel Euro-American taste and power. Consider a shattered River Burnished pitcher recovered from a privy that stood adjacent to the kitchen quarter and behind an eighteenth-century Church Street town house (see figure 1). The pitcher's shards were found with a mass of English manufactured ceramic dishes, mugs, chamber pots, and other pottery vessels as well as a wealth of bottles and table glass. The archaeological context of discovery immediately blurs social and cultural categories. The privy straddled the domestic spheres of both city quarter and dwelling, and its ceramic contexts easily reflect the two possibilities. However, we need to set the pitcher in motion, placing it in the worlds of both masters and servants.

The appropriation of Euro-American ceramic forms through African and Native American technologies, ornament, and use into the precincts of the town house quarter speaks not only to the strength of African traditions in repressive environments but also to the ways in which African American Charlestonians were able to critique the world of Euro-American manners. As a container, possibly used for mixing and dispensing African medicines, the pitcher became a prominent fixture in the maintenance of African traditions and identity. However, the pitcher can also be placed in the master's and mistress's house. The

FIG. 1. Colonoware. Courtesy of Collections of the Charleston Museum, Charleston, South Carolina

Euro-American fascination with natural and cultural exotica was very much a part of late eighteenth-century households, not only in Charleston but throughout the North Atlantic rim.[21] Silver-inlaid coconut cups, gold-mounted ostrich eggs, and cowry shell snuff boxes were objects that imported "foreign" cultures into the polite precincts of the house and symbolized the ability to contain and domesticate the exotic. Perched on a parlor mantelpiece or lodged in a specimen cabinet, the pitcher affirmed a particular sense of cultural authority. Still, even as elites presumed possession, they missed the point that River Burnished colonoware was intended by its makers for exchange and represented on one level a thoughtful and critical reading of "white" desire. Thus, the possible histories represented by this colonoware pitcher are open-ended. The object possesses no fixed meanings both because of and despite its archaeological associations with a particular time and place. The pitcher opens up a world where individuals employed all sorts of objects in the constant negotiation of their everyday lives. In this sense, colonoware achieves its greatest resonance in the ambiguities its possible readings create. Like a poem, it communicates before it is understood.

If ambiguity creates the slippage that enables us to invest multiple meanings in the colono pottery of Charleston, where do we find the lyric nature of space? Colonoware achieves its critical authority through its ability to colonize the historical imagination; it existed (and continues to exist) in very real circumstances that we know only through archaeological remains. In the absence of functional certainties colonoware offers a semiotic looseness. What we tend to lose sight of, though, is the fact that colonoware (and by extension all objects) defines architectural spaces through practice. This is where the notion of comportment in the material world comes into play. Comportment denotes the visual, spatial, and mental relationships that people perceive, construct, and experience between buildings, settings, objects, and selves.[22] Comportment is about the ways in which people stand in relationship to one another and the worlds they inhabit. Comportment may be thought of as an evocation of the etiquette of everyday life. Because the idea of comportment stems from relationships, it scrutinizes the interstices between objects and people. Thus, comportment is about the perceptual and performative spaces that join and divide experience.[23] The colonoware recovered from a number of excavated features at 14 Legare Street (better known as the Pineapple Gate House) gets at the process of comportment and its interstitial nature, its *in-betweenness.* The nature of the problem (and of our assumptions), however, crystallizes around a single feature, number 226—the remains of what was apparently a trash pile.[24]

Before the construction of the present house in the early 1800s, 14 Legare Street was an empty lot attached to the Miles Brewton house at 46 King Street and was separated from it by a low, marshy area. Through a series of property acquisitions, new surveys, and lot clearances, the plot at 14 Legare Street was developed and furnished with a large neoclassically inspired Charleston single house. The site history prior to the house, however, is where we begin. The back lot apparently provided a meeting place and social refuge for enslaved African Americans associated with 46 King Street. It was also a dump for household debris associated with the mansion on King Street (see figure 2). Both functions are recorded in the ceramics discarded on the site.

The trash pile behind 46 King Street contained not only colonoware but also an array of European refined body earthenware, porcelain, table glass, bottles, oyster shell, and bones recording a diet that included beef, pork, and mutton. A wine bottle bearing the seal "Mbrewton" and a button monogrammed "JB" link the debris to the great house across the marshy slough. The volume and diversity of ceramics and other artifacts are standard for later eighteenth-century urban sites. Yet we tend to miss a central point of this mass of artifactual evidence. As Martha Zierden notes, the trash deposition could have come into being for any number of reasons—for example, cleaning the yard of 46 King Street between owners or following the British occupation of the city. What is clear is that the physical objects within the trash pile are inextricably bound together in earth and time. When we segregate the colonoware from the blue decorated delft bowls or Chinese export porcelain saucer that accompanied it into the ground, we commit a crime of certainty—we presume a kind of material discretion at work in the world, and we perpetuate unstated assumptions and reified structures of cultural power. The only certainty we possess, in fact, is that all of these objects

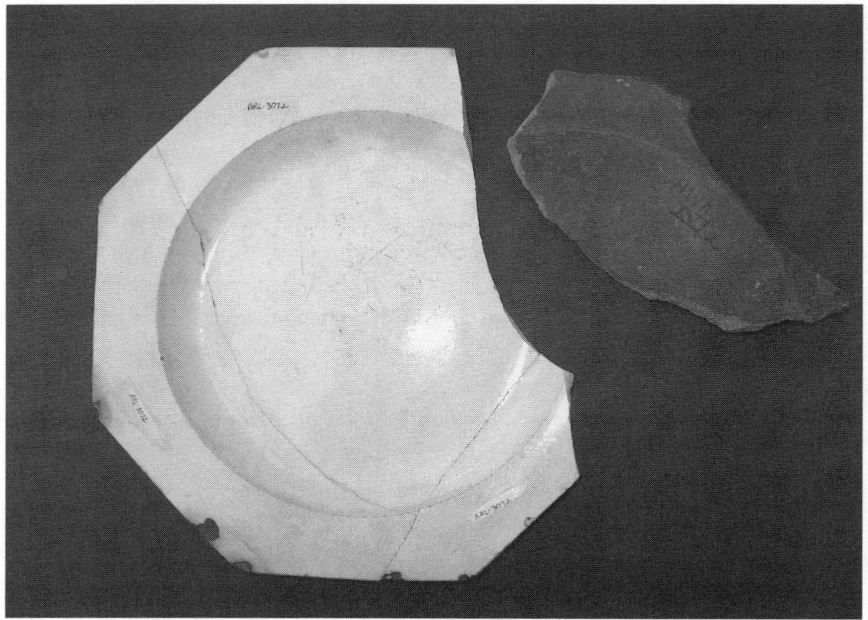

Fig. 2. Comparative samples of colonoware and imported ceramics. Courtesy of Collections of the Charleston Museum, Charleston, South Carolina

coexisted and were gathered together, discarded on the ground as rubbish, and preserved in an archaeological feature.

The jumble of ceramic forms in the trash pile at 14 Legare Street creates a critical space between things, a crevice that enables us to peer into and eavesdrop on the cadences of other aspects of Charleston city life. Consider an account of a dining room penned by Timothy Ford in the 1780s: "one or more servants (in many places) plant themselves in the corners of the room where they stand & upon the slightest occasion they are called. . . . At dinner it wd Seem as if the appetite were to be whetted & the victuals receive it's relish in proportion to the number in attendance. They surround the table like a cohort of black guards & here it appears there is a superfluity; for no sooner is a call made than there is a considerable delay either from all rushing at once; or all waiting for one another to do the business."[25] Or reflect on Billy Robinson's defense during his trial for complicity in the Denmark Vesey conspiracy of 1822. Billy Robinson argued his innocence from the position that, because he lived in a world of white surveillance, he could not have conspired as charged. Four white witnesses supported his defense only to see it undone by an alleged coconspirator and Billy Robinson exiled from South Carolina for life with the added penalty of death should he attempt to return. What makes these occasions significant is that they describe worlds where boundaries are routinely transgressed. Urban space "is a state of mind as much as a particular place"; it is the "domain of aesthetic contention."[26]

How, then, does a colonoware vessel reveal a poetics of urban space? In its telling. A poetics of urban space relies for its composition on the ambiguities and lyricism intrinsic to the people, buildings, streets, and objects that populate and define the city. The poetical city is, in turn, the "exemplary poem" that "carries its own encoded instructions, enacting its subject, pointing to its own operation." Like Edward Hirsch's definition of a poem, the poetical city "enacts what it is about," it is "a made thing that indicates the nature of its own making." Interpreting the materiality of the poetical city, engaging its sensuousness, its projective voice, its transgressive nature—that is our task.

Notes

I am indebted to David Shields, Martha Zierden, Maurie McInnis, David Brody, and Fredrika Jacobs for their help and insightful comments. Martha Zierden has been a great friend and an invaluable colleague, freely sharing field data and her rich store of knowledge on the archaeology of Charleston.

1. Charles Olson, "Olson Letter 4," in Peter Anastas, ed., *Charles Olson: Maximus to Gloucester; The Letters and Poems of Charles Olson to the Editor of the Gloucester Daily Times, 1962–1969* (Gloucester: Ten Pound Island Books, 1992), 93.

2. Edward Hirsch, *How to Read a Poem: And Fall in Love with Poetry* (New York: Harcourt Brace and Co., 1999), 31.

3. Italo Calvino, *Invisible Cities,* trans. William Weaver (New York: Harcourt Brace Jovanovich, 1972), 135–36.

4. Dell Upton, "Ethnicity, Authenticity, and Invented Traditions," *Historical Archaeology* 30, no. 2 (1996): 1–7.

5. Susan Stewart, "Lyric Possession," *Critical Inquiry* 22, no. 1 (Autumn 1995): 34–63.

6. Michel de Certeau, *The Practice of Everyday Life* (Berkeley: University of California Press, 1984); Erving Goffman, *The Presentation of Self in Everyday Life* (New York: Doubleday Anchor Books, 1959).

7. Charles Olson, "Projective Verse," in Olson, *Selected Writings of Charles Olson,* ed. Robert Creeley (New York: New Directions, 1966), 15–30; Peter Jukes, *A Shout in the Street: An Excursion into the Modern City* (Berkeley: University of California Press, 1991), 159–75.

8. Charles Olson, *Proprioception* (San Francisco: Four Seasons Foundation, 1965), 1.

9. Charles Olson, *Maximus Poems* (London: Cape Goliard Press, 1960), n.p.

10. Robert Plant Armstrong, *The Affecting Presence: An Essay in Humanistic Anthropology* (Urbana: University of Illinois Press, 1971), 4.

11. Ibid., 4–5. For debates on this relationship, see Michael Owen Jones, *The Hand Made Object and Its Maker* (Los Angeles: University of California Press, 1975), 202–42; Henry Glassie, *Material Culture* (Bloomington: Indiana University Press, 1999), 120–26.

12. David S. Shields, *Civil Tongues and Polite Letters in British America* (Chapel Hill: University of North Carolina Press for the Institute for Early American History and Culture, 1997), xvi–ix; Max Beicher, Svend Holsoe, and Bernard L. Herman, *A Land and Life Remembered: Americo-Liberian Folk Architecture* (Athens: University of Georgia Press, 1988), 127–29.

13. Michel Foucault, ed., *I, Pierre Riviere, Having Slaughtered My Mother, My Sister, and My Brother . . .: A Case of Parricide in the Nineteenth Century,* trans. Frank Jellinek (Lincoln: University of Nebraska Press, 1975), 269–73.

14. A useful summary of colonoware appears in Nicole Isenbarger, "Analysis of Colonoware in the Eighteenth Century Deposits," in Martha A. Zierden, *Excavations at 14 Legare Street, Charleston, South Carolina,* archaeological contribution no. 28 (Charleston, S.C.: Charleston Museum, 2001), 8:14–25.

15. Leland G. Ferguson, *Uncommon Ground: Archaeology and Early Africa America, 1650–1800* (Washington, D.C.: Smithsonian Institution Press, 1992), 18–32, 82–107, 110–16; Theresa A. Singleton, "The Archaeology of Slave Life," in *Before Freedom Came: African-American Life in the Antebellum South,* ed. Edward D. C. Campbell Jr. and Kym S. Rice (Richmond: University Press of Virginia for the Museum of the Confederacy, 1991), 159–6l. See also James Deetz, *In Small Things Forgotten: The Archaeology of Early American Life* (Garden City, N.Y.: Anchor Press / Doubleday, 1977), 138–54.

16. Brian Crane, "Suffered to Cook, Bake . . . and Otherwise Traffic . . . in the Public Markets and Streets of Charlestown': Colon Wares and Trade in Colonial South Carolina" (paper presented at the annual meeting of the Society for Historical Archaeology, Kansas City, Mo., 1993).

17. Ferguson, *Uncommon Ground,* 82–107.

18. Isenbarger, "Analysis of Colonoware," 8:17–19.

19. Martha A. Zierden, personal communication with author.

20. Crane, "Suffered to Cook"; Isenbarger, "Analysis of Colonoware," 8:15–16.

21. For an overview on the origins for concepts of collecting and curiosities, see Lorraine Daston and Katharine Parks, *Wonders and the Order of Nature, 1150–1750* (New York: Zone Books, 1998). For a discussion on the relationship between the exotic and the construction of the primitive, see Mark Antliff and Patricia Leighten, "Primitive," in *Critical Terms for Art History,* ed. Robert S. Nelson and Richard Shiff (Chicago: University of Chicago Press, 1996), 170–84; Marianna Torgovnik, *Gone Primitive: Savage Intellects. Modern Lives* (Chicago: University of Chicago Press, 1990), 3–41.

22. For a parallel discussion of comportment as a strategy for the interpretation of material culture, see Bernard L. Herman, *The Stolen House* (Charlottesville: University Press of Virginia, 1992), 9–10, 54–55. The idea of comportment draws on an extended discussion of context in material culture. See Ian Hodder, *Reading the Past: Current Approaches to Interpretation in Archaeology,* 2d ed. (Cambridge: Cambridge University Press, 1991), 121–55; Henry Glassie, "Studying Material Culture Today," in *Living in a Material World: Canadian and American Approaches to Material Culture,* ed. Gerald L. Pocius (St. John's: Institute of Social and Economic Research, Memorial University of Newfoundland, 1991), 253–66; Lu Ann De Cunzo, "Introduction: People, Material Culture, Context, and Culture in Historical Archaeology," in *Historical Archaeology and the Study of American*

Culture, ed. Lu Ann De Cunzo and Bernard L. Herman (Winterthur: Henry Francis du Pont Winterthur Museum, 1996), 1–17. This idea owes much to Upton's discussion of style and mode in *Holy Things and Profane,* 101–2, which in turn draws on Basil Bernstein's formulation of restricted and elaborated codes in *Class, Codes, and Control: Theoretical Studies towards a Sociology of Language* (New York: Schocken Books, 1975), 125–30.

23. Herman, *The Stolen House,* 9–10, 54–55.

24. Zierden, *Excavations at* 14 *Legare Street,* 3:1–59.

25. Timothy Ford, "Diary of Timothy Ford, 1785–1786," ed. Joseph W. Barnwell, *SCHM* 13, no. 3 (July 1912): 142–43.

26. Jukes, *Shout in the Street,* xv, xvii.

Building Charleston

The Expansion of an Eighteenth-Century British Atlantic Town

Emma Hart

Colonial American towns experienced significant expansion during the seventeenth and eighteenth centuries. Boston, New York, Philadelphia, and later Baltimore all grew from villages with a few hundred residents to bustling port cities with populations of thousands in the space of only a hundred years. The rate of growth in these early towns was nothing short of spectacular, and soon they were among the twenty largest cities in the eighteenth-century British Atlantic world, even exceeding English towns such as Sheffield, Portsmouth, and Leeds in size by midcentury.[1] In addition to being impressive, this urban growth was important. Growing towns reflected and fostered increases in trade; they nurtured industrial and consumer revolution; and they played host to new intellectual and leisure pursuits. As scholars of both Britain and America in the eighteenth century have shown, the expanding town was a pivotal site for understanding many of the changes that occurred in the eighteenth-century Anglophone world.[2]

Charleston was no exception to this growth trend. By the 1770s the lowcountry town had been transformed from an unstable village of only one thousand people in circa 1690 into a mature settlement with over twelve thousand residents. In a little over eighty years a disease- and fire-ravaged outpost had become the fourth-largest town in colonial America and a major player in the British Empire with a social scene, public buildings, harbor, and private mansions to match. As two familiar maps of the city show, the "Grand Modell," the initial grid plan laid out by the proprietors in 1672, was rapidly extended, with creeks and marshland drained and laid out so that by 1788 virtually the entire eastern tip of the peninsula had been brought under control by settlers.

Charleston's expansion has as much to tell us about the lowcountry as the growth of places such as Philadelphia and Liverpool has revealed about Pennsylvania and northwest England, respectively.[3] Indeed, scholars have already pointed out some significant implications of Charleston's rise. We know, for example, that increasing slave and free-black domination of the town's market reveals much about the position that some African Americans had carved out for themselves in the lowcountry. Likewise, Robert Olwell has shown that the planter-assemblymen who commissioned and financed the town's grand public landmarks used such edifices to display and assert their power over the city and the region.[4] However, as a result of these observations, Charleston has become an urban anomaly, often ignored in more general discussions of the early American town. Whereas other places are perceived to have had increasingly lively domestic economies and wide-ranging cultural scenes, Charleston's development in both of these areas is thought to have been stunted by a cultural hegemony of the elite and a staple economy. As a town, Charleston has become stranded in a lonely southern colonial world.[5]

However, just as the Exchange and the planter's mansion have turned Charleston into an anomaly, so were they anomalous within the contemporary urban landscape. For sure, buildings such as St. Michael's Church were prominent, important landmarks, but they occupied only small corners of the town. On the whole, the streets were lined by a far more mundane assortment of houses, shops, tenements, stables, and outbuildings—buildings that almost exclusively crowded Charleston's many back alleys and lanes. Recent scholarship has drawn more attention to this variety of structures that made up the city. In particular, the careful research undertaken by Jonathan Poston and the Historic Charleston Foundation has introduced us to some key features of privately sponsored urban growth—namely, the activities of major urban landowners and developers such as Christopher Gadsden, George Anson, and Daniel Cannon.[6] However, streetscapes—the bulk of the town—still have a lot more to tell us about Charleston and the lowcountry. Perhaps, by looking at the way in which Charleston's more usual spaces were developed, we can find ways in which the city was not so unusual after all.[7] By uncovering who was responsible for the town's physical development, along with the methods they used to further this expansion, we can start to understand better where the town fit into a British colonial urban scheme. What is more, through an understanding of who owned and controlled the town's everyday spaces, we can also obtain a new perspective on the structure of lowcountry society as a whole.

Constructing an eighteenth-century townscape from scratch involved three key processes. These processes promoted urban expansion throughout the eighteenth-century (and present-day) Anglophone world, and they comprised the purchase of land, the financing of its development with buildings, and the actual process of construction. Focusing on these phases of growth can discern who bought, sold, and owned land as well as who built and owned the houses, shops, and warehouses that constituted the built environment. Thus, rather than looking for stylistic trends of the buildings themselves, analysis will concentrate instead on ownership patterns and their implications for the development of the townscape as a whole.

Although buying land and building on it were central to Charleston's expansion, other forces prevailed upon the settlers who engaged in these processes. The first of these was the Grand Modell, a grid plan that had been laid out by the original proprietors in 1680. This model's grid plan was followed as streets extended further to the south and west, with settlers also using its lot division and numbering to describe town land throughout the eighteenth century. Indeed, it was not until the last quarter of this century that increasingly complicated plot division and ownership patterns ended reliance on the model's lot numbers.

Because of its hold on the overall form of Charleston, the Grand Modell was crucial to the town's development. The model was also important in that it had been laid out on what Europeans considered to be virgin land. This situation lay in direct contrast to the Old World, where town lands were controlled by a smaller, and more elite, group of society. These ancient ownership patterns meant that newly monied men in Britain would often find it hard to buy a central piece of city property outright, as the title was simply not up for sale. If men wished to invest their money in speculative building schemes, they further found themselves bound by the wishes of aristocratic or corporate landowners, who often worked with the promoters and developers of their choice to build up town lands according to their wishes. Even in towns such as Bristol and Hull, where aristocracy and corporations owned little land, development by smallholders was still limited to the edge of long-established town centers.[8] However, this situation hardly ever arose in the first decades of Charleston's history, with price the only barrier to the permanent ownership of any piece of land anywhere in the city. Overall, the Charleston land market privileged the rights of the individual, independent landowner to a far greater extent than was possible in the Old World town.

These ownership advantages also extended to the legal methods used to convey land between buyer and seller. The vast majority of Charleston transactions involved sale by "lease and release," meaning that a lot was leased to the buyer for a year, after which the title passed to him in perpetuity. This type of title was an inheritance from English common law, but its popularity in the purchase of urban lands in Charleston was somewhat unique. Because of the aforementioned ownership patterns, English urban land that was sold, especially in London and Liverpool, was sold only on a leasehold/building lease—often for a ninety-nine-year period. Overall only 50 percent of urban land was available for purchase on a freehold title, and the remainder still ultimately belonged to its ancient owner. However, when Charleston landowners bought a plot, they could do what they liked with it, free of annual rents, stringent landowner restrictions about how the property should be used, or standards to which new buildings should conform.[9] Therefore, development of Charleston's lots rested to a great extent with the individual, his building plans, or his decisions about how else he might use or divide the plot.

Hence, before Charleston had even begun to expand, it was already destined to develop as a British American town. Although its freehold lands and spacious grid plan lay in stark contrast to the layers of ownership rights and medieval streets of the English town, the English common law still dictated what kind of property title owners would hold. In addition, the emerging principles of classical urban planning had influenced the South Carolina proprietors as they carefully marked out their broad, majestic streets. How did this balanced inheritance influence the actual development of the town when it came to buying, investing, and developing these lands?

Between 1680 and 1783 pieces of land in Charleston changed hands hundreds, if not thousands, of times. Original Grand Modell lots were subdivided and sold off in sections, and developers laid out new streets in the southwest of the town. Because of this large number of surviving transaction records, a sample consisting of the deeds recorded between 1767 and 1773 has been selected for analysis. The 189 deeds included suggest that while property ownership was the preserve of the one-fourth of settlers who were free white males, among those who could legally buy town lands, a wide variety did so.[10] The profile of urban land buyers in table 1 below reveals that Charleston lots were mostly traded among artisans, service workers, and merchants, with planters showing a much lower level of interest in the town's land market. Thus, it would appear that although planters spent significant periods in Charleston socializing, actual ownership of the urban landscape was the preserve of settlers who lived and worked in the town all year round—the people who were, in the Old World, the traditional town dwellers. Moreover, information gathered by Poston in *The Buildings of Charleston* suggests that those who bought and sold land also formed the majority of those who owned it. In a survey of the builders or owners of almost 160 surviving residential properties in the heart of the eighteenth-century town, merchants and artisans were again in the majority, with 50 percent of houses constructed and owned by artisans, 40 percent by merchants, and only 10 percent by planters.[11]

This notably high level of merchant and artisan interest in urban land also manifested itself in some of Charleston's major eighteenth-century speculative developments. Two particularly notable schemes were those initiated by Daniel Cannon and Henry Laurens. Both in the laying out of the village of Hampstead by Henry Laurens and in the founding of Cannonborough by Daniel Cannon, the money and initiative of the city's craftsmen and merchants proved to be especially important.

Stated Occupations of Parties in Conveyances of Charleston Lands, 1767–73

	SELLERS	BUYERS
Craftsmen/Service Workers	70	83
Merchants	45	40
Planters	31	24
Professionals	17	13
Gentlemen/Esquires	16	15
Women and Spinsters	7	10
Unknown	3	4
TOTAL	189	189

Source: Clara A. Langley, *South Carolina Deed Abstracts, 1767–1773* (Greenville, S.C.: Southern Historical Press, 1983).

The contractor and carpenter Daniel Cannon was one of Charleston's wealthiest artisans, spending his entire working life in the city until his death in 1802. He was also one of the town's more substantial urban property holders, with about forty-five land transactions to his name. Cannon bought or sold city property throughout the eighteenth century and, in his capacity as churchwarden, was also responsible for the development of the St. Philip's Parish glebe land on Coming Street. Many of Cannon's private transactions involved land in the town center, but a large number were associated with his most ambitious enterprise, the development of the suburban Cannonborough tract. Cannonborough was most likely laid out in lots around 1794, as the first land was sold in 1795. By the time of his death, Cannon had managed to sell about half of the seventy lots he had planned. With their location at the city boundary, the lots were relatively cheap, and most of them seem to have been sold to their first owners for about one hundred pounds sterling. These initial landholders, many of whom put up houses or workshops on their property, were mostly artisans; they included a harness maker, metalworkers, carpenters, butchers, and a free black man named John Sheppard. Other buyers were merchants, such as Thomas Doughty, who bought a number of lots, thus continuing on a smaller scale the speculative process that Cannon had started. Doughty's investment turned out to be a good one, as the antebellum era saw Cannonborough transformed from a lower-class district to a suburb that contained the mansions of many of the lowcountry's wealthiest planters.[12]

A high level of artisanal and merchant participation is also evident in Henry Laurens's Hampstead development. The original plat of this suburban project dates from 1769, and it included 140 lots, some complete with wharves and access to Stone Creek, an inlet that flowed into the Cooper River. Laurens financed the venture by selling bonds to a group of twenty-one local investors made up of nine artisans, eight merchants, and four planters. In September 1770 Laurens sold a half-share in his venture to the merchant William Bampfield, making him the holder of the largest number of lots. However, most of the other lot owners were artisans. These craftsmen consisted of buyers who had originally put money into the scheme or others, such as the upholsterer Edward Weyman and his Fellowship Society, who had bought land soon after Laurens put it on the market. Subsequent transactions of lots suggest that artisans continued to sink their money into the scheme. The painter George Flagg added a lot to his already substantial downtown holdings, and other carpenters and bricklayers working in Charleston in the last part of the century bought and sold village land. Some, such as the gardener Charles Gross and the carpenter Betje Hendrickson, even developed their lots with tenements and houses to rent.[13] Although Laurens's scheme does not seem to have been a great success, with only 68 of the 140 lots sold during his lifetime, it is clear that of the land that was sold, most went to the merchants and artisans of Charleston.

Investigating these urban land transactions and speculative projects has already revealed some key characteristics of landownership in Charleston. First, lots were more likely to be bought and owned by merchants and artisans than they were by planters. Outside of their mansions and churches, therefore, planters could claim less influence over the shape of the town because, unlike their elite British contemporaries, they had no historic claims on the land. However, these ownership patterns also suggest that, as in other British and American towns of the period, Charleston was home to a distinct group of urbanites, who not only lived and worked in the city but also chose to invest in it using customary tools of speculative development.[14] Thus, at the first stage in the process of expansion, colonial and British, but not southern, influences played important roles.

However, in a town, land is usually only the foundation for a building. It was only a matter of time before lots in the center of Charleston became cluttered with all sorts of buildings. Yet we still do not really know who financed and constructed this assortment of houses, tenements, warehouses, kitchens, workshops, and stables. Again, land records can provide a window into the methods used by settlers to build houses. First, these records reveal that Charlestonians used building leases to construct houses. These agreements, deployed widely by developers in the growing towns of Britain, permitted the owner of a property to let it out to a builder on the understanding that the latter would develop the plot and receive any profits from his efforts until the lease was up. One of the earliest such agreements was between the carpenter John Vaun and Francis Guichard, "clerk pastor of the Church of French Protestants." Taking a fifty-year lease on a city lot at a yearly ground rent of £10.4.0, Vaun agreed to "erect and build upon the said part of the said lot . . . a good firm and substantial brick house of good materials and of at least fifteen feet in front" and to keep it in good repair.[15] A year later, having built the required house and two additional tenements, Vaun advertised the properties for let, expecting that they would be "entirely suitable for a carpenter or a private family."[16]

Later documents show building leases to have been a means of urban development after the Revolution as well. At a meeting of the College of Charleston's board of trustees in 1786, the committee elected to let out the city land it owned on "repairing leases" for seven years, with a view to improving the value and profitability of the tenements thereon.[17] Similarly, in 1789 Greenhill and Morrison, a partnership of house carpenters, signed an agreement with Miss Amarinthea Elliott of Charleston to build a house on Legare Street. The document was specifically termed a "building lease" from Elliott to the builders.[18] What followed was a contract that still used established English custom as a template but, as with the college's agreement, established a limited lease for less than ten years.[19] Furthermore, at the end of the stipulated nine-year period, Amarinthea Elliott was to decide whether she would pay a "fair value" for the house or rent it out, with all rents going to Morrison and Greenhill until it was paid for. Clearly, this shorter type of contract was still financially beneficial to both parties. The carpenters, who obtained land that they could build on, were assured of payment for the house and could offset their building costs with the rents they might obtain during the nine years of their lease. Elliott, meanwhile, had the ground rent and city taxes paid on her property for nine years, a period after which she would own a lot improved with a new house. An adapted form of the building lease was deployed by others, such as the merchant Christopher Gadsden, who in 1769 divided up his town lands into lots and put them up for private sale. Although purchasers bought by lease and release, they nonetheless had to "promise to improve [the lots] within a year or eighteen months." However, buyers would be assisted by Gadsden as he would allow them to "have their timber, bricks, lime and other materials for building said lots, landed at either of his wharves . . . FREE OF CHARGE."[20]

Rather than hand responsibility for development over to someone else, a second group of urban landowners chose to supervise the development of their lots themselves, often then selling off the completed houses and plots. A significant number of landowners undertook these small-scale speculations. Two such developers were the block maker Barnard Beekman and the blacksmith Tunis Tebout, who in 1761 laid out £5,010 S.C. currency for a prime lot on Bay Street. A few months later the two craftsmen were able to sell the estate, complete with the "now erected long brick building containing many shops and stores" to the merchant Benjamin Smith for £10,000.[21] Even in the less prosperous post-Revolutionary years, Charlestonians still bought, developed, and sold lots in similarly short periods of time. The modest lot on the edge of town purchased by the house carpenter Gilbert Chalmers for £2,800 in May 1796 realized £4,200 a few months later, when the grocer John Gennerick bought it complete with its new wooden buildings.[22]

Some town landowners took out mortgages and used them to sponsor house construction on a larger scale. One of the clearest examples of this practice was the activity of Robert Deans, a house carpenter and general contractor who came to Charleston from Scotland in about 1750. Deans started out by buying an acre of land, lots 119 and 120, on Queen Street. To pay for the land, Deans took out a mortgage for £1,400 of its value with the seller Thomas Boone. In 1763, once the original sum had been paid off, Deans remortgaged the property to the merchant Thomas Buckle, this time for £5,000. This second loan was almost certainly taken out by the carpenter to fund the development of his property because when the silversmith Alexander Petrie took over the management of the lots for Deans (who was visiting Scotland) in late 1764, they were known as "Deans' Square." Petrie was commanded to "view and examine the condition of all real estate including houses, messuages, tenements, and hereditaments and to make necessary repairs . . . [and] collect due rents." During his management, Petrie was also allowed to sell the property if a profitable opportunity arose. Within the year the silversmith had managed to dispose of the development for a total of £10,100.[23]

Through the activities of men such as Petrie and Deans, homes and commercial premises became available to Charlestonians who needed space but did not wish to build themselves. However, some settlers did not wish to buy, and others could not afford to do so. Thus, a third group of urban dwellers chose to buy land, develop it, and then rent it out. Often these rental properties were erected with the goal of accommodating as many occupants as possible and were described as tenements by owners and renters alike. Records show that wealthy men, such as the planter Benjamin Huger, could own rows of tenements that were rented out to shopkeepers and artisans who could not afford their own homes. Henry Gray had similar holdings at the corner of Meeting and Guignard streets, "consisting of two tenements . . . having four good rooms and a large garret in each . . . is a corner house, high and pleasantly situated, has a good well, kitchen garden, stables, and chair house, for each tenement."[24] Charleston's major churches also owned similar properties, with both the St. Philip's vestry and the Congregationalists building blocks of tenements that were rented out to poorer citizens.

Records suggest, however, that the Charleston rental market extended beyond tenement housing to include all types of town properties. One of the most impressive property portfolios was that sold off by the merchant-planter Barnard Elliott in 1774. Elliott appears to have owned a house on the bay occupied by the businesses of a wine merchant and a printer, a large residential property on Queen Street, a smaller house on the same thoroughfare, a lot on which the town fire station stood, a retail shop, a barber's shop, a gunsmith's shop, and an inn.[25] What is more, Elliott was not unique in the level of his property holdings. In 1769 the silversmith John Paul Grimke advertised no fewer than four centrally located homes that would soon be available for rent: a "new-finished house . . . next to the Hon., Egerton Leigh Esq."; a "three-story brick house . . . next to Mr. Thomas Adam"; and also "two three-story brick houses . . . each with good cellars, garrets, a two-story brick kitchen, wash-room, coach-house, and stables for two horses."[26] The shipwright Thomas Rose's holdings almost matched those of Grimke; in 1782 he had a three-story brick house, two tenements, a wooden house, a brick house, and a wharf and store, all situated in town.[27] While not all Charlestonians owned as much property as these men did, there is evidence to suggest that less wealthy town dwellers also entered the rental market, though on a more modest scale. The shipwright George Noddings, for example, owned only one extra property, a "pleasant, airy, and commodious house on Trott's Point containing six good rooms . . . suitable for a private family," which he advertised for rent in 1771.[28]

Furthermore, renting appears to have been popular with Charlestonians from across the social and occupational spectrum. The large merchant firm of Faesch and Guerard rented a town house from the contractor Richard Moncrieff, and after the Revolution, Judge James Waties was a tenant of the builders Greenhill and Morrison.[29] One of the aforementioned tenements owned by Henry Gray was let out to the Reverend Mr. Martyn, and a Dr. Haley was the resident of Barnard Elliott's largest property. Indeed, by the end of the third quarter of the eighteenth century, renting had become so customary that some house sale advertisements included notes about the sums for which they usually rented. Barnard Elliott's holdings brought in an estimated £1,570 per annum in rent, and the silversmith Jonathan Sarrazin's house "usually let at £350 year"; his corner tenement on Broad Street, "if it was to let, would no doubt command a very great rent." The bricklayer Anthony Toomer was also keen to inform the public that his Archdale Street tenements, up for sale in 1773, "can be let for £350 per annum."[30]

Among Charlestonians who lived and worked in the town, the imperative of investing in housing was evidently as strong as the trend for buying urban lands. Why did so many town dwellers choose to focus their investment activities on the town and not the vast tracts of cheap rural land? Perhaps the most obvious reason would be the potential profitability of such a decision, as illustrated by the account book of the cabinetmaker Thomas Elfe, one of Charleston's best-known mechanics. Elfe operated on a grand scale. At the opening of accounts in 1768, he was in possession of five town properties: two houses and lots on Friend and Broad streets, a pair of tenements on Broad Street, a lot containing his shop on King Street, and an empty lot situated on Queen Street. For the entirety of this period Elfe rented his town home from the merchant and planter Othoniel Beale. Both the houses and tenements were rented out, and constant occupancy of all four properties meant that in the space of eight years they brought in a total of £8,720. Of course, this sum did not amount to a straight profit, as Elfe was frequently making repairs and improvements to his holdings. He spent small sums, usually under £40 for each job, installing pumps, drains, and wells; putting up fences; painting and glazing windows; and maintaining the brickwork. The cabinetmaker also undertook some larger improvement projects. He spent £551 on a new kitchen for the Broad Street tenements and £50 on a coach house adjacent to his workshop on King Street. However, Elfe was also interested in further increasing his holdings and, if possible, acquiring more rental properties. In 1773, after having made £3,750 from selling off a portion of his Queen Street lot, Elfe embarked on the construction of another house. The house, built by the local bricklayer Benjamin Baker, cost £1,979 and was completed at the beginning of 1774; by 1775 Elfe had increased his income by renting it out for £330 a year. In April 1774 the cabinetmaker made his last major investment of this period; he purchased a fifth rental property in the suburbs of Charleston and let it for £330. At the end of his accounts in late 1775, Elfe was receiving £660 more in rent a year and, despite substantial expenditure on his holdings, was £6,224 better off. Being a landlord in Charleston was a profitable business.[31]

Furthermore, it seems that some Charleston residents might have favored such holdings because they constituted future security for their families. When Elfe died, the properties meant that his wife and their four children could look forward to a secure financial future, free from the uncertainty that the loss of the main breadwinner might otherwise have brought. The widow Elfe was to live in the Broad Street house, daughter Hannah on Broad Street, son Thomas on Broad Street, son George on Friend Street, and son Benjamin on Queen Street. Furthermore, because not all of the children had yet reached their majority at their father's death, the rents from their future homes could be used for their support and education until they were married or working.[32]

Another artisan, the bricklayer Anthony Toomer, was engaged in developing a similarly substantial set of town holdings at his death in the 1790s. In his will Toomer instructed his executors to "compleat [the] buildings in Hazell Street according to the plan that is known to my family" and also "to improve the lands which I purchased of Mr. Cannon to the best of their judgment."[33] The Hazell Street property of Toomer is detailed in the plat drawn up shortly before the bricklayer's death; quite possibly this is the plan with which the deceased's family was familiar.[34] The plat illustrates a twenty-seven-thousand-square-foot holding situated on the edge of Charleston as it stood in the last quarter of the eighteenth century and divided up into seven developed lots. Descriptions of the buildings (to be) laid out on these lots suggest that Toomer was planning a substantial development. Each piece of land bore a "house three stories with cellars of brick and covered with slate roof, kitchen and washroom two stories with cellars of brick, covered with slate, stable and carriage house one story with lofts of brick covered with tiles." These properties were clearly destined for occupants of some wealth, who would be willing either to rent or to buy for a handsome sum, a sum that would support Toomer's widow and their sons well into the future.

Through investment in lots and buildings merchants and artisans, along with a small number of planters, became responsible for Charleston's expansion. At the heart of their activities lay English law, making for a town that had grown through the deployment of techniques common throughout the urban British Atlantic. However, although merchants and artisans were able to control urban land and property in the broadest sense, most did not have the skills to construct their houses themselves. Therefore, in order to complete this investigation of Charleston's eighteenth-century development, we need to know more about the people who provided the labor needed to build a house, a shop, or a warehouse. Who were the builders in eighteenth-century Charleston, how did they interact with their clients, and can the lowcountry building trade be compared to its Atlantic counterparts? Such questions are especially relevant as in the British eighteenth-century town changes in the ways that land was purchased and developed were accompanied by transformations in the relationships between builders of various trades and between artisans and their clients. In the first instance the building contractor, an artisan-cum-manager who directed a project, emerged as a common figure from the 1680s onward. [35] Also taking shape at this time was the role of architect; a function that could be performed by the contractor, the customer (or "gentleman-architect"), or both in collaboration.[36] Were Charleston's builders also experiencing these professionalization processes?

Although there were free as well as slave artisans working in early Charleston, research to date has suggested that skilled whites faced stiff competition from skilled blacks. However, the deployment of the building lease and the activities of building artisans such as Anthony Toomer and Daniel Cannon suggest that there were enough white mechanics to insure a transfer of knowledge and techniques from the Old World. Indeed, records have yielded details of over seven hundred free white bricklayers and carpenters who worked in eighteenth-century Charleston.[37] Some of these men were essential to the construction of two of Charleston's best-known pre-Revolutionary edifices, the Miles Brewton house and St. Michael's Church. Here the building contractors Richard Moncrieff and Samuel Cardy directed the works, managing slave labor as well as a variety of subcontractors appointed to complete brickwork, carving, and painting.[38] Such "prestige projects," however, differed greatly from the more mundane work that went into putting up a house or a store, not least because we would expect professional builders to be put in charge of churches and mansions. However, the evidence suggests that similar men played an important role in Charleston's smaller, private building activity as well.

Overall, the vast majority of Charleston house-building accounts include bills for work performed by white craftsmen. Moreover, it is clear that the types of functions fulfilled by these men did change as the eighteenth century progressed. In one of the earliest recorded instances of town tenement construction, the executors of the widow Elizabeth Sindrey took it upon themselves in 1712 to erect a number of houses and shops in Charleston. Labor for the project came from the indentured servants and slaves belonging to William Rhett, a family friend. The indentured carpenters Charles Crouch, Matthew Toole, and Charles Brewer were paid by the day for their work, which was undertaken alongside hired slaves, and performed according to the directions of the executors.[39] Such low reliance on free white artisans may partly have been a function of their scarcity in the town during the earliest part of the eighteenth century, a situation that persisted until after the fire of 1740.[40]

However, the building activities of Peter Manigault during the 1760s and 1770s betray a much higher reliance on the labor of white carpenters and bricklayers. Particularly illustrative of the growing reliance on free artisans was Manigault's reasoning behind an unusual decision to deploy his own slave bricklayers on the construction of a tenement. Writing to the future resident of the property, Daniel Blake, Manigault explained that he had "not employed Young about the brickwork, because he and Gordon never agree, but had put my own bricklayers to work." Clearly, a poor working relationship between the carpenter James Gordon and his contemporary Thomas Young while engaged on a previous contract for Manigault had persuaded him that it would be expeditious to give only one of them responsibility for this particular project. What is more, Manigault's logic suggests that he was a regular customer of these builders and that, while working for him, any decisions regarding the planning and management of his projects were the preserve of Gordon and Young.[41] The merchant's regular employment of white builders is underlined by a 1771 demand that a man pressed into military service should be released, as he was a "landsman carpenter" working on the construction of Manigault's new town house.[42] Manigault also recruited local craftsmen to work on the projects that he supervised on behalf of friends. In 1765 the merchant set about the construction of a substantial city house for the then-absent

Ralph Izard. Manigault took the lead in the overall design of the house and kept Izard abreast of the works with letters and plans of his future residence.[43] Having drawn up a ground plan and dabbled in the early phases of planning, however, Manigault handed over the project to the house carpenter and contractor Daniel Cannon, who managed the necessary labor and materials and saw the house through to its completion.[44]

This interaction between Manigault and Cannon in the construction of Izard's house is not only notable for the responsibility assigned to the white craftsman; it is also important because the building was realized by a contractor working with a drawn plan. Both of these characteristics indicate that as the century progressed, Charleston building custom did increasingly resemble similar practices that had been developing in Britain's cities. Manigault, a gentleman-architect, gave his instructions to Cannon, a general contractor, who then took on the responsibility of managing the work of free and slave craftsmen.

These roles, it seems, were not confined to Peter Manigault's construction ventures. A number of surviving building contracts from eighteenth-century Charleston suggest that this burgeoning role of building undertaker was so firmly rooted on both sides of the Atlantic as to have become customary in house construction in the colonial lowcountry. If a Charleston merchant or planter wanted to build, he would have to negotiate his terms with a professional. In 1750 Charles Pinckney had chosen to direct the building of a house himself. Having bought a city house and lot that were in a state of some disrepair, he called in the carpenter-contractor John Williams to manage this new project. Using a simple scale elevation and a sketch of the design to be implemented for a new Dutch dormer roof, Pinckney conveyed the outline of the proposed work to Williams. Pinckney supplemented this drawing with a written "memorandum of carpenter's work to be done." The memorandum, essentially a contract, contained many detailed demands. The doors on the first and second floors were required to have six panels, and the windows were to have plain window seats under them. However, the contract also left much to the imagination of Williams. The final design of the roof was to be "as shall be judged best," and although the stairs were to be built "without ramp or twist," the shape of the banisters was left open to interpretation. Furthermore, the memorandum closed with a formulaic statement often inserted into such contracts, namely that "the whole [should] be completed and finished in a workmanlike, handsome and substantial manner." Overall, it was the interplay of the gentleman's ideas with the craftsman's specialist knowledge and skill that produced even the most mundane of town rental properties. Although we have no way of knowing in what ways the finished house differed from Pinckney's original plan, the accompanying accounts show the carpenter Williams executing his commission with the authority of a contractor. He found all of the necessary materials for the job and organized the slave labor, presenting Pinckney with a bill for the project once it had been completed.[45]

Although Pinckney's memorandum is clear evidence that the role and responsibilities of a Charleston contractor precisely matched those of his English counterpart, it does not feature the legal requirements that came to be part of such agreements. In Charleston, as in Britain, the eighteenth century witnessed the introduction of procedures that ensured that both parties signing a building contract might have recourse in law should one of them fail to fulfill his obligations. The ubiquity of such contracts not only changed the relationship between craftsman and customers but also affected the way an artisan might receive remuneration for his work. Before the advent of the formal contract, the craftsman received a daily wage, or was paid according to the amount of house he had completed (by the measure). However, a third option was payment in the form of a lump sum, received in installments throughout the period of construction. In addition, as the role of the building undertaker became more widespread, so did the instances when a preagreed price was paid to this superintendent. Contemporaries termed this process "by the great."[46]

A number of Charleston contracts strongly suggest that these contractual changes also had an Atlantic resonance. One such document was drawn up in May 1770 between the bricklayers/carpenters Axson and Gaborial and the planter William Clay Snipes. With Thomas Lowder as their witness, Axson and Gaborial agreed that they should build a Charleston residence for Snipes "with outhouses and other appurtenances agreeable to a plan given in and signed by the said John Gaborial." The house was "to be finished in a compleat perfect workmanlike manner on or before 6th November 1770," with Axson and Gaborial receiving half of their £3,500 fee when the house was "inclosed" and the other half when it was completed. For their money, the partners undertook to provide "all the materials and workmanship" and to pay a penal sum of £500 if the building was not completed on time.[47] The agreement was clearly couched in formulaic terms, implying that its writing was a familiar process for the builders. Furthermore, this was a language that recurred throughout contemporary documents. The contractor Thomas Robinson noted that he had built a shed "as per agreement" for Luke Stoutenburgh, and Ann Middleton similarly recorded an "agreement with Andrew Gordon for building a house."[48]

By 1770 Charleston's builders were key players in the construction of urban properties. They were responsible both for the style of a house and the marshaling of the materials and labor necessary to its construction. Although in some cases the peculiarities of the local economy might encroach on the role of the building undertaker, as it would have been perceived in contemporary Britain, the essential developments in building practice had made it across the Atlantic.

This successful transplantation meant that, on the most basic level, the New World urban environment was being developed with the Old World tools of urban growth.

Plainly, there were some striking similarities in the ways that houses were built in Charleston and in the contemporary English town. At every stage of the development process—land purchase, construction, and building occupancy—Old World law and custom dictated the mode in which buyers and sellers functioned. Put simply, Charleston's settlers had created an urban land market similar to those that were to be found in many growing towns across Britain in the eighteenth century. Yet the tale of Charleston's expansion is not a straight retelling of an old story. In comparison to the mother country, a wider sector of the free, white, male population could claim a stake in their cityscape. These eclectic ownership patterns did not, however, result in a disorganized city, as development was carried out on the terms laid down by South Carolina's founders.

Finding such convergence in the methods used to build Charleston, and those deployed in the development of other towns across America and Britain, points to new ways in which early lowcountry society shared a British Atlantic world during the eighteenth century. There is no denying that with its huge slave population, hot climate, and palmetto-lined streets the town stood alone in several very important ways. However, in order to create the townscape that was home to these peculiarities, settlers had revealed their British inheritance. For sure, adaptations were made to this legacy, but they consisted more of adjustments to a colonial, rather than a southern, location. Therefore, in its very fabric, Charleston was first a British provincial town, second a colonial British American town, and only third a southern anomaly.

Notes

1. Gary Nash, "The Social Evolution of Preindustrial American Cities, 1700–1820: Reflections and New Directions," *Journal of Urban History* 13, no. 2 (1987): 117, table 1.

2. Among the most prominent works on this topic are Peter Borsay, *The English Urban Renaissance: Culture and Society in the Provincial Town, 1660–1770* (Oxford: Clarendon Press, 1989); Peter Borsay, ed., *The Eighteenth-Century Town: A Reader in English Urban History, 1688–1820* (London & New York: Longman, 1990); C. W. Chalklin, *The Provincial Towns of Georgian England: A Study of the Building Process, 1740–1820,* Studies in Urban History Series (London: Edward Arnold, 1974); P. J. Corfield, *The Impact of English Towns, 1700–1800* (Oxford: Oxford University Press, 1982); M. J. Daunton, "Towns and Economic Growth in 18th Century England," in *Towns in Societies: Essays in Economic History and Historical Sociology,* ed. P. Abrams and E. A. Wrigley (Cambridge: Cambridge University Press, 1978), 245–77; Peter Earle, *The Making of the English Middle Class: Business, Society and Family Life in London, 1660–1730* (Berkeley: University of California Press, 1990); Timothy Mowl, *To Build the Second City: Architects and Craftsmen of*

Georgian Bristol (London: Redcliffe Press, 1991); Jon Stobart, "An 18th Century Revolution? Urban Growth in North-West England, 1614–1801," *Urban History* 23 (May 1996): 26–47; R. A. Houston, *Social Change in the Age of Enlightenment: Edinburgh, 1660–1760* (Oxford: Clarendon Press, 1994).

3. Donna Rilling, *Making Houses, Crafting Capitalism: Builders in Philadelphia, 1790–1850* (Philadelphia: University of Pennsylvania Press, 2001); Paul Clemens, "The Rise of Liverpool, 1665–1750," *Economic History Review* 29, no. 2 (1976): 211–24; Chalklin, *Provincial Towns.*

4. Philip Morgan, "Black Life in Eighteenth-Century Charleston," in *Perspectives in American History,* n.s., 1, ed. Bernard Bailyn and Donald Fleming (Cambridge, 1984), 205; Robert Olwell, *Masters, Slaves, and Subjects: The Culture of Power in the South Carolina Lowcountry, 1740–1790* (Ithaca, N.Y.: Cornell University Press, 1998).

5. For the English story, see Borsay, *English Urban Renaissance.* American developments are best outlined by Gary Nash, *The Urban Crucible: Social Change, Political Consciousness, and the Origins of the American Revolution* (Cambridge, Mass.: Harvard University Press, 1979); Carl Bridenbaugh, *Cities in the Wilderness: The First Century of Urban Life in America, 1625–1742* (New York: Ronald Press, 1938); and Carl Bridenbaugh, *Cities in Revolt: Urban Life in America, 1743–1776* (New York: Oxford University Press, 1955). Charleston appears especially unusual in Richard Waterhouse, "The Development of Elite Culture in the Colonial American South: A Study of Charles Town," *Australian Journal of Politics and History* 28 (1982): 391–404; and Olwell, *Masters, Slaves, and Subjects.*

6. Jonathan H. Poston for the Historic Charleston Foundation, *The Buildings of Charleston: A Guide to the City's Architecture* (Columbia: University of South Carolina Press, 1997), 197.

7. In particular, work on the construction of cities in early America and Britain provides an excellent context for our discussion. Donna Rilling's study of early national Philadelphia artisans in the building trades shows how America's first city was expanded by a group of entrepreneurial, capitalistic craftsmen who were willing to take financial risks in the name of speculative projects. Such practices would, of course, strike the historian of the eighteenth-century British city as familiar. As Chalklin and, more recently, Elizabeth McKellar have demonstrated, large- and small-scale speculation also lay at the heart of Old World urban growth during this period. See Rilling, *Making Houses;* Elizabeth McKellar, *The Birth of Modern London: The Development and Design of the City, 1660–1720* (Manchester: Palgrave, 1999); Chalklin, *Provincial Towns.*

8. Chalklin, *Provincial Towns.*

9. It should be noted that restrictions on building in Charleston did come in the form of an act of assembly that followed the disastrous 1740 fire. This act required "that all the out-side of all buildings hereafter to be erected . . . of brick or stone"; however, the current appearance of Charleston is telling of how little effect this regulation had in the long term. See "An Act for Regulating the Buildings Hereafter to Be Erected or Built in Charles-Town . . . ," *SCG,* December 18, 1740.

10. Significantly, some sales were recorded many years after the event. Therefore, although this is not a complete record of every city land sale, the sample has omitted sales on a fair basis.

11. Poston, *Buildings of Charleston,* 47–293. With regard to sale and ownership, one needs to take into account that planters could have owned large tracts of land that they chose never to sell, thus making them a force in the ownership of the town without showing up in land records. However, the patterns of ownership recorded in Poston make this unlikely.

12. For all transactions relating to Cannonborough, see Charleston County Register of Mesne Conveyance excerpts in the Index of Southern Artists and Artisans, Museum of Southern Decorative Arts, Winston-Salem, N.C.. The transformation of Cannonborough into a rich suburb is discussed in Poston, *Buildings of Charleston,* 617.

13. For an outline of the Hampstead scheme, including the original plat, see *The Papers of Henry Laurens,* vol. 7, ed. David R. Chesnutt (Columbia: University of South Carolina Press, 1979), 589–95, app. A.

14. A good frame of reference here might be the merchants of eighteenth-century Philadelphia. See Thomas Doerflinger, *A Vigorous Spirit of Enterprise: Merchants and Economic Development in Revolutionary Philadelphia* (Chapel Hill: University of North Carolina Press, 1986).

15. Charleston County Register of Mesne Conveyance, book NN, 389–94, October 1, 1742, agreement between Francis Guichard and John Vaun.

16. Advertisement of John Vaun, *SCG* (Charleston), March 5, 1743/44. A tenement usually referred to a property erected for rental. The tenement would usually be smaller than average and would probably be attached to its neighbors.

17. Board of trustees meeting of April 28, 1786, College of Charleston trustee minutes, vol. 1, 1785–1817, Special Collections of the Robert Small Library, College of Charleston.

18. The agreement is recorded in Charleston County Register of Mesne Conveyance, Land Records Miscellaneous, part 87, books R6–S6, 1796–98, 246–51, South Carolina Department of Archives and History [hereafter cited as SCDAH].

19. At least one other building lease from this post-Revolutionary period also ran for a seven-year period. See Charleston County Register of Mesne Conveyance, part 75, book Y5, 64–66, January 1, 1786, lease between George Ross and Robert Haig/Alexander Don, SCDAH.

20. Advertisement of Christopher Gadsden, *SCG,* July 6, 1769.

21. Charleston Register of Mesne Conveyance, part 35, book ZZ, 1761, 201, May 17, 1761, Barnard Elliot and Thomas Lamboll lease and release to Barnard Beekman and Tunis Thebout as tenants in common; and part 35, book ZZ, 216, June 10, 1761, Thebout and Beekman to Benjamin Smith Esquire, SCDAH.

22. Mesne Conveyances, part 87, book R6, 369, May 23, 1796; and ibid., 375, November 4, 1796, SCDAH. Chalmers advertised the real estate in the *Charleston Gazette and Daily Advertiser* in November 1796 as "a lot of land . . . at the corner of Boundary and King with all the buildings."

23. Land Records, part 32, book B3, 565, October 24, 1758; part 30, book WW, 526, February 6, 1759; part 32, book A3, 91, May 19, 1763; part 32, book B3, 316, March 28, 1764; part 33, book C3, 426, July 12, 1764; part 33, book C3, 545, December 18, 1764; part 34, book E3, 260, October 21, 1765, SCDAH.

24. Advertisement of Henry Gray, *SCG,* October 22, 1763.

25. Advertisement of Barnard Elliott, *South Carolina Gazette and Country Journal,* May 24, 1774.

26. Advertisement of John Paul Grimke, *SCG,* September 28, 1769.

27. Claims to the Loyalist Commission in the British Public Record Office, AO13, claim of John Rose Volume 132(2), reel 134, microfilm, Library of Congress.

28. Advertisement of George Noddings, *SCG,* July 11, 1771.

29. Entries for April and September 1758, William Ancrum Account Book and Letterbook; and Judge James Waties Papers, South Caroliniana Library, University of South Carolina, Columbia.

30. Advertisement for Jonathan Sarrazin's property, *South Carolina and American General Gazette,* September 18, 1777; advertisement of Anthony Toomer, *South Carolina Gazette and Country Journal,* January 26, 1773.

31. All figures derived from the Thomas Elfe Account Book, MSS, Charleston Library Society.

32. Will of Thomas Elfe, book B, 1776–84, 71, WPA transcripts, South Carolina Room, Charleston Public Library (hereafter cited as CPL).

33. Will of Anthony Toomer, book 507, 1784–90, WPA transcripts, CPL.

34. Plat number 182, Plan of the Lands of Anthony Toomer, McCrady Plat Collection, SCDAH.

35. McKellar, *Birth of Modern London,* chap. 5.

36. Chalklin, *Provincial Towns,* chap. 5.

37. Figure derived from the Index of Early Southern Artists and Artisans at the Museum of Early Southern Decorative Art, Winston-Salem, N.C..

38. Commissioners' accounts, Records of St. Michael's Church, SCHS; advertisement of Ezra Waite, *South Carolina and American General Gazette* (Charleston), August 18, 1769; Caroline Wyche Dixon, "The Miles Brewton House: Ezra Waite's Architectural Books and Other Possible Design Sources," *SCHM* 82 (April 1981): 118–43.

39. Elizabeth Sindrey account book, MSS 34/355, SCHS.

40. Shortly after the devastating fire of 1740, the merchant Robert Pringle wrote to Andrew Pringle, his brother, "I am again to desire you'll endeavour to procure me a carpenter servant, & instead of two as mention'd in my last, to procure me a bricklayer in the room of one of them. They may depend on good encouragement" (Robert Pringle to Andrew Pringle, Charleston, December 29, 1740, in *The Letterbook of Robert Pringle,* ed. Walter Edgar [Columbia: University of South Carolina Press, 1972]).

41. Peter Manigault to Daniel Blake, Charleston, March 6, 1770, Peter Manigault Letterbook, transposed copy by Maurice A. Crowse, library at the Museum of Early Southern Decorative Arts, Winston-Salem, N.C.

42. Peter Manigault to Capt. William Hay, April 3, 1771, Peter Manigault Letterbook.

43. Peter Manigault to Ralph Izard Esq., not dated but estimated September 1765, Peter Manigault Letterbook.

44. Peter Manigault to Ralph Izard Esq., Charleston, October 9, 1765, Peter Manigault Letterbook.

45. Memorandum and sketches dated February 19, 1750, Papers of Charles Pinckney, MSS 1127, 2104, and 3900, South Caroliniana Library, University of South Carolina.

46. For a full explanation of this process, see McKellar, *Birth of Modern London,* esp. 81–89.

47. South Carolina Judgement Rolls, Jacob Axson Jr. vs. William Clay Snipes, 1771, vol. 99A, no. 255A, SCDAH.

48. South Carolina Judgement Rolls, Thomas Robinson vs. Luke Stoutenburgh Esq., 1768, vol. 88A, no. 173A, SCDAH; Expense of Building Mrs Ann Middleton's House and Kitchen, 1799–1800, MSS 43/118, SCHS.

Domestic Material Culture and Consumer Demand in the British Atlantic World

Colonial South Carolina, 1670–1770

R. C. Nash

Until the 1980s little research was undertaken on consumerism in Britain and British America in the seventeenth and eighteenth centuries. However, since then the subject has generated impressive work on consumer demand and on the production and marketing of consumer goods. For Britain, the major issue at stake was the part played by the growth of the home consumer market in the onset of industrialization. The most ambitious interpretation holds that a "consumer revolution" erupted in the mid–eighteenth century, a demand-side shift that paralleled and accelerated the revolutionary supply-side changes occurring in the scale of industrial production and technology. The central feature of this supposed revolution was that for the first time the "middling sort" and the laboring classes became regular consumers of manufactured consumer goods. New levels of prosperity created by the growth of commerce and industry and reinforced by the higher earnings of the army of women and children who entered manufacturing employment converted the latent desires of middling and lower-class consumers to engage in socially competitive spending into an effective demand for consumer products.[1]

The concept of a "consumer revolution" has focused attention on the great significance of the home market to industrialization, but it also had a number of critics. First, while it was agreed that the laboring classes in eighteenth-century England became mass consumers of tobacco, tea, and other groceries, many historians doubt that their real wages and general living standards increased from circa 1750 or that systematic evidence existed to show that they formed the basis of a mass market for consumer manufactures.[2] Second, the view that the mid-eighteenth century represented a watershed in the history of consumption was rejected. The origins of a consumer society had deep roots in the sixteenth and seventeenth centuries, when English rural industry was reorganized to produce a much-diversified range of import-substituting textiles and of other manufactures for the expanding home market. If there was a decisive turning point in the development of the consumer market for manufactures, it lay not in the mid-eighteenth but in the late seventeenth century, a period when the middling, though *not* the laboring, classes adopted new consumer items, including tableware, ceramics, and furnishings, on a widespread basis.[3]

The concept of a "consumer revolution" influenced studies of the development of consumerism in British America, although it was not linked there to a debate about industrialization. Rather, the focus of study was the late colonial growth of population and of the incomes generated from staple-export production, which together created a mass demand for manufactures. Despite the claims of earlier historians, this demand could not be met by self-sufficient household production, which was limited in extent; nor was it satisfied by indigenous industry, which largely consisted of artisans involved in the handicraft production of low-grade textiles, shoes, and furniture.[4] Instead, colonial consumers preferred the greater variety and the higher quality of British and European goods. As a consequence, the booming colonial economy sucked in imports from Britain and Europe, a flow which reached unprecedented proportions from the late 1740s: "This consumer revolution affected the lives of all Americans." The mechanisms that drove it were the same as those that underpinned demand in Britain—that is, competitive and emulative spending on products, which conferred social status on the purchasers. The post-1750 flood of imports from Britain tied the colonies ever more firmly to the metropolitan economy and swamped America with goods of the same type as those consumed by the middling and gentry classes in Britain. Colonial tastes in textiles, tableware, furnishings, and other consumer goods became thoroughly anglicized, creating an "empire of goods" and a new and remarkable unity in the character of British American consumer culture.[5]

The notion of an eighteenth-century "consumer revolution" has received a much warmer reception among American than British historians, and the argument that a colonial mass market for imported manufactures had come into existence by the Revolutionary era has commanded general acceptance.[6] Criticisms of the thesis in the colonial context have amounted to qualifications of the argument, and of its periodization, rather than to its outright rejection. Most notably, regional studies, drawing on the evidence of probate inventories and extending their coverage back into the seventeenth century, have demonstrated that the emergence of consumer markets until circa 1720 was a slow process, although it did provide the essential foundations for the faster development of consumerism in the late colonial period.

The geographical coverage of these regional studies, however, has been uneven. While New England and especially the Chesapeake have generated comprehensive research, the region studied in this essay, South Carolina, has been mentioned only in passing.[7] Yet we know that South Carolina's economy, based on the plantation production of rice and later indigo, expanded at a faster rate than that in any other colonial region in the eighteenth century and that its white population achieved levels of wealth and an access to imported British commodities that far surpassed those found elsewhere in British North America.[8] This raises an obvious question: did South Carolina's rapid economic growth and great wealth lead it to develop a distinctive consumer culture, one which diverged significantly from that found in less wealthy colonies such as the Chesapeake and New England?

First, a discussion of current research on New England and the Chesapeake provides a comparative context for the study of consumerism in South Carolina and surveys a number of key issues concerning sources and methodology. Second, probate data are used to explore the distinctive features of South Carolina's consumer culture, concluding that the tempo at which consumerism spread in South Carolina was more rapid than that in other regions and that the South Carolina elite came, in the late colonial period, to engage in conspicuous consumption to a degree not paralleled in other colonial societies. Third, South Carolina's exceptionalism is explained in terms of its greater wealth, the high degree of integration of its urban and rural societies, and the role played in consumption by its unique systems for importing and distributing consumer goods. Fourth, while earlier studies have relied on the use of probate inventories to examine patterns of consumption, these sources have to be supplemented by the evidence of trade data and mercantile sources if anything like a full picture of consumer expenditures is to be established.

Analyzing Probate Inventories

Regional studies of colonial consumption have used probate inventories as their main source. It is useful, before summarizing the main conclusions of this research, to investigate the methodology used to analyze the inventories, a methodology that, in the next section, provides the basis for exploring South Carolina's consumer culture. Current research into probate inventories has been directed to two main ends. First, historians have calculated the monetary value of consumer goods recorded in inventories and compared this with the value of the three categories of nonconsumer property that comprised the rest of the property listed: producer goods, such as livestock, crops, and tools; slaves and other bonded labor; and business inventories and financial assets.[9] From these sources historians have been able to estimate both the absolute value of household consumer possessions and their relative significance in total personal wealth compared with those resources that were devoted to production, to bonded labor, and to financial investment.

Second, within the consumer category, historians have recorded the incidence in probate inventories both of "traditional" goods, those which had long been in common usage, and of new "consumerist" goods, such as tea-ware and tableware, those which reflected new forms of personal and social conduct within the household. One way of assessing the relative significance of old and new goods in inventoried estates is simply to count the percentage of households that possessed certain goods. However, a more sophisticated approach is to construct indexes of bundles of goods that reflect different aspects of consumer behavior and measure the scores achieved by these indexes in samples of inventoried estates. Carr and Walsh, in their exhaustive studies of Chesapeake consumption, use two main indexes (which are employed in the next section in analyzing consumer behavior in South Carolina). The first, a "modern" index, comprises those essential goods that a modern household would perceive as necessary even for the most rudimentary of domestic lifestyles, such as beds, tables and cooking pots. This index allows us to assess the degree to which households achieved traditional standards of comfort and convenience—that is, standards of consumption regarded in early modern society as conventional for households that existed at levels above mere subsistence. The second, an "amenities" index, is comprised mainly of new consumer goods such as tea-ware, cutlery, silverware, pictures, and secular books.[10] This index assesses the rates of diffusion of ownership of goods associated with new forms of eating and drinking, leisure, and social display in the period. It represents the degree to which households participated in the new modes of "polite" behavior and civilized domesticity that historians have identified as the crucial social underpinnings of the eighteenth-century expansion of consumerism.

The application of these approaches to the Chesapeake and New England has brought household living standards in these regions into a sharp focus. In one crucial respect, of course, both regions enjoyed a high standard of life compared with that of the mass of the English population. The colonists, after the period of initial settlement, always had enough cultivated land to produce ample food supplies and a high standard of nutrition, so that by circa 1700 American adults were several inches taller than their English counterparts.[11] However, while Americans were well fed compared with the average Briton, the mass of colonists experienced standards of domestic comfort and convenience, at least as represented by their household consumer possessions, that were no better, and for large sections of the population considerably worse, than those prevailing in low-income British households.

The patterns of consumerism that emerged in America reflected the regional character of migration, rates of population growth, and household formation.

The great majority of migrants to New England were free persons rather than indentured servants, and they brought with them some capital and possessions, including consumer goods. They came largely in family groups, and this, combined with the region's low rates of mortality and high rates of fertility, promoted a rapid population growth and the predominance in society of families that were large even by the standards of preindustrial society. These sizable households had ample supplies of land and labor, agricultural resources that were boosted by the wealth they brought from England or, in the case of later generations, by the substantial property that newly married couples received from their parents. New England households therefore had the means of satisfying their needs for basic consumer goods. As early as circa 1650, probate inventories record an average of thirty pounds of consumer goods per household, a monetary value similar to that found in inventoried farming households in England and one that, for New England, was not to change substantially over the entire colonial period (see table 1[A]).[12] New England families therefore owned a reasonable complement of basic consumer goods, although the high costs of imported manufactures meant that their domestic possessions were scantier than those found in English households with an equivalent value of goods. Thus, about half of all households were seriously deficient in essential consumer possessions as measured by the "modern" index, including furniture and equipment such as beds, chairs, and drinking vessels. Moreover, as late as circa 1720 the great mass of New England households entirely lacked those amenities that historians have associated with more refined forms of domesticity and leisure, such as fine earthenware, tea- or coffee-making equipment, and secular books.[13]

The majority of seventeenth-century migrants to the Chesapeake, on the other hand, were young, penniless, male indentured servants who performed several years' unpaid labor growing tobacco for their colonial employers in exchange for the costs of their passage. Once freed, ex-servants possessed few resources other than an allotment of unimproved land, and as tobacco producers they struggled to make a living in an industry that suffered from frequent overproduction crises in the later seventeenth century. These bleak economic prospects, combined with high rates of adult mortality and the gender imbalance among migrants, meant that many Chesapeake households were impoverished and that a high proportion were composed of a single, poor male adult or a single widow or widower with children. As late as circa 1680 the average value of consumer goods held by the poorer Chesapeake households, the great majority, was only about ten pounds, one-third of the average value of such goods found in New England households. The majority of the population was therefore deprived of many basic household goods such as tables, earthenware, and linen, a starkness in material possessions that compared unfavorably with even the poorest households in England. The expansion of the native-born element of the population,

Table 1. Average Personal and Consumer Goods Wealth in Worcester, England; Virginia; Massachusetts; Maryland; Rural Pennsylvania; and South Carolina, c. 1670–c. 1770

	AVERAGE PERSONAL WEALTH		AVERAGE VALUE OF CONSUMER GOODS		% OF WEALTH IN CONSUMER GOODS
	Current £	*Constant £*	*Current £*	*Constant £*	
(A)					
England					
S. WORCESTER, c. 1670	£104*	£104	£29	£29	28%
S. WORCESTER, c. 1720	£154	£154	£31	£31	20%
Colonies					
VIRGINIA, c. 1670	£140	£140	£26	£26	19%
VIRGINIA, c. 1730	£104	£104	£28	£28	27%
VIRGINIA, 1774	£412	£310	£33	£25	8%
MASSACHUSETTS, c. 1670	£105	£105	£35	£35	33%
MASSACHUSETTS, 1774	£190	£143	£40	£30	21%
MARYLAND, c. 1670	n.a.		£23	£23	n.a.
MARYLAND, c. 1720	n.a.		£27	£27	n.a.
RURAL PENNSYLVANIA, c. 1690	n.a.		£30	£30	n.a.
RURAL PENNSYLVANIA, c. 1730	n.a.		£21	£21	n.a.

	AVERAGE PERSONAL WEALTH		AVERAGE VALUE OF CONSUMER GOODS		% OF WEALTH IN CONSUMER GOODS
	Current £	*Constant £*	*Current £*	*Constant £*	
(B)					
SOUTH CAROLINA, c. 1700	£265	£265	n.a.		n.a.
SOUTH CAROLINA, c. 1730	£436	£436	£28	£28	6%
SOUTH CAROLINA, c. 1745	£565	£528	£30	£28	5%
SOUTH CAROLINA, 1773/74	£1707	£1283	£78	£59	5%

*All values are in £s sterling. For the conversion of current to constant values, see Shammas, *Pre-Industrial Consumer,* 303–4. Base years, 1660–74.

Sources: (A) Carole Shammas, *The Pre-Industrial Consumer in England and America* (Oxford: Oxford University Press, 1990), 87, 94–95. (B) For c. 1700, Peter M. Coclanis, *The Shadow of a Dream: Economic Life and Death in the South Carolina Low Country, 1670–1920* (New York: Oxford University Press, 1989), 79. For all other dates, see "Note on Sources," p. 256–57.

which inherited some property, including improved land, and which experienced much lower levels of mortality than the migrant population, increased the number of sizable, better-off households. However, it was not until circa 1720 that Chesapeake consumption standards caught up with those current in New England in circa 1650 (see table 1[A]). The middling and well-to-do tobacco planters did enjoy a more comfortable existence, but by circa 1720 only a small proportion of them possessed even a modicum of the more refined amenities. Their consumption therefore differed in degree rather than in kind from those of the poorer households. The Chesapeake in the early eighteenth century had a "broadly shared material condition and cultural attitude that was distinctly premodern. . . . The region's wealthiest men and women had not yet adopted an integrated lifestyle which set them off from that of other groups."[14]

From the early eighteenth century there was an overall increase in both the quantity and the diversity of the consumer goods owned by households in the two regions, a process which has been measured with a fair degree of precision using the indexes of consumption specified above. In the Chesapeake the average "amenities score" per estate increased from two amenities (out of twelve) in 1700 to about five per estate in the early 1770s. In New England the trend in the ownership of amenities was uncannily similar: the average number held by households was two in 1675–1700 and five in the years 1760–74. There were differences between the two regions, however, in the rate of the diffusion of these goods by social class. In the Chesapeake the process of dissemination commenced with the richer households from the early eighteenth century and then spread to the generality of households in the 1740s and 1750s. In rural New England all wealth groups improved their positions at a similar rate from the early eighteenth century, although with a much quicker pace of progress from the 1740s to the 1770s.[15]

Colonial Americans, then, achieved new, and some historians have argued also revolutionized, standards of consumerism in the eighteenth century with respect both to the quantity and to the diversity of their consumer possessions. What caused this expansion in consumption? The most important factor encouraging its growth was increasing wealth. At any one time there was a close association between the hierarchy of wealth and that of consumption. In the Chesapeake, for example, the richest households, circa 1720, invested several times as much in consumption goods as did the poorest ones.[16] One would therefore have expected that the eighteenth-century growth both in colonial wealth and in consumption would be reflected in a steady increase in the value of consumer possessions recorded in household inventories.[17] In fact, recent research has shown the opposite: the absolute value of household consumer goods rose to circa 1700 but then stagnated in the eighteenth century, despite the fact that consumerism was spreading in the colonies at a fast pace (see table 2[A]). For example, in Virginia the total personal wealth of the planters trebled from 1730 to 1774, mainly because the number and the value of the slaves they owned were increasing. At the same time they increased the quantity and diversity of consumer goods in their possession, and yet the value of these possessions remained unchanged.

How can we account for the fact that consumption became more widespread while the value of consumer goods held by households stagnated? The answer lies in the long-term changes that occurred in consumer preferences and in the quality and prices of consumer goods. The notable trend in consumer preferences in England and America in the early modern period was the substitution of "traditional" goods, which had provided an enduring or even a lifetime's use, with less durable products—for example, pottery and glass were substituted for pewter and wooden-ware, and lightweight cottons replaced heavy-duty woolens. Consumers came to prefer goods that were finished in more attractive styles or patterns and that were less cumbersome to use or more comfortable to wear. These substitutes were cheaper, often much cheaper, than the goods they replaced. Furthermore, there was a general fall in the prices of consumer goods, both old and new, from the late seventeenth to the late eighteenth century; textiles, for example, including broadcloth, kerseys, and standard linen fabrics, fell in price by between 30 percent and 50 percent.[18] These factors meant that a stock of goods in circa 1770, containing a significant element of new consumer products, comprised a much-increased *quantity* of possessions compared with a stock of traditional goods of the same monetary value a century earlier. As Shammas has commented, "A combination of falling prices and substitutions of less permanent goods for more durable ones probably disguises most of the increased accumulation of consumer goods in the eighteenth century."[19]

The question is, why did the colonists, as their wealth increased, supposedly not spend more on consumer goods, especially given the claims made by historians that they had a whole-hearted commitment to new forms of consumerism?[20] The answer is that they did indeed spend more on consumption, something which again is concealed by the unchanging value of consumer goods held in probate inventories. The probate records give us a snapshot of the stocks of consumer goods held in inventoried estates at any one time, but they tell us little about important changes in household expenditure patterns over time. First, as noted, the new consumerist goods had a limited durability compared with the traditional manufactures they superseded, and hence they had to be replaced more frequently. Furthermore, the more often goods were replaced, the greater the opportunities for new product fashions to be marketed and adopted; that is, household purchasing decisions came to be heavily influenced by short-term fashion considerations as well as by a practical need to replace goods that had worn out or broken. Thus, the annual expenditure required to maintain a

Table 2. South Carolina Inventories

(A) PROPORTIONS OF SOUTH CAROLINA, COLONIAL, AND ENGLISH INVENTORIES WITH NEW COMMODITIES, 1730–1774

	Knives/ Forks	*Glassware*	*Ceramics*	*Tea Equip.*	*Coffee Equip.*	*Mahogany Furniture*	*Secular Books*	*Riding Carriages*
c. 1730								
SOUTH CAROLINA	32%	17%	37%	35%	14%	3%	45%	2%
VIRGINIA	16%	9%	3%	3%	1%	?	?*	?
ENGLAND	10%	?	57%		15%	?	22%	?
LONDON	19%	17%	39%	32%	23%	?	52%	?
1774								
SOUTH CAROLINA	47%	32%	54%	52%	22%	38%	53%	31%
VIRGINIA	71%	46%	36%	49%	20%	3%	?	?
MASSACHUSETTS	53%	56%	35%	56%	24%	12%	?	?
MASSACHUSETTS LOW WEALTH	40%	46%	24%	48%	19%	?	?	?

*The Virginia sample used in this table does not include books; however, we know that the possession of secular books in Maryland and in York County, Virginia, was on an exiguous scale, c. 1730; see Lois Green Carr and Lorena S. Walsh, "Changing Lifestyles and Consumer Behaviour in the Colonial Chesapeake," in *Of Consuming Interests: The Style of Life in the Eighteenth Century*, ed. Cary Carson, Ronald Hoffman, and Peter J. Albert, 59–166 (Charlottesville: University Press of Virginia, 1990).

(B) PROPORTIONS OF SOUTH CAROLINA INVENTORIES WITH NEW COMMODITIES*

	Knives/ Forks	*Glassware*	*Ceramics*	*Tea Equip.*	*Coffee Equip.*	*Mahogany Furniture*	*Secular Books*	*Riding Carriages*
c. 1730								
UPPER	41%	24%	70%	59%	29%	4%	41%	10%
MIDDLE	43%	18%	44%	50%	15%	2%	57%	0%
LOWER	21%	12%	26%	17%	9%	0%	36%	0%
1773/74								
UPPER	68%	58%	90%	78%	35%	72%	77%	74%
MIDDLE	46%	24%	59%	55%	18%	30%	47%	20%
LOWER	24%	15%	19%	34%	14%	12%	32%	6%

*Wealth groups fall within the following range of inventoried personal wealth: lower, £1–200; middle, £201–1,000; upper, £1001– .

Sources: For South Carolina see table 1. For Virginia, Massachusetts, and London see Carole Shammas, *The Pre-Industrial Consumer in England and America* (Oxford: Oxford University Press, 1990), 12, 182–84. For England and for London (ownership of books only), see Lorna Weatherill, *Consumer Behaviour & Material Culture in Britain, 1660–1760*, 2d ed. (London: Routledge, 1996), 26, 49.

stock of goods circa 1770 comprised of semidurable consumer goods was inevitably higher than the expenditure needed to sustain a stock of the same value in circa 1670 but composed of sturdier, traditional items.[21]

Probate inventories (especially those of South Carolina) significantly underrecorded two categories of goods that comprised the major categories of consumer expenditures but that have largely been ignored in modern studies of consumerism in colonial America: textiles and clothing and consumer perishables, principally groceries, goods imported from Britain and the West Indies. A fuller picture of household spending has to include expenditure on these imports, which experienced a substantial per capita increase in the eighteenth century. Given the absence of information on such goods in probate inventories and the general lack of data on household budgets, such expenditures can be reconstructed only by analyzing trends in the volume and composition of imports of European and Caribbean consumer goods. (For South Carolina this task is undertaken in the section titled "Consumption Data for South Carolina" below.)

In addition to the economic factor of wealth, historians have emphasized two other major cultural and social forces as key and competing explanations of changes in consumer behavior: status competition between social classes leading to emulative spending; and the effects of urbanization. The "emulation thesis" sees consumer innovation as a top-down process. It was initiated by high-status, landed elites seeking to differentiate themselves from the lower orders but whose novelties then achieved a widespread and, from the elites' point of view, unwelcome circulation as they were progressively imitated down the social scale, thus in turn setting off another cycle of elite differentiation and "lower-order" imitation. Research on the Chesapeake has focused attention on social emulation rather than urbanization as the major cause of the expansion of consumerism in the region. Towns in the Chesapeake did indeed adopt new consumer goods at an earlier stage, and to a greater extent, than did the rural areas, and yet they had little influence on the countryside. Chesapeake towns before circa 1750 were few in number and small in size compared with those in New England and the other northern colonies. They sold few goods to farming households, and the "display" effects of their higher standards of consumption had little influence on rural consumers, even those within their immediate hinterlands. The pioneers in consumer innovation in the rural areas were found not in the towns but among the rural elite. The "tobacco gentry" became, in the early eighteenth century, the first rural social group to adopt new goods, which they imported directly from the merchants in England to whom they consigned their crops. Their consumption habits were then taken up, in the 1740s and 1750s, first by the middling class and eventually by the lower class of tobacco planters, groups which obtained their consumer products from the thick clusters of rural stores that sprang up in the Chesapeake in the same decades.[22]

In recent years, however, a strong reaction has set in against the emulation thesis.[23] Cultural historians have argued that the motivations of consumers cannot be determined from the mere fact of the ownership of possessions as recorded in probate inventories and, furthermore, that consumers had reasons for acquiring goods other than a desire to emulate their betters. Middle-class women, for example, cherished their possessions more for private and sentimental reasons than because they provided an opportunity for social display. Moreover, middle- and lower-class consumers, in general, resisted elite fashions when these were seen as extravagant or overblown, remaining loyal to traditional fashions or generating independent styles in clothing and furnishings that were free of elite influences.[24]

The emphasis on urbanization as a key influence on consumer behavior has also been developed as a critical response to the "emulation thesis." Weatherill has argued that for England in the period 1675–1725, there was no direct link between social status and consumer innovation; indeed, urban craftsmen and merchants adopted new consumer products, such as fine china and tea-ware, with more alacrity than did higher-status rural farmers or gentry. Carson has shown that for British America, the first colonial users of new types of furniture or tableware invariably were town dwellers. Towns were quicker to adopt new consumer goods than rural areas were for three main reasons. First, consumer goods were more readily available in towns, acting as they did as the chief centers for marketing and manufactures. Second, townspeople engaged in more frequent and more elaborate social interactions than did country dwellers, which stimulated the use of consumer props such as tableware and the participation in social rituals such as tea drinking. Third, towns were more anonymous than rural communities were; hence, townspeople were eager to display portfolios of fashionable goods to signal their status to other town dwellers.[25] This shaping influence of towns in consumerism is evident in New England, where new consumer goods made their first appearance in Boston in the 1680s; became commonplace in middling Boston households by 1720; but did not bulk large in rural New England inventories until the 1740s or 1750s. The diffusion of consumer goods in rural New England was also dictated by the towns, which acted as the principal centers for importation and distribution. Indeed, the geographical take-up of consumer goods in the countryside closely followed the pattern of the waterway and other transport routes that connected Boston and other coastal towns to communities in the interior.[26]

In summary, a consumer revolution, or something close to it, occurred in America in the eighteenth century: the new consumerism was centered on the adoption of cheap substitutes for traditional goods, whose prices fell substantially over the period; hence there was no increase in the absolute value of the stocks of consumer goods held by colonial households at any one time. However, expenditures on consumer goods rose over time in association with the colonists' growing wealth, both because the new goods required more frequent replacements and because spending increased on imported textiles and groceries, trends in spending for which probate inventories provide an inadequate guide. The mechanisms driving the new consumerism, however, differed markedly between regions. In New England the towns pioneered new consumer tastes and also acted as the means by which the new goods were diffused in the rural areas. Towns in the Chesapeake, on the other hand, while they adopted new goods with gusto, had a negligible impact on the countryside. Here the pacesetters in consumer tastes were the wealthy and high-status rural gentry, whose new consumer habits were emulated a generation later by their middle- and lower-class neighbors. New England and the Chesapeake, then, provide two divergent models of the development of consumerism. The next section shows that colonial South Carolina followed neither model but instead developed a distinctive consumer culture of its own.

Consumption Data for South Carolina

Research on the material culture of domestic households in the British American colonies has neglected South Carolina. We know a fair amount about the lifestyle of Charleston's richest inhabitants in the late colonial period, but there are no systematic studies of consumption to parallel those for the Chesapeake and New England.[27] This section provides such data, drawn from probate inventories, for the lowcountry area of South Carolina, the economically unified plantation region that dominated the colony's economy. Estimates of the total personal wealth and of the consumer wealth of inventoried South Carolina estates in the eighteenth century are presented in table 1(B). These estimates confirm the well-known fact that the average wealth of South Carolinians was much higher than that possessed by the residents of the other mainland colonies, a contrast quite obvious by circa 1700 and even more marked in the eighteenth century. Thus, while probated estates in South Carolina were worth, on average, twice as much as those in Virginia and Massachusetts in circa 1700, by the time of the Revolution they held four times as much wealth as those in Virginia and ten times that found in Massachusetts. However, until the mid–eighteenth century, despite their notably greater resources, South Carolina's inventoried wealth-holders, on average, possessed consumer goods of no greater value than that of their less affluent neighbors in the other colonies. As they were much richer than their fellow colonists, this means that the proportion of their wealth held in consumer goods was extremely low by American or British standards.

The great concentration of South Carolina's wealth in slaves and other productive assets, circa 1730, reflected the investment priorities dictated by the hectic expansion of the lowcountry's plantation economy in the early eighteenth century. South Carolina was an unusual colony in that a substantial proportion of the migrants who founded it came not from Europe but from the other British colonies in America, especially from the West Indies. The latter brought slaves with them, and hence, unlike in the Chesapeake, slaves formed an important part of the colony's labor force from its first settlement. To begin with, these slaves were employed in conventional rural activities, in livestock farming, and in the lumber business. From 1710, however, slaves, who now came mainly from Africa, were employed on plantations producing naval stores and especially rice; by the late 1720s rice production dominated what had become, in two generations, an important regional export economy. The massive investment in improving land and above all in importing slaves clearly restricted the resources available for consumption. Thus, from circa 1700 to circa 1730 South Carolina's exports of plantation staples increased tenfold, while imports of slaves increased fourteenfold; yet imports from Britain, the overwhelming source of consumer goods, increased only fivefold. Export earnings generated by plantation production were spent not on consumer imports but on slaves and other investments in plantations.[28]

Table 3. Distribution of Resources between Productive Assets and Consumer Goods, South Carolina Estates, c. 1730

SLAVES	PRODUCER GOODS*	FINANCIAL ASSETS†	CONSUMER GOODS
48%	33%	13%	6%

*Includes livestock, producer durables and perishables such as field crops, stored grain, etc., and business inventories.

†Includes cash as well as mortgages, bonds, and notes.

Source: See table 1(B).

Nevertheless, while the demands of plantation production appear to have restricted South Carolinians' consumption to modest levels, given their total wealth, consumer behavior in the region circa 1730 differed from that in other colonial regions in a number of important ways. First, historians have identified certain goods such as pottery, glassware, and tea- and coffee-drinking equipment as the key components in the transformation of domestic consumer culture in the eighteenth-century American colonies. As Shammas comments, "What really marked the mid–eighteenth century off from previous periods, then, was the diffusion of eating and drinking goods into the ordinary household."[29] It is notable that the incidence of these goods in South Carolina was much higher as early as circa 1730 than it was in Virginia or indeed in provincial England (see table 2[A]). That South Carolinians made a greater and more precocious use of these goods than colonists in the Chesapeake is confirmed by evidence from a quite different source, the colony's (white) per capita imports of tea, china, and earthenware and glass, which far exceeded comparable imports into Virginia and Maryland in the same years.

Table 4. White Population's Per Capita Imports of Tea and of China, Glass, and Earthenware: Carolina and Virginia and Maryland, 1733–37 (Annual Averages)

	TEA (LBS)	CHINA & GLASS/ EARTHENWARE (PIECES)
Carolina	0.53	9.7
Virginia & Maryland	0.10	1.6

Sources: For imports, see Customs 3, vols. 33–37, Inspectors'-General, Ledgers of Imports and Exports, National Archives, England. For population, see John J. McCusker and Russell R. Menard, *The Economy of British America, 1607–1789* (Chapel Hill: University of North Carolina Press, 1985), 136; Coclanis, *Shadow of a Dream,* 64.

Second, we can further confirm the precocious development of consumerism in South Carolina by organizing the inventory data for the colony using the Carr and Walsh and the Weatherill indexes expressing the changing distribution of consumer goods in terms of the percentage of the three indexes (bundles of goods) held in inventoried estates. This reveals that circa 1730 the numbers of "modern" items—that is, basic and traditional household goods such as mattresses, tables, and cooking pots—recorded in South Carolina and in Chesapeake inventories were equal: each group of households possessed about 6 "modern" items per unit.[30] However, at the same time, the number of "amenities" per South Carolina estate was 4.5, while in both the Chesapeake and New England it averaged just fewer than 3 items per unit (see table 5). South Carolinians had more novel items connected to leisure, to civilized comforts, and to display than did their fellow colonists. They were more eager, it appears, to engage in fashionable forms of domestic behavior than they were to acquire the full range of basic facilities, although the acquisition of the latter was clearly within their economic means.

In fact a more useful point of comparison between consumerism in South Carolina and consumerism elsewhere in the early eighteenth century is not with the other plantation colonies, or indeed with the English provinces, but with London, which was of course the center of fashionable consumption in the Anglo-American world at this time. Peter Earle notes, for example, "the dual invasion of coffee and tea-making equipment into London homes. This was rare before the 1690s but, as with so many other innovations, what was rare or unknown in the 1680s becomes commonplace in the reign of Queen Anne."[31] Remarkably, South Carolina was not far behind (see table 2[A]). By circa 1730 the incidence in South Carolina inventories of ceramics, glassware, cutlery, tea and coffee equipment, and secular books matched or exceeded that found in London inventories (predominantly those of middle-class traders and tradesmen). Rather surprisingly, then, we find that South Carolinian standards of consumption were metropolitan rather than provincial. Consumer culture in South Carolina, defined in terms of new "polite" forms of behavior and of civilized domesticity, was as early as the colony's second generation in close step with developments among London's middle classes and some years ahead of those prevailing in the rest of American colonial society.

Table 5. Possession of Consumer Goods in South Carolina Estates as Measured by Three Indexes

	AMENITIES	WEATHERILL'S	MODERN	AVERAGE % SCORE	% OF ESTATES
1729–31, 1735					
UPPER	47%	54%	73%	58%	11%
MIDDLE	34%	48%	67%	50%	39%
LOWER	20%	24%	37%	27%	50%
ALL	34%	42%	59%	45%	100%
1773–74					
UPPER	56%	69%	84%	70%	34%
MIDDLE	33%	38%	57%	43%	34%
LOWER	19%	21%	31%	24%	32%
ALL	36%	43%	57%	45%	100%

Sources: See table 1 and "Note on Sources," pp. 256–57

From the 1730s, however, the rate at which South Carolinian households adopted new commodities slowed down. By the 1770s Virginia residents, for example, had caught up with and in some respects had even overtaken South Carolina's levels of consumption. So tea and coffee drinking, which scarcely register in the Virginia samples for circa 1730, had by the 1770s become as popular there as in South Carolina, while tableware items such as cutlery and glassware were more commonly encountered in Virginian (and indeed in New England) than in South Carolinian households (see table 2[A]). The more detailed index scores tell the same story. The average number of "amenities" and "modern" items per South Carolina household changed little from circa 1730 to the mid-1770s, whereas in the Chesapeake the scores of both the "modern" and especially the "amenities" indexes increased substantially; by the early 1770s the Chesapeake scores in these respects very nearly equaled the South Carolinian ones.[32]

However, it would be misleading to suggest that South Carolina's consumption patterns evolved quickly in the first two generations of settlement and then stagnated. There was a major change in consumption in South Carolina in the later colonial period: the average value of consumer goods held by South Carolinian estates grew rapidly, trebling in the forty years from midcentury to the Revolution from twenty-eight pounds to seventy-eight pounds per inventory. In Virginia and Massachusetts, in the same period, the value of inventoried consumer goods increased respectively from twenty-eight pounds to thirty-three pounds and from twenty-seven pounds to thirty-four pounds per household. (table 1). The standard pattern observed for other colonies, which is now regarded as the orthodoxy, in which from the early eighteenth century to the Revolution the monetary value of consumer goods in estates stagnated or fell, is not found in South Carolina.

However, South Carolina's divergence from other societies cannot be understood by focusing on the "average" probated estate. We must ask instead whether the precocious use of new consumer goods circa 1730 and the increase after 1750 in the value of consumer goods held by households occurred among all social groups or whether it was stratified by social class and occupation and by urban and rural residence. This requires the disaggregation of our sample of inventoried wealth-holders into more refined categories organized around wealth levels, occupations, and places of residence.[33]

The probate data for South Carolina have therefore been classified into upper, middle, and lower wealth groups in order to provide information of the average value of estates in different wealth classes and of the consumer component within them (see table 6). The upper group (those with estates valued at more than one thousand pounds) was dominated by planters producing rice and later indigo for the export sector, who made up about 80 percent of the class. It also included rich farmers—those using large slave-labor forces to produce livestock and grain for the internal South Carolina market rather than for the external market. These planters and farmers owned nearly half of all inventoried slaves circa 1730 and 90 percent of them in the early 1770s. The upper group was rounded off by a small number of foreign-trade merchants, by high-ranking professionals, and by rentiers whose chief form of income was money lending. Farmers made up the largest category in the middle group (estates valued from one hundred to one thousand pounds), alongside planters, professionals—including lawyers, public officials, schoolmasters, and doctors—and rentiers. Farmers were also the largest element in the lowest wealth class (one to one hundred pounds), although it should be said that farmers in this category were almost all petty agriculturalists with few if any slaves and little livestock.[34] The other major occupation in the lower group was that of trades of low status, comprising shopkeepers and artisans such as carpenters and tailors. Twenty percent of those in the lowest wealth group had no identifiable occupation, although it is certain that these were nonagriculturalists, namely, mariners, overseers, laborers, retired males and widows, and the unemployed and the indigent.[35]

What specific patterns of consumption were associated with the various wealth groups, and how did wealth differences shape the distinctive features of South Carolina's consumer culture? The hierarchy of wealth and of occupations, and thus of status, it goes without saying, was related to the consumption hierarchy. Around 1730, for example, the upper wealth group held total wealth four to five times as great as that held by the middle group and consumer goods worth twice as much (see table 6). However, this made surprisingly little difference to the profile of consumer goods held by the two groups. The upper group owned more new consumer goods than did the middle group, but the differences were small ones. In addition, with respect to two commodities, cutlery and secular books, the middle households had higher proportions of these goods than did the upper ones (see table 2[B]). Likewise the upper and middle groups both held quite similar bundles of the basic and the nonessential goods that comprise the "modern," the "amenities," and the Weatherill indexes.[36] In qualitative terms, then, both groups owned a similar range of possessions; the rich merely had rather more of them. The two groups, it could be said, shared a common material culture.[37] The social line of division in terms of consumption lay not between the elite and everyone else but rather between the upper *and* middle groups on the one hand and the lowest wealth category on the other. The latter were too poor to reach the monetary threshold needed to acquire more than a modicum of basic goods, a threshold set circa 1730 at twenty-five to thirty pounds per household. However, while the low-wealth households possessed many fewer basic goods and amenities than did the middle and upper ones, they nevertheless did share in the fashion for some new commodities, and in this respect they easily outdid comparable Virginia households. So tea or coffee drinking was found in about one in four households of the lowest wealth category in South Carolina in circa 1730, while such habits were almost nonexistent in any other than the very wealthiest households in the Chesapeake samples of the same period.[38]

What major changes occurred in the social distribution of consumption in the later colonial period? The consumption patterns of the middle and lower groups experienced no change. By the mid-1770s the values of consumer goods held by these two groups stood at almost exactly the same level as those of the early 1730s.[39] Moreover, neither group experienced any improvement in the range of basic goods and amenities in its possession, as measured by the indexes, and neither increased its possession of "new" commodities beyond the precocious levels achieved forty years earlier. This contrasts with low- and middle-wealth households in New England and the Chesapeake, which improved their consumer standards most rapidly in the period from the 1730s to the Revolution.

Table 6. Distribution of Inventoried Wealth and Consumer Goods among South Carolina Estates, c. 1730, c. 1745, c. 1774

	AV. WEALTH	AV. CONSUMER GOODS	CONSUMER GOODS AS % OF WEALTH	% OF TOTAL ESTATES	% OF TOTAL WEALTH
1729–31, 1735					
UPPER	£1,904	£71	4%	11%	48%
MIDDLE	£482	£34	7%	39%	43%
LOWER	£80	£13	16%	50%	9%
ALL ESTATES	£436	£28	6%	100%	100%
1746–48					
UPPER	£2,291	£78	3%	15%	60%
MIDDLE	£475	£31	7%	39%	33%
LOWER	£81	£14	17%	46%	7%
ALL ESTATES	£565	£30	5%	100%	100%
1773–74					
UPPER	£4,539	£186	4%	34%	90%
MIDDLE	£443	£32	7%	34%	9%
LOWER	£73	£14	28%	32%	1%
ALL ESTATES	£1,707	£78	5%	100%	100%

Source: See table 1. Wealth Groups fall within the following range of inventoried personal wealth: lower, £1–200; middle, £201–1,000; upper, £1001– .

The upper group of South Carolina households, on the other hand, increased its average total and consumer goods wealth by more than two and one-half times from circa 1730 to the 1770s and further extended both the range of amenities in its possession and its ownership of new consumer goods. Moreover, the percentage of all inventoried estates made up by the highest wealth class increased from 11 percent in 1730 to 34 percent by the early 1770s, by which time the upper group of estates effectively monopolized inventoried personal wealth, holding 90 percent of the total (see table 6).

Table 7. Distribution of Resources between Productive Assets and Consumer Goods, South Carolina Estates, 1773–74

ESTATE VALUE	SLAVES	PRODUCER GOODS*	FINANCIAL ASSETS†	CONSUMER GOODS
£2001–	59%	19%	18%	4%
£1001–2,000	70%	15%	9%	6%
£201–1,000	55%	19%	2%	7%
£1–200	43%	26%	3%	28%

*Includes livestock, producer durables and perishables such as field crops, stored grain, etc., and business inventories.

†Includes cash as well as mortgages, bonds, and notes.

Source: See table 1(B).

This upgrading of wealth levels was caused by South Carolina's rapid economic growth in the late colonial era. The value of rice exports slumped in the wartime depression of the 1740s, but they boomed from the end of the war until the 1770s, years in which they were supplemented by indigo exports, which commenced in the 1740s and thereafter enjoyed a spectacular rate of progress. This surge in exports was based on a growth in the scale and intensity of plantation production, as planters reinvested their export earnings in more slaves and required their labor forces to produce both rice and indigo on their reorganized estates. The average numbers of slaves owned on plantations increased by one-half from the late 1740s to the early 1770s; furthermore the high demand for slaves and their enhanced productivity raised their average value by about 40 percent in the same period.[40] The late colonial boom in plantation production and exports was therefore accompanied by a further massive increase in the value of slaves and other productive assets, forms of wealth that continued to dominate the planters' portfolios (see table 7). Moreover, the growth in the elite's wealth was so rapid that rich households were able to increase their investments both in production *and* in consumption. In the early 1730s the upper wealth class held an average of £71 of consumer goods per estate; by the early 1770s this had increased to £186 per estate (see table 6).

By the 1770s, indeed, the richer households, especially those with total wealth above two thousand pounds, stood out by their ownership of four types of goods (see table 8). The first was wrought silver, which in the early eighteenth century had been held in the form of conventional plate but by the 1770s was invariably encountered as tea, coffee, dining, and cutlery services and was owned, at least in households worth more than two thousand pounds, in the quantity of hundreds of ounces.[41] The second was furniture, including mahogany tables, chairs, desks, chests of drawers, clothes presses, and gaming tables; cheaper items, although in lesser quantities, made from walnut, cedar, cypress, hickory, and more uncommonly from maple, sycamore, and oak; as well as much basic furniture in pine.[42] The third category included riding chairs, chariots, and chaises, that is, light two- and four-wheeled vehicles, some of which were manufactured in South Carolina but most of which were imported from London.[43] The fourth included masses of household linen and tableware: mounds of sheets, napkins, and tablecloths; numerous pieces of china and other ceramics—for example, matched sets such as Wedgwood Queensware and delftware—for serving tea and meals; and multiple sets of specialized glasses and decanters, for wine and spirits.

From circa 1750, then, the South Carolina elite fashioned for itself a domestic milieu of conspicuous display based on an abundance of high-status goods, a milieu different in character from the domestic environment found in the houses of middle or lower wealth-holders or in Chesapeake estates.[44] Before 1750 the boundary between the rich and the middling groups by consumption had not been clearly defined. By the 1770s the elites had distinguished themselves from the lower social groups by the number, quality, and value of their possessions. They had constructed portfolios of consumer goods that were regarded as the indispensable components not just of "polite" but also of "genteel" society, ones that were beyond the monetary reach of middling wealth-holders, signifying a style of life that was the distinctive property of upper-class households.

South Carolina consumption patterns, then, were heavily influenced by wealth and social class, but they were also affected by urbanization and occupation. By the early 1770s rural estates were worth, on average, about 12 percent more than Charleston estates, and yet their holdings of consumer goods were worth about 15 percent less (see table 9[A]). This distinction between town and country was most obvious at the lower and upper ends of the wealth scale and much less noticeable in the middle register. In the richest category, for example, the city residents held estates worth, on average, 40 percent more than their rural equivalents, while their holdings of consumer goods were worth 80 percent more. It appears, then, that Charleston's elite residents demonstrated a lavishness of consumption that exceeded even that of their richest rural counterparts, while the city's poorer households strove to achieve a level of consumption that marked them distinctive from their rural counterparts.

Table 8. Distribution of Major Categories of Consumer Goods Held by Four Wealth Groups, 1729–31, 1735, and 1773/74*

ESTATE CATEGORY	APPAREL	BEDS/LINEN	FURNITURE	KITCHEN GOODS	WROUGHT SILVER	RIDING CARRIAGES
A. £2,001–						
Average Value						
1729–31/35	£0	£18	£26	£18	£28	£5
1773/74	£5	£55	£67	£42	£70	£26
B. £1001–£2,000						
Average Value						
1729–31/35	£8	£22	£9	£8	£11	—
1773/74–	£2	£23	£16	£11	£11	£7
C. £201–£1,000						
Average Value						
1729–31/35	£2	£13	£5	£7	£6	—
1773/74	£2	£10	£8	£6	£3	£1
D. £1–£200						
Average Value						
1729–31/35	£5	£3	£2	£2	£2	—
1773/74	£4	£4	£2	£2	£3	—

*The data excludes various miscellaneous goods that made up about 2 percent of the value of all consumer possessions. The sample also omits estates in which consumer goods are not valued or are valued as a whole but not specified in detail.

Source: See table 1.

In addition to place of residence, occupation had an important influence on consumption. By far the greater part of South Carolina's wealth was held by its agriculturalists. In 1773/74 planters and farmers comprised 58 percent of inventoried wealth-holders, and yet they held 76 percent of all personal wealth. In contrast, nonagricultural households made up 42 percent of estates and yet held only 24 percent of total wealth. However, the nonagriculturalists were greater consumers than were the planters and farmers (see table 9[B]). Thus those identified with occupations of high status, such as merchants, were much less wealthy on average than their agricultural equivalents, the rice and indigo planters, and yet they possessed the more richly appointed households. Likewise, those in low-status trades were the poorest of the occupational groups identified, and yet these tradesmen owned consumer goods of a disproportionately high value. Of course, the distinctions made here between urban and rural inventoried estates and between those following agricultural occupations and those with nonagricultural ones are overlapping. The great majority of the planters and farmers were resident in the rural areas, while most of the nonagriculturalists were located in Charleston. Indeed, the categories of "urban" and "rural" were elastic in the South Carolina context.

Consumption and Urbanity in South Carolina

What explains South Carolina's distinctive patterns of consumerism in the colonial period compared with those of other colonial regions? In particular, how can we account for the precocious standards of consumption achieved in the early eighteenth century, the surge of elite consumerism after circa 1750, and the differences that existed in levels of consumption between urban and rural and between agricultural and nonagricultural households. The obvious answer to these questions is that South Carolina was much wealthier than other colonies and that wealth was the decisive influence shaping consumption.[45] However, the growth of wealth alone cannot explain the distinctive features of South Carolina's consumer culture. First, as noted above, South Carolina consumers in the early eighteenth century, at *all* wealth levels, had a higher propensity to acquire new consumer goods than did Virginian households. Second, while the growing wealth created by the booming economic trends of the late colonial era was a precondition for the surge in elite consumption that occurred after 1750, it was not a sufficient condition for that expenditure to occur. In fact, in other colonial societies sharp increases in average wealth in the late colonial period were accompanied by *falling* levels of consumption. In the upper echelon of Chesapeake and New England inventoried estates the value of consumer possessions reached a peak in circa 1720, leveled out until circa 1750, and then actually fell in the twenty or thirty years before the Revolution—the opposite of the pattern that prevailed

Table 9. Distribution of Personal and Consumer Goods Wealth between Charleston and Non-Charleston and between Agricultural and Nonagricultural Estates in South Carolina, 1773–74

(A) RURAL V. URBAN*

	Wealth Categories					
	Average Wealth £1–200		Average Wealth £201–1000		Average Wealth £1000–	
	Personal	*Consumer*	*Personal*	*Consumer*	*Personal*	*Consumer*
Charleston	£42	£20	£423	£35	£5096	£277
Non-Charleston	£78	£12	£406	£34	£3640	£156

(B) OCCUPATIONS

	Agricultural v. Nonagricultural Occupations							
	PLANTERS OF STATUS Average Wealth		FARMERS Average Wealth		HIGH-STATUS TRADES Average Wealth		LOW-STATUS TRADES Average Wealth	
Estate Size	*Personal*	*Consumer*	*Personal*	*Consumer*	*Personal*	*Consumer*	*Personal*	*Consumer*
£1–200	£81	£2	£84	£3	£135	£63	£60	£15
£201–1000	£475	£20	£446	£30	£452	£51	£366	£20
£1001–	£4215	£147	£2094	£64	£5963	£324	—	—
All Estates	£3416	£120	£509	£23	£1927	£128	£145	£16

*South Carolina inventories seldom give the residence of the deceased. However, the location of the great majority of estates can be established from the evidence of wills, jury lists, newspaper advertisements of the post-mortem sale of estates, the known residence of estate appraisers, and from other miscellaneous sources. Estates for which no location could be established are excluded from panel A. Likewise, those estates for which no occupation could be established are excluded from panel B.

Source: See table 1.

among South Carolina's elite.[46] Third, the wealthiest households were not always the most frenetic consumers. Thus, urban consumers, and those in nonagricultural occupations generally, had lower average wealth than their rural and agricultural counterparts, and yet they spent more on consumption.

The key to integrating nonwealth factors into the explanation of the distinctive characteristics of South Carolina's consumerism lies in the recognition that nowhere in colonial North America were the boundaries between the town and the countryside more fluid and nowhere was there such a high degree of integration of the urban and rural economies and societies as in South Carolina. Thus, many of the richest Charleston households were the homes of planters more or less permanently resident in the city, of merchants and professionals who combined commercial and professional occupations with the ownership of plantations, and of city rentiers who did not own plantations but who held sheaves of mortgages and bonded debts from planters. Conversely, many planters whose principal domiciles were on their plantations were resident in Charleston for part of the year, transacting business and politics or in the pursuit of leisure, entertainment, and consumer goods.[47] Even those South Carolina planters who did not take up temporary residence in Charleston were *urban* consumers in the sense that they bought their consumer goods from the city's large-scale and specialized suppliers rather than from rural retailers. Consumption tends to be viewed in terms of the cultural demands and preferences exercised by the consuming groups and of the economic means that they possessed to make those demands effective ones. However, consumption was also critically influenced by the means of supply, and in South Carolina nearly all households, not just those of the elite, learned and satisfied their consumer demands in a metropolitan market that had no counterpart in the other plantation colonies.

Indeed it is notable that the consumerism of South Carolina's highest wealth groups, whether in town or country, bears a much closer comparison with that of the mercantile and gentlemanly elite of the northern mainland cities than it does with the wealthy planters of the Chesapeake.[48] In eighteenth-century Philadelphia, for example, there was in the houses of the richer merchants and gentlemen the same profusion of mahogany furniture, silver, and riding carriages as that among the Carolina planters.[49] One should not, therefore, make too much of the differences in levels of consumption in South Carolina between rural and urban or between agricultural and nonagricultural households. South Carolina's rich households, whether in town or country, adopted a "high-style" consumerism that in other colonial regions was associated with an urban culture and marketing system and that, to seek comparisons further afield, closely resembled the domestic lifestyle of London's bourgeois merchants and tradesmen.[50] The interplay between urban and rural life in elite consumerism is conveyed in the following advertisement in the *South Carolina Gazette* of May 1773 announcing the sale of the country property of the rich, Huguenot-descended planter Benjamin Guerard, which summed up the gentlemanly ideal: "A *delightful* RETREAT, Eight miles by land or water from [Charles] Town . . . open to several parts of that beautiful River, *Ashley River*. . . . With which will be Sold, The large Quantity of very genteel furniture. . . . A very easy and desirable Distance for a Carriage and Four or Six Horses, as a Gentleman may come to his Business in Town in the Morning, and return to his Family in the Evening."

What functions did this carefully cultivated urban or quasi-urban lifestyle play in buttressing the elite's position at the head of South Carolina society? In general, historians have interpreted the social behavior and consumption of elites in the colonial Anglo-American world in terms of their pursuit of gentility. The key eighteenth-century development was that the status of gentleman came to be defined less by birth and more by manners and education, that is, by acquired rather than by inherited traits.[51] In America, where birth counted far less than in England, elite gentlemen emphasized the gulf between themselves and the "meaner sorts" by presenting themselves and their domestic surroundings in styles that were abreast of the highest and latest fashions. Stylish goods thus displaced possessions that reflected the old-fashioned virtues of antiquity and dynastic tradition. Fashion replaced the "patina of age" as the key indicator of the individual's social worth, at least as defined by his possessions.[52] However, while the obvious costliness of the elite's clothes and possessions displayed wealth and hence status, these were things that prosperous members of the lower social groups could attempt to imitate or counterfeit. Hence, as a second tactic in fashioning themselves as a socially exclusive caste, the elite sought to create a complex code of genteel, dignified, and restrained manners and social rituals, which only they had the necessary education and leisure time to acquire and perfect: "as gentility became more a matter of manner, society placed less emphasis on material display."[53]

The South Carolina inventories provide evidence of the first rather than the second tactic that is testimony of a greater conspicuous consumption as opposed to a retreat from material display. The wealthy elite was the only social class in South Carolina to increase its investment in consumer goods from the 1740s. This meant, inevitably, that the material expression of social distinctions between the elite and everyone else came to rest on a greater degree of visible differences in the possessions owned by them and by other social groups (see tables 6 and 8). Rich South Carolina families lavished their main consumer investment on luxury, high-status goods such as riding carriages, silver tableware, and mahogany furniture, thus emphasizing the social distance that existed between them and the middle and lower classes. In doing so, these households were clearly driven by a desire to exhibit the latest fashions, generally English or rather London ones.

Riding carriages, for example, became popular among London middle-class and urban gentry families from the late seventeenth century, where they played an unrivaled role in "genteel" *urban* social communication between upper and middle-class families, particularly between their female members. Although rare in South Carolina estates before circa 1750, carriages then came to play a similar role in the province's rural and urban social life. By the 1760s and 1770s, indeed, they were de rigueur in rich households, being found in 85 percent of estates with personal wealth valued above two thousand pounds, in 60 percent of estates worth more than one thousand pounds, but in only 20 percent of estates of the middling category. Carriages became the ultimate status possessions for elite families, acting, alongside silver tableware and fine mahogany furniture, as one of the three "badges of distinction that set apart the very rich from the merely wealthy." Imported carriages were widely advertised in the *South Carolina Gazette,* invariably with the tag that they were "of the latest London fashion," replete with details of their accoutrement and decoration.[54] The adoption of the metropolitan vogue for mahogany furniture, on the other hand, occurred much more quickly. Fashionable in England from the 1710s and 1720s, mahogany furniture was found in 3 percent of all South Carolina estates circa 1730, a proportion that rose to 24 percent by the mid-1740s and to 38 percent by the mid-1770s.[55] Additional evidence suggests that South Carolina consumers in the 1760s and 1770s followed London furniture fashions closely, as the taste developed for a more restrained style of mahogany furniture based on simpler lines and less elaborate carving. However, while mahogany furniture by the 1770s was invariably found in estates worth more than one thousand pounds, it was rarely encountered in rural estates below this value.[56]

The South Carolina elite, then, had quasi-urban standards of consumption. However, the closeness of the links between town and country meant that South Carolina consumers of *all* classes tapped into Charleston's supply and distribution system. The importance of the centralization of the lowcountry's marketing system, and the shaping influence it had on consumption, can best be brought out by comparing it with the rural-based marketing structure of the Chesapeake. There, until the 1730s, the generality of planters bought their imported goods not from towns but from stores kept by great planters or by "country" merchants who acted largely as factors for merchants in the British outports. The supply of goods offered by these stores was limited and intermittent. The wealthier planters, who consigned tobacco on their own account to London, therefore satisfied their demand for better-quality goods by placing direct orders with their London correspondents. From the 1740s the distribution system in the Chesapeake was transformed by the appearance of chains of well-stocked rural stores run by factors for English and Scottish principals and by indigenous rural merchants who imported large cargoes of manufactures on credit from London suppliers. This revolution in distribution has been credited as one of the major causes of the region's proliferating consumerism in the mid–eighteenth century, which brought it up in many respects to South Carolinian standards.[57]

South Carolina had, in contrast and from its foundation, a highly centralized and urbanized system of merchandising and distribution. Thus a high proportion of the small number of surviving probate inventories for South Carolina in the years from 1670 to 1700 are of merchants, nearly all of them resident in Charleston. However, although one or two of these firms carried large and varied stocks of goods, the majority of them were petty shopkeepers and dealers, and none of the mercantile inventories for the period included any modish consumer goods such as tea, pottery, or cutlery and other forms of tableware.[58] From 1700 the rise of the naval stores and rice industries focused the colony's trade on Charleston to an extraordinary degree. South Carolina planters, unlike the wealthier tobacco producers, did not consign their crops to England on their own account, nor did they sell them to rural stores, in the manner of the poorer tobacco planters; rather they disposed of them in Charleston, from whence they also obtained their consumer goods.[59] The distribution system for imports was therefore, as in the other plantation colonies, intimately linked to the export trades, but it created an urban rather than a rural marketing structure.

By the years 1733–37, when imports from England averaged eighty-four thousand pounds per year, of which a high proportion (72 percent) came from London, a large business community of at least seventy-four merchants and shopkeepers sold dry goods in Charleston.[60] These dealers held quite modest inventories of trade goods, which averaged only about two hundred to three hundred pounds per trader, although these stocks, unlike those of the first generation of merchants, now invariably included new items of consumption such as teaware, pottery, glassware, cutlery, and secular books.[61] There was also a scattering of retailers in the countryside, but in South Carolina rural dealers never achieved a fraction of the significance they possessed in the Chesapeake or in Pennsylvania and Massachusetts, and in any case, they were mainly subsidiaries of Charleston firms.[62] Charleston's dominance in the distribution of manufactures was underpinned by the compactness of the lowcountry's settlement: as late as 1720 over 75 percent of white settlers lived in a central zone bounded by the Edisto River to the south and by the upper branches of the Cooper River to the north, and hence few households were located more than twenty or thirty miles from Charleston.[63] The city's firms had numerous rural as well as urban customers, and it is clear that Charleston was the overwhelming point of supply for consumer goods throughout the province. Rural clients were supplied by urban merchants on credit, undertaking to repay their debts in cash or in rice and other goods delivered to Charleston; the absence of such credit arrangements in the Chesapeake seems to have precluded the tobacco region from generating significant urban-rural consumption links.[64]

The post-1750 surge in consumerism was underpinned by a further elaboration of the Charleston marketing system. In the 1760s there were about 120 merchants and shopkeepers advertising the sale of imported dry goods in Charleston.[65] The probate records reveal that merchants now held much larger trading stocks than those that had been common in the 1720s and 1730s—business inventories that averaged fifteen hundred to two thousand pounds per firm, similar in value to those held by Philadelphia merchants or by the larger of the rural Scotch stores trading in the Chesapeake at this time.[66] There were also many more specialized city dealers in luxury imports than in the 1730s: in wine, wrought silver and jewelry, furniture, and riding carriages. For example, in the 1760s there were forty-two and in the early 1770s over fifty Charleston dealers in wine and spirits, compared with sixteen traders in the 1730s.[67] In addition, the demand for basic linens and cottons prompted the opening of Charleston "warehouses" from the late 1760s, in which a number of separate merchant-retailers sold these and other goods cheaply for cash or on short credits.[68] By the 1760s rural settlement had spread considerably outside the central region of the low-country in both the northward and southward directions, but these areas were supplied by a well-articulated system of roads and above all water-borne distribution that flowed out from Charleston's wharves. For example, James Poyas, whose general Charleston dry goods and groceries business supplied over sixty rural customers in the mid-1760s, distributed his goods by wagon and through the use of twelve different owners of schooners and boats.[69]

Textiles and Clothing as Consumer Goods

The study of South Carolina's distribution system for imported manufactures helps to explain the "urbanized" patterns of consumption observed in probate inventories, but it further makes clear that the story of consumption told by the inventories is incomplete. First, the inventories tell us little about the quotidian flows of household incomes and expenditure and about the proportion of income spent on consumer products. The probate records give us a static representation of the kinetic process of consumption. Second, while inventories provide an excellent record of durable items found in the households, they tend to omit or underrepresent two less durable components that nevertheless represented the principal items of consumer expenditure: that is, they exclude most forms of textiles and clothing as well as foodstuffs that were purchased rather than produced within the household, which in South Carolina were groceries rather than basic food items.[70] The significance of these expenditures cannot be grasped from probate inventories but only from an analysis of the flow of consumer imports into the Charleston market from Britain and the West Indies, which supplied by far the greater part of South Carolina's textiles, clothing, and groceries.

Table 10. Composition of "Carolina" Imports from England, 1771–74

CONSUMER GOODS				
linens/cottons	*woollens*	*silks*	*clothing/haberdashery*	*subtotal*
32%	16%	3%	8%	59%
food/drugs	*domestic hardware**	*silver plate*	*other*	*subtotal*
6%	2%	1%	15%	83%
PRODUCER GOODS			GRAND TOTALS	
metal goods	*other*			*average value*
7%	10%		100%	£395,000

*Includes, glass, earthenware, china, and pewter. There are two customs' categories, wrought metal goods and the catch-all and expanding category of "goods several sorts," which cannot be readily classified as either consumer or producer goods. I have therefore assumed that these goods were divided equally between the two classifications. For a recent discussion of the composition of the English export trades to the North American colonies, see S. D. Smith, "The Market for Manufactures in the Thirteen Continental Colonies, 1698–1776," *Economic History Review* 51 (1998): 678–708.

Source: Customs 3, vols. 71–74, Inspectors'-General, Ledgers of Imports and Exports, National Archives, England. Total value in sterling.

White per capita consumption of imported English goods in the South Carolina lowcountry in circa 1770 has been estimated at fourteen pounds per year, which assuming an average household size of 4.22 whites, indicates household expenditures on English imports of sixty pounds per year.[71] This was the prime cost of these goods in England, but by the time they reached the South Carolina consumer their prices had been increased by at least 25 percent to accommodate the costs of freights, insurance, mercantile profits, and the granting of credit to the customer.[72] Analysis of the composition of these imports (table 10) suggests that 83 percent of them can be classified as consumer goods and hence that annual household expenditure on English *consumer* imports amounted to sixty-two pounds (£60 x 1.25 x 0.83).

Goods imported from the West Indies circa 1770 amounted to about another eight pounds per household, virtually all of which can be classified under the heading of consumer foodstuffs.[73] In other words, *annual* household expenditure on imported consumer products stood at seventy pounds in circa 1770, close to the value of a household's *lifetime* accumulation of such goods in 1773/74, namely seventy-eight pounds, as estimated from probate inventories. The data for the early 1770s can be compared with expenditures on consumer-goods' imports, circa 1730, of about twenty-three pounds per lowcountry household, indicating that household spending on consumer imports increased three and one-half–fold over the period.[74] Part of this spending, however, was on textiles and other imported manufactured goods for the use of slaves and which therefore counts as producer rather than consumer expenditures. The value of textile imports earmarked for slaves in the early 1770s can be roughly estimated at thirty thousand to forty thousand pounds per annum—that is, about 10 percent of total imports.[75]

The probate inventories and other sources reveal that there was also an indigenous production of consumer goods: "homespun" textile production for household use; a plantation output of other basic goods, such as "negro shoes"; and a Charleston production of luxury goods such as fine wood furniture, silverware, and riding carriages. However, the value of this internal output was minute compared with the value of stocks of imports found in mercantile inventories. Moreover, South Carolina's production of silverware, pottery, paper, textiles, and other consumer goods in the late colonial period ranked at a low level compared with that in the northern colonies, which means that South Carolina was more dependent on imports than other colonial regions were.[76] One suspects, indeed, that the largest indigenous South Carolina contribution to consumer "production" was the making of the several million yards of textiles that were imported every year into clothing.[77]

The major category of imports from Britain was textiles, led by linens and cottons but among which woolens and silks played a prominent part, as did clothing items and accessories such as gloves, hats, stockings, and haberdashery; the less sizable imports from the West Indies were composed principally of rum, sugar, and other foodstuffs. The goods that have most interested historians of consumerism, on the other hand, such as furniture, silver, china, glass, earthenware, cutlery, and other domestic utensils, made up a much less important component of consumer imports.[78] There is, then, a great difference between the types of consumer goods that predominate in South Carolina inventories and those that were imported and distributed through the colony's transatlantic trade networks, although nearly all studies of consumerism have privileged consumer durables over textiles, clothes, and accessories.[79] This basic mismatch between the pattern of consumption revealed by probate sources and what people actually spent their money on is confirmed by the contents of the business inventories held by Charleston merchants, a number of which are summarized in table 11.

Mercantile inventories, in fact, provide a more accurate account of consumption than is derived from the English customs records, both because they include all types of imports and because the more detailed descriptions of goods

Table 11. Composition of Sample of Mercantile Inventories Held by South Carolina Merchants, 1720–35, 1745–75

	CONSUMER GOODS						
	textiles	*clothing/haberdashery*	*bedding*	*domestic hardware*	*groceries*	*books*	*other*
1720–35	52%	6%	1%	2%	22%	*	2%
1745–75	50%	11%	6%	3%	14%	1%	5%

	PRODUCER GOODS		TOTAL £S	
	hardware/tools	*other*	*no.*	*Average value*
1720–35	9%	6%	7	£288
1745–75	5%	5%	9	£2,020

*Less than 0.5%

Sources: South Carolina Probate Records, 1720–35: inventories for Andrew Dupuy (1723), James Du Poids D'Or (1725), Timothy Bellamy (1726), Francis Holmes Sr. (1726), Albert Muller (1727), Jacob Satur (1729), Joseph Warmingham (1729); 1745–75: inventories for John Laurens (1747), John Dart (1755), Samuel Perroneau (1756), Samuel Winborn (1762), John Jones (1764), Samuel Perroneau (1766), William Ioor (1767?), Thomas Gadsden (1770), Nathanial Stoll (1772). The inventories for Gadsden and Ioor provide figures of total stocks held but not of the individual commodities. They are included as evidence of the total size of mercantile inventories.

in inventories allow them to be classified more precisely. The source once again highlights the long-term dominance in distribution of textiles, and of clothing and clothing accessories, and the low value of domestic hardware and utensils. Consumers demanded a huge variety of textiles, the means to turn this raw material into clothing, and an assortment of ready-made clothes and items of personal adornment. Merchants and retailers shaped their stocks to meet these requirements, and hence, to take one example, their inventories generally carried a greater value of stocks of buttons than they did of all the new tableware commodities put together. This reflected the standard gentleman's costume of the period, consisting of a long waistcoat and outer coat, with single or double lines of narrowly spaced buttons running from the collar to the hem.[80] Foodstuffs and groceries form a higher proportion of the mercantile inventories than they do of imports from England, because the inventories include West Indian and Philadelphia goods as well as imports of food from England.

Table 12. James Poyas's Retail and Wholesale Sales, March 1764–February 1765, September 1765–February 1766*

CONSUMER GOODS						
textiles	*clothing/ haberdashery*	*bedding*†	*domestic hardware*‡	*groceries*	*books*§	*other*
53%	15%	9%	2%	15%	1%	1%

PRODUCER GOODS		TOTAL VALUE OF SALES
hardware/tools	*other*	
4%	1%	£4,510

*The source is largely illegible for the period March–August 1765.

†This is comprised of textiles, mainly woollen blankets, but includes mattresses, ticks, and miscellaneous items such as gauze for mosquito netting.

‡Includes all forms of tableware, cutlery, cooking and cleaning utensils, and miscellaneous equipment.

§Includes writing materials.

Source: Merchant's Day Book [James Poyas], 1764–66 (photocopy), 34–325, South Carolina Historical Society, Charleston, South Carolina.

Of course, mercantile inventories of wholesalers and retailers, like probate inventories in general, record stocks of goods rather than flows of sales and expenditure. Therefore, a particular item might represent only a modest percentage of a merchant's stock of goods, but if its turnover was rapid, then its contribution to merchandising and consumer expenditure would be much higher than its proportionate share of the inventory would suggest. A more accurate picture of the flow of expenditure and consumption would therefore be gained from mercantile records of sales to customers. However, for South Carolina, unlike, say, Philadelphia, mercantile accounts are thin on the ground, scarcer even than surviving collections of mercantile correspondence. Indeed, there is only one extant set of accounts for a Charleston merchant-retailer in the late colonial period, the daybooks of James Poyas for the years 1762–67. Poyas was a Charleston rice and indigo factor who sold the planters' crops in Charleston on commission and retailed to them and to many other Charleston and country customers a full range of imported commodities from Britain, the West Indies, and elsewhere.[81] Poyas's sales for an eighteenth-month period are summarized in table 12.

What Poyas's business reveals is the dominance of sales of textiles, clothing and haberdashery, and groceries and the low significance of the turnover of domestic hardware and other consumer goods of the type that predominate in probate inventories. Poyas's customers spent most of their money on textiles and groceries, goods which they bought on a monthly or more frequent basis. Their purchases of domestic hardware and producer goods were much less important and were made only two or three times a year.

In conclusion: the distinctive features of South Carolina's consumerism in the eighteenth century, as revealed by probate inventories, lay in its early adoption of new consumer goods, in the rising tide of consumer expenditures found in wealthier households from midcentury, and in the differential patterns of consumption found in urban and rural households. However, South Carolina households spent a far higher proportion of their incomes on imported textiles, clothing, and groceries than they did on newfangled commodities or high-status possessions, goods which have been the motifs of recent research into early modern consumer culture. Consumerism, in other words, combined two quite different sorts of expenditure: first, spending on consumer durables, which leaves clear evidence in post-mortem inventories; and second, the buying of textiles and clothes, a pattern of spending which is heavily underrepresented in the probate records. The first kind of expenditure was an intermittent one. The formation of new households gave rise to a large expenditure on consumer durables of the type recorded in probate inventories. Subsequently, however, such purchases made up a small and noticeably irregular part of household spending.[82] Of course, in their efforts to keep abreast of fashion, the richer households in South Carolina renewed or extended the range of their domestic possessions after marriage. However, much of the elite's increased expenditure in this category in the late colonial period was on silver, mahogany furniture, and other luxury goods. The fashion characteristics embodied in these goods formed a large part of their appeal, but so did their longevity in use and their transmission by inheritance, attributes that embodied an important part of their function as objects proclaiming high status.[83] Indeed, the symbolic value imparted to high-status goods by the "patina of age" probably did not lose its significance as quickly as has been claimed, meaning that these goods were replaced at infrequent intervals.

The second, and much more important, form of expenditure, as has been demonstrated through an analysis of trade and mercantile records, was on textiles, clothing, and items of personal adornment. The replacement rate for these goods was higher than for consumer durables, partly because more lightweight textiles came into fashion and had to be replaced more often, and partly because consumers were more sensitized to new fashions in clothes than they were in household goods. De Vries, in his idealized model of changing replacement rates for consumer goods in the eighteenth century, assumes that the rate of replacement for textiles might accelerate from every ten years to every five years, that for tableware from every thirty to every fifteen years, while that for furniture and silver remained static at thirty years.[84] As another historian of eighteenth-century consumerism has commented, "metropolitan *chic* was more highly prized in clothing than in tableware, in tableware than in furniture and in furniture than in kitchenware."[85]

South Carolina households spent about sixty pounds per annum on British imports, the greater part of it on textiles and clothing. Peter Earle's study of well-to-do London families in the period 1675–1725, whose consumption patterns were in many other ways similar to those of South Carolina households, suggests that they spent roughly the same amount on clothing, that is, sixty pounds per annum.[86] Moreover, the mercantile records of one merchant (James Poyas) suggest that South Carolinians shopped far more frequently for textiles and clothing than they did for consumer durables. Indeed, it may well be that South Carolina's upper-class consumers asserted their status through a dual strategy: first, they renewed their claims to high fashion on a season-to-season basis through their clothes and other personal adornments, upon which they, like everyone else, concentrated their consumer expenditures; second, they used possessions such as mahogany furniture, silver tea services, and riding carriages to emphasize the time-honored nature of their families' claims to high social status. The focus of consumption for eighteenth-century South Carolinians, however, remained dominant throughout the early modern period: they purchased the textiles, clothing, and numerous personal accessories used to adorn their bodies rather than the new consumerist objects designed to adorn their houses.

A Note on Sources

Tables 1, 2, 5, 6, 8, and 9 are based on an analysis of probate inventories for the following periods: June 1729–May 1731 and 1735 (156 inventories); 1746–48 (154 inventories); 1773–74 (263 inventories).[87] They represent about 11 percent of all the extant South Carolina inventories for the period 1730–74. The first set of years was chosen because the inventories were fairly numerous and in reasonable or good condition and because these years allowed comparisons to be made with data currently available for Chesapeake households. The other sets of data were chosen as representative of the mid- and late colonial periods. In 1746–48 the South Carolina economy was beginning to recover from the war-induced depression of the early and mid-1740s, while in 1773 and 1774 economic conditions were in a largely favorable conjuncture, although overshadowed in 1774 by the impending conflict with Britain. All the inventories for the period until 1748, as far as I have been able to establish, are for the lowcountry. A small number of the inventories for 1773–74 are for the backcountry, although in the end these have been included in the sample.

I have not attempted to assess the degree to which the wealth of the inventoried population was representative of the population at large because the scantiness of tax and demographic data for South Carolina means that we lack the information about the age and family structure of both the inventoried and the wider population that is required for such an exercise. There is no reason to believe that the range of deceased individuals subject to probate inventories was markedly different in 1773–74 than in earlier years.

It should be noted that eighty-four of the inventories for 1774 have been printed in Jones's well-known study, a sample used by historians to provide evidence of average inventoried wealth in the South Carolina lowcountry in the late colonial period.[88] However, her sample was taken solely from the Charleston District for 1774, in which households were on average wealthier than in the other two lowcountry districts of Beaufort and Georgetown.[89] This does not materially affect Jones's methodology, which used a randomly selected sample of districts covering all the colonial regions, and she took steps to correct for the Charleston District's heavy concentration of personal wealth when arriving at her final figures of British American per capita wealth.[90] However, it does mean that her data, when used in isolation, give an exaggerated, although far from wholly distorting, picture of the lowcountry's wealth on the eve of the Revolution. Consequently, the figures of average personal wealth presented above, which are drawn from all lowcountry districts, are somewhat lower than those given in the sources quoted above and elsewhere. It also means that any comparisons made between Jones's data and those for earlier years, which draw on all South Carolina districts—for example, Bentley's comprehensive study—are not strictly comparing like with like.[91] A final note: all values given in the tables and in the text are in pounds sterling and are, with the exception of table 1, current rather than constant.

Notes

I would like to thank my colleagues Steve Rigby and Natalie Zacek for their very helpful comments on an earlier draft of this chapter.

1. Neil McKendrick, "The Consumer Revolution in Eighteenth-Century England," in *The Birth of a Consumer Society: The Commercialisation of Eighteenth-Century England,* ed. McKendrick, John Brewer, and J. H. Plumb (Bloomington: Indiana University Press, 1982); Neil McKendrick, "Home Demand and Economic Growth: A New View of the Role of Women and Children in the Industrial Revolution," in *Historical Perspectives: Studies in English Thought and Society in Honour of J. H. Plumb,* ed. McKendrick (London: Europa, 1974).

2. See Ben Fine and Ellen Leopold, "Consumerism and the Industrial Revolution," *Social History* 15 (1990): esp. 172–76; Pat Hudson, *The Industrial Revolution* (New York: Oxford University Press, 1992), 173–80; Jan De Vries, "Between Purchasing Power and the World of Goods: Understanding the Household Economy in Early Modern Europe," in *Consumption and the World of Goods,* ed. John Brewer and Roy Porter (London: Routledge, 1993), 87–98; Carole Shammas, *The Pre-Industrial Consumer in England and America* (Oxford: Oxford University Press, 1990), 77–86. For a more optimistic view of mass living standards after 1750 and of the working-class contribution to a mass market for cotton textiles, see Beverly Lemire, *Fashion's Favourite: The Cotton Trade and the Consumer in Britain, 1660–1800* (Oxford: Oxford University Press, 1991), 46–54, 97–106.

3. Joan Thirsk, *Economic Policy and Projects: The Development of a Consumer Society in Early Modern England* (Oxford: Oxford University Press, 1978); Margaret Spufford, *The Great Reclothing of Rural England: Petty Chapmen and Their Wares in the Seventeenth Century* (London: Continuum, 1984); Lorna Weatherill, *Consumer Behaviour & Material Culture in Britain, 1660–1760,* 2d ed. (London: Routledge, 1996); Peter Earle, *The Making of the English Middle Class: Business, Society, and Family Life in London, 1660–1730* (Berkeley: University of California Press, 1989).

4. Carole Shammas, "How Self-Sufficient Was Early America," *Journal of Interdisciplinary History* 13 (1982): 247–72; Shammas, *Pre-Industrial Consumer,* 57–69; John J. McCusker and Russell R. Menard, *The Economy of British America, 1607–1789* (Chapel Hill: University of North Carolina Press, 1985), 280–94.

5. T. H. Breen, "An Empire of Goods: The Anglicization of Colonial America, 1690–1776," *Journal of British Studies* 25 (1986): 467–99, quote from 487; T. H. Breen, "'Baubles of Britain': The American and Consumer Revolutions of the Eighteenth Century," *Past and Present* 119 (1988): 73–87.

6. See, for example, John-Christophe Agnew, "Coming Up for Air: Consumer Culture in Historical Perspective," in *Consumption,* ed. Brewer and Porter, 31–33; Lois Green Carr and Lorena S. Walsh, "The Standard of Living in the Colonial Chesapeake," *William and Mary Quarterly* 45 (1988): 142–43.

7. For recent research on consumerism in British America and its relative neglect of South Carolina, see Cary Carson, Ronald Hoffman, and Peter J. Albert, eds., *Of Consuming Interests: The Style of Life in the Eighteenth Century* (Charlottesville: University Press of Virginia, 1990); Shammas, *Pre-Industrial Consumer;* Brewer and Porter, eds., *Consumption.* There has also been little study of consumerism in the British Caribbean colonies, although see Nuala Zahedieh, "London and the Colonial Consumer in the Late Seventeenth Century," *Economic History Review* 48 (1994): 239–61. For a brief comparative survey of late

seventeenth-century Caribbean and mainland consumption standards, see Lois Green Carr, Russell R. Menard, and Lorena S. Walsh, *Robert Cole's World: Agriculture and Society in Early Maryland* (Chapel Hill: University of North Carolina Press, 1991), 114–17.

8. See McCusker and Menard, *Economy of British America,* 168–88; Peter M. Coclanis, *The Shadow of a Dream* (New York: Oxford University Press, 1989), 63–110.

9. Probate inventories, other than those for New England, seldom include valuations of real property, i.e., land and buildings. The figures of wealth given in this chapter therefore refer to personal or movable wealth.

10. Lois Green Carr and Lorena S. Walsh, "Changing Lifestyles and Consumer Behaviour in the Colonial Chesapeake," in *Of Consuming Interests,* ed. Carson et al., 69, 133–34. A third index, which is used for comparative purposes in the next section, can be derived from Weatherill's studies of English consumerism in *Consumer Behaviour,* app. 1, 201–7; in essence, it combines the Carr/Walsh "modern" and "amenities" indexes.

11. Lorena S. Walsh, "Toward a History of the Standard of Living in British North America," *William and Mary Quarterly* 45 (1988): 117–18; Carr and Walsh, "Standard of Living," 135–36; Sarah McMahon, "A Comfortable Subsistence: The Changing Composition of Diet in Rural New England, 1620–1840," *William and Mary Quarterly* 42 (1985): 25–65.

12. McCusker and Menard, *Economy of British America,* 103–5; Kenneth A. Lockridge, *A New England Town: The First Hundred Years* (New York: Norton, 1970), esp. 65–75; Gloria L. Main, "The Standard of Living in Colonial Massachusetts," *Journal of Economic History* 43 (1983): 101–8; Gloria L. Main, "The Standard of Living in Southern New England, 1640–1773," *William and Mary Quarterly* 45 (1988): 124–34; Jackson Turner Main, "Summary: The Hereafter," *William and Mary Quarterly* 45 (1988): 160–61; Gloria L. Main and Jackson Turner Main, "Economic Growth and the Standard of Living in Southern New England," *Journal of Economic History* 48 (1988): 27–46; Jackson Turner Main, "Standards of Living and the Life Cycle in Colonial Connecticut," *Journal of Economic History* 43 (1983): 159–74.

13. See table 1(A); Jackson Turner Main and Gloria Main, "Living Standards in Colonial New England," 39–45; Jackson Turner Main, *Society and Economy in Colonial Connecticut* (Princeton: Princeton University Press, 1985), esp. 88–114; John Demos, *A Little Commonwealth: Family Life in Plymouth Colony* (New York: Oxford University Press, 1970), 24–58.

14. McCusker and Menard, *Economy of British America,* 35–40; Carr and Walsh, "Changing Lifestyles," 63–65, 71–77, 123–29, quote from 64; Carr and Walsh, "Standard of Living," 135–59; Gloria L. Main, *Tobacco Colony: Life in Early Maryland, 1650–1720* (Princeton: Princeton University Press, 1982), 167–266; James Horn, *Adapting to a New World: English Society in the Seventeenth-Century Chesapeake* (Chapel Hill: University of North Carolina Press, Omohundro Institute for Early American History and Culture, 1994), esp. 31–48, 293–333.

15. Carr and Walsh, "Changing Lifestyles," 65–67, 71–75, 130–31; Main and Main, "Living Standards in Colonial New England," 39–45.

16. Carr and Walsh, "Changing Lifestyles," 72–77.

17. For example, Carole Shammas, "The Domestic Environment in Early Modern England and America," *Journal of Social History* 14 (1980): 18, states: "Over the three century period [1500–1800] the same wealth groups progressively invested a higher proportion of their wealth in consumer goods."

18. Shammas, *Pre-Industrial Consumer,* 95–100, 116; Carole Shammas, "The Decline of Textile Prices in England and British America prior to Industrialization," *Economic History Review* 47 (1994): 483–507; Weatherill, *Consumer Behaviour,* 109–11.

19. Shammas, *Pre-Industrial Consumer,* 112.

20. See Billy G. Smith, "Comment," *William and Mary Quarterly* 45 (1988): 163–66.

21. De Vries, "Purchasing Power and the World of Goods," 100–104; Shammas, *Pre-Industrial Consumer,* 95–96.

22. Carr and Walsh, "Changing Lifestyles," 65–68, 102–9, 116–18, 134, 144–45.

23. For critical discussions, see, for example, Grant McCracken, *Culture and Consumption: New Approaches to the Symbolic Character of Consumer Goods and Activities* (Bloomington & Indianapolis: Indiana University Press, 1988), 93–96; Amanda Vickery, "Women and the World of Goods: A Lancashire Consumer and Her Possessions," in *Consumption,* ed. Brewer and Porter, 274–77.

24. Vickery, "Women and the World of Goods," 289–94; Hudson, *Industrial Revolution,* 177–79; Fine and Leopold, "Consumerism," 166–73.

25. Weatherill, *Consumer Behaviour,* esp. 167–89; Carson, "The Consumer Revolution in Colonial America," in *Of Consuming Interests,* 67–121; Carr and Walsh, "Changing Lifestyles," 91–102.

26. Main and Main, "Living Standards in Colonial New England," 40–41.

27. For late colonial Charleston, see George C. Rogers Jr., *Charleston in the Age of the Pinckneys* (Norman: University of Oklahoma Press, 1969); Bridenbaugh, *Cities in Revolt,* 336–37.

28. Coclanis, *Shadow of a Dream,* 74–75; Wood, *Black Majority,* 28–37, 55–62, 95–124; Peter Wood, "'More Like a Negro Country': Demographic Patterns in Colonial South Carolina, 1700–1740," in *Race and Slavery in the Western Hemisphere: Quantitative Studies,* ed. Stanley L. Engerman and Eugene D. Genovese (Princeton: Princeton University Press, 1975), 72. Slave imports increased fourteenfold between the decades 1706–15 and 1726–35.

29. Shammas, "Domestic Environment," 14.

30. For the Chesapeake, see Carr and Walsh, "Changing Lifestyles," 71–77, figs. 1–7. For South Carolina, see table 5. To arrive at the number of "modern" items per household, divide by ten.

31. See table 2(A); Earle, *Making of the English Middle-Class,* 294–300, quote from 295. Weatherill, *Consumer Behaviour,* 49, 88, also shows that the incidence of new goods in London inventories was low until the 1690s and then spread rapidly.

32. See tables 2(A) and 5; Carr and Walsh, "Changing Lifestyles," esp. 68–71.

33. Probate inventories, at least for South Carolina, rarely give the occupation of the deceased, and even these designations are not always accurate ones; hence the great majority of occupational descriptions are drawn from the internal evidence of the inventories themselves.

34. Note that in 1773/74 the lower wealth group owned only 1 percent of all slaves in the sample.

35. Agricultural occupations are easy to spot in the inventories as these invariably listed holdings of crops, livestock, and farming tools and equipment.

36. Compare the first two lines of the upper panel of table 2(B).

37. As Kevin M. Sweeney comments on the American colonies generally in the early eighteenth century: "the homes of the wealthy were more likely to be distinguished by a greater number of rooms and greater quantities of goods than by the character or quality of the furnishings" (Sweeney, "High-Style Vernacular: Lifestyles of the Colonial Elite," in *Of Consuming Interests,* ed. Carson et al., 4).

38. See table 2(B); Carr and Walsh, "Changing Lifestyles," 78–90.

39. One would not, of course, expect much alteration in the average wealth of those in the middle and lower categories as their wealth was defined within strict and unchanging bands; however, it would have been perfectly possible for households possessed of an unchanging average personal wealth to have increased or, indeed, decreased their holdings of consumer goods.

40. Peter C. Mancall, Joshua L. Rosenbloom, and Thomas Weiss, "Slave Prices and the South-Carolina Economy, 1722–1809," *Journal of Economic History* 61 (2001): esp. 620, 625.

41. At prevailing valuations, the average seventy pounds worth of wrought silver owned by the richest households was equivalent to about three hundred ounces. The growing use of silver tableware followed English fashions; see Earle, *Making of the English Middle-Class,* 298; Sweeney, "High-Style Venacular," 3–5. In the inventories of rich households one also notes the ubiquitous presence of silver and gold watches and the much less common occurrence, at least in the inventories, of gold and silver jewelry and other items of personal adornment.

42. South Carolina inventories, unlike those in other colonies, invariably record whether furniture, even items such as chests or boxes, was made from pine or one of the finer woods. Where a particular wood was not specified, I have assumed that the furniture was made of pine; certainly, unclassified furniture wood was much cheaper than other kinds.

43. This statement is made judging by advertisements in the *SCG* for the years 1770–74, which more commonly feature imported carriages than locally made ones.

44. For consumer possessions in Chesapeake estates, see Alice Hanson Jones, *American Colonial Wealth: Documents and Methods,* 3 vols. (New York: Arno Press, 1977), vol. 2. For a brief comparison between the richest South Carolina estates and those of the Chesapeake, see Alice Hanson Jones, *Wealth of a Nation to Be: The American Colonies on the Eve of the Revolution* (New York: Columbia University Press, 1980), 335–36.

45. See table 1(B). For an analysis of the growing wealth of colonial South Carolina's plantation society, see Russell R. Menard, "Slavery, Economic Growth and Revolutionary Ideology in the South Carolina Low Country," in *The Economy of Early America: The Revolutionary Period, 1763–1790,* ed. Hoffman, McCusker, Menard, and Albert (Charlottesville, 1988), esp. 263–71.

46. See table 1(A); Main, "Standard of Living in Southern New England," 131; Carr and Walsh, "Changing Lifestyles," 72–73, figs. 2 and 3, 117. The Chesapeake elite did shift

their spending preferences toward more luxurious goods in the late colonial period, although they apparently did so while the aggregate value of their consumer goods' holdings declined.

47. Rogers, *Charleston;* Bridenbaugh, *Cities in Revolt,* 340; R. C. Nash, "The Organization of Trade and Finance in the Atlantic Economy," in *Money, Trade and Power: The Evolution of Colonial South Carolina's Plantation Society,* ed. Jack P. Greene, Rosemary Brana-Shute, and Randy J. Sparks (Columbia: University of South Carolina Press, 2001), 94–97; Russell R. Menard, "Financing the Lowcountry Export Boom: Capital and Growth in Early South Carolina," *William and Mary Quarterly* 51 (1984): 659–76; Menard, "Slavery, Economic Growth and Revolutionary Ideology," 261–62.

48. For the idea that a common culture embraced the elites of Charleston and of the northern cities, see Bridenbaugh, *Cities in Revolt,* 346–49.

49. Doerflinger, *Vigorous Spirit,* 20–26, 129–31, 375–81. Doerflinger's sample of late colonial Philadelphia merchants were wealthier than the upper group of South Carolina estates but owned roughly the same value of household consumer goods. Among a larger sample of merchants for 1789, the richer traders owned riding carriages and silver plate, although not in the same proportions as wealthy South Carolinians did in the early 1770s. For the high values of consumer goods held in Boston estates compared with those in rural New England, see Main and Main, "Living Standards in Colonial New England," 38; Main, "Standard of Living," 130–31.

50. For the northern seaports as the settings for the most developed forms of luxury consumerism in the late colonial period, see Sweeney, "High-Style Vernacular," 24–26. For advanced levels of consumption in a Caribbean city, Port Royal, Jamaica, see Zahedieh, "London and the Colonial Consumer," 252–56.

51. For a recent discussion, in the English context, of changing conceptions of gentility and of the "middling sort," see Henry French, "'Ingenious & Learned Gentlemen'—Social Perceptions and Self-fashioning among Parish Elites in Essex, 1680–1740," *Social History* 25 (2001): 44–66; Henry French, "The Search for the Middle Sort of People in England, 1600–1800," *Historical Journal* 43 (2001): 277–93.

52. McCracken, *Culture and Consumption,* 31–41.

53. Sweeney, "High-Style Vernacular," 8–10; Carson, "Consumer Revolution," 520–21; Karin Calvert, "The Function of Fashion in Eighteenth-Century America," in *Of Consuming Interests,* ed. Carson et al., 260–63, 270–75, quote from 274; Richard L. Bushman, "American High-Style and Vernacular Cultures," in *Colonial British America: Essays in the New History of the Early Modern Era,* ed. Jack P. Greene and J. R. Pole (Baltimore: Johns Hopkins University Press, 1984), esp. 352–67.

54. See table 2. For the high status, and costs, associated with riding carriages, see Sweeney, "High-Style Vernacular," 37–38, quote from 37; Bridenbaugh, *Cities in Revolt,* 340–42; Earle, *Making of the English Middle-Class,* 301; Susan E. Whyman, *Sociability and Power in Late-Stuart England: The Cultural World of the Verneys, 1660–1720* (Oxford: Oxford University Press, 1999), 87–109. Carriages were also luxuries in England because they were accompanied by dedicated carriage horses and liveried servants. Carriage horses are quite often specified in South Carolina inventories; slave coachmen much less so. For

advertisements for imported carriages, see, for example, *SCG,* January 17, October 31, and November 21, 1774.

55. Before c. 1750 mahogany furniture was almost all tables; chairs and other forms of furniture did not become widespread until the 1760s and 1770s. For English and colonial styles and production, see Ambrose Heal, *The London Furniture Makers* (London: Batsford, 1953); Earle, *Making of the English Middle-Class,* 27–28; E. T. Joy, "The Overseas Trade in Furniture in the Eighteenth Century," *Furniture History* 1 (1965); Weatherill, *Consumer Behaviour,* 32–33; Bushman, "American High-Style," 363–67.

56. This was true except in a fair proportion of Charleston and of nonagricultural households of middling wealth, illustrating the influence of urban residence and of occupations on consumption patterns.

57. See Lois Green Carr, "The Metropolis of Maryland: A Comment on Town Development along the Tobacco Coast," *Maryland Historical Magazine* 69 (1974): esp. 139–45; Carr and Walsh, "Changing Lifestyles," 105–11; Richard L. Bushman, "Shopping and Advertising in Colonial America," in *Of Consuming Interests,* ed. Carson et al., 236–37; Shammas, *Pre-Industrial Consumer,* 283–84; Jacob M. Price, "Economic Function and the Growth of American Port Towns in the Eighteenth Century," *Perspectives in American History* 8 (1974): 163–73; Jacob M. Price, "Buchanan and Simson, 1758–1763: A Different Kind of Glasgow Firm Trading to the Chesapeake," *William and Mary Quarterly* 40 (1983): 3–41. For the greater choice offered by urban over rural stores, see Carson, "Consumer Revolution," 608–9, esp. n193. In the late colonial period the location of Chesapeake stores continued to follow a riverine rather than an urban pattern, and the town network never dominated the distribution of goods to rural customers.

58. This refers to the inventories of James Beamer, Margaret Clifford, Wilson Dunston, Richard Fowell, John Harris, Samuel Osborn, Lewis Pedriau, Alexander Pepin, John Van Aersien, John Vansusteren, and Nathanial Williamson, all in Records of the Secretary of the Province [hereafter cited as Records of the Sec.], 1675–95, and Records of the Sec., 1692–1700, SCDAH.

59. Nash, "Organization of Trade and Finance," 77–81.

60. Ibid., 83, 86. This includes only dealers who advertised in the *SCG* in these years. Of course many traders seldom advertised—for example, Gabriel Manigault, one of the great South Carolina merchants in the period; see Maurice A. Crouse, "Gabriel Manigault: Charleston Merchant," *SCHM* 68 (1967): 220.

61. For these mercantile inventories, see notes to table 11.

62. See Nash, "Organization of Trade and Finance," 81–83; R. C. Nash, "Urbanization in the Colonial South: Charleston, South Carolina, as a Case Study," *Journal of Urban History* 19 (November 1992): 14–15. For the Chesapeake, see above note 57. For Pennsylvania and Massachusetts, see Thomas Doerflinger, "Farmers and Dry Goods in the Philadelphia Market Area, 1750–1800," in *Economy of Early America,* ed. Hoffman et al., 167–78; Shammas, *Pre-Industrial Consumer,* 266–85.

63. See Wood, "More Like a Negro Country," 134–40.

64. For examples of Charleston merchants with a large rural clientele, supplied on credit, see inventories of Capt. Albert Muller, John Cawood, and George Atcheson,

Records of the Sec., vol. E, 1726–27, 423–29, 531–34; Records of the Sec., vol. F, 1727–29, 358–59, SCDAH. For the 1760s, the business accounts of James Poyas, see note 81 below.

65. For the period 1762–67, see Jeanne A. Calhoun, Elizabeth A. Paysinger, and Martha A. Zierden, "A Survey of Economic Activity in Charleston, 1732–1770" (Charleston Museum, 1982), 92–96.

66. Shammas, *Pre-Industrial Consumer,* 268–69; Doerflinger, *Vigorous Spirit,* 129–30.

67. For sources, see above notes 59, 60, 65.

68. For advertisements for warehouses, see, for example, the *SCG,* August 1 and 22, 1771; June 4, 1772, supplement.

69. For Poyas, see below note 81.

70. For an acknowledgment of the importance of textiles and more ephemeral items in household expenditures, see Weatherill, *Consumer Behaviour,* 112–36; John Styles, "Manufacturing, Consumption and Design in Eighteenth-Century England," in *Consumption,* ed. Brewer and Porter, 538–39; De Vries, "Purchasing Power and the World of Goods," 102–3.

71. For per capita imports, see Coclanis, *Shadow of a Dream,* 75–77, 248–49n79. I have assumed that household size in 1770 in the lowcountry was the same as in the first census of 1790, that is, 4.22; see *Heads of Families at the First Census of the United States Taken in the Year 1790* (Baltimore, Md.: Genealogical Publishing Company Inc., 1978), 9. For the South as a whole, in 1774, see Jones, *Wealth of a Nation to Be,* 37, which estimates that there were 4.26 free persons per wealth holder, which is approximately the same as household size, although as she points out, some households had two or more wealth-holders.

72. Shammas, *Pre-Industrial Consumer,* 74–75; and Jacob M. Price, *Capital and Credit in British Overseas Trade: The View from the Chesapeake, 1700–1776* (Cambridge, Mass.: Harvard University Press, 1980), 149–50, suggest much higher markups than this for retail transactions in the colonies. However, Charleston's market was a highly competitive and efficient one, and in the late colonial period dry goods were sold on credit there in retail transactions at an advance of 9:1 on the English invoice price, which, taking into account the difference in currencies, represented an advance of 28.5 percent. See, for example, advertisements for dry goods in the *SCG,* January 3, 1771; June 14, 1773; January 17 and March 28, 1774.

73. For West India imports, see Nash, "Urbanization in the Colonial South," 7.

74. The figures for c. 1730 (1728–32) were estimated on the same basis as those for 1771–74, above.

75. Morgan, *Slave Counterpoint,* 125–26, estimates that South Carolina slaves received five yards of "negro cloth" (plains = cheapest woolens) and a pair of shoes per year. Henry Laurens allotted his slaves about ten yards of "negro cloth" per year in the mid-1760s plus shoes; see *The Papers of Henry Laurens,* ed. David R. Chesnutt et al., 16 vols. (Columbia, S.C., 1968–2002), 4:493, 634, 661, 665; 5:3–4, 6, 11, 19, 57, 73, 93, 95, 161. Imports of woolens to provide slaves with ten yards each would have cost approximately forty thousand pounds per annum at Charleston retail prices in the early 1770s, or less than 10 percent of the total value of imports from England. Slaves acquired other goods, such as pipes and caps, but as generally they had to pay for these, they cannot have owned them

in large quantities. For further discussion of slave consumption of imported goods, see Robert S. DuPlessis, "Cloth and the Emergence of the Atlantic Economy," in *The Atlantic Economy during the Seventeenth and Eighteenth Centuries,* ed. Peter A. Coclanis (Columbia: University of South Carolina Press, 2005), 80.

76. For the limited extent of consumer production in the British American colonies, see Shammas, *Pre-Industrial Consumer,* 3–4, 62–69. On craft production in Charleston, see Bridenbaugh, *Cities in Revolt,* 271–75; Calhoun et al., "Survey of Economic Activity." Numerous advertisements in the *SCG* show that craftsmen, especially those in the luxury trades, sold imported goods as well as their own products.

77. Note the importance of "haberdashery," which mainly consisted of thread and other articles needed to make clothes.

78. For the importance of textiles compared with consumer durables in London's export trade to the West Indies in the late seventeenth century, see Zahedieh, "London and the Colonial Consumer," 250–51.

79. For the great significance of imported goods to British American consumption as a whole, see Shammas, *Pre-Industrial Consumer,* 62–69.

80. Sales of buttons by Philadelphia merchants to rural shopkeepers exceeded in value those of eating utensils; see Doerflinger, "Farmers and Dry Goods," 178. Bushman, "Shopping and Advertising," 236–38, also notes the prominence of stocks of buttons in shopkeepers' inventories.

81. There are two surviving daybooks for Poyas's business: Merchant's Day Book [James Poyas], 1761–64, Charleston Museum Archives, Charleston, which is now regarded as too fragile for archival use; and Merchant's Day Book [James Poyas], 1764–66, SCHS, 34–325, available only in the form of a photocopy, the copy used here. Poyas imported cargoes of manufactures from a number of major London merchants; he also imported flour and other provisions from Philadelphia, while his West India goods were bought at auctions in Charleston.

82. For this theme, see especially Weatherill, *Consumer Behaviour,* 113–33. A study of outgoings on a Maryland tobacco plantation, 1662–72, shows that expenditure on clothing exceeded that on other imported manufactures by a factor of at least ten to one, although the trustee managing the estate in these years was little concerned to replace consumer durables; see Carr et al., *Robert Cole's World,* 80–86.

83. As Vickery, "Women and the World of Goods," 290, 292, comments on a Lancashire gentry family in the middle decades of the eighteenth century, "it appears that furniture was bought once in a life-time and expected to last for generations" and that "Large or expensive items [of furniture], bought new or inherited, were suggestive of history and lineage."

84. De Vries, "Purchasing Power and the World of Goods," 101–4.

85. Vickery, "Women and the World of Goods," 292.

86. Earle, *Making of the English Middle-Class,* 283–90.

87. Records of the Sec., vol. F, 1727–29, vol. G, 1729–31, vol. H, 1730–31; Inventories, WPA Transcripts, vols. 112–14 (1746–48); Miscellaneous Records: Inventories, vol. CC, (1732–36); Inventories, vol. MM (1746–48); Inventories, vol. Z (1771–74); vol. & (1772–76); vol. AA (1774–85), SCDAH. See also Jones, *American Colonial Wealth,* 3:1473–1619.

88. See previous note for Jones's data. For examples of their use, see Menard, "Slavery, Economic Growth, and Revolutionary Ideology," 265–67; Coclanis, *Shadow of a Dream,* 89–91.

89. As noted by Coclanis, *Shadow of a Dream,* 90–91. In fact Jones did not use all the inventories for 1774, even for the Charleston district.

90. See Jones, *Wealth of a Nation to Be,* 352–62.

91. William G. Bentley, "Wealth Distribution in Colonial South Carolina" (Ph.D. thesis, Georgia State University, 1977).

The Archaeological Signature of Eighteenth-Century Charleston

Martha A. Zierden

The first British settlement in the Carolina colony, Charleston is well known as the social and intellectual center of a successful plantation economy. The accumulation of great wealth through trade in staples, supported by slave labor, peaked in the late eighteenth century, when Charleston was the wealthiest city (per capita) in the American colonies and the fourth-largest commercial center. The city's success as a commercial center was matched by her role as a center for the cultures of gentility and sociability among the white elite, an entrepôt for the flow of goods, ideas, and people from throughout the Atlantic rim. However, the first generations of colonists experienced Charleston as a struggling frontier community where luxury and leisure were relatively unknown. Efforts to expand the fledgling colony's economy were tempered by outside threats from neighboring Spanish and French colonial settlements; from Native Americans, both on the coast and on the interior; and from the growing population of enslaved African people within the settlement. The recovery of archaeological assemblages that span the eighteenth century has provided a tangible measure of these trends.

Archaeology is one of several disciplines that provide a more complex picture of Charleston's evolution. The excavations have uncovered material culture that reflects the purchasing power of Charleston's elite. They also reveal evidence of the difficulties of daily life in an urban setting and call attention to the city's middling and poor, particularly the enslaved people who maintained the elite residents. The artifacts that dominate archaeological assemblages, such as ceramic and glass containers, are infrequently mentioned in diaries and rarely enumerated in advertisements. An assortment of the material items common in the living world find their way into the archaeological record after use, some in by-product form. Nails, building hardware, bits of personal items such as fans, and small decorative items from household furnishings are there only occasionally but in a consistent enough fashion to derive meaning. At the same time, Charleston's archaeological record contains only rarely the idiosyncracies and personalized objects of individuals; instead it contains listings of artifacts of a sameness found on sites across eastern North America, from cosmopolitan seaport cities to small backcountry villages. Residents of both drank and served tea in the same porcelain and pearl-ware tea cups. These artifacts signify the global connectedness of small frontier towns, bustling colonial seaports, and England's industrial centers, reflecting a world economy. Though only a fraction of the material goods used by urban dwellers, the citywide archaeological sample provides a baseline to measure trends of interaction, acquisition, use, and discard by a diverse colonial population.

Archaeological evidence may generally be divided into three categories: material culture (the cultural artifacts), stratigraphy (the layered deposition of earth and trash), and environmental evidence (plant and animal remains). The latter two categories have been used in previous studies to explore the evolution of Charleston's landscape, with particular focus on the late eighteenth and early nineteenth centuries.[1] The material culture recovered from controlled excavations may be used to explore issues of trade and international relations, cultural diversity and self- and group identity, and socioeconomic classification. Previous material culture studies in Charleston have, again, focused on the late eighteenth and nineteenth centuries.[2] The current study explores the lesser-known colonial period.[3]

This study utilizes all aspects of archaeological material culture, but the discussion focuses particularly on ceramics. Though only a small portion of the material goods of colonial people, ceramics dominate the archaeological record. They are durable, easily recognized, and well documented. Ceramics are used here to measure the flow of goods, people, and ideas and to measure changes in these through time.

A recent opportunity to examine the relation of the British colonial settlement to Spanish St. Augustine was the impetus to reexamine the archaeological data for early eighteenth-century Charleston.[4] Eighteenth-century provenances were divided into periods (1680–1720, 1720–40, 1740–60, and 1760–90). These newly derived figures frame the first discussion. However, there is more to the discussion than mere numbers. In a recent volume archaeologists argue that eighteenth-century Carolina was more diverse, socially and ethnically, than in the post-Revolutionary period.[5] The materials from the pre-1760 periods support this idea.

The second period of discussion, roughly the 1770 to 1800 period, is the era of acquisition for Charlestonians, and much of this overflows into the ground. The density and indeed the sheer volume of archaeological materials increase dramatically for this time period, and the finery acquired by the wealthy planter class

Fig. 1. Example of archaeological deposits in Charleston. The soil profile reveals (from top to bottom) a deep layer of topsoil deposited in the twentieth century; a series of thin, working, or driving surfaces of crushed shell and compacted sand, dating to the nineteenth century; and a deep refuse-filled pit deposited in the last quarter of the eighteenth century. The soil profile is from the excavations at 14 Legare Street, a property first occupied in 1800. Courtesy of the Collections of the Charleston Museum, Charleston, South Carolina

is reflected in the archaeological record. That same series of soil deposits contains the more muted remains of the African bondsmen, their refuse mixed with that of their owners. Charlestonians begin to divide themselves simply into black and white, rather than the myriad groups of the colonial period, as their physical proximity becomes less separate. For this late eighteenth-century period individual assemblages datable to single decades, and discussed in detail, follow a general discussion of a citywide assemblages.

The Archaeological Data

Since 1982 nearly thirty excavation projects of varying sizes, ranging from a single test unit to large block excavations, have been conducted by the author. Eighteen of the most relevant sites have been retabulated. In addition, data from excavations conducted by others working in Charleston were incorporated, where their data sets are comparable.[6]

Five of the excavated sites are located within the limits of the walled city, and three more are immediately adjacent to the wall locations. Five more are in areas developed by the mid–eighteenth century. The remainder are located in what would be considered, through time, suburban residential areas, gradually occupied and urbanized in the late eighteenth century, the early nineteenth century, and the mid–nineteenth century respectively. Taken together, the sites excavated produced 1,916 temporally defined provenances and 183,700 artifacts.

The temporal division into specific periods is a revision of previous classification by three broad eras (1720–60, 1760–1830, 1830–80), which corresponded to historical development and technological advances in material culture.[7] Archaeological association with these events was uneven. The first period, 1680 to 1720, is considered Charleston's frontier stage. Only the Judicial Center site, outside the city gates, produced 2 provenances with 104 artifacts. The earliest period of archaeological representation is 1720–40, for which six sites (two of them outside the city walls) produced 63 provenances and 5,080 artifacts. Archaeological representation expands considerably in the next period, 1740–60, with 144 provenances and 31,500 artifacts from nine sites. The period considered Charleston's economic golden age, 1760–90, is well represented archaeologically. Ten sites produced 223 provenances and 35,900 artifacts. The nineteenth century is considerably noisier. The post-Revolutionary period of prosperity, 1790 to 1820, yielded 647 provenances from twenty sites and more than 55,000 artifacts. The remainder of the nineteenth century produced 861 provenances from seventeen sites and nearly 100,000 artifacts.

The Material Culture of Early Charleston

For the purposes of initial analysis, the data for each period were divided into the eight traditional artifact categories proposed by Stanley South for his Carolina artifact pattern, a principal used to organize the Charleston data for twenty years.[8] The artifact proportions generally conform to the Carolina pattern, and to each other, and do not change through time. The one variation is an increase in architectural items in the 1740–60 period. This may reflect the rebuilding after two city-destroying events, the 1740 fire and the hurricane of 1752, an observation supported by Louis Nelson's recent research.[9] Likewise, the newly acquired wealth from rice production prompted a building boom, as planters "needed" new, stylish houses.[10]

Artifacts related to affairs of the kitchen dominate the archaeological assemblages from throughout the eighteenth century, averaging 55 percent to 60 percent of all artifacts. Ceramic vessels and glass containers are the most common artifacts, and their relative proportions remain constant. Nearly 42 percent of the ceramics from the early century consists of the mundane earthenware of food preparation and storage and possibly consumption. Coarse earthenware items include North Devon wares, Buckley earthenware, and an infinite variety of lead-glazed redware from England. These sturdy vessels included cream pans and crocks of all kinds. The lead-glazed earthenware, such as manganese mottled ware and slip-coated ware, also includes smaller vessels—tankards, bowls, cups—for individual consumption of food and beverage. Likewise, the most common utilitarian ware, combed and trailed slipware, comes in large bowls for food preparation and small cups and pitchers for individual consumption. This range of forms is mirrored in utilitarian stoneware from the Rhineland, imported through England. Jugs, crocks, tankards, and chamber wares predominate.

Ceramics and other artifact categories were used to measure material diversity in the eighteenth century. As a British colony, Carolina was expected to import manufactured goods exclusively British.[11] The residential population, though, hailed from a number of locations throughout Europe, Africa, and the Caribbean. These people shared the colony with Native American groups already in the midst of cultural upheaval. The archaeological record suggests that, on regular occasion, goods as well as people arrived in the port town.

There is, from early on, a newly discovered Caribbean presence in the Charleston ceramics. Over the years a few isolated ceramics have been identified as Caribbean in origin. More recently Michael Stoner has identified lead-glazed earthenware from Charles Town Landing (site of the original 1670 settlement) as Barbadian in origin. These wares were recovered in kiln sites on Barbados and at the 1664 Charles Fort settlement in North Carolina. Lead-glazed wares from the Judicial Center site and from the Heyward-Washington house appear similar to Stoner's Barbadian samples and are currently undergoing chemical testing to determine if they were used after the town moved from Albemarle Point to Oyster Point. This is the first material manifestation of the Barbadian connection of the earliest settlers.[12]

An initially illicit trade between Charleston and Spanish St. Augustine during the first half of the eighteenth century evidently included inexpensive material goods. Archaeology suggests that ceramics and glass, as well as provisions, were shipped to St. Augustine. Non-Spanish wares become a significant component of the St. Augustine archaeological record by the second quarter of the eighteenth century.[13] The ships evidently returned to Charleston with few material goods. Joyce Harmon's tables list many returning with ballast and some with provisions, particularly oranges.[14] Spanish ceramics are a small component of the archaeological record (less than 0.5 percent) in Charleston after 1720 and peak in the 1790s records, principally from a waterfront deposit that contained a number of Spanish and Caribbean artifacts. This assemblage consists principally of the most common Hispanic coarse earthenware—olive jar, followed by El Morro, Spanish storage jar, and Mexican painted wares, along with a small number of late seventeenth- and eighteenth-century majolicas (tin-glazed tableware).

French ceramics also make up a measurable component of the Charleston ceramic collection. A green-glazed earthenware found on almost all eighteenth-century lowcountry sites has recently been identified as French. Smaller numbers

FIG. 2. An El Morro–ware bowl recovered from the waterfront deposits at the Atlantic Wharf site. El Morro is a Spanish ceramic, possibly produced in North America. It is recovered in Charleston provenances dating to the second half of the eighteenth century. Courtesy of the Collections of the Charleston Museum, Charleston, South Carolina

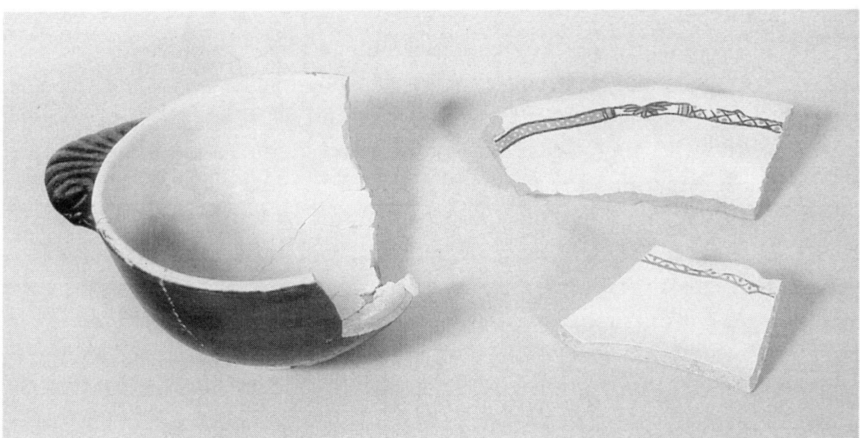

FIG. 3. Examples of French faience, usually recovered from late eighteenth-century provenances in Charleston. The porringer is an example of the faience brune wares, featuring a brown-glazed exterior. Courtesy of the Collections of the Charleston Museum, Charleston, South Carolina

of Saintonge and Provence earthenware have also come from early eighteenth-century deposits.[15] In contrast to these utilitarian wares, French faience tableware items are common only in late eighteenth-century components.[16] These French and Spanish wares are present in similar proportions on contemporary low-country plantation sites as well, reflecting their distribution through the Carolina economy upon arrival in Charleston.

The most notable sign of diversity of the Charleston population is colonoware, attributed principally to African residents. In the records these wares are present from the beginning, peak in the 1740–60 period at 24 percent of ceramics, decline gradually from 1760 through 1800, and are only a minor component thereafter. Most researchers involved in the study of colonoware now note a significant mixing of Native American characteristics in general and in particular vessels, and they suggest that the wares are the products of both peoples or at least an interaction of both peoples.[17] Further, some exhibit European form or decoration.

Native American slaves have been largely overlooked in historical studies and are seemingly invisible in the archaeological record as well. However, the historian William Ramsey has recently noted that Native Americans made up a sizable portion of the slave population from about 1700 until the Yamassee War.[18] He further suggests that Carolina governor James Moore's raids of St. Augustine in 1702 and the Spanish missions of Apalachee in 1704 were largely responsible for the tremendous increase in Indian slaves, from 10 percent of the slave population in 1703 to 25 percent by 1709. The majority of these slaves, Ramsey notes, were women, and many worked as domestic servants. Native Americans largely disappear from the lowcountry records following the Yamassee War of 1714, but some remain as enslaved laborers or in small enclaves of "neighbor Indians." Some scholars, principally Ronald Anthony, have recently discovered a significant amount of early eighteenth-century colonoware with paste characteristic of historic Native American pottery. Anthony's study of colonoware from a 1740–80 plantation on the Edisto River revealed a third of the collection with grit-tempered paste.[19] The Heyward-Washington house on Church Street in Charleston also produced measurable amounts of grit-tempered colonoware. Four reconstructable vessels from Charleston that are clearly historic southeastern Native American come not from the earliest contexts but from those dating to the 1740s. These may have been used in Charleston kitchens during the early years of the eighteenth century. The majority of the colonoware, though, was likely made and used by people of African descent.

Ironically, and perhaps symbolically, the most common non-English artifacts recovered in Charleston are silver coins. Whereas Spanish ceramics make up less than 0.4 percent of the total ceramics, Spanish coins constitute 30 percent of all colonial coinage recovered in Charleston. The presence of these coins peaks in

Fig. 4. Colonoware is a major component of Charleston ceramic assemblages. Globular jars, such as these, are the most common form. From excavations at the Heyward-Washington house and 14 Legare Street. Courtesy of the Collections of the Charleston Museum, Charleston, South Carolina

the 1770s records: the Revolutionary-era coin assemblage for the city consists of two-thirds British half-pennies and one-third Spanish two-real pieces. However, even for the earlier years, when coinage was scarcer, Spanish coins are one-eighth of the total numismatic assemblage. Ivor Noël Hume and others have suggested that specie was generally rare in the colonies and that any currency was acceptable, particularly silver coins from Spain and France. While the proportion of Spanish coins in other British colonial settings is unknown, it would seem that Charleston's eighteenth-century trade ties to St. Augustine and the Caribbean could account for the frequency in the city. Spanish coins were also recovered on lowcountry plantation sites in similar proportions. Interestingly, nearly all of the Spanish coins and none of the British coins are pierced to be worn as charms.

Recent excavation of tightly dated refuse-bearing zones at the Heyward-Washington house on lower Church Street provides a new look at the material assemblage of the 1730s and from the catastrophic fire of 1740 and new refuse from the 1740s to 1750s. The lot at 86 Church Street was first occupied in 1730 by John Milner, a gunsmith of modest means. He operated his gunsmith business behind a wooden house that fronted on Church Street. His house burned in the 1740 fire, which destroyed most of the town at that time (over three hundred buildings). Milner and his son, John Milner Jr., evidently continued the gunsmith business on the property after the fire. John Milner Jr. inherited the property upon

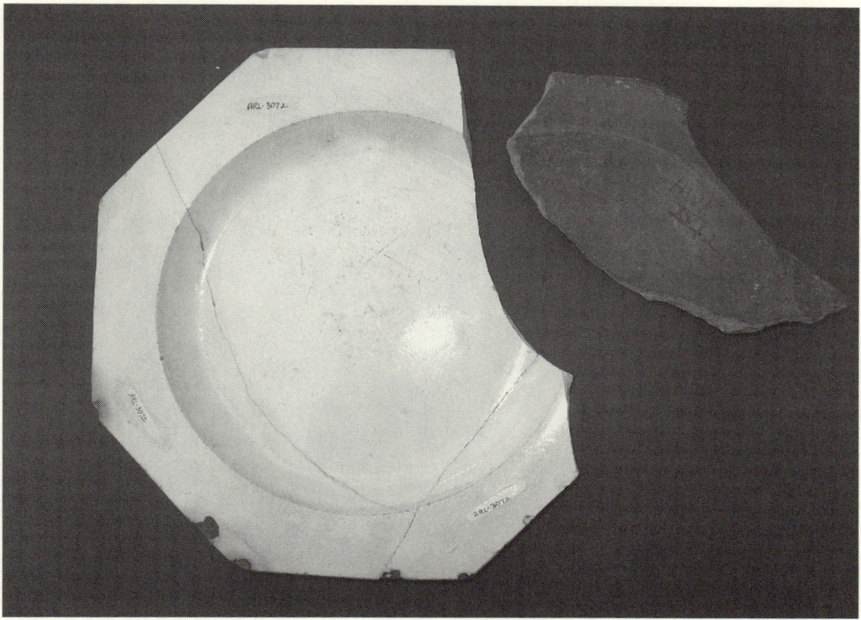

Fig. 5. Colonoware is occasionally produced in European forms. Here a piece of colonoware is shown with a comparable form in creamware from Staffordshire. Both vessels are from Church Street. Courtesy of the Collections of the Charleston Museum, Charleston, South Carolina

his father's death in 1749 and then built a new brick single house and outbuildings on the lot. Archaeological excavations inside the circa 1750 stable building revealed sealed layers dating to Milner's occupation from 1730 to 1740, a layer of ash from the 1740 fire, and a second midden dating 1740 to 1750, sealed by a construction layer for the stable in 1750. These contexts provide a small but reliable sample to examine the archaeological signature of these two decades.

Both assemblages conform somewhat to the averages that reflect the Carolina artifact pattern. Kitchen materials are 53 percent of the 1730 assemblage, while architectural items make up 34 percent. This relatively large proportion of architectural items may reflect the "newness" of the site, as construction of the house and outbuildings overshadows a relatively short accumulation of daily refuse, reflected in the kitchen group. The opposite occurs in the 1740s assemblage. We know from documents and archaeology that this layer does not include any construction activities but simply reflects a continuation of trade and living. Kitchen materials make up 65 percent of this assemblage and architecture 24 percent. Tobacco pipe fragments represent 10 percent of each assemblage, suggesting a continuation of this leisure activity. The 1740s assemblage is twice as large and,

FIG. 6. Native American vessel from Heyward-Washington house, possibly Yamassee. The exterior features complicated stamped designs, while the interior is burnished with a red-filmed rim. Courtesy of the Collections of the Charleston Museum, Charleston, South Carolina

for the first time, includes some luxury items, such as clothing artifacts and personal objects. Likewise, Chinese export porcelains increase in proportion for the 1740s; they comprise 6 percent of the ceramics, compared to 3 percent for the earlier decade. These may replace the English white stoneware items, which drop from 5 percent to 3 percent of the ceramics. Tin-enameled delft tableware also declines in frequency, from 24 percent in the 1730s to 10 percent in the 1740s. Colonoware, including that attributed to Native Americans, is a fairly consistent presence, dropping only slightly from 27 percent of the ceramics to 23 percent. Native American wares make up nearly 2 percent of each assemblage. The most interesting figure is the near absence of French and Spanish ceramics in the 1730s assemblage and their rise to 3.3 percent in the 1740s. The latter figure includes equal amounts of French and Spanish utilitarian earthenware.

The paucity of the archaeological record for the early eighteenth century and its near absence for the late seventeenth century, compared to that of the second half of the colonial period, were surprising. Recent reconsiderations of the archaeological, cartographic, and documentary evidence suggest that the phenomenal urban growth that was under way by 1739, as documented in the Roberts and Toms map of that year, appears to have occurred principally after

Fig. 7. Delft punch bowl proclaiming "Success to Trade," recovered from the waterfront deposits at the Exchange Building. Courtesy of the Collections of the Charleston Museum, Charleston, South Carolina

1720.[20] Consideration of this period may also be hampered by small sample size (only five sites within the confines of the city wall) and lack of access to those remains. Joseph's work at the Charleston Judicial Center suggests that early deposits may be clustered near the streetfronts, areas covered with new buildings by the late eighteenth century.[21]

The Late Eighteenth Century

The acquisition of material goods by Charlestonians, particularly those of the upper class, accelerated in the second half of the eighteenth century. These goods include new houses in the single-house or double-house style, furniture, plates, paintings, books, and a few items that survive in archaeological contexts. For the archaeologist, these are principally ceramics from the merchant-planters' dinner and tea tables, along with some embellishments from clothing and furniture. Consumption may also be measured through the remains from architectural expansion and renovation and from gardening.

The late eighteenth-century assemblage is denser and noisier archaeologically. Not only do absolute numbers of artifacts and provenances increase, but so does the density of archaeological deposits. Early eighteenth-century deposits, on average, contain 122 artifacts per provenance. The figure increases to 139 per provenance by the late eighteenth century. Early nineteenth-century provenances average 180 artifacts, while late nineteenth-century provenances average only 22 artifacts, suggesting that much less refuse was cycled into the individual archaeological site during this era. By the end of the antebellum period, off-site refuse disposal appears to be the norm. In the late eighteenth century Charleston yards were still utilized for disposal and for a number of activities, reflected in both artifact density and the large number of depositional events.

Proportions of artifacts traditionally considered status indicators are remarkably consistent through time. These include Chinese porcelain and table glass, as well as the remains of clothing, personal possessions, and furniture. These groups, however, get more diverse through time, beginning in the 1760s; porcelain remains a large percentage of the ceramics, for example, even though the later assemblages are filled with the new English refined earthenware. People evidently bought and used more porcelain, proportionally. The outstanding statistic is that people simply acquired more goods as the eighteenth century progressed, and almost all of them were English. Import statistics suggest that from 1700 until 1775 South Carolina's dry-goods imports multiplied twentyfold, increasing from 3 percent of all American imports to 11 percent.

In the category of kitchen items, a variety of fine wares for food serving, consuming, and entertaining explode on the scene for the late eighteenth century. The proportion of the rough utilitarian ware artifacts drops from 42 percent to only 18 percent. It appears that the actual number and range of types remain fairly consistent; instead, quantities of new tableware are added to the assemblage. British refined earthenware dominates the ceramic assemblages of late eighteenth-century households. These were available in a variety of styles and price ranges, from the mass-produced dinnerware to the elaborately decorated serving and tea wares. Creamware makes up nearly 20 percent of late eighteenth-century ceramics and 15 percent of nineteenth-century ones. Creamware augments but does not replace Chinese porcelain at town-house sites. Porcelain jumps from 10 percent of the early eighteenth-century ceramics to 18 percent for the late part of that century and declines only slightly to 14 percent for the nineteenth century. The flood of tableware, generally, overwhelms what appears to be a relatively stable number of utilitarian ceramics. French and Spanish ceramics remain a small but consistent component of the ceramic collections.

Colonoware also remains a significant component of the ceramic assemblage, reflecting both the African American presence and the continuing role of colonoware in Charleston households. Colonoware comprises 17–20 percent of the early eighteenth-century ceramics but drops to 5 percent for the late eighteenth century. It does not completely disappear for the early nineteenth century (comprising 6.5 percent in the 1790–1820 period), though; the Aiken-Rhett house, first occupied in 1818, included .2 percent colonoware in the nineteenth-century assemblage. Ongoing excavations reinforce the notion that the archaeological material culture of African Americans cannot be separated from that of European Americans in the city. As Bernard Herman suggests in this volume, scholars should avoid such exercises; they imply a false physical—and social—separation. Artifact collections of the late eighteenth century reinforce the mixing of colonoware and porcelains in city households.

Excavations in the formal garden at the Miles Brewton site produced both unique stratigraphy and a distinctive artifact assemblage. Unlike the rest of the yard, particularly the work area, the artifacts in the garden appear to be a single depositional event, described by archaeologists as a "horizon." Here the dense deposit of bone, architectural rubble, and kitchen artifacts appeared to be deliberately deposited for drainage and fertilizer, presumably soon after completion of the house in 1769. The majority of the artifacts consist of kitchenware, though the overall assemblage is comparable to South's Carolina artifact pattern, suggesting generalized domestic refuse. Over a dozen plates of Chinese export porcelain, each of a different design, were reassembled.[22] The same excavation units revealed a set of nested delft platters, octagonal in shape and decorated in blue. The table glass included enamel-twist goblet stems, various candlestick and decanter fragments, and a number of large tumblers in a molded diamond pattern. Other trenches revealed a lead-glazed redware cream pan broken in place and a brown salt-glazed stoneware jug. Architectural materials included nails, window glass, and delft tiles.

Utilitarian wares included slipware, American-made earthenware, and a variety of stoneware. Colonoware comprised 10 percent of the Brewton assemblage. No artifacts directly attributable to Miles Brewton were recovered. A single personalized wine bottle seal belonged to fellow Charlestonian Charles Pinckney. An identical seal was recovered at Pinckney's Snee Farm plantation in Mt. Pleasant.

Additional deposits of Miles Brewton's tableware were discovered a decade later on an adjoining property. The lot at 14 Legare Street currently features a town house built in 1800 and renovated in 1818. In the late eighteenth century, though, the property was a vacant lot separated from the Brewton lot by a finger of marsh or low-lying swampy land. Brewton or his servants discarded household refuse there.[23]

The eighteenth-century trash deposits contained English and Chinese porcelain tea wares, elaborate new-style creamware, and a variety of colonoware, including decorated globular jars and large bowls. The feature contained a green wine bottle with a personalized seal that read "Mbrewton." A second pit contained a silver teaspoon handle engraved "M*B."

A privy pit from the South Carolina Society Hall site, dated 1760–70, yielded an unparalleled set of vessels used and discarded together, including Whieldon-ware plates, plates in white salt-glazed stoneware, and blue-on-white porcelain plates. Porcelain tea wares featured Imari-style overglazing. Chamber pots were delft or combed and trailed slipware. The teapots were sprigged creamware, a red Chinese stoneware, and Elers ware. More unusual was a French bowl of Provence yellow on white faience and a Spanish storage jar. Utilitarian wares included a black lead-glazed redware bowl and a brown-glazed cooking cup. Also present was the ubiquitous colonoware, a large, well-fired bowl.

The increased availability of consumer goods and the financial ability to consume them are reflected in a rise in quantity and variety of those artifacts associated with clothing, personal possession, and furniture. They remain minor components of the archaeological assemblage but increase in both frequency and variety for the late colonial period. Furniture assemblages are dominated by upholstery tacks, curtain rings, and the lost or discarded drawer pulls or locks. Clothing items include a large variety of buttons and buckles. Items likely belonging to African residents include silver coins pierced to be worn as charms, cowrie shells, and quartz crystals, in addition to the more anonymous European goods.[24]

Conclusion

The explosion of consumer goods, mass-produced in the industrial era, by the end of the eighteenth century mean that artifacts begin to lose some of their

Fig. 8. Whieldon-ware tea wares in the form of a pineapple, from the Charleston County Judicial Center site. Courtesy of the Collections of the Charleston Museum, Charleston, South Carolina

FIG. 9. Ceramics recovered from the privy at South Carolina Society Hall, including feather-edged creamware, Chinese export porcelain, and Whieldon ware. The ceramics date to the third quarter of the eighteenth century and were likely discarded in the 1770s. Courtesy of the Collections of the Charleston Museum, Charleston, South Carolina

shared meaning. The archaeological record gets "noisy" as population pressure mounts in Charleston. Sanitation and health become critical issues, and the archaeological record on domestic sites literally disappears, as off-site refuse disposal replaces on-site accumulation. Gradually artifacts, from all members of Charleston society, do not make it to the archaeological record in quantifiable amounts.

The dominance of mass-produced British ceramics around the world likewise smothers the products of individual countries and regions that characterize the archaeological assemblage of the early eighteenth century. The quantity of material goods in the archaeological record of the late eighteenth century provides more to read, but its message may be less clear, for the assemblage is clearly dominated by the refuse of those who could afford to count human beings as well as tea wares among their possessions.

The archaeological record of the earlier colonial period, in contrast, suggests a more fluid society where settlers from a number of cultures and countries met and interacted. People from across Europe and Africa met with native peoples from a variety of groups. The urban society that would by the late eighteenth century become "Charleston" sprang from these cultural encounters a century earlier.[25] Though relatively sparse, the archaeological record of the early eighteenth century reflects the contributions by people from a variety of backgrounds to the creation of this urban society. The interactions among Native Americans and African, English, Caribbean, French, and Spanish setters are reflected in the development of colonoware, the limited presence of Native American pottery, and the trade in various European ceramics.

Notes

1. Archaeological discussion of the Charleston landscape may be found in Martha Zierden and Bernard Herman, "Charleston Townhouses: Archaeology, Architecture, and the Urban Landscape, 1750–1850," in *Landscape Archaeology: Reading and Interpreting the American Historical Landscape,* ed. Rebecca Yamin and Karen Metheny (Knoxville: University of Tennessee Press, 1996), 197–227; Martha Zierden, "The Urban Landscape, the Work Yard, and Archaeological Site Formation Processes in Charleston, South Carolina," in *Historical Archaeology and the Study of American Culture,* ed. Bernard L. Herman and Lu Ann De Cunzo (Winterthur: Winterthur Museum Publications, University of Tennessee Press, 1996), 285–315; Martha Zierden, "The Urban Landscape in South Carolina," in *Carolina's Historical Landscapes: Archaeological Perspectives,* ed. Linda Stine, Martha Zierden, Lesley Drucker, and Christopher Judge (Knoxville: University of Tennessee Press, 1997), 161–74; Martha Zierden, "Charleston's Powder Magazine and the Development of a Southern City," in *Archaeology of Southern Urban Landscapes,* ed. Amy Young (Tuscaloosa: University of Alabama Press, 2000), 92–108.

2. Martha Zierden, ed., "Charleston in the Context of Trans-Atlantic Culture," *Historical Archaeology* 33, no. 3 (1999): 73–87.

3. Another recent study of early eighteenth-century Charleston is J. W. Joseph, "From Colonist to Charlestonian: The Crafting of Identity in a Colonial Southern City," in *Another's Country,* ed. Joseph and Zierden, 215–34.

4. Martha A. Zierden and Elizabeth J. Reitz, "Eighteenth Century Charleston: Aftermath of the Siege of St. Augustine," *Firestorm and Ashes: The Siege of 1702, El Escribano* (St. Augustine Historical Society) (2002).

5. Joseph and Zierden, eds., *Another's Country.*

6. Of particular relevance are the excavations at the Heyward-Washington house on lower Church Street (occupied from 1730 to the present), conducted by Elaine Herold, formerly of the Charleston Museum, in the 1970s (additional areas of this site were recently excavated by the author), and the Charleston Judicial Center site, immediately outside of the city gates at Meeting and Broad streets (occupied by the 1710s), excavated by J. W. Joseph of New South Associates, Atlanta.

7. For a discussion of Charleston artifact assemblages by temporal association, see Martha Zierden, "Big House / Back Lot: An Archaeological Study of the Nathaniel Russell House," Archaeological Contributions 25 (Charleston: Charleston Museum, 1996).

8. Stanley South, *Method and Theory in Historical Archaeology* (New York: Academic Press, 1977).

9. Louis Nelson, Department of History, University of Virginia, personal communication with author, June 2002.

10. Poston's *Buildings of Charleston* lays out the general trends in building styles for the city; see also Zierden and Herman, "Charleston Townhouses."

11. Import statistics suggest that from 1700 to 1775, South Carolina's dry goods imports increased twentyfold, increasing from 3 percent of all American imports to 11 percent; see Nash, "Organization of Trade," 74–107.

12. Michael Stoner and Stanley South, *Exploring 1670 Charles Town: Final Archaeology Report* (Columbia: Research Manuscript Series 230, South Carolina Institute of Archaeology and Anthropology, 2001); Michael Stoner, "Codrington Plantation: A History of a Barbadian Ceramic Industry (M.A. thesis, Armstrong Atlantic State University, 2000).

13. For a discussion of English goods in archaeological contexts in St. Augustine, see Kathleen Deagan, *Spanish St. Augustine: The Archaeology of a Colonial Creole Community* (New York: Academic Press, 1983); and Carl Halbirt, "Conflagration and Exchange: The Impact of the Carolina Colony on the Development of the 18th Century Presidio de San Augustin, Florida," *El Escribano* (2002). Spanish ceramics and other material culture are discussed in Deagan, *Artifacts of the Spanish Colonies.*

14. The most complete study of the illicit trade between Charleston and St. Augustine is Joyce Harmon, *Trade and Privateering in Spanish Florida, 1732–1763* (St. Augustine: St. Augustine Historical Society, 1969). Kathleen Deagan has recently reanalyzed the trade between St. Augustine and Charleston and discovered evidence that the trade was legalized in the late eighteenth century (Deagan, "Eliciting Contraband through Archaeology: Illicit Trade in Eighteenth-Century St. Augustine," *Historical Archaeology* 41, no. 4 [2007]: 98–116.). Greg Waselkov and his colleagues note a similar discrepancy between the documented trade in foodstuffs between the Spanish and French in the lower Gulf Coast and the recovery of Spanish ceramics and other material goods in Old Mobile; see Gregory A. Waselkov, ed., "French Colonial Archaeology at Old Mobile: Selected Studies," *Historical Archaeology* 36, no. 1 (2002): 3–12.

15. Gregory Waselkov and Bonnie Gums, University of South Alabama, personal communication with author, October 2002. See also Waselkov, ed., "French Colonial Archaeology."

16. Ivor Noël Hume, *A Guide to Artifacts of Colonial America* (Philadelphia: University of Pennsylvania Press, 2001), suggests that French faience arrived in America during the Revolutionary years, when trade with Britain was interrupted.

17. For an ongoing discussion of the origins of colonoware, see Ronald Anthony, "Tangible Interaction: Evidence from Stobo Plantation," in *Another's Country,* ed. Joseph and Zierden, 45–64; Ferguson, *Uncommon Ground.*

18. William Ramsey, "All & Singular the Slaves: A Demographic Profile of Indian Slavery in Colonial South Carolina," in *Money, Trade and Power,* ed. Greene et al., 166–86.

19. Anthony, "Tangible Interaction."

20. Katherine Saunders has suggested that a series of maps produced through 1721 indicates that the walled city remained through this date. This, plus recent architectural research, indicates that much of the building we see on the 1739 map was relatively recent. See Katherine Saunders, "'As regular and fformidable as any such woorke in America': The Walled City of Charles Town," in *Another's Country,* ed. Joseph and Zierden. For a historical summary of the city at the turn of the eighteenth century, see Robert Weir,

"Charles Town circa 1702: On the Cusp," *El Escribano* (2002): 65–79, in which Weir portrays the turn-of-the-century port as a tenuous settlement, at best.

21. Joseph, "From Colonist to Charlestonian," 215–34.

22. Some scholars have suggested that these unmatched plates would have been used together on a late eighteenth-century dining table. This concentration of porcelain plates, though, in a yard full of refuse, calls into question the source of this rubbish. Was it all discards from the Brewton household, carefully saved for deposition in the garden, or possibly a collection of refuse from a central urban dump, deliberately introduced to prepare garden beds?

23. For a more detailed discussion of the movement of refuse from Miles Brewton's lot to the 14 Legare site, see Martha Zierden "The Journey of Miles Brewton's Bottle," www.common-place.org/vol-01/no-04/lessons (accessed February 16, 2009).

24. For a discussion of artifacts associated with African American beliefs and practices, see Barbara Heath, *Hidden Lives: The Archaeology of Slave Life at Thomas Jefferson's Poplar Forest* (Charlottesville: University of Virginia Press, 1999); Patricia Samford, "The Archaeology of African American Slavery and Material Culture," *William and Mary Quarterly* 53, no. 1 (1995): 87–114; Singleton, "Archaeology of Slave Life."

25. See J. W. Joseph and Martha Zierden, "Cultural Diversity in the Southern Colonies," in *Another's Country*, ed. Joseph and Zierden, 1–12.

Changing Our Habitation

Henry Laurens, Rattray Green, and the Revolutionary Movement in Charleston's Domestic Spaces

Benjamin L. Carp

Lightning struck a fine house in the suburb of Ansonborough, north of Charleston, on November 14, 1771. The blast shattered a large china bowl, a pair of tureens, several glass toys, three large looking glasses, a thermometer, and two sconce glasses; splintered a closet door, shelves, and the top of a chest of drawers; cracked some of the wainscoting and plaster; ruined a portrait frame; drove glass shards into a mahogany desk; damaged two clocks, the chimney, and some prints; and melted pewter dishes and the silver handles of knives and other plate, as well as "a Brass warming Pan and a Tin japanned Waiter." Bed quilts flew from the closet. A harpsichord was, incredibly, unharmed. The glass panes of a book case were in shards, but the case itself survived. Of the nine or ten people on the property, only one sustained serious injury: a black slave, "Satira—had her right Arm & hand much burn'd by the Lightning" as she was working near the chimney in a separate kitchen building.[1]

Chaos and destruction had torn through the opulence of Henry Laurens's home, not for the first time and not for the last. Laurens wept with joy that on this occasion his brother's family and most of "their innocent Dependants" had been "miraculously preserv'd."[2] Yet in less than five years chaos would return to Charleston. Like the bolt of lightning that scorched the interior of Laurens's estate, the Revolutionary fervor electrified all segments of society. The storm of war would wreak much more havoc on Laurens, his home, and his family than the 1771 thunderbolt had. Laurens's imprisonment in the Tower of London and the death of his eldest son, John, in battle are well known. These tragedies were analogous to the toll on Laurens's home after the British capture of Charleston in 1780: "The stable & Kitchen is entirely down, the House barely worths repairing, the Garden entirely destroyed."[3]

The household was a site of conflict, a poignant metaphor, and a critical venue for the Revolutionary movement in Charleston. Laurens and his contemporaries infused their households with many layers of significance and meaning.[4] In its most basic respect, the house was a place of security: shelter from the weather (in its mundane and cataclysmic forms) and security from intruders. The household comprised the most basic social unit—the family. Among wealthy Carolinians, the family generally included extended kin networks (such as the family of Laurens's brother) and black slaves (such as the wounded Satira). In the traditional, hierarchical world of colonial South Carolina, the household was a place of paternal protection and deference and a place to manage and contain chattel slaves. The household was also property—an estate for transmission to one's heirs and a place to affirm one's status through the conspicuous display of objects, such as the opulent furnishings that had been damaged by the lightning. The household was a place to receive guests: to offer hospitality and extend one's shelter to visitors. South Carolina planters making a fortune in rice (and later indigo) often split their time between Charleston town houses and country plantations. As a result, many planters attempted to replicate the social patterns of the plantation household on their urban house lots in Charleston.[5]

The owners of these town houses discovered that city life presented a very different landscape, which militated against an exact duplication of the patterns of plantation life. With roughly twelve thousand residents on the eve of the Revolution, Charleston by far contained the greatest concentration of people in the South; the wealthiest families in all of North America; more black slaves than Boston, New York, and Philadelphia combined; a unique aggregation of free black people; and more nonslaveholding whites than any parish in the lowcountry.[6] Charleston was more than just a demographic concentration; it was also the political center of South Carolina and its principal commercial entrepôt.[7] In an urban setting elite Charlestonians sought connections with their neighbors for trade and sociability and with more far-flung trading partners, visitors, and correspondents in the Carolina hinterland and overseas. Thus the politics, economy, sociability, and demography of the city would provide unique opportunities and challenges for the wealthy leaders of Charleston.

During the colonial period Charleston's gentry sat relatively unified atop the pyramid of social, political, and economic control in the city and the country (see figure 1). They extended their power over the wider community as civic leaders, over their families as patriarchs, and over their slaves as masters. With their economic success and cultural achievements, these Charlestonians also expected to enjoy liberty under the British constitution and their rightful share of social dignity. South Carolina's leaders surrounded themselves with objects of luxury that bespoke the grandeur and refinement of their metropolitan exports, their cosmopolitan membership in a transatlantic empire, and their preeminent status within

Fig. 1. Henry Laurens, portrait by John Singleton Copley. National Portrait Gallery, Smithsonian Institution

that empire. Elite Charlestonians needed to identify one another and distinguish themselves from the lower orders of society, while the abundance of urban neighbors and visitors provided more opportunities for the conspicuous and aggressive display of objects of refinement and authority. The members of the Charleston gentry also kept their own *political* objects in view, one of which was to protect their status and authority.[8] In other cities and towns the tavern might be a place for social organization, the courthouse for political authority, the marketplace for economic management, the church and schoolhouse for cultural fulfillment and perpetuation, and the streets for identity formation.[9] In Charleston the household was the most important site for all of these functions. Its leaders sought to further their political objectives using the built spaces and household goods around them.

The household as a polity also framed the contentious social relations of a patriarchal slave society. In the urban landscape the crowded streets teemed with potential intruders, external threats that might undermine the gentry's authority. The ferment of the Revolutionary era subjected the urban household to new challenges and threats: from within their own households among women and slaves, from their neighbors in the backcountry and among less wealthy white city dwellers, and from imperial authority overseas. The household was the place where Charlestonians in power sought to mediate between man and woman, parent and child, master and slave, black and white, metropolis and province, city and hinterland. In a burgeoning republican society Charlestonians might have to adopt new notions about the household as the basis of their society and polity. Excessive luxury, enslavement of blacks, a military conflict against Great Britain, and social challenges from women, urban artisans, or farmers from the Carolina backcountry caused anxieties among the Charleston planters, even as these planters maintained a striking degree of social cohesion by the end of the eighteenth century.[10] Although lightning had struck, with sufficient wealth and power the gentry found it conceivable to rebuild their households, perhaps even stronger than before.

After the fire of 1740 and the hurricane of 1752, Charleston was teeming with newly built houses. Moses Lopez believed in 1764 that the city had doubled in size since he had last been there in 1742: "One cannot go anywhere where one does not see new buildings and large and small houses started, half finished, and almost finished."[11] Charlestonians were building to accommodate their families and slaves or to rent properties (at exorbitant rates) to less wealthy neighbors. They fashioned work spaces in their back lots, where they hoped to supervise their bound laborers. They imported the finest furniture, tableware, and clothing or had local craftsmen closely emulate such imports and conspicuously displayed the Englishness of their fine wares within their households. As they played host to visitors and travelers throughout the Atlantic world and the Carolina hinterland, they positioned themselves as the leading members of their society and as Anglicized consumers in the transatlantic economy.[12] Families living in spacious double houses or the upper parts of single houses maintained some privacy and restriction in the rear and upper rooms; however, even the inner recesses of the household were never far from the noisy world of commerce, where one observed "a perpetual moving scene of what is doing at the wharfs and in the street below."[13] Streets bustled with customers moving in and out of Charleston buildings, which reinforced both the power of the wealthiest Charlestonians and their proximity to the contentious streets.

In the middle of the eighteenth century Henry Laurens conducted his successful commercial enterprise from a Bay Street countinghouse while maintaining a residence on Broad Street.[14] In this part of Charleston he would have observed a city that was noisy, sweltering, dirty, crowded, cramped, noisome, squalid, and prone to fires.[15] Residents complained that their neighbors threw rubbish in the streets, built uncovered necessary houses for their slaves, or sold spirits to blacks at disorderly houses.[16] Travelers noted that Charlestonians "must generally keep their windows open all the time because of the great heat," but open windows meant that sand from the roads would annoy anyone in the front rooms "together with swarms of mosqueto's and flies," which were "excessive troublesome and disagreeable all the warm weather season."[17] To escape the heat, Charleston residents generally located their bedrooms and dining rooms on the second floor, and the wealthiest tried to build houses at a distance from their neighbors: a German visitor wrote, "In proportion to its circumference, Charleston could really have more houses. However, . . . the houses are mostly built so far apart that the breeze can blow into the streets from all sides."[18] Although the Charleston gentry boasted "large handsome modern built brick houses," there were also merely "decent looking large houses," and "the greatest part are middling looking wooden ones."[19] Charleston offered a diverse array of households, where the estates of the wealthiest were prominent landmarks amid a complex urban landscape.

By the early 1760s Laurens was ready to retire from the stresses of mercantile life and city living as he devoted more of his assets to plantation lands. To signify his retirement and his new landed lifestyle, he began construction of a house on a sprawling four-acre property in the suburb of Ansonborough (see figure 2). Charleston was expanding northward into this area during these years as residents sought new lots just outside the crowded confines of the old walled city.[20] Laurens had a Scottish carpenter named Robert Deans build the new house, and the Laurens family was occupying it by the beginning of 1764. Since the Laurens house (which he initially called Rattray Green after a previous owner of the property) was demolished in 1916, architectural historians have not devoted much time to its analysis. Nevertheless the account of the 1771 lightning strike, a description by Laurens's biographer, photographs in the possession of descendants, and other documentary evidence can help us reconstruct some of the house's characteristics.[21]

Like its even more elaborate neighbor, the Pinckney house, Rattray Green was an elevated house with four rooms per floor and a jerkin-head roof (see figure 3). Distinguished visitors entering the house probably first encountered the hall (the largest room on the first floor) or the ornate library; for meals they might be invited upstairs to the dining room or withdrawing room. Servants coming from the work yard probably entered through a rear door, where subsidiary rooms were probably located. As in most wealthy South Carolina households, urban as well as rural, many subsidiary functions at Rattray Green were relegated to outbuildings, such as the stabling of horses, the preparation of food, and Laurens's reduced level of business transactions in the countinghouse.[22]

Laurens regarded Rattray Green as a country house in the fashion of an English squire, and he emphasized its rural qualities. The pride of the Ansonborough property was not the house so much as the gardens, reminiscent of villas along the Thames.[23] Laurens wrote, "Mrs. Laurens takes great delight in Gardening & we content ourselves upon moderate Fare in a quiet rural Life. . . . And I am so well contented with my Situation that no other Motive but the Good of my Country or Family could tempt me to remove from it."[24] As Laurens was returning from his long trip to London, he urged his brother to stay in his house as long as he needed to, since the gardens were "all the property or possession I ever had." Laurens looked forward to the experimental products of his garden providing "public benefit," as he shared in the scientific endeavors that occupied many gentlemen of his day.[25] He appreciated another significant benefit of his new rural location during a heat wave in 1765: "I am now as cool as a cucumber & not a moist thread, while the People who come from below say that those in the midst of the Town are suffocating."[26] Rattray Green still stood close to Charleston proper, and Laurens encouraged his friends to stay there on their way downtown.[27] Thus, Rattray Green served all the functions of the southern and Charlestonian household: it provided security and shelter for the family; it supervised the labor of slaves; it allowed Henry Laurens to demonstrate his paternal authority and his patriarchal status and to offer hospitality to guests; and it helped maintain his connections to Charleston and its networks of communication, socialization, governance, gentility, science, and trade. Yet, Laurens had not lived in his new house long when the internal and external threats to the Charleston household became vividly apparent.

Opening the Front Door to Turmoil: Stamp Act Unrest

The Laurens home was located at some distance from the bustle of Charleston but still within reach. When building his house, therefore, Laurens needed to consider questions of access. The floor plan of Rattray Green probably included a formal means of access for the processional welcoming of distinguished guests. Laurens did not mention his house much in his correspondence, even when he first moved in; when he did, it was to invite visitors to stay with him during their travels to Charleston.[28] Thus the unwritten rules of hospitality and access to the house, known to all South Carolinians, were at the forefront of Laurens's mind. His neighbors' violation of these rules during the Stamp Act crisis, therefore, must have struck him as a terrible affront.

On October 19, 1765, crowds had smashed the windows of the stamp distributor George Saxby's house; four days later the crowd focused on Henry Laurens. Laurens opposed the Stamp Act, although unlike the more radical Christopher Gadsden, he was not yet ready to gamble his "clear Estate" on a rash defiance of Parliament.[29] At midnight on October 23 Laurens "heard a most violent thumping & confus'd Noise at my Western door & Chamber Window, & soon distinguish'd the sounds of *Liberty, Liberty & Stamp'd Paper, Open your doors* & let us Search your House & *Cellars.*" Confronting a crowd of sixty to eighty sailors and townsmen (many of whom he recognized), Laurens claimed that he had no stamped paper, and "when I found that no fair words would pacify them I

FIG. 2. Map of Charlestown showing Laurens's city garden on the northeast corner of the street grid, 1780. From William Gordon, *History of the Rise, Progress and Establishment of the Independence of the United States . . .*, 4 vols. (London: Charles Dilly, 1788), 3: facing 358. Courtesy of Thomas Cooper Library, University of South Carolina, Columbia

FIG. 3. Photograph of Henry Laurens's house, c. 1919. The view is from the northwest. The fenestration in the photographs indicates the location of the two stairways. A piazza is visible, but it is unknown whether this was an original feature of the house. Courtesy of John Laurens, Charleston, South Carolina

accused them with cruelty to a poor Sick Woman far gone with Child & produced Mrs. Laurens shrieking & wringing her hands." The crowd assured him that they merely wanted to *search* his house, not damage it, its contents, or its inhabitants. Laurens, still offended at this affront to his elite status, hesitated until it seemed the crowd was two minutes away from beating down his door. The rioters conducted a superficial search of his house, countinghouse, cellar, and stable and tried unsuccessfully to compel from him either an oath or a renunciation of certain friendships. As they retired, they gave Laurens three cheers, wished him good night, and said, "We hope the poor Lady will do well." Laurens was amazed that the drunk, armed crowd "did not do one penny damage to my Garden" and not fifteen shillings damage to his fence, gate, or house. At the same time, the event had so distressed his pregnant wife that Laurens spent the next few days giving her constant attention at home. The child, James, died ten years later, and Laurens would recall the 1765 incident and lament that misfortune had followed the boy since before his birth.[30] Laurens was mortified that these uninvited guests had compelled him to allow a search of his house and grounds. In his own home the crowd had threatened the standing that he should have enjoyed as a Charleston patriarch.[31]

The Politics of Material Luxury: The Debates over Nonimportation

During the Stamp Act crisis the gentry's homes and estates faced threats from both unconstitutional British taxation, on the one hand, and unlawful mobbish destruction, on the other. The goal during subsequent conflicts with Britain would be to restrain the latter while combating the more enduring threat from the former. In the aftermath of the Townshend duties, Charlestonians formed committees to enforce nonimportation of British goods. The household became a crucial battlefield as they debated whether to continue consuming their cherished British household goods and thereby reinforce their connection to Great Britain. Henry Laurens's house spilled over with an abundance of these expensive goods: his china, clocks, silver plate, mahogany furniture, and looking glasses represented the epitome of expense and elegance.[32] By conveying the dominance of the gentry, these objects had enduring political importance; during the nonimportation crisis the political character of material goods took on a more controversial cast.

In 1769 South Carolinians protested the Revenue Acts by resolving to promote North American manufactures and refrain from importing most British goods: "We will use the utmost OECONOMY, in our Persons, Families, Houses, and Furniture." Charlestonians thought of nonimportation in terms of family. One writer asked his "Brother" planters, "How can we look at our children" if Carolinians did not protest the Revenue Acts by means of nonimportation? "Let us then, AT LAST, follow the example of our brother sufferers in the Northern Colonies, and encourage the making our own manufactures."[33] Radicals enjoined each other as brothers, for the sake of their children, to defend their right to be taxed only by their own elected representatives.

Radicals needed to make strident appeals because consumption was at the center of Charleston's household life. Ebenezer Hazard wrote that Charlestonians "appear to pay more attention to dress than any thing else."[34] In the ninth of his famous *Letters from an American Farmer* (1782), J. Hector St. John de Crèvecoeur remarked on "the elegance of their houses, their sumptuous furniture, as well as the magnificence of their tables," while Carl Bauer in 1780 could attest, "We seldom entered a house in which we did not find almost all furniture of mahogany and also very much silverware." Gov. James Glen wrote in 1751 of the "many houses that have cost a thousand and twelve hundred pound sterling. The furniture in those houses must be very considerable and plate begins to shine upon their side boards, and in proportion as they thrive they delight to have good things from England."[35] Wealthy Charlestonians conspicuously displayed the English trappings of their fine wares within the households and out of doors; David Ramsay feared they were becoming "fond of British manners even to excess."[36] As a result of their strong attachments to a life of consumption, many Charlestonians retained their fondness for new and imported clothing after the nonimportation agreements went into effect. When asked to wear homespun, they replied, "*That's not the thing,*" and they resisted the critics of fashionable culture.[37] Thus, Charlestonians continued to consume, at least initially, raising once again the concern among radicals and moralists that luxury was polluting the city. Eventually, through extralegal policing and the drawing up of subscription lists, South Carolinians convinced more and more merchants to forgo importing British goods. While some were reluctant to suspend consumption for the sake of country, Charlestonians sought to remind their neighbors of the importance of uniting for the public good.[38]

During the nonimportation debates, Charleston Whig patriarchs attempted to enlist the help of women. Gadsden wrote that it would be "impossible to succeed" without the help of women, and he was optimistic about their participation. "None in the world are better œconomists, make better wives, or more tender mothers, than *ours,*" he wrote. "Only let their husbands point out the necessity of such a conduct; convince them, that it is the only thing that can save them and their children, from distress, slavery, and disgrace; their affections will then soon be awakened, and co-operate with their reason." Women, with their interest in preserving the family and the household, would see the logic of the Whigs' arguments. Even as Gadsden elevated these virtuous women, the stipulation that husbands would "point out" the advantages of nonimportation may better reflect the reality of how household decisions were made. Gadsden insisted that women "are not such absolute slaves to dress as hath been too often and too sneeringly represented." Women would obey their husbands, therefore, or they would be likened to slaves. An opponent of Gadsden's, meanwhile, mocked women's "entire complaisance to their Lords and Masters" and wrote satirically that he did not doubt that their dutifulness, obedience, hospitality, and diligent attendance to "domestic affairs, will lead them to be directors in matters of the highest consequences; and by their frequent attendance upon political debates, and being so often admitted to the gentlemen's council, they certainly will be much the properest persons to manage an affair of so much consequence to the American world."[39] Radicals attempted to enlist women in their cause, even if it entailed subtle coercion, while their opponents made it clear that women, as subordinate, nonpolitical beings, did not matter at all. To many, attention to domestic affairs and admittance to "gentlemen's council" were mutually exclusive.

One writer, posing as "MARGERY DISTAFF—CONDITIONALLY," used nonimportation as a vehicle for criticizing the luxurious and sinful life of Carolina men: "*Women* think, it would tend to but very little good Purpose, were they to *card* and *spin,* whilst the *Men* are racking their Brains, in contriving how to *dissipate* their *Time* and *Money,* in what they call PARTIES OF PLEASURE." Distaff lamented that each night of the week men would frequent clubs or taverns, gamble away their money on cock fights and horse races, stay up late, and "*impair their Healths* by the intemperate Use of Spiritous Liquors." Women, by contrast, pursued "innocent Amusements" such as attending balls or assemblies, spending time with acquaintances, and attending to their families. Thus women's spinning of homespun cloth would be contingent, the author wrote, on men's less profligate behavior and improved economy.[40] The household had become a key site in the battle over nonimportation, where firm commitments to virtue and economy were crucial for staving off the pernicious influence of British goods and government.

Women's role became particularly important during the tea boycott in 1774. Tea tables were fixtures in Charleston households, including Laurens's, where multiple "tea tables" were mentioned as having been damaged in 1771.[41] In the *South Carolina Gazette and Country Journal,* the Presbyterian minister William Tennent addressed "the Ladies of South Carolina" as "an admirer of your sex" and urged them to learn about the dispute surrounding the 1773 Tea Act. Knowing the effects of "long habit," British officials judged that rather than give up the "darling tea-dish ceremony," Charleston women would "suffer this empire to be enslaved and your husbands throats to be cut." Tennent reminded them, therefore, "It is tea that has kept all America trembling for years. It is tea that has brought vengeance upon Boston; and you may thank your tea-tables that thousands are now cruelly deprived of their bread." As he appealed to their compassion, fear, and love of family, Tennent insisted that he was not asking women to give up their comfort or daily necessities but only "a mere ceremony—worse, a time consuming poison; a thing which no one can pretend ever did any good." Boycotting tea would chastise Parliament and the East India Company, "convince them that American patriotism extends even to the fair sex, and discourage any future attempts to enslave us." A grateful nation of husbands would add their respect to "the deliverers of their country" to their usual tenderness as husbands and lovers. Tennent's epistle lacks the sarcasm or coercion of earlier appeals to women; instead he evinces gratitude as he criticizes the tea ceremony rather than its matrons.[42]

South Carolina leaders, while allowing that women might have more political agency than they had suspected in 1769, still expected to draft women into the measures against Britain. Men needed women, and their decision-making power now seemed to count. Women used this opportunity to enter the public sphere, harness their household responsibilities to imperial resistance, and promote the tea boycott. Henry Laurens paid a visit to Gabriel Manigault on June 7, 1775, and found that the aging patrician had reluctantly signed the articles for participating in the Continental Association, which prohibited trade with Britain and restricted consumption. Referring to Manigault's wife Anne, Laurens wrote: "the poor old Lady!, from expressions which She dropped, I concluded her persuasions had prevailed."[43] If many Charlestonians had embraced nonimportation and limits on consumption with reluctance, some women used the agreements as opportunities to reform the patriarchal household.

Expulsion from the Garden? Challenges to Provincial Authority

During the imperial crisis Laurens's retirement to rural life at Rattray Green itself became an issue. By challenging his new life of comfort, the supporters of British government also challenged the position of provincial authority that Laurens and his peers had previously enjoyed. Laurens purported to decry objects of imported luxury during his quarrel with British authorities over the seizure of his ship *Ann,* since these articles "tend to impoverish the Community, by promoting Luxury, Idleness and Debauchery."[44] The Loyalist judge Egerton Leigh, in turn, attacked Laurens's hypocritical sanctimony. Laurens professed to have retired from the slave trade for moral reasons, while having built Rattray Green with his mercantile wealth (including that from slave imports). Now Laurens lived aloof as "the first man in a new street," casting an "idle gaze from his parlour window" at the world. Leigh suggested that his opponent's ungentlemanly actions made him better suited for "lodging in the common goal of Charles-Town" than the "*pure air* which Ansonborough affords."[45] Laurens scorned this empty threat as a "vague swaggering Assumption of Power which was never vested in him," though he seemed defensive about Leigh's remarks on the slave trade.[46] By mocking Laurens's idleness, comfort, and hypocrisy, Leigh challenged Laurens's authority over his own household and over the province. The judge implied that any Whig who resisted imperial policy was similarly unfit to enjoy his seat of power.

Laurens resisted the criticisms of imperial sympathizers such as Leigh; on the contrary, he believed that his success entitled him to his rural life, his comfort, his house and gardens, his liberty, and his authority. When he returned from England in 1774, all Laurens wanted was to be "left with the Freedom of an English Man, encouraged to plant & Cultivate my Vine & my Fig Tree, from a well grounded assurance that I may Sit quietly under them & enjoy the fruit of my Labour, as my own property, not to be taken from me but by my own Consent."[47] Yet a year later Laurens found that he and his fellow lowcountry planters were "miserably Situated between two Fires." One danger was "Kingly tyranny," and the other was "popular" tyranny. Charleston's enlightened patriarchs would need "Skilful pilotage" to steer between the two. Laurens feared that "habit & Custom" would reconcile the people to royal tyranny—that British goods coupled with imperial prerogative would corrupt Americans. Having experienced mob disturbances in his own home during the Stamp Act encounter, Laurens believed popular tyranny to be even worse since it was more violent, although at least mob disturbances were "only temporary."[48] The events of the Revolutionary crisis repeatedly taught Charleston planters that their households were under assault, either from the British goods within, the violence of popular elements without, or the abuse of imperial power withal.

In this particular discussion of "popular tyranny" Laurens referred to backcountry agitators, although he might just as easily have been discussing urban crowds. As violence began to rage throughout the colonies, Charleston planters hoped to be able to turn to their white neighbors, the residents of the Carolina backcountry. Unfortunately, since 1765 backcountry Regulators had fumed at Charleston's predominance, castigating "the Selfish Views of those, whose Fortune and Estates, are in or near *Charlestown*—which makes them endeavour, That all Matters and Things shall center there, however detrimental to the Body Politic."[49] The selfishness of Laurens and his fellow Charlestonians had left "the Back Country without Law, Gospel, or the least Advantage, of Civil or Religious Life—No Churches, Ministers, Schools, Order, Discipline No Roads Cut—Bridges built—Causeys made for them."[50] Thus during the Stamp Act crisis Christopher Gadsden had written that "very little depends on the Example of the Towns in any part of the unpensioned part of the Continent."[51] Where Charleston patriarchs did not perform their obligations, casting only an idle gaze from their parlor windows, they could not expect dutiful neighbors.

Laurens and his fellow aristocrats did not want backcountry residents breaking windows and trampling gardens in Charleston, and so they made political concessions that they hoped would pacify their fellow colonists upriver. During a 1775 debate in the General Assembly over measures against Great Britain, Laurens called upon his backcountry "Brethren" and emphasized the importance of staving off "disunion." The backcountry residents "murmured against delay & procrastination," suspecting that "the Rich Rice-Planter & the Towns-people had Schemed to weary them out in order to thin the House & transact business their own way." To ward off these complaints, Laurens "proceeded to make an offer of my own House for the accomodation of any whose pockets were not Sufficiently Stored for defraying the expence of Town Lodgings." The backcountry men responded positively: "Several Voices were heard as in a Shout they were Satisfied contented & determined to Sit out the necessary time." Laurens may have intended this as a sincere expression of goodwill or a gambit for extracting obedience in return for paternal hospitality. In either case, the exchange is significant because Laurens displayed his willingness to share his house, as well as the larger house of a burgeoning republican South Carolina, with these underrepresented farmers.[52] Months later the Council of Safety (Henry Laurens presiding) sent William Henry Drayton and the Reverend Tennent with the Baptist minister Oliver Hart to recruit backcountry farmers for support of the new Provincial Congress.[53] Laurens had learned that it was not enough to enjoy the fruits of his life's labor from Rattray Green: he needed to extend paternal protection to his neighbors too if he wanted to retain his household authority.

Grumblings in the Work Yard: The Threat of Slave Uprisings

Meanwhile the Charleston gentry had to contend with a group of South Carolinians who already shared their households. A Hessian officer observed that in Charleston, "Everything is done by Negroes, whom one finds in great numbers in all houses, and to excess in many. Those who serve their masters in the city and in the country are kept well." These slaves lived "either in the house with the master, or else an adjacent house serves as their dwelling."[54] The fantastic wealth and aristocratic style of the gentry depended on the labor of slaves, and Charleston was the urban center of slave trading and slave households more than any other city in British North America. As elite slave owners divided their time between their plantations in the Carolina hinterland and their Charleston town houses, they often maintained paternalistic control at a distance from their plantations.[55] While in Charleston, these white masters also supervised slave laborers in the yards and kitchens: urban "plantations" within a geographically constrained landscape. Whites and blacks probably experienced different "embedded" landscapes on a Charleston estate. Whites had access to normal avenues of movement through entrance halls, drawing rooms, and dining rooms. Blacks either used the same routes (though invisibly) or used less formal routes of access such as the passageways between rooms and the carriage ways outdoors, routes that provided them with intimate access to the household even as whites intended them to remain subordinate.[56]

Blacks often enjoyed a certain degree of privacy in the urban spaces and interstices where they congregated, which left them time and space for a certain degree of freedom and for activities their masters regarded as subversive. With greater economic and socializing opportunities, Charleston's black residents seemed to "have a peculiar kind of pride and bearing; without degenerating into insolence, it at least gives the impression that they regard a man who is not their master simply as a man, not a tyrant."[57] White Carolinians imagined that they could maintain the same stable supervision over black people in the city as they did on the plantations. Yet disruptive urban conditions often frustrated their pretensions to control. Henry Laurens famously admonished his brother's slaves "to behave with great circumspection" and warned them against the "treatchery of pretended freinds & false witnesses" if they associated with blacks outside the family.[58] Years before, his slave John (also called Footbea) had "Strolled away from my house, about midnight" in an almost casual way. Since Footbea spoke no English, "he is supposed to have been decoyed away by some other negro."[59] Just as customers and families penetrated the boundaries between street and household, so the free blacks who were often seen gaming in the streets might form contacts with domestic servants inside the masters' domains. Laurens hoped that by sending his errant slave Abram "away from some pernicious connexions that he has made with Slaves in Charles Town I do believe he will behave much better and become a Valuable Slave."[60] Laurens idealized the patriarchal relationship he had with his slaves, where he exchanged humane protection for dutiful and grateful obedience. Thus when a slave was recalcitrant or ran away, he blamed the outside influences of the urban black community.[61] While such an attitude may have been self-serving, this interplay between the city's broader social forces and the household was a key factor in Charleston's domestic life.

Henry Laurens's views on slavery were in some ways more moderate than those of his neighbors, although he too expected obedience from his slaves and declined to manumit them and thus deprive his children of an inherited "Estate."[62] Not choosing to free their slaves, therefore, planters needed to use the traditional means of coercion to keep their households in order. Charlestonians had long suspected that blacks were holding secret councils outside of town or within the city proper, at dram shops, "the houses of *free negroes,* apartments *hired to slaves,* or the *kitchens* of such Gentlemen as frequently retire, with their families, into the country, for a few days."[63] These urban spaces and other interstices could become seedbeds of slave revolt if they were not cautiously monitored and patrolled. As Christopher Gadsden wrote to Samuel Adams, "We are a weak Colony from the Number of Negroes we have amongst us, and therefore exposed to more formid[able?] ministerial Tricks."[64] Especially in 1775 and 1776 blacks were paying attention to the language of liberty that rolled off presses and tongues, and they were taking advantage of wartime chaos with all its potential interruptions of authority. Whites anxiously swapped rumors of possible insurrections and sought to patrol the streets even more diligently.[65] Maintaining control over slaves would protect Charleston's domestic tranquillity and, not incidentally, the patriarchal power of Charleston's elite planters.

Charlestonians responded harshly when they suspected a black person of plotting revolt, as they demonstrated in 1776 during the case of Thomas Jeremiah, or "Jerry." The authorities accused Jeremiah, a successful free black man, of insurrection when he voiced his anticipation of a "great war coming" that would "help the poor Negroes." A number of prominent whites believed Jeremiah's protestations of innocence, among them Gov. William Campbell. Henry Laurens, who might have intervened on Jerry's behalf as president of the Council of Safety, was not among them. Part of his reason for upholding Jerry's conviction and execution was not a fear of urban blacks but a fear of urban whites. "Although I know none of the out of Door Secrets of the people, & carefully avoid Such knowledge," he wrote, "yet I had heard enough to fill me with horror from a prospect of what might be done by Men enraged as Men would have been if a pardon had been Issued." Laurens did not want to repeat the events of

1765, when the resentment of Charleston crowds had threatened the sanctity of his home in retaliation for his unpopular actions. Instead Laurens sought to maintain the domestic order as the prevailing opinion of Charleston understood it. Slaves would remain in humble submission or face physical coercion or even execution.[66]

The Charleston gentry tried to retain dominance atop the urban social system, continuing to enjoy a preponderance of wealth, status, and political power even as they encountered the fluidity and disruption inherent in urban life. Visitors noted of Charleston's gentry, "accustomed to tyrannize from their infancy, they carry with them a disposition to treat all mankind in the same manner they have been used to treat their Negroes."[67] Henry Laurens might have agreed. "We cannot trust any other eyes or judgement but our own in every minute article," he wrote. "Negroes are faithless, & Workmen exceedingly careless."[68] Elite Charlestonians wanted to avoid the dangerous possibility of a disorderly city where workers and blacks asserted themselves, and so they needed to use their legal, political, economic, and social power to keep their extended urban families in check.

Historians have long remarked on the connection between Carolinians' fear of British enslavement and their own possession of blacks as chattel. Christopher Gadsden, like his neighbors, sought to avoid "the abject Slavery intended for us and our posterity."[69] Slave owners ferociously defended their liberty because they witnessed the suppression of blacks firsthand. Charlestonians most likely perceived this issue in terms of domestic space and domestic order. More than anywhere else in the colony, Charleston planters stood at the nexus of connections to Great Britain and connections to the rural plantations in the city's vast southern hinterland. The threat of slave insurrection and the impending break from Great Britain both loomed large in Charlestonians' minds. Therefore, Charlestonians sought to maintain order in their own households precisely because they knew they were about to cause significant disruption in the imperial household.

Foundations of the Household: Adopting a New Society and Polity

With the building of each grand household, Rattray Green among them, Charlestonians loudly announced that another family, another building block would comprise South Carolina's high society. Thus their ideas about the ordering of their society and polity often had significant overtones of domesticity. The ministers of Charleston's two Anglican churches each deployed domestic ideology as a means to keep afloat during the turbulent Revolutionary period. In February 1775 the Reverend Robert Smith of St. Philip's Church enjoined his parishioners to ask themselves, "Whatever is my part in life, do I act it well,—and contribute my share to public happiness? As a member of *the Community,* a parent, a master, or a servant; is my behaviour such as the eye of Heaven can approve?" He continued, "Let each of us in our sphere & station contribute our share.—let those on whom *a kind Providence* has lavish'd her favours, *Men of large fortunes and extensive influence* lead the way, & thousands will catch the fashion from them. . . . they will find it in the willing obedience of their children, in the duty & faithfulness of their dependents; . . . in the *love &* approbation of their country;—and the admiration & fear of their enemies." Moderation and reverence for God would help men of influence maintain a mighty household in which dependents and neighbors obediently took their cues from their masters and betters.[70] Laurens had called upon his "Country Men, the Rich & opulent" to make a "virtuous opposition" to Parliament.[71] Smith had armed the wealthy members of his Charleston congregation with the ideological weaponry that would help them retain control.

John Bullman, the rector of St. Michael's Church, had given an earlier sermon that proved to be much less palatable to his audience. In August 1774 he railed against the sedition of the "illeterate Mechanic," a man "who cannot perhaps govern his own household" or pay his debts, and who "presumes he is qualified to dictate how the State should be governed." Such men had no right to take advantage of urban proximity and pry into his "Neighbour's Secrets." When Bullman offered some of the same distaste for crowds as Laurens had expressed, most parishioners resented Bullman's implication that white mechanics had any less ability to govern their households and voice their opinions in government. The vestry had Bullman summarily dismissed from his pulpit. It was one thing to invoke slaves and Indian tribes to play upon the fears of white Carolinians; it was quite another to impugn the white mechanics, backcountry men, and (to a lesser extent) women who were gradually gaining acceptance as members of the emerging provincial polity.[72]

When the Continental Congress signed the Declaration of Independence in Philadelphia, Laurens used household metaphors to describe his reaction: "Can we change our habitation remove our effects from one House to another without Some trouble, without some damage to the furniture or without Some Struggle among the branches of the family for the best apartments in the new Mansion? Surely not can we expect then to change Governors to establish a new System & to have no murmuring in so large a family?"[73] Laurens captured the dual position of the Charleston gentry: on the one hand, revolutionaries were moving to a republican household to replace the imperial house they had outgrown; on the other hand, provincial patriarchs were trying to maintain control over the dissident, "murmuring" elements of South Carolina society—disenfranchised backcountry residents, despised mechanics, haughty Loyalists, and oppressed blacks. As he worried about these squabbles, Laurens waxed nostalgic about the royal house he left behind. "Even at this Moment," he wrote, "my heart is full of the lively sensations of a dutiful Son, thrust by the hand of violence out of a Father's House into the wide World."[74] This use of a paternal metaphor rather than the more common maternal metaphor was significant: in the aftermath of the Declaration of Independence, it was not just the ministers in the vaguely defined "mother country" that had abandoned them.

Two years earlier Christopher Gadsden limited himself to a criticism of "our Mother-in-Law's Intentions" toward Boston, while William Henry Drayton lamented, "alas! instead of parental tenderness, we experience a step-mother's severity—instead of justice, we receive marks of the most unfeeling ingratitude!"[75] Now, in the year of Thomas Paine's king-killing harangues, it was the king and father who had violently brought America to sword point. Although Laurens objected to Britain's methods for chastising America "as a Child," he looked forward to the possibility that Anglo-Americans could "restore mutual Love & a happy intercourse between the Roots & the transplanted branches of the family."[76] Charleston's ruling aristocracy, masters of their domains, tried to reconcile a whirlwind of domestic conflicts with their own desire to retain power in the American republic. The royal, paternal, imperial household was the only one that they had known, and yet they were becoming increasingly unified in their rejection of British control.

The planters knew it was time to abandon the royal household. As early as February 1775 Henry Laurens was having visions of his "pretty Garden" as "the parading Ground of Some Scots Regiment & my House occupied by a half Score Red Coats their Motto 'down with America.'"[77] A relative moderate compared to radicals such as Drayton and Gadsden, Laurens advocated "compassion & indulgence" to those slow to embrace the Revolutionary cause. "Some people live in a House contentedly till it is disjointed & ready to tumble about their Ears, they Say it will last their time without the trouble or expence of repairs an Instance of great Indolence, but tis generally found in quiet in offensive people."[78] The lifelong cultural, economic, and political attachments to Britain were hard to shake; nevertheless, Laurens and his fellow Whigs became more aggressive about repairs—they knew the time had come to tear down the old house and erect a "new Mansion." By 1776 Great Britain could no longer be called "home."

As war escalated, female Charlestonians found their roles as consumers, wives, and mothers reach profound importance, as Americans reevaluated their economic and political relationship to Great Britain and set about building a new republican household. Working Charlestonians and backcountry Carolinians saw the Revolution as an opportunity to expand the polity, so that South Carolina's political world might no longer be the exclusive dwelling of the lowcountry gentry. Black Charlestonians saw the Revolution as an opportunity to resist, escape, or otherwise assert greater control over their own lives. At the same time, the household was the repository of tradition, and although slaves and women found occasions for escaping their bonds, old ways of treating women and slaves persisted after peace returned.[79] These traditions included authoritarian displays of power as well as safety valves of freedom or quasi-freedom. Where Charleston elites could, they attempted to tighten their authority. Where they could not, they grudgingly permitted new liberties or allowed new groups to assert their rights within the republican household.

Charlestonians were accustomed to ordering their world along the lines of master and servant, black and white, man and woman, adult and child, elite, middling, and humble. Although the turbulence of the Revolutionary era invited challenges to this political and social order, Charleston planters (minus some of the outright Tories) remained atop their perch after the formation of the United States. Unified politically and socially, they were better placed than the legislators in most of the other thirteen colonies to rule without much dissent. They owed their dominance in part to their ownership of the most enviable houses in the city and country; from their management of plantations they had learned how to extract obedience, through negotiated persuasion or concession where possible and through coercion as an ever-present last resort.[80]

Perhaps it is fitting that the final chapter of lasting royal government in Charleston took place in one of its finest houses in the summer of 1775, the home of the slave trader Miles Brewton. According to a family legend, Brewton and Laurens met with Lord William Campbell, South Carolina's last royal governor, warning him that it would be dangerous to remain in the city. Charleston's most radical Whigs were itching to place the governor under house arrest. Brewton sympathized with the British, while Laurens probably mused over his own encounters with Charleston crowds a decade before. One wonders if Campbell noted the irony of these Charleston grandees heralding the collapse of British government in Brewton's sumptuous home, one of the most opulent examples of Georgian architecture, fashionable craftsmanship, and imported furnishings in the city—"the grandest hall" Josiah Quincy had "ever beheld." Although Charlestonians would continue to import consumer goods into their homes after the Revolution, after the destructive years of war and occupation they would forever decline the hospitality and authority of the Crown. The fearful Campbell took refuge aboard the HMS *Tamar* in Charleston harbor on September 15, and Brewton would perish at sea later that year. Laurens remained with his fellow gentry rebels to manage the "new Mansion," and the slaves Brewton and his competitors had sold them, to their satisfaction. They trusted, as Reverend Smith had promised, that men of opulence and influence would lead the way.[81]

Notes

1. For two accounts, see "Newspaper Account" from *South Caroline Gazette,* November 28, 1771; and James Laurens to John Laurens, December 5, 1771—both in *The Papers of Henry Laurens* [hereafter cited as *PHL*], 16 vols. (Columbia: University of South Carolina Press, 1968–2002), 8:61–62, 80–84.

2. Henry Laurens to James Laurens, December 26, 1771, in *PHL,* 8:123–25.

3. James Custer to Henry Laurens, June 1780, in *PHL,* 15:301–4.

4. I prefer "household," which Elizabeth Fox-Genovese calls a "basic social unit in which people, whether voluntarily or under compulsion, pool their income and resources," to "house" because the urban lot included outbuildings, working spaces, and gardens. The great house itself provided the vantage point for most of the literate figures who were able to record their thoughts for posterity, and so the historical record often focuses on houses themselves. I also want to use the terms "household" and "home" in a broad sense and to take note of when these terms are used to refer to Charleston, S.C., North America, or Great Britain. See Elizabeth Fox-Genovese, *Within the Plantation Household: Black and White Women of the Old South* (Chapel Hill: University of North Carolina Press, 1988), 31–32, 82–92.

5. Zierden and Herman, "Charleston Townhouses," 205; David R. Goldfield, *Cotton Fields and Skyscrapers: Southern City and Region, 1607–1980* (Baton Rouge: Louisiana State University Press, 1982), 17–18; Crowley, *Invention of Comfort,* 102–5. Fox-Genovese ignores urban households, pointing to the rural character of the South and the decline of Charleston during the nineteenth century. I support her contention that southern households drew their characteristics from the rural slave society of the South but argue that these patterns can provide a useful framework for interpreting urban households as well. See Fox-Genovese, *Within the Plantation Household,* 70–81.

6. For contemporary population estimates, see William Bull to the Earl of Hillsborough, November 30, 1770, in H. Roy Merrens, ed., *The Colonial South Carolina Scene: Contemporary Views, 1697–1774* (Columbia: University of South Carolina Press, 1977), 262. Nine of the ten richest men in British North America were South Carolinians, and Charleston District was the wealthiest in North America, with a mean aggregate wealth per inventoried estate that tripled the mean of its closest rival. See Morgan, "Black Life in Eighteenth-Century Charleston," 188–89; Ira Berlin, *Many Thousands Gone: The First Two Centuries of Slavery in North America* (Cambridge, Mass.: Harvard University Press, Belknap Press, 1998), 144–45, 151–57; Walter Edgar, *South Carolina: A History* (Columbia: University of South Carolina Press, 1998), 151–53.

7. McCusker and Menard, *Economy of British America,* 184–85; Kenneth E. Lewis, "The Metropolis and the Backcountry: The Making of a Colonial Landscape on the South Carolina Frontier," *Historical Archaeology* 33 (1999): 3–13; Goldfield, *Cotton Fields and Skyscrapers,* 17–21, 24–26; Robert M. Weir, "'The Harmony We Were Famous for': An Interpretation of Pre-Revolutionary South Carolina Politics," *William and Mary Quarterly* 26 (1969): 473–501; Lorri Glover, *All Our Relations: Blood Ties and Emotional Bonds among the Early South Carolina Gentry* (Baltimore: Johns Hopkins University Press, 2000).

8. Morgan, *Slave Counterpoint,* 257–300; Olwell, *Masters, Slaves, and Subjects,* 187–219; Isaac, *Transformation of Virginia,* 70–79; Edward Pearson, "'Planters Full of Money': The Self-Fashioning of the Eighteenth-Century South Carolina Elite," in *Money, Trade, and Power,* ed. Greene et al., 299–321.

9. For the interactions in public spaces, see David W. Conroy, *In Public Houses: Drink and the Revolution of Authority in Colonial Massachusetts* (Chapel Hill: University of North

Carolina Press, 1995); Paul A. Gilje, *The Road to Mobocracy: Popular Disorder in New York City, 1763–1784* (Chapel Hill: University of North Carolina Press, 1987); Dirk Hoerder, *Crowd Action in Revolutionary Massachusetts, 1765–1780* (New York: Academic Press, 1977); Cornelia Hughes Dayton, *Women before the Bar: Gender, Law, and Society in Connecticut, 1639–1789* (Chapel Hill: University of North Carolina Press, 1995); Isaac, *Transformation of Virginia;* Peter Thompson, *Rum Punch and Revolution: Taverngoing and Public Life in Eighteenth-Century Philadelphia* (Philadelphia: University of Pennsylvania Press, 1999); Upton, *Holy Things and Profane.*

10. Berlin, *Many Thousands Gone,* 290–324; Olwell, *Masters, Slaves, and Subjects,* 221–70; Sylvia R. Frey, *Water from the Rock: Black Resistance in a Revolutionary Age* (Princeton, N.J.: Princeton University Press, 1991), 108–42; Richard Walsh, *Charleston's Sons of Liberty: A Study of the Artisans, 1763–1789* (Columbia: University of South Carolina Press, 1959); Rachel N. Klein, *Unification of a Slave State: The Rise of the Planter Class in the South Carolina Backcountry, 1760–1808* (Chapel Hill: University of North Carolina Press, 1990); Robert Stansbury Lambert, *South Carolina Loyalists in the American Revolution* (Columbia: University of South Carolina Press, 1987); Cynthia A. Kierner, *Beyond the Household: Women's Place in the Early South, 1700–1835* (Ithaca, N.Y.: Cornell University Press, 1998).

11. *SCG,* November 20, 27, and December 25, 1740; Moses Lopez to Aaron Lopez, May 3, 1764, in Tobias, ed., "Charles Town in 1764," 67–68; Bridenbaugh, *Cities in Revolt,* 18–19, 227–28, 336–37; Carl Bridenbaugh, *Myths and Realities: Societies of the Colonial South* (New York: Atheneum, 1965), 76–77.

12. T. H. Breen, *The Marketplace of Revolution: How Consumer Politics Shaped American Independence* (Oxford: Oxford University Press, 2004); T. H. Breen, "'Baubles of Britain': The American and Consumer Revolutions of the Eighteenth Century," in *Of Consuming Interests,* ed. Carson et al., 444–82; Pelatiah Webster, "Journal of a Voiage [*sic*] from Philadelphia to Charlestown in So. Carolina, begun May 15, 1765," in Merrens, ed., *Colonial South Carolina Scene,* 221–24; Josiah Quincy Jr., "Journal of Josiah Quincy, Junior, 1773," ed. Mark Antony De Wolfe Howe, *Proceedings of the Massachusetts Historical Society* 49 (1916): 442–51; Waterhouse, *New World Gentry,* 92–96; Rogers, *Charleston,* 81–83; Alice R. Huger Smith and D. E. Huger Smith, *The Dwelling Houses of Charleston, South Carolina* (Philadelphia: J. B. Lippincott Co., 1917), 183; Maurie D. McInnis et al., *In Pursuit of Refinement: Charlestonians Abroad, 1740–1860* (Columbia: University of South Carolina Press, 1999); Ronald L. Hurst and Jonathan Prown, *Southern Furniture, 1680–1830: The Colonial Williamsburg Collection* (New York: Colonial Williamsburg Foundation and Harry N. Abrams, 1997), 23–33, 83–85, 282–84, 308–10, 359, 382, passim.

13. Gov. James Glen to Lords Commissioners for Trade and Plantations, March 1751, in Merrens, *Colonial South Carolina Scene,* 189–91, 281. See also Zierden and Herman, "Charleston Townhouses," 204.

14. Henry Laurens to Thomas Osborne, February 8, 1763, in *PHL,* 3:241.

15. John A. Hall, "'Nefarious Wretches, Insidious Villains, and Evil-Minded Persons': Urban Crime Reported in Charleston's *City Gazette,* in 1788," *SCHM* 88 (July 1987): 154; Rogers, *Charleston,* 26–30, 86–88.

16. *SCG,* May 9, 1768, June 21, 1772.

17. George Fenwick Jones, "The 1780 Siege of Charleston as Expressed by a Hessian Officer," part 2, *SCHM* 88 (1987): 71; Merrens, *Colonial South Carolina Scene,* 286. See also Crowley, *Invention of Comfort,* 232–34.

18. Jones, "Siege of Charleston," 71. See also Smith and Smith, *Dwelling Houses of Charleston;* H. Roy Merrens, ed., "A View of Coastal South Carolina in 1778: The Journal of Ebenezer Hazard," *SCHM* 73 (October 1972): 183.

19. Merrens, *Colonial South Carolina Scene,* 282–83. See also Peter A. Coclanis, "The Sociology of Architecture in Colonial Charleston: Pattern and Process in an Eighteenth-Century Southern City," *Journal of Social History* 18 (Summer 1985): 610–14.

20. Bridenbaugh, *Cities in Revolt,* 232, 236–37.

21. *PHL,* 4:9n; Henry Laurens to Robert Deans, December 2, 1763, in *PHL,* 4:65; Henry Laurens to John Ettwein, March 13, 1764, in *PHL,* 4:209.

22. Henry Laurens to William Keith, [June 1764,] in *PHL,* 4:297.

23. See C. Allan Brown, "Eighteenth-Century Virginia Plantation Gardens: Translating an Ancient Idyll," in *Regional Garden Design in the United States,* ed. Therese O'Malley and Marc Treib (Washington, D.C.: Dumbarton Oaks Research Library and Collection, 1995), 125–62.

24. Henry Laurens to Benjamin Addison, May 26, 1768, in *PHL,* 5:702. Laurens was prescient about his motives, since he removed to London for three years for the sake of his sons' education, and to Philadelphia and Europe during the Revolutionary War for business with the Continental Congress.

25. Henry Laurens to James Laurens, April 15, 1774, in *PHL* 9:408; Richard Drayton, *Nature's Government: Science, Imperial Britain, and the 'Improvement' of the World* (New Haven, Conn.: Yale University Press, 2000), 59–67.

26. Henry Laurens to Joseph Brown, August 19, 1765, in *PHL,* 4:664.

27. Henry Laurens to John Ettwein, March 13, 1764, in *PHL,* 4:209; Henry Laurens to Lachlan McIntosh, August 15, 1764, in *PHL,* 4:368.

28. Ibid.; Henry Laurens to John Rutherford, February 7, 1764, in *PHL,* 4:162.

29. Christopher Gadsden to James Pearson, February 13, 1766, in "Two Letters by Christopher Gadsden, February 1766," ed. Robert M. Weir, *SCHM* 73 (July 1974): 173.

30. Henry Laurens to Joseph Brown, October 28, 1765, in *PHL,* 5:29–32; Henry Laurens to James Grant, November 1, 1765, in *PHL,* 5:37–40. See also Pauline Maier, *From Resistance to Revolution: Colonial Radicals and the Development of American Opposition to Britain, 1765–1776* (New York: Alfred A. Knopf, 1972), 66–67.

31. See Robert Blair St. George, *Conversing by Signs: Poetics of Implication in Colonial New England Culture* (Chapel Hill: University of North Carolina Press, 1998), 206–8, 242–95, although I disagree with St. George's strong emphasis on class conflict.

32. See Henry Laurens to Isaac King, March 15, 1764, in *PHL,* 4:211; Crowley, *Invention of Comfort,* 122–30; Robert A. Leith, "'After the Chinese Taste': Chinese Export Porcelain and Chinoiserie Decoration in Eighteenth-Century Charleston" [title taken from table of contents], *Historical Archaeology* 33 (1999): 48–61.

33. *SCG,* February 2, March 23, June 1, June 29, July 6, July 13, 1769; December 27, 1770.

34. This also held true for the black and mulatto women who catered to white gentlemen at "black dances" in Charleston; see Merrens, "Journal of Hazard," 186, 190. One newspaper contributor was distressed by the freedoms this habit encouraged; see "The STRANGER," *SCG,* September 24, 1770. See also "The Presentments of the Grand Jurors for the District of Charles-Town," *SCG,* May 24, 1773, June 3, 1774.

35. Jones, "Siege of Charleston," 73. Glen to Lords of Trade, in Merrens, *Colonial South Carolina Scene,* 180.

36. David Ramsay, quoted by William Henry Drayton in Robert M. Weir, ed., *The Letters of Freemen, Etc.: Essays on the Nonimportation Movement in South Carolina* (Columbia: University of South Carolina Press, 1977), xxiii, quoted in Olwell, *Masters, Slaves, and Subjects,* 39–40.

37. PRO GEGE ET REGE [Christopher Gadsden], "To the PLANTERS, MECHANICKS and FREEHOLDERS of the province of SOUTH CAROLINE, no ways concerned in the importation of British manufactures," *SCG,* June 22, 1769.

38. Breen, *Marketplace of Revolution,* 271–75.

39. PRO GEGE ET REGE, "To the PLANTERS"; PRO LIBERTATE ET LEGE, *SCG,* July 13, 1769.

40. MARGERY DISTAFF—CONDITIONALLY, *SCG,* October 5, 1769.

41. James Laurens to John Laurens, December 5, 1771, in *PHL,* 8:82.

42. The Husband of the Planter's Wife [William Tennent] to the Ladies of South Carolina, in William Tennent, "Writings of the Reverend William Tennent, 1740–1777," ed. Newton B. Jones, *SCHM* 61 (July 1960): 136–37 [this letter also appeared in *South Carolina Gazette and Country Journal,* August 2, 1774]. For more on tea ceremonies, see Rodris Roth, "Tea-Drinking in Eighteenth-Century America: Its Etiquette and Equipage," in *Material Life in America,* ed. St. George, 439–62.

43. Henry Laurens to John Laurens, June 8, 1775, in *PHL,* 10:168; Kierner, *Beyond the Household,* 80–81.

44. Henry Laurens, EXTRACTS from the Proceedings of the High Court of Vice-Admiralty . . . (1769), repr. in *PHL,* 6:370.

45. Egerton Leigh, *The Man Unmasked* (1769), repr. in *PHL,* 6:489, 528.

46. Henry Laurens, APPENDIX to the EXTRACTS from the Proceedings of the High Court of Vice-Admiralty in Charlestown, South-Carolina, &c. (1769), repr. in *PHL,* 7:57, 99–100. See also Daniel J. McDonough, *Christopher Gadsden and Henry Laurens: The Parallel Lives of Two American Patriots* (Sellinsgrove, Pa.: Susquehanna University Press, 2000), 23–25, 94–95. The two men later quarreled over domestic matters when Leigh impregnated his own sister-in-law—Leigh's wife and her sister were Laurens's nieces (McDonough, *Gadsden and Laurens,* 96–98).

47. Henry Laurens to James Laurens, April 15, 1774, in *PHL,* 9:408. This passage paraphrases 1 Kings 4:25, 2 Kings 18:31, Isa. 36:16, and Mic. 4:3–4; generations of Anglo-American gentlemen had echoed these idyllic sentiments, laying out their own gardens as an expression of the ideal landscape of peace, prosperity, retirement, comfort, virtue, and order. See Brown, "Eighteenth-Century Virginia Plantation Gardens," 125n1, 125–26, 154–55, 159–62.

48. Henry Laurens to John Laurens, January 22, 1775, in *PHL,* 10:40.

49. Charles Woodmason, "The Remonstrance," in *The Carolina Backcountry on the Eve of the Revolution: The Journal and Other Writings of Charles Woodmason, Anglican Itinerant,* ed. Richard J. Hooker (Chapel Hill: University of North Carolina Press, 1953), 221.

50. Ibid., 239.

51. Gadsden to Pearson, in "Two Letters," ed. Weir, 172.

52. Henry Laurens to John Laurens, January 22, 1775, 10:39–40.

53. These three joined the Camden-area merchant Joseph Kershaw and Prince Frederick County Cherokee fighter Col. Richard Richardson. See Jerome J. Nadelhaft, *The Disorders of War: The Revolution in South Carolina* (Orono: University of Maine at Orono Press, 1981), 20; John Wesley Brinsfield Jr., *Religion and Politics in Colonial South Carolina* (Charleston: Southern Historical Press, 1983), 92–103.

54. Jones, "Siege of Charleston," 71–72.

55. Morgan, *Slave Counterpoint,* 95–101; Berlin, *Many Thousands Gone,* 144–45, 152–57; McCusker and Menard, *Economy of British America,* 181–82.

56. Bernard L. Herman, "Slave and Servant Housing in Charleston, 1770–1820," *Historical Archaeology* 33 (1999): 88–101; Herman, "Embedded Landscapes," 45–48, 52–54; Gina Haney, "In Complete Order: Social Control and Architectural Organization in the Charleston Back Lot" (M.Arch. thesis, University of Virginia, 1996), 25–27; Dell Upton, "White and Black Landscapes in Eighteenth-Century Virginia," in *Material Life in America,* ed. St. George, 357–69.

57. Edward D. Seeber, ed. and trans., *On the Threshold of Liberty: Journal of a Frenchman's Tour of the American Colonies in 1777* (Bloomington, Ind., 1959), 14–15; quoted in Morgan, "Black Life in Eighteenth-Century Charleston," 187; Olwell, *Masters, Slaves, and Subjects,* 141–80.

58. Henry Laurens to James Laurens, June 7, 1775, in *PHL,* 10:163.

59. *SCG,* September 3, 1753; repr. in *PHL,* 1:242.

60. Henry Laurens to George Dick, June 1764, in *PHL,* 4:299.

61. See also "The STRANGER," *SCG,* September 17, 24, 1772.

62. Henry Laurens to John Laurens, August 14, 1776, in *PHL,* 11:223–25.

63. "The STRANGER," *SCG,* September 17, 24, 1772.

64. Christopher Gadsden to Samuel Adams, May 23, 1774, in *The Writings of Christopher Gadsden, 1746–1805,* ed. Richard Walsh (Columbia: University of South Carolina Press, 1966), 93.

65. See Olwell, *Masters, Slaves, and Subjects,* 187–219, 229–43; Robert A. Olwell, "'Domestick Enemies': Slavery and Political Independence in South Carolina, May 1775–March 1776," *Journal of Southern History* 55 (February 1989): 21–48; "The Presentments of the Grand Jurors for the District of Charles-Town," *SCG,* May 24, 1773.

66. Henry Laurens to John Laurens, August 20, 1775, in *PHL,* 10:321–23; Robert M. Weir, *Colonial South Carolina: A History* (Columbia: University of South Carolina Press, 1983), 200–203; Morgan, "Black Life in Eighteenth-Century Charleston," 213; Kinloch Bull Jr., *The Oligarchs in Colonial and Revolutionary Charleston: Lieutenant Governor William Bull II and His Family* (Columbia: University of South Carolina Press, 1991), 238–39.

67. Merrens, "Journal of Hazard," 190.

68. Henry Laurens to John Knight, December 24, 1764, in *PHL*, 4:556.

69. Jack P. Greene, "'Slavery or Independence': Some Reflections on the Relationship among Liberty, Black Bondage, and Equality in Revolutionary South Carolina," in Greene, *Imperatives, Behaviors and Identities*, 268–89; Christopher Gadsden to Samuel Adams, June 5, 1774, in *Writings of Gadsden*, ed. Walsh, 95.

70. C. P. Seabrook Wilkinson, ed., "A Declaration of Dependence: Robert Smith's 1775 Humiliation Sermon," *SCHM* 100 (July 1999): 13, 17–18.

71. Henry Laurens to James Laurens, April 15, 1774, in *PHL*, 9:408.

72. George W. Williams, *St. Michael's, Charleston, 1751–1951* (Columbia: University of South Carolina Press, 1951), 30–39; Robert M. Weir, "Who Shall Rule at Home: The American Revolution as a Crisis of Legitimacy for the Colonial Elite," in Weir, *"The Last of American Freemen": Studies in the Political Culture of the Colonial and Revolutionary South* (Macon, Ga.: Mercer University Press, 1986), 63–87.

73. Henry Laurens to Jonas Baird, August 16, 1776, in *PHL*, 11:246.

74. Henry Laurens to John Laurens, August 14, 1776, in *PHL*, 11:228.

75. Gadsden to Adams, May 23, 1774, in *Writings of Gadsden*, ed. Walsh, 94; William Henry Drayton, "A Letter from 'Freeman' of South Carolina to the Deputies of North America . . . ," in *Documentary History of the American Revolution*, ed. Robert W. Gibbes, 3 vols. (1853–57); repr., 3 vols. in 1 (New York: Kraus Reprint, 1971), 37; quoted in J. Russell Snapp, "William Henry Drayton: The Making of a Conservative Revolutionary," *Journal of Southern History* 57 (November 1991): 653. For Drayton, whose father had married the sixteen-year-old Rebecca Perry against his son's will, this familial analogy was particularly poignant.

76. Henry Laurens to Jonas Baird, August 16, 1776, in *PHL*, 11:247.

77. Henry Laurens to Robert Deans, February 6, 1775, in *PHL*, 10:53.

78. Henry Laurens to Jonas Baird, August 16, 1776, in *PHL*, 11:247.

79. See Eliza Wilkinson, *Letters of Eliza Wilkinson*, ed. Caroline Gilman (New York: Samuel Colman, 1839; repr., New York: Arno Press, 1969), 17; Mary Beth Norton, *Liberty's Daughters: The Revolutionary Experience of American Women, 1750–1800* (Ithaca, N.Y.: Cornell University Press, 1980); Linda K. Kerber, *Women of the Republic: Intellect and Ideology in Revolutionary America* (Chapel Hill: University of North Carolina Press, 1980); Kierner, *Beyond the Household;* Olwell, *Masters, Slaves, and Subjects*, 243–83; George Smith McCowen Jr., *The British Occupation of Charleston, 1780–82* (Columbia: University of South Carolina Press, 1972), chap. 5; Frey, *Water from the Rock*, 108–42.

80. Nadelhaft, *Disorders of War*, 4–5, 8–11; Weir, "Harmony," 473–501; Klein, *Unification of a Slave State*, 84–86; Glover, *All Our Relations*, 140–45.

81. Bull, *Oligarchs*, 241; Henry Laurens to John Laurens, June 18, 1775, in *PHL*, 10:184; Henry Laurens to John Laurens, June 23, 1775, in *PHL*, 10:194–95; Leila Sellers, *Charleston Business on the Eve of the American Revolution* (New York: Arno Press, 1970), 131, 144, 211–12; Rogers, *Charleston*, 30, 38, 69–70; Dixon, "Miles Brewton House"; Maurie D. McInnis, "'An Idea of Grandeur': Furnishing the Classical Interior in Charleston, 1815–1840," *Historical Archaeology* 33 (1999): 32–47; Quincy, "Journal," ed. Howe, 444; Smith and Smith, *Dwelling Houses of Charleston*, 93–103, 105–10.

Raphaelle Peale's *Still Life with Oranges*

Status, Ritual, and the Illusion of Mastery

Maurie D. McInnis

Raphaelle Peale's *Still Life with Oranges* (see figure 1) is a deceptively simple picture. As an early American example of this least valued genre of painting, Raphaelle's painting at first appears to be little more than an aesthetic exercise, a pleasing illusionistic rendering of fruit and wine that has embedded within it playful trompe l'oeil devices such as the table on which the composition rests and the punning trail of orange peel, playing on the artist's surname. Although Raphaelle is considerably less famous than his father or his other artist brothers, art historians have been intrigued with his still lifes, asking questions ranging from what they visualize about America's expanding democracy, to what they tell us about the artist's relationship to his domineering father, to what they disclose about his personal struggle with the vice of intemperance.[1] The unusual quality of Raphaelle's paintings have mostly led scholars to pursue the artist, but what about the patron(s)? What was appealing about these paintings to the individuals who supported the artist? For the most part we know little about Raphaelle's patrons. In the case of this painting, however, the painter inscribed the work to "John A. Alston Esq.r The Patron of Living American Artists." By exploring the connections between painter and patron, it is possible to speculate about just why the hauntingly evocative and illusionistic works may have appealed to Alston, a rice planter in the South Carolina lowcountry.

Still Life with Oranges is a seemingly innocent picture, a still-life composition that delights in the illusionistic rendering of color, surfaces, and textures. In the pearlware fruit-basket oranges, nuts, raisins, and grapes are artfully arranged. Lying diagonally across the top is a branch suggesting the freshness of the selection before us. Green grapes and raisins spill over in abundance, and in the foreground an orange has been cut in half, its trailing peel suggesting a dessert course just under way. At left a full glass of wine, as yet untasted, waits in the shadows, there but somehow just out of our easy reach. Laid on the table before us, tempting us with the juiciness of the freshly cut orange, is the final round, the summation of a sumptuous meal.

Painted around 1820 for John Ashe Alston, one of Charleston's most active art collectors in the first half of the nineteenth century, *Still Life with Oranges* offers provocative commentary on status and ritual in antebellum Charleston and a multiplicity of inferred associations regarding indulgence and excess. On one level this painting was itself a status symbol. It was but one work in a much larger collection that served in the early nineteenth century to distinguish Alston's place among other rice planters who were already secure in their elite status. Works of art were, after all, the ultimate status object, above all other luxury consumer items because assembling a painting collection required taste, knowledge, and connoisseurship. On another level this picture referred to such social rituals as dining, in which this and numerous consumer objects gained their cultural significance and, at the same time, acted to establish or solidify an owner's status. On yet another level, in light of Raphaelle's immoderate lifestyle and Charleston's hedonistic reputation, this painting of a dessert course comments on the vice of intemperance and is, therefore, closely linked with cultural criticisms leveled at the city during the antebellum era.

Raphaelle Peale was the eldest son of the artist Charles Willson Peale. He devoted most of his career to the painting of still lifes in an era when there was little support for the genre. Charles Willson constantly admonished his son to devote himself to "loftier" pursuits, such as painting portraits, but Raphaelle persisted, producing a body of still-life paintings that, ironically, receive considerably more attention from scholars today than the more artistically elevated works created by his siblings.[2] Raphaelle struggled professionally. After 1815 he continued to paint mostly still lifes, shunning more lucrative portrait commissions, even though he had few buyers and significant debts. His still-life paintings often sold for only fifteen dollars each, while his brother's portraits cost one hundred dollars, and yet he remained attached to still-life painting.[3]

The artist visited Charleston on at least three different occasions: in 1795–96 with his brother Rembrandt when they exhibited portraits of Revolutionary-era patriots; in 1804, when he was principally employed in making silhouettes from the physiognotrace, the invention to which he had exclusive American rights; and in 1823, when he told his father before his trip that he had one or two sitters already engaged and advertised for commissions for portraits in oil, miniatures, still lifes, and colored profiles.[4] Alston's acquaintance with and patronage of Raphaelle probably dates to one of these trips, likely the last, a period when he was particularly active as a collector. For example, in the three years that Samuel

FIG. 1. Raphaelle Peale (American, 1744–1825), *Still Life with Oranges*, c. 1818. Oil on panel, 18 5/8 × 22 × 15/16 in. Purchased with funds from the Florence Scott Libbey Bequest in memory of her father, Maurice A. Scott. Toledo Museum of Art, Toledo, Ohio

F. B. Morse was in Charleston (1818–21), Alston commissioned from him nineteen portraits. Only a few of these survive, including a small-scale portrait of Alston (see figure 2).[5] He owned at least four "fruit piece" paintings by Raphaelle, which may have made him one of the artist's most notable patrons and may well explain the inscription on the bottom of the painting, "Painted for the Collection of John A. Alston, The Patron of Living American Artists."[6]

Alston was a knowledgeable, demanding patron. In a letter to Morse, Alston asked the artist to marshal all the lessons he learned from the Old Masters. "May you exhibit . . . the learning of Michael Angelo," he implored, "the grace of Correggio, the colouring of Titian, but *above all* I invoke the spirit of 'the divine Raphael' to inspire you with the *attitude*."[7] Alston's collection was extensive. In addition to a large number of European paintings, he had works by American artists. In his letters to Morse he mentioned owning Thomas Sully's *Washington Crossing the Delaware* and Benjamin West's *Venus and Cupid* and hoping to acquire paintings by John Vanderlyn, Gilbert Stuart, Alvan Fisher, and Washington Allston, a distant cousin.[8]

Like Alston's "fruit piece[s]," Raphaelle's surviving still-life paintings focus almost entirely on the dessert course, with restrained but luscious and sensuous displays of fruits, nuts, cake, and wine. As the art historian Brandon Brame Fortune has argued, his decision to focus on dessert rather than flowers, game, or other established still-life subject matter is intriguing, given the artist's biography. Raphaelle suffered from gout, a painful inflammation of the toes and fingers that his father believed was caused by excessive drink and overindulgence in rich foods.[9] Writing at length to his son about the evils of excess, Charles Willson echoed many Anglo-American commentators who warned against overindulgence. "When we set down at the Table, perhaps loaded with a variety of unnecessary articles," the domineering father reproached his son, "two or three things is realy all that is needful . . . resolve that taste shall not be superior to reason."[10] Given his father's frequent admonitions, it is notable that Raphaelle's paintings focus on delights that speak more to "taste" than to the sobriety of "reason." There is a tension between the luxury that they represent and the moderation of their display. They thus become illusionistic essays in which Raphaelle crafts his illusion of mastery and control over the vices that tempted him.[11] However, the subject matter undeniably affirms a longing for indulgence and perhaps reveals not only Raphaelle's desires but also his affinity for Charleston.

FIG. 2. Samuel F. B. Morse, *John Ashe Alston*, c. 1820. Oil on canvas. Photograph by Rich Rhodes. Courtesy of the Historic Charleston Foundation, Charleston, South Carolina

The South Carolina lowcountry was well acquainted with extravagance. In George Roupell's 1768 drawing of *Mr. Peter Manigault and His Friends* (see figure 3) the men clearly enjoy the beverages and the fellowship following dinner, now stretching late into the evening. Of all the objects on display in Roupell's drawing, none is more evident than the decanters and glasses, as a vigorous round of toasting is under way. With Charleston's hospitable reputation firmly entrenched, when Raphaelle returned in 1823, he felt it necessary to assure his father that he would "be industrious, and prudent."[12] Such a quotidian existence was, however, difficult for the painter. Understanding his son only too well, Charles Willson wrote in response, "when you write to me say nothing about your drinking only water, as some that see your letters will not give credit to you. It is better to practice and not speak of it, as the result of good conduct will be more powerful than words to do you justice."[13] While none of the painter's letters from Charleston survive, it seems hard to imagine that he found it easy to maintain the prudent and temperate lifestyle his father recommended. Certainly Raphaelle's still lifes, with their emphasis on the dessert course and their frequently full glasses or decanters, speak of indulgences waiting to be enjoyed.

The display of fruits, nuts, and wine seen in the painting owned by Alston would have marked either the final course of an elaborate ball or, more likely given its moderate display, a dessert course following a customary all-male dinner party.[14] These gatherings, which began at three or four in the afternoon and continued until nine or ten in the evening, were an intricate component of the social fabric in Charleston, part of the social glue that held the city together. Elaborately conceived and executed with seeming grace, thanks to the highly specialized and well-trained domestic slave labor, such temporal entertainments were what gave the city's elite its social cohesion in a period of outside cultural scrutiny. Typically composed of either all men or the women of the family with invited male guests, they were part conviviality, part business. They were where society and politics were discussed, where perspectives were exchanged, where opinions were cemented.

For all the social exchange implied by the dessert course, art historians David C. Ward and Sidney Hart have noted how most of Raphaelle's still lifes seem to deny the social world. The paintings only gesture toward the way in which the objects within intersected with social intercourse. Most of Peale's still lifes are marked by their hermeticism.[15] The picture Raphaelle painted for Alston, however, is unusual in the number of markers that suggest human agency and consumption. The artist's inscription implies that he painted this work specifically for Alston, perhaps in gratitude for previous patronage. Alston's four still-life paintings by Raphaelle were joined by another three unidentified in the patron's partially surviving inventory. Except for one described as a game piece, all were fruit pieces. Some, if not all, of these paintings probably hung in the dining room

FIG. 3. George Roupell, *Mr. Peter Manigault and His Friends*, c. 1760. Drawing on paper. Courtesy of Winterthur Museum and Country Estate, Wilmington, Delaware

at Alston's rice plantation. A contemporary depiction of the Charleston dining room of the rice planter Arthur Middleton, drawn by his brother Thomas Middleton, (see figure 4) likely represents a similar interior where an extensive collection of pictures fills the walls of a room otherwise devoted to social pleasures. These consumer goods established the appropriate setting where erudite conversation and exuberant conviviality cemented class allegiances. Given the artist's familiarity with both his patron and Charleston, it seems that he painted a work likely to appeal to his benefactor. Both the trailing end of the orange peel and the glass of wine speak of a celebration under way and a promise of future pleasures.

Charleston's penchant for extravagant and frequent dinner parties was widely acknowledged by nineteenth-century visitors. The proper presentation of such events was considered so vital to establishing one's social rank that Charlestonian John Berkeley Grimball recorded the details of dinner parties he attended in order to guide him in the performance of his own, often including small sketches with careful illustrations of how the tables were arranged (see figure 5). When the eleven guests arrived for dinner at Charles Alston's in 1832, a great display was set before them on the table, a mark of status, wealth, and power.[16] Following

Fig. 4. Thomas Middleton, *Friends and Amateurs in Musick*, 1827. Wash drawing with touches of white on paper. Courtesy of the Gibbes Museum of Art / Carolina Art Association, Charleston, South Carolina

the expected custom, the dishes were presented to maximize effect. Turtle soup at the ends was joined by an abundant and symmetrical arrangement of the other meats—boiled mutton, boiled ham, turtle steak and fins, and oysters. A large plate of macaroni stood in the center, and vegetables were placed in the four corners. After the guests were offered soup, it was removed and a haunch of venison and a roast turkey were put in its stead where the host often performed the carving.[17]

When it was time for the next course, slaves would have removed the dishes and the top tablecloth and then set the table with the next course. It was quite common for the second course to be another meat and vegetable course. At Alston's party, however, the second course was a dessert course with ice cream in the center, bread pudding and pie at each end, and blanc mange and jelly in between. For the final course, yet another dessert course, the second tablecloth was removed, leaving only a bare mahogany table, and the table was set with bananas, apples, oranges, nuts, and other delicacies, whose vibrant colors reflected off the brilliantly polished surface.[18]

The primary goal of these events was the correct performative orchestration of abundant food, luxury objects, and personal comportment. Beginning in the eighteenth century and continuing into the nineteenth century, there was a great

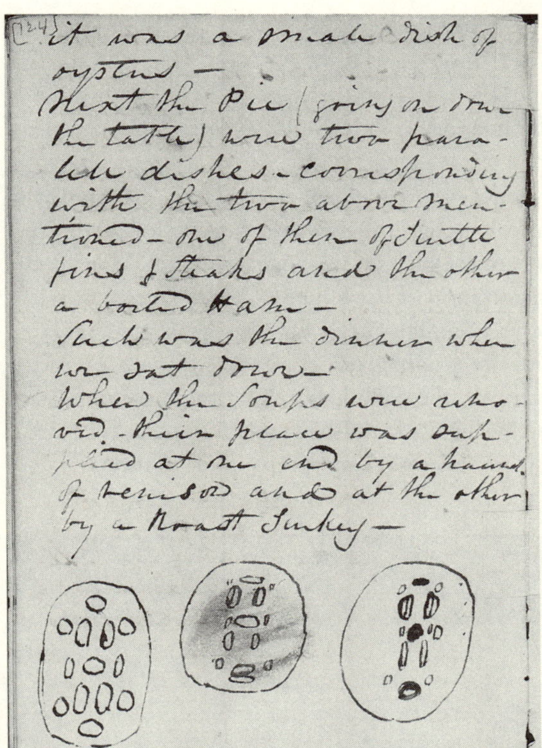
it was a small dish of
oysters —
Next the Pie (going on down
the table) were two para-
lell dishes – corresponding
with the two above men-
tioned – one of them of Turtle
fins & Steaks and the other
a boiled Ham —
Such was the dinner when
we sat down —
When the Soups were remo-
ved – their place was supplied at one end by a haunch
of venison and at the other
by a Roast Turkey —

FIG. 5. Excerpt from the diary of John Berkeley Grimball, showing a diagram for a dinner party at the home of Charles Alston, October 15, 1832. Courtesy of the Southern Historical Collection, Wilson Library, University of North Carolina at Chapel Hill

proliferation of specialized items for the ritual display of food. Elite Charlestonian inventories are replete with long lists of items intended to establish both lineage and refinement, such as the Chinese export porcelain ordered by Charles Izard Manigault when he was in Canton in 1820 (see figure 6). The 381-piece service in the Fitzhugh pattern with the Manigault crest emblazoned in the center was remarkable in its scope and size even in elite households.[19]

Most elite families had many sets of china. In 1834 Mary Motte Alston Pringle, who lived at the Miles Brewton house (see figure 7) and was John Ashe Alston's half sister, began an inventory book to keep track of her many sets of china and her extensive silver collection. Some she had inherited, such as a set of Dresden china, but others she purchased new, such as a complete set of French porcelain that included a dinner set and a dessert and fruit set, likely similar in style to these fruit coolers from the Pinckney family (see figure 8).[20] Grimball's diary entries about the dinner parties he attended often made note of the serving dishes, pointing to the importance of these items in the orchestration of a proper meal. At one dinner given by a "Gentleman of taste," he noted the "beautiful &

large China vase filled with flowers" between two "silver wine coolers" in the center of the table, surrounded by the "tureen and dishes of silver" that held the first course. At the conclusion of his description of the meal he noted with satisfaction, "Plate was in great profusion, and the China—white with a very deep border of green, richly gilt."[21]

While Charleston dinner parties were largely all-male affairs, the woman of the house played an important role because she was responsible for supervising the domestic slaves whose labors made such events possible. At the Miles Brewton house Mary tackled the organization of her household with an almost scientific precision, maintaining a series of notebooks to assist her vigilant surveillance over the household supplies and the activities of her slaves.[22] In preparing for a large dinner party or an evening ball, the cook held one of the most important jobs. While the work was done by the cook and his assistants, Mary (like other slave-owning women) supervised the planning and preparation of meals.

FIG. 6. Miles Brewton house, 27 King Street, 1769, northeast parlor on the first floor. This room was used as a dining room in the antebellum period. On the table is part of the armorial dinner service in the brown Fitzhugh pattern ordered by Charles Izard Manigault when he was in Canton in 1820. The bread basket in the center of the table was made by Hester Bateman, London, 1788–89, and is engraved with William Alston's crest. Photograph by Erik Kvalsvik. Courtesy of the owner

FIG. 7. Miles Brewton house (1769) and carriage house (1769), 27 King Street, with facade altered c. 1840s. Photograph by Louis I. Schwartz, 1940. Courtesy of Historic American Buildings Survey, Prints and Photographs Division, Library of Congress

FIG. 8. Paris porcelain fruit cooler, c. 1820, originally owned by the Pinckney family. Courtesy of the Collections of the Charleston Museum, Charleston, South Carolina

Preparing for an elaborate dinner party was, at a minimum, an all-day task. Chickens had to be killed and plucked; cows had to be butchered; fish had to be scaled. Much of this would have occurred just outside the kitchen in the area of the work yard and would have been either done or supervised by the cook. Inside the kitchen, where the cooking would have principally been done in the open fireplace, the work was dangerous, smoky, and hot, especially during the oppressively sultry summer months.[23]

In the house the butler and footmen were responsible for the preparations. Mack, the Pringles' butler, was responsible for supervising the four footmen—Yellow, Cornelius, Thomas, and Ishmael—as well as all those duties associated with dining and entertaining. In this role he was well versed in the rituals of refinement, such as how to set a table properly, how to prepare the evening tea, and how to care for the Pringles' extensive collection of silver, china, and glassware. Yellow's responsibilities included the grand second-floor drawing room and the care and cleaning of the silver, an extensive collection. Mary's 1840 list of silver in use at the house included some that was inherited from her parents, such as the dozens of spoons and forks all marked "WA." for her father, William Alston. It also included silver recently purchased, such as the flatware marked "WBP" for her husband, William Bull Pringle. A long list of serving items makes it evident that the Pringles were well equipped for large-scale and ostentatious entertaining.[24] Such extensive collections of silver allowed the Pringles to surround themselves with elegance and to demonstrate their refined taste at lavish entertainments (see figure 9). In preparation for a dinner party, Yellow polished the silver, Thomas washed the glasses, and Ishmael prepared the dining room. Here he would have been expected to "rub down the table until it reflected the glass and silver upon it when they removed the cloth for dessert."[25]

Yet when Mack, Yellow, Cornelius, Thomas, and Ishmael, after waiting the table during the meal and clearing dishes afterward, were finally allowed to return to the kitchen for their own meals, they faced a dramatically different material reality. Instead of the mahogany table in the dining room, they would probably have eaten off a pine table, where light would have been provided not with Corinthian-column silver candelabra but with tin candlesticks. Instead of the extensive selection of imported china, they would have eaten off of cheap crockery, such as the few "green edge" plates and dishes in the cook kitchen of Alexander Christie. These were probably shell-edged pearlware, by far the most common ceramic now found in archaeological contexts. Instead of the silver serving pieces, they likely served directly from the iron cooking pots.[26]

Significantly dinners in Charleston continued along the line of service *à la anglais,* where the dishes are all set out on the table and diners served themselves, even while much of the rest of the nation was adopting service *à la français.*[27] In the latter, dishes were placed on the sideboard and were constantly supplied and

FIG. 9. Henry Sargent (American, 1770–1845), *The Dinner Party*, about 1821. Oil on canvas, 61⅝ × 49¾ in. Gift of Mrs. Horatio Appleton Lamb in memory of Mr. and Mrs. Winthrop Sargent. Photograph ©2006, Museum of Fine Arts, Boston

passed by a larger retinue of servants. While other regions were increasing the presence of servants, in antebellum Charleston changes were made to household service to diminish the number and visibility of slaves in the public spaces of the house, significantly reducing the impression of the "cohort of black guards" noted by an eighteenth-century visitor and depicted in Roupell's drawing (see figure 3).[28] Slaves who waited on table had long been an important source for political information, and many Charleston slave owners consciously tried to limit their access to such information. They had reason to be wary. As a former slave recalled, "the arrangement had been made with Jake that as soon as possible after dinner, he was to run down and tell them any news he might gather during that meal." To deflect slave-owner suspicion, Jake feigned incompetence.

"Jake, as a possible gatherer of news!" the narrator continued, "Why that was absurd! He was spry enough about the house and dining-room, but otherwise he was as dense as a block of stone. At least, that was what his master would have said of him. This density on the part of the Negro was, in fact, a weapon of defense—the only one he had."[29] Such an act was another way in which Charleston's slaves subverted their masters' control. Despite the fewer number of slaves immediately present, whites still desired seemingly effortless, unobtrusive, and silent service—"their automatic noiseless perfection of training," as it was described by Mary Chesnut.[30] To accommodate this, many antebellum houses installed elaborate call-bell systems, allowing slave owners to summon slaves at all hours.

Charleston's slave owners were dependent on their slaves for the success of their social engagements. As such, these were perfect opportunities for enslaved cooks and footmen, through small acts of resistance, to jeopardize their slave owners' entertainments and thus challenge their owners' mastery over both their social world and their slave household. On February 6, 1861, Ann Morris Vanderhorst began to prepare for her party, but her slave Peter, the cook, whom she described as "my whole dependence," claimed he was sick and "could do nothing more." So instead Ann found herself fixing the chicken salad, paté, and sweetmeats; dusting the drawing room; carrying gilt plates and dishes up and down the stairs; and arranging the flowers. At the end she claimed that she was "perfectly exhausted." Her salvation was Ben, a man who belonged to a friend and was sent to assist. He took over preparing the other room that was to be set with the heavy supper as well as getting the ice; making the ice cream; preparing the oysters, wild turkey, and pheasant; and later sending up the tea and coffee.[31] Without his assistance, Ann would have been greatly embarrassed. Such frequent challenges to slave-owner authority demonstrated the centrality of slaves' labors as cultural signifiers of elite status.

Social gatherings were the backbone of a genteel life in nineteenth-century America. Yet those held in Charleston often had a flair distinct from those in other regions of the country. Both the visual and textual records reveal significant differences. Henry Sargent's 1821 painting of the Bostonian dinner party (see figure 9) and Thomas Middleton's 1827 drawing of the Charlestonian equivalent, *Friends and Amateurs in Musick* (see figure 4), reveal striking differences. In contrast to the decorum demonstrated in Sargent's late-afternoon gathering for dinner, Middleton's work unveiled a scene of debauched amusement. As the inscription on the back explained, that event was a rather typical summer afternoon gathering "[of] a number of gentlemen friends and Amateurs in musick, [who] frequently met at each others['] houses to beguile away the time in listening to the soothing strains of their own music." While the pursuit of musical accomplishment served as a cultural signifier of refinement, this was not a serious musical gathering. As Middleton commented, the gentleman on the far right is "at his old trick, instead of playing on his Clarinet he is endeavoring to excite our laughter by imitating the Bass upon my Guitar case." The greatest contributor to the relaxed and humorous atmosphere of the afternoon, and another signifier of class, is represented by the collection of decanters and glasses on the table. As Middleton clarified, "I have to apologize for the representation of certain glass, both black and white on the table, but it was in Vain to remonstrate. No. 6 said he must himself vanish if those respectable warmers of the blood (spirits and wine) were not produced, and even Nos. 4, 5, & 7 join'd in for the admission at all events for the Black holder of Sparkly."[32]

To Charlestonians, wine and champagne were considered important components of the cultured life of the upper class and their liberal dispensing the mark of a good host. In fact, such customs were important markers in the rituals of gentility. To outsiders, Charlestonians were often accused of a "great intemperance in drinking." As one visitor speculated, this was likely due to the poor quality of Charleston's drinking water, but he concluded that while most Charlestonians seemed accustomed to such levels of drink and in general remained within the bounds of "moderation," foreigners, "who have not been accustomed to such continual soaking are much more liable to suffer from its effects than those who are well seasoned."[33] Others were less generous in their assessments of Charlestonian immoderation, and justly so. According to elite Charlestonians, proper entertaining required a ready and prodigious supply of wine. Most kept plenty on hand. One representative inventory included more than 140 dozen bottles of Madeira, nine dozen bottles of French and German wines, and several demijohns of other liquors.[34] At one of the dinner parties recorded by Grimball, he noted the wines with each course: sauterne, Madeira, and champagne during dinner; porter with the cheeses; chambertin next; and Chateaux Margaux and Madeira with the dessert course.[35] The importance of wine is confirmed in Raphaelle's *Still Life with Oranges* and in Middleton's drawing, where there were not only bottles and decanters on the table but also a sideboard and a wooden case on the dining table available for the storage of more. As in other American cities, demarcations were clearly made between the drinking of the city's elites and that of the other classes.[36] Whereas elites drank wine mostly in the privacy of their homes, the "retailers of spirituous liquors" who served Charleston's nonelite whites were heavily regulated. The most distinct dividing line, however, was race. It was illegal to serve any alcoholic beverage to an African American, free or slave, and they were not even allowed to assemble in shops where drinks were sold.[37] Frequent commentary in the newspaper, however, makes it clear that such prohibitions were often circumvented.

Returning to the starting point of this essay, Raphaelle Peale's *Still Life with Oranges* is a surprisingly resonant cultural artifact, allowing for an exploration of cultural context and issues of status, social ritual, performance, and temperance, and it also provides a metaphorical examination of tension and contradiction. On one level the painting is about gentility and refinement: the cultural erudition of an early and important painting collector; the refinement of the ritual of dining that in Charleston occupied particularly rarefied heights; and the gentility of cultural and political interchange that solidified Charleston's social stance. Yet the painting also embodies many tensions and contrasts. Formally, the tensions are created by the strong competing diagonals established by the impossibly balanced branch running one way and the light source falling the other; the procession from plump grape, to shriveled raisin, to glass of wine; the straight lines of the basket against the circular forms of the fruit; and the looming empty space in the right rear. In terms of subject matter, the contradictions are suggested by the choice implied by the dessert course set before us: to indulge or be moderate; to choose vice or to choose virtue. It is in the contrasts and tensions that the painting's strongest metaphorical statement is made. More than anything else, Charleston's observers in the antebellum period saw the city as the seat of inexplicable contradictions, with the level of refinement and gentility and the level of indulgence and hospitality standing in stark contrast to the brutality of slavery. In the 1820s Adam Hodgson commented on the contradictions he perceived: "the mixture of gaiety and splendour with misery and degradation, is too incongrous."[38] This, ultimately, is the place where Raphaelle's still life leaves us, with the question posed by the city's cultural critics, such as the British abolitionist James Redpath, who inquired, "How is it . . . that this infernal institution exists, when surrounded by such much nobility of nature."[39]

Raphaelle's paintings were, most simply, illusions. That is, they were illusionistic renderings of space and materiality. At the same time, however, as Fortune has demonstrated, in their careful balance of moderation and indulgence they were illusions of mastery and control—in this case of Raphaelle's own struggle with intemperance. Yet perhaps it was this illusion that gave these paintings such cultural resonance in their lowcountry setting. As Grimball's diary suggests, Charleston's social rituals served several functions. They were intended to establish one's mastery over a complex array of performative orchestrations. In doing thus, they also confirmed one's mastery over one's enslaved household. Yet, clearly, such mastery was not as absolute as slave owners wished and assured the outside world that it was. Part of the performance was mastering the proper assemblage of consumer items and paintings that were intended to enhance their owners' statements of authority. A large painting collection confirmed mastery among other elites, but it was also one element that asserted mastery over their slaves. As such, paintings often became targets of subversion. When the slaves of

Charles Izard Manigault learned of their emancipation, one of their first acts was symbolically to overturn Manigault's authority by removing his paintings from his home. Most of the pictures they took to their own cabins; some they scattered on the lawn. One painting, a portrait of Manigault by Thomas Sully, was given by his driver to a freedwoman visiting from a distant plantation, who told her "that she must take this portrait home with her, to remember him!!" In such acts former lowcountry slaves asserted that the slave owners' sense of mastery was only an illusion.[40]

Notes

1. Nicolai Cikovsky Jr., "Democratic Illusions," in Cikovsky, Linda Bantel, and John Wilmerding, *Raphaelle Peale Still Lifes* (Washington, D.C.: National Gallery of Art, 1988), 31–72; Lillian B. Miller, "Father and Son: The Relationship of Charles Willson Peale and Raphaelle Peale," *American Art Journal* 25, nos. 1–2 (1993): 4–61; David C. Ward and Sidney Hart, "Subversion and Illusion in the Life and Art of Raphaelle Peale," *American Art* 8, nos. 3–4 (Summer/Fall 1994): 97–120; Brandon Brame Fortune, "A Delicate Balance: Raphaelle Peale's Still-Life Paintings and the Ideal of Temperance," in *The Peale Family: Creation of a Legacy, 1770–1870*, ed. Lillian B. Miller (New York: Abbeville Press, 1996); Alexander Nemerov, *The Body of Raphaelle Peale: Still Life and Selfhood, 1812–1824* (Berkeley: University of California Press, 2001).

2. For more on Charles Willson's admonitions to his son to paint portraits, see Fortune, "Delicate Balance," 138–41.

3. There is little known about Raphaelle's patronage. His father once mentioned the sum of fifteen dollars in one of his letters to Raphaelle. See Ward and Hart, "Subversion and Illusion," 108–10.

4. Anna Wells Rutledge, *Artists in the Life of Charleston through Colony and State from Restoration to Reconstruction* (1949; repr., Columbia: University of South Carolina Press, 1980), 214–15; Charles Willson Peale to Rubens Peale, November 23, 1823, Peale-Sellers Papers, *Collected Papers,* microfiche, series II-A, card 69, line E, space 11. For general biographic information, see Linda Bantel, "Raphaelle Peale in Philadelphia," in *Raphaelle Peale Still Lifes,* 15–30.

5. Paul Staiti, "John Ashe Alston: Patron of Samuel F. B. Morse," in *Art in the Lives of South Carolinians: Nineteenth-Century Chapters* (Charleston: Carolina Art Association, 1979), PSa-1–PSa-13. For more on Morse's years in Charleston, see also Paul Staiti, "Samuel F. B. Morse in Charleston, 1818–1821," *SCHM* 79 (January 1978): 87–112; Paul Staiti, *Samuel F. B. Morse* (Cambridge: Cambridge University Press, 1989), 46–70. For more on Alston's collection, see Maurie D. McInnis, "'Picture Mania': Collectors and Collections in Charleston," in McInnis et al., *In Pursuit of Refinement,* 39–53.

6. Unfortunately, the complete inventory of Alston's collection does not survive, but the first page, likely compiled for the auction of his estate, does. It lists four paintings by "Rembrandt Peale" as "fruit piece" and another two fruit pieces and a game piece with no artist's name listed. The misidentification of the paintings as being by Rembrandt Peale is probably due to Rembrandt's greater fame. See "List of Pictures &c belonging to the Estate of Col. J. A. Alston," Cheves-Middleton Papers, SCHS.

7. John Ashe Alston to Samuel F. B. Morse, Georgetown, S.C., January 30, 1819, Samuel F. B. Morse Papers, Library of Congress.

8. John Ashe Alston to Samuel F. B. Morse, Georgetown, S.C., March 15, 1820; December 28, 1818, Samuel F. B. Morse Papers, Library of Congress.

9. Fortune, "Delicate Balance," 135–38, 144.

10. Charles Willson Peale to Raphaelle Peale, July 4, 1820, quoted in Fortune, "Delicate Balance," 136.

11. Ibid.

12. Charles Willson Peale to Rubens Peale, Philadelphia, November 30, 1823, printed in "Texts and Documents," in Cikovsky, *Raphaelle Peale Still Lifes,* 112.

13. Charles Willson Peale to Raphaelle Peale, February 21, 1824, printed in "Texts and Documents," in Cikovsky, *Raphaelle Peale Still Lifes,* 115.

14. For more on such events in other cities, see Barbara G. Carson, *Ambitious Appetites: Dining, Behavior, and Patterns of Consumption in Federal Washington* (Washington, D.C.: American Institutes of Architects Press, 1990), 118–22, 124–30.

15. Ward and Hart, "Subversion and Illusion," 115.

16. Louise Conway Belden, *The Festive Tradition: Table Decoration and Desserts in America, 1650–1900* (New York: Norton, 1983), 5. Charles Alston was John Ashe Alston's half brother.

17. John Berkeley Grimball, diary, October 15, 1832, Southern Historical Collection, University of North Carolina, Chapel Hill. For more on nineteenth-century dining practices, see Belden, *Festive Tradition,* 19–27.

18. Ibid.

19. McInnis et al., *In Pursuit of Refinement,* 293.

20. Ibid., 294.

21. Grimball, diary, October 29, 1852.

22. Mary Motte Alston Pringle, Household Inventory book, 1834–65, Alston-Pringle-Frost Papers, SCHS.

23. Susan Strasser, *Never Done: A History of American Housework* (New York: Pantheon Books, 1982), 32–36.

24. Pringle, Household Inventory book.

25. In the eighteenth century the dining room at the Miles Brewton house, and other Charleston homes, was on the second floor. By the nineteenth century, in most Charleston households, the dining room had shifted to the first floor. See Alicia Hopton Middleton, *Life in Carolina and New England during the Nineteenth Century* (Bristol, R.I.: privately printed, 1929), 101.

26. Shell-edged pearl ware was generally the least expensive ceramic widely available in the early nineteenth century. For more, see Ivor Noël Hume, *A Guide to Artifacts of Colonial America* (New York: Alfred A. Knopf, 1970), 129–33; George L. Miller, "Classification and Economic Scaling of Nineteenth-Century Ceramics," *Historical Archaeology* 14 (1980): 1–40; Inventory of Alexander Christie, October 8, 1823, Charleston County Inventories, book F, 1819–24, 572–74. Most kitchen inventories list only the pots, pans, and others supplies used in cooking. A few mention pine tables. Christie's provides the most complete kitchen inventory in the antebellum period. From the contents, it appears to

include both the cook and the wash kitchen: "1 frying pan, 1 griddle, 1 stewing pan, 3 dutch ovens, 2 tea kettles, 1 grid iron, 1 tin callender, 2 chopping knives, 2 spits, 6 iron pots, pr tongs, hangers, 1 dripping pan, 3 tin pans, 1 sieve, 2 pine tables, 2 pewter basins, 2 coffee mills, 5 washing tubs, 5 cloathes horses, 6 irons, 1 copper kettle, 1 iron stand, 1 pair iron dogs, 1 coffee kettle, 1 iron stand, 1 pair iron dogs, 1 coffee bigging, tin tureen, 1 pepper mill, 3 tin candlesticks, cheese toaster, lanthern, bread toaster, 1 axe, 4 step ladders, 1 wheel barrow, corn mill, 2 market baskets, 6 piazza chairs, 8 doz. empty bottles, 6 stone jars, 1 spice box, brass seals & weights, 8 demijohns, 1 brass pestle & mortar, 1 green edge tureen, 2 doz. Green edge plates, 3 green edge dishes." The entire contents were valued at ten dollars. At the same time, the "1 Blue sett table china, 2 blue water pitches" used in the main house were valued at ten dollars.

27. Carson, *Ambitious Appetites,* 115–17.

28. Ford, "Diary," ed. Barnwell, 142, quoted in Bernard L. Herman, "Slave and Servant Housing in Charleston, 1770–1820," *Historical Archaeology* 33, no. 3 (1999): 97.

29. Sam Aleckson, *Before the War, and After the Union: An Autobiography* (Boston: Gold Mine Publishing Co., 1929), 78.

30. C. Vann Woodward, ed., *Mary Chesnut's Civil War* (New Haven, Conn., and London: Yale University Press, 1981), 488.

31. Ann Morris Vanderhorst, diary, February 6, 1861, Vanderhorst Papers, SCHS.

32. Quotations from Thomas Middleton, inscription on *Friends and Amateurs in Musick* (1827), Carolina Art Association, Gibbes Museum of Art, Charleston, S.C.

33. Peter Neilson, *Recollections of a Six Years' Residence in the United States of America* (Glasgow: David Robertson, 1830), 307.

34. Col. Thomas Pinckney, inventory, Thomas Pinckney estate papers, Charleston [S.C.] Library Society.

35. Grimball, diary, June 13, 1832.

36. See also Mark Edward Lender and James Kirby Martin, *Drinking in America: A History* (New York: Free Press, 1987); W. J. Rorabaugh, *The Alcoholic Republic: An American Tradition* (New York: Oxford University Press, 1979); Peter Thompson, "'The Friendly Glass': Drink and Gentility in Colonial Philadelphia," *Pennsylvania Magazine of History and Biography* 113, no. 4 (October 1989): 549–73.

37. George B. Eckhard, *A Digest of the Ordinances of the City Council of Charleston, from the Year 1783 to Oct. 1844* (Charleston, S.C.: Walker & Burke, 1844), 219–30.

38. Adam Hodgson, *Remarks during a Journey through North America in the Years 1819, 1820, and 1821 in a Series of Letters* (New York: Samuel Whiting, 1823), 124.

39. James Redpath, *The Roving Editor, or Talks with Slave in the Southern States,* ed. John R. McKivigan (1859; repr., University Park: Pennsylvania State University Press, 1996), 67.

40. For more on Manigault's collection, see McInnis, "Picture Mania," 48–49; Charles Izard Manigault, "Description of Paintings, at No. 6 Gibbs Street, Charleston, So.Ca. the property of Charles Manigault, 1867," Carolina Art Association, Gibbes Museum of Art, Charleston, S.C.

Urban Plantations in the National City

Slavery, Republican Ideology, and Conflict on the Streets of Early Washington

Laura Croghan Kamoie

Throughout its history the city of Washington has been characterized by conflict and contradictions. Is the city a local or national place? Is it northern or southern? Is it inhabited by longtime residents or only newcomers and transients? Is it just a company town or do *real* people live there? Should the inhabitants have voting rights and self-government or should Congress manage the district's affairs?[1] Many of these questions arose with Washington's founding in 1790. Then it was both everyone's city and also the city of just a few. It was a planned municipality, in fact the largest of its time, and yet remained largely undeveloped with vast expanses of wilderness until the late nineteenth century. The public buildings, particularly the Capitol and the White House, were built to express the values of the new republican government. In 1789 the architect Peter Charles L'Enfant poignantly described the rare opportunity that the United States possessed when he pointed out to George Washington that "No nation had ever before the opportunity offered them of deliberately deciding on the spot where their Capital City should be fixed" and what it should represent. These questions were passionately debated on the national stage.

Yet local architectural traditions, particularly the Georgian plantation home, were equally important in expressing the city's identity. Private residents, mostly from surrounding Virginia and Maryland, began purchasing lots in Washington City during the 1790s. These individuals brought with them specific ideas about what constituted appropriate homes, yards, and communities. Having been influenced by the material culture of plantation slavery, many early Washingtonians re-created the plantation landscape in the city, redefining it only to meet the restrictions and limitations imposed by Washington's street, square, and lot grid system. Interestingly, private residents determined the symbolic message that Washington's architecture would communicate without the debates that characterized the design and construction of the city's layout and public buildings. That message, largely shaped by the creation and re-creation of urban plantations, emphasized southern values, aspirations, and ideologies. Indeed, it was part of the regional culture of the Chesapeake and even of the whole South.

The material culture of early Washington embodied these tensions. On the one hand, the classical style of architecture in which the public buildings were constructed emphasized order, justice, equality, and virtue. On the other hand, the architecture of the urban plantations represented a world built on disparate power relationships and social and racial hierarchy. The high brick walls that separated the private sphere of these urban plantations from public access also reveal a world built on appearances and enforced social order. The one harkened back to classical Greece and Rome, the other to colonial aristocratic and even monarchical society. The fundamental ideological tensions inherent in the Constitution over the institution of slavery thus revealed themselves in the various architectural styles that came to predominate on Washington's streets. This ideological and architectural tension heightened as Washington became further engaged in supporting and maintaining the institution of slavery through the domestic slave trade. Consequently antislavery forces recognized the symbolic message that the material culture of the national city was sending and focused on the goal of destroying slavery and the slave trade there. In so doing, they hoped to resolve the ideological tension and thereby disarm the architectural one.

Buildings represent culture in its most persuasive physical form. The city of Washington, virtually built from scratch, presented the Founding Fathers with an opportunity to write the values of the new nation into the built environment.[2] Indeed, the idea that architecture contained messages that were obvious to its viewers and clearly expressed abstract concepts was an Enlightenment idea that the Founding Fathers accepted, spread, and used.[3] Washington's hand-picked architect, Peter Charles L'Enfant, created a design for the city that embodied the new Constitution and emphasized national unity and identity. As early as 1784 L'Enfant articulated his vision for the city; he desired "to give an idea of the greatness of the empire as well as to engrave in every mind that sense of respect that is due to a place which is the seat of supreme sovereignty."[4] "The idea of . . . greatness" that men such as Washington, Jefferson, and L'Enfant had in mind would enshrine American republicanism, at least as the Federalists interpreted it. Using monumental architectural scale, they wanted the city to reflect important ideas of the new government: national union, government of and by the people, equal access to all Americans, individual liberty, the good of the whole, virtue, justice, and freedom from tyranny. To physically express these ideas, the Founding Fathers looked to the past, particularly to the classical architecture of Rome

FIG. 1. Thomas Crawford, *Freedom Triumphant in War and Peace.* Courtesy of Library of Congress

and also Greece.[5] Through this lens Washington, Jefferson, and others conceived of the American capital as a new Rome, "'the mistress of the western world, the patroness of science and arts, the dispenser of freedom, justice and peace to unborn millions,' a new Byzantium, 'the seat of science, manufacturing and commerce for ages to come.'"[6]

In thinking about the future, values, and meaning of the new United States, officials' references to and associations with antiquity were common. During the constitutional debates, delegates frequently cited the Roman Republic as the best model for America's government. Additionally, Americans "shared the visual and written heritage of Greco-Roman antiquity," despite their social, religious, or political divisions. Thus, Americans understood what was being represented in the late eighteenth century when the figure of "Columbia" or "American Liberty" became a popular symbol for the new nation. Columbia was a female usually depicted wearing Roman robes and a liberty cap, or sometimes a feathered headdress, and carrying a shield, sword, pike, olive branch, or fasces (bundles of rods that were the insignia of Roman senators). She was a composite figure of at least two symbolic personifications: "America" and "Minerva." Europeans created America during the age of discovery as an allegorical figure of the New World; she was usually depicted as a Native American wearing traditional clothing and feathers and accompanied by native plants or animals. Minerva was the Roman version of the Greek warrior goddess Athena, both of whom represented strength and civic virtue. The historian Pamela Scott credits Benjamin Franklin with creating the new composite figure of Columbia, who represented American liberty through representative government.[7] The Statue of Freedom, placed atop the Capitol dome in 1863, embodies the symbolism of Columbia (see figure 1).

The public building that best expressed these ideas and values and demonstrated these classical influences was the Capitol of the United States. Scott argues that, "Like the Declaration of Independence, the Constitution, and the Bill of Rights, the Capitol was a tangible expression of the ideas of the Founding Fathers."[8] Washington and Jefferson wanted America's political ideals to be permanently enshrined in the city's public architecture, but particularly in the Capitol. They trusted that an emphasis on America's classical connections would offer additional authority, legitimacy, and the weight of history to the new nation's republican ideals. Physical permanence of these symbolically represented ideas, they hoped, would help guarantee their acceptance and endurance. Jefferson instructed L'Enfant, "whenever it is proposed to prepare plans for the Capitol, I should prefer the adoption of some one of the models of antiquity which have had the approbation of thousands of years." In full agreement, L'Enfant knew it was not enough to include such messages and that they also needed to be widely and easily visible (see figure 2). Therefore he planned a "Capitol . . . situated on a most beautiful eminence, commanding a complete view of every part of the city, and of a considerable part of the country around." Jenkin's Hill, the location L'Enfant chose for the Capitol, was the highest ridge in Washington and, he argued, "stand[s] as a pedestal waiting for a monument."[9]

Though others preceded him, the early nineteenth-century architect who most pursued these goals was English-born and European-trained Benjamin Henry Latrobe. Hired by Thomas Jefferson in 1803, Latrobe represented his neoclassical vision for the Capitol through its stone colonnades, vaults, porticoes, Rotunda, and dome. Jefferson, for one, was pleased with how his approach was turning out. In 1809 he congratulated Latrobe, saying, "I think the work when finished will be a durable and honorable memorial to our infant republic, and will bear favorable comparison with the remains of the same kind in the antient republics of Greece and Rome."[10] Latrobe strove to make the connection

FIG. 2. City of Washington, view beyond the navy yard. Courtesy of Library of Congress

obvious. As early as 1803 he began adding a variety of Greek architectural elements to both the interior and exterior of the building. He perfected the dome, first proposed for the building by the architect William Thornton (see figure 3), that was the Capitol's central element and was inspired by the Roman Pantheon (see figure 4). In 1811 he added a frieze of relief sculpture to the drum of the dome. His drawing for this frieze shows figures in classical dress and recalls the famous frieze at the Parthenon, which depicts the most famous annual civic event in Athens, the Panathenaic process. At the same time he proposed to add a propylaea (see figure 5), or classical gateway in the form of a temple, as the entrance to the Capitol. Though never built, this gateway would have been a six-columned Greek Doric portico resembling the Athenian Acropolis's Propylaea, through which one passes to enter the Parthenon, one of the temples in Athens dedicated to Athena, the founder of Athens and of civic strength and virtue.[11]

The President's House, or White House, as it became known probably during Jefferson's administration, also represented the nation's republican values and classical connections. Representing an important tension in the message, however, L'Enfant envisioned a sumptuous palace nearly five times the size of the house ultimately built that would be convenient to the Capitol and have "the agreeableness of a country seat."[12] Outraged by the seeming monarchical connections of L'Enfant's plan, Thomas Jefferson and others stepped in and revised the

FIG. 3. Elevation drawing of the Capitol. Courtesy of Library of Congress

FIG. 4. The Pantheon, Rome. Courtesy of Library of Congress

house to represent more republican values. Still, while none of the architects who submitted designs for it devised ordinary houses, the English country house and even the Georgian plantation house seemed the most significant influences.[13] Designed by the Irish-born and trained architect James Hoban, who had been practicing in Charleston when he won the design contest for the President's House and used an Irish country estate as inspiration, the house came to embody republican values perhaps more through its function than its size and architecture. During his presidency Jefferson did the most to ensure the house's republican character. As early as May 1801 he ordered the doors open every day so that citizens could have access to the state rooms, hoping to "modify the grandeur of

Fig. 5. Benjamin H. Latrobe, *West Elevation of the Capitol U.S. Washington.* Courtesy of Library of Congress

the Federalist palace," as the historian William Seale has described his intentions. Within months his plan seemed to have been working, as the White House became the most popular tourist attraction in the city, and citizens made regular use of their right to walk through.[14] Additionally, Latrobe, inspired as he was by ancient Greece, attempted to clarify the message of the material culture of the White House by introducing Grecian-style furniture to the Madisons and installing a variety of Greek ornamentation and architectural devices throughout the interior of the house.[15]

Unhappily for Latrobe and the city of Washington, war broke out between the United States and Britain in 1812. Appropriations for projects throughout the city slowed, and in August 1814 the British invaded the capital. In retaliation for the American destruction of York (now Toronto) and because of the building's symbolic importance, British troops headed first to destroy the Capitol. Before doing so, however, they toured the building and were awed by its dignified and noble interiors. After torching the Capitol, they moved next to the President's House (see figure 6), where they again wandered through like tourists and admired the building's splendor before shoving torches through the mansion's many windows. Over the course of two days British troops burned all the public buildings in Washington except the Patent Office, saved by the architect William Thornton when he persuaded a British commander that most of its contents were private property and that destroying irreplaceable inventions would be barbaric.[16]

With the city's major public buildings in ruin in 1814, Congress once again faced the question of the capital's location. Those who had opposed its Potomac

FIG. 6. View of the President's House, August 24, 1814. Courtesy of Library of Congress

location all along saw its destruction as an opportunity to generate support for the government's removal. The British, however, had unintentionally done the city a favor. When the British burned the city's public buildings, they admitted their understanding of the republican messages embedded in them and therefore ascribed to them a significance perhaps taken for granted by many Americans. Because the British saw the buildings as embodying America's ideals, politicians of various backgrounds rose to the city's defense in its role as the seat of government. North Carolina representative Joseph Pearson represented many politicians' positions when he posed the question, "Shall we go off in a panic from a place not even menaced by the enemy? To do so would be ten times more degrading than the result of the late incursion."[17] After Andrew Jackson's victory against the British at New Orleans, the Federalist Party was essentially destroyed because of its opposition to the war. Demonstrating how important the classical public buildings had become across party lines, the Republicans took the lead in meticulously reconstructing one of the foremost Federalist symbols, the White House. President Madison ordered that they must "not deviate from the models destroyed" in building the new Capitol and White House, and construction began by March 1815. America's victory over Britain not only increased its stature among the European powers but also boosted America's self-confidence and renewed its desire to articulate its values and identity.[18]

Construction activity on the public buildings permeated the city again during the late 1810s and 1820s. Latrobe gutted the Capitol building in August 1815 and left extensive plans for its rebuilding when he resigned in 1817. His plans included a "comprehensive iconographic scheme intended to be comprehensible to the common man that fused both European and American symbols and personifications." Figures of Liberty, Justice, History, and the Genius of the Constitution, along with figures representing the original thirteen states, were to impress upon the building's users and visitors its significance. In the 1820s later architects and artists contributed a series of frescoes and sculptures depicting America's history, starting with Columbus's exploration of the New World. Thirty-four years after it was first planned, the Capitol was completed in 1826. Presidents James Monroe and John Quincy Adams requested that the dome be enlarged so that the building would be visible from an even greater distance, which was finally accomplished during the 1860s.[19] At the White House, President Monroe actively participated in the designing and decorating of the restored building. During his administration, the White House not only represented the power and authority of the executive but also symbolized triumph, unity, and the country's emergence as an international power. Planned porticoes were added, and long-overdue landscaping was completed as well. By 1830 workers made the last addition to the building until the early twentieth century, when they built the monumental Greek-revival north portico. By then Americans were in the mood to honor and glorify their president again, the newly elected Andrew Jackson, and wanted to give him a respectable and polished residence (see figure 7). The historian William Seale quipped, "What had been a palace for John Quincy Adams was too shabby and run down for the hero-president to occupy."[20]

Fig. 7. Andrew Jackson's home as president. Courtesy of Library of Congress

The government also turned to reconstructing other important public buildings that the British had burned during the war. During the late 1790s the Treasury Department and War Office buildings, designed in a complementary Georgian style with some classical elements, were erected on either side of the White House. After the war, construction crews rebuilt Treasury and War and added State and Navy department buildings to the president's complex (by 1820) (see figure 8). New Treasury and Patent Office buildings were begun in the 1830s. City Hall was completed in 1820 and ultimately formed the center portion of the group of federal and district court buildings that became Judiciary Square (wings were completed in 1826 and 1849). The City Hall, Treasury, and Patent Office buildings represented some of the finest examples of Greek-revival architecture in Washington, with their Greek Ionic porticoes set above a terraced stepped base. The architect Robert Mills designed the new Treasury building (1836–71) (see figure 9) and drew his inspiration from the Erechtheum on the Acropolis. Together these other public buildings demonstrate the pervasiveness of the republican-classical connection in physically representing America's ideals and identity.[21]

At the same time that national leaders were debating the actual and symbolic significance of the government's location and architecture, another perhaps smaller but equally important flurry of construction activity was taking place in Washington. Planters, politicians, and entrepreneurs from Virginia and Maryland were building houses in the new city. Some came to pursue politics, others to participate in the social life of the city, others yet to speculate in any number

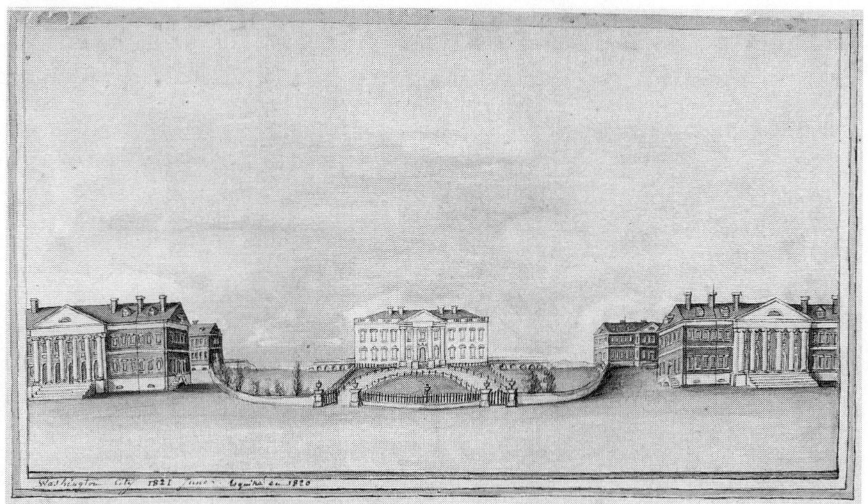

FIG. 8. Washington City, 1821. Courtesy of New York Public Library, Astor, Lenox and Tilden Foundations

Fig. 9. The United States Treasury Building. Courtesy of Library of Congress

Fig. 10. Home of Daniel Carroll of Duddington. Courtesy of Library of Congress

Fig. 11. Decatur House, front view. Courtesy of Library of Congress

Fig. 12. Decatur House, rear courtyard. Courtesy of Library of Congress

Fig. 13. Baroness Hyde de Neuville's drawing of "le coin de E Street Washington vis a vis notre Maison ete de 1817." Courtesy of New York Public Library, Astor, Lenox and Tilden Foundations

of business ventures. One similarity many of these new city residents shared was the type of home they built in Washington. Drawing on the architectural traditions of the regional plantation landscape, these newcomers built urban plantations based on the Georgian style of architecture and including an array of outbuildings. This was by no means a new occurrence in a southern city—the older cities of Alexandria, Fredericksburg, Richmond, Norfolk, and Charleston incorporated similar architectural styles because of their connections to the slave countryside.[22] The street plan that represented national union, the classical style and symbolism of the towering public buildings, and the city's intended function as "a temple erected to liberty" apparently had little influence on the local architecture of Washington or on older established Georgetown. Moreover, local domestic architecture remained conservative even several decades after the city's founding. The Greek-revival style of architecture became nationally popular during the 1830s and yet was not widely popular among the domestic architecture in Washington City.[23]

Washington's urban plantations condensed the plantation complex into smaller lots defined by the city's grid system. The houses were frequently situated immediately along the street, though because Washington was underdeveloped for so long, it was not unusual to find seemingly rural-style plantations within

FIG. 14. Commodore John Rodgers's house, 1831, called the "Club-House" in 1859. Courtesy of Library of Congress

FIG. 15. Octagon House. Courtesy of Library of Congress

the city, not to mention the district.[24] The outbuildings on an urban plantation were frequently fewer than those of their rural counterparts and included buildings such as stables, carriage houses, smokehouses, dairies, ice houses, laundries, and servants' quarters. In the countryside sheer space separated one plantation from the next and helped the master control the movement of his servants and slaves. In the city, as Bernard Herman has shown, masters had to construct a physical barrier to enforce social order and control and ensure privacy, and therefore avert public challenges to private authority, within the domestic realm. In Washington as in other southern cities, these physical barriers could take the form of tall wooden fences, brick walls, or even dependent structures that connected to the side of the main house to form an "L" that ran down the street. Herman has argued that these barriers served three functions: to remove the backyard from the view of the street; to regulate the movement of servants and slaves; and to force onlookers' attention to the orderly front of the house.[25]

A number of examples from the first decades of Washington's existence illustrate the arrangement and pervasiveness of this style of architecture. Duddington, located near Capitol Hill at F and Second streets, S.E., was the residence of Daniel Carroll of Duddington (see figure 10). Built in 1793 on four acres, it was enclosed by a six-foot-high brick wall and contained numerous outbuildings, including a spring house, a meat house, a stable, and servants' quarters. At the time Daniel Carroll was the largest landowner in the district and a member of the powerful Carroll family of Maryland.[26] Like Duddington, Tudor Place, completed in 1816 by William Thornton, was another rural-style urban plantation. Located in Georgetown, it included an array of large agricultural outbuildings, slave quarters, and gardens. Inspired as he was by neoclassical architecture, Thornton added classical elements such as a domed portico to the otherwise Georgian mansion.[27]

When space was more restricted, some builders chose to construct L-shaped buildings that maximized the building space on the lot and simultaneously blocked the interior yard from view. The Sewall-Belmont house on Capitol Hill, constructed in 1800, represents this arrangement. The Ruppert House at New York Avenue and Bladensburg Road, N.E., used a similar layout. The main house was constructed in 1775 and enlarged in 1800 by Jonathan Slater. In this case the dependency did not create an L but instead blocked an elongated lot from view of the fronting street. Behind the connected structures were long sheds for curing meat, a greenhouse, a kitchen, and a stable. A final example of this approach to domestic organization is the Decatur house, built one block from the White House in 1817 (see figures 11 and 12). The first residence on Lafayette Square, the Decatur house was built by Benjamin Henry Latrobe in an L-shape that created a large inner yard with multiple outbuildings and spaces for domestic functions in the dependency.[28]

A final approach employed by many residents was to construct a tall brick wall to separate the public world of the street from the private world of the yard. This approach was employed when the John Thomson Mason house was built in 1797, creating a huge yard running down Thirty-fourth Street that was completely blocked from view. A house in what would become the downtown sketched by the Baroness Hyde de Neuville in 1821 also used this arrangement (see figure 13). The baroness's sketch is interesting because it offers a glimpse into the private world of this house. Laundry is hanging out to dry from one of the windows, and African American servants carrying bundles pause to speak outside a gate leading through the brick wall (making one wonder how much control the wall really offered slave masters). The Rodgers house (see figure 14), built by Commodore John Rodgers in 1831 on the opposite side of Lafayette Square from the Decatur house, appears to have used a board fence to achieve a similar effect. Like the downtown house, this privacy fence also includes a door to the outside world that the planter may or may not have been able to control.[29]

A final example of the walled approach was the Octagon (see figure 15), built just south of the President's House between 1799 and 1801 by John Tayloe III of Virginia. Tayloe spent upward of thirty thousand dollars constructing his new city house, which was designed by William Thornton, the same architect who submitted the winning design for the Capitol. Outbuildings included two two-story buildings housing the laundry, servants' quarters, stables, and carriage house, a smokehouse, a chicken coop, a shed, and an ice house (see figures 16 and 17). He also dug a well to create a convenient water supply. A man with business and political ambitions, Tayloe hoped to pursue a number of advantageous arrangements from his new Washington home. To do so, he began residing in Washington half of each year, from approximately March to October.

Tayloe's new large house and his large family (which included thirteen surviving children) required an equally large staff of servants. Between 1802 and 1817, the years when the Tayloes conducted their seasonal moving, some of the Tayloes' many domestic slaves moved back and forth with them, disrupting both their family ties on the plantation and their new relationships in the city. In late 1817 Tayloe decided to relocate permanently to Washington City and leave his rural plantations in his adult sons' care. Following city law, he certified that the fifteen slaves he was bringing with him were for his personal use. These slaves ranged in age from twelve to sixty-three; the men worked as coachmen, hostlers, butlers, and cooks, and the women as spinners, laundresses, nurses, and domestic servants. Others of his slaves, such as the carpenters, joiners, masons, or jockeys, resided temporarily in the city to work on specific jobs. Tayloe's son William recalled the house and grounds as they related to the slaves: "A private Stairs run back of the Dining room from basement to the Upper floors. In the Basement is the House Keepers room, store rooms, Wine cellars, Servants Hall, Kitchen with

Fig. 16. Octagon House outbuildings. Courtesy of Library of Congress

Fig. 17. Drawing of the Octagon House and its outbuildings. National Historic Building Survey. Courtesy of the Octagon House, American Institute of Architects

a Well. . . . The Garden is inclosed with a Brick Wall. . . . In its rear is a two Story House for the Laundry & Servants rooms."[30]

As his construction of the city house and his later permanent move to Washington demonstrate, Tayloe was an enterprising man interested in pursuing new social and especially economic opportunities. Consequently he moved slaves around as he needed, even though he professed to wish to avoid disrupting slave families when possible. He also sold slaves when they were disruptive, not useful, or could provide ready money for some need or investment. In 1816 alone Tayloe made ten thousand dollars when he sold twenty-six slaves, mostly women and children, through the active domestic slave trade centered in the city.[31] Like many Washingtonians, Tayloe participated in the most controversial aspect of slavery in the nation's capital. The market had existed in the city since at least 1808 and by the 1830s became one of the largest slave depots in the country.

Increasingly a number of Americans saw the vigorous, accepted, and pervasive institution of slavery in the national capital as a major conflict with the national ideals the capital was supposed to represent. Indeed, it was such a fundamental conflict that it was embodied in writing in the Constitution, which refers to slavery in three places without calling it by name, and it was recorded permanently in the physical form of the city's architecture. Antislavery activists and abolitionist leaders became increasingly incensed by the contradiction and focused their energies on ending the institution, or at least the hated slave trade, where it was occurring under the shadow of the Capitol. Between the 1810s and 1830s abolitionists published a variety of broadsides, books, and pamphlets arguing that slavery was "utterly incompatible with the free institutions of Republican Government." In illustrations a favorite technique was to visually represent the contradiction by showing slave coffles manacled at the wrists and ankles either being marched by or seemingly pleading to the Capitol (see figures 18, 19, and 20). The Philadelphia physician and abolitionist Jesse Torrey described such a scene: on his way to a session of Congress, his "agreeable reverie was suddenly interrupted by a voice of a stammering boy, who, as he was coming into the house, from the street, exclaimed, 'There goes the Ge-Ge-orgy men with a drove o' niggers chained together two and two.'" He then saw "a light colored wagon a procession of men, women, and children resembling that of a funeral. . . . They were [slaves] bound together in pairs, some with ropes, and some with iron chains." Shocked, Torrey had "supposed that the instances of the streets of the city consecrated to freedom, being paraded with people led in captivity were rare," but he soon realized that in fact "they were quite frequent, that several hundred people, including not legal slaves only, but many kidnapped freemen and youth bound to service for a term of years, and unlawfully sold as slaves for life, are annually collected at Washington (as it were an emporium of slavery) for transportation to the slave regions."[32]

Not all of the protests originated from outsiders, as those sympathetic to slavery argued. In 1827 more than one thousand Washingtonians signed a petition for the gradual end to slavery, arguing that it "impairs prosperity and happiness of this District and casts the reproach of inconsistency upon the free institutions established among us." Abolitionist agitation on this issue not only led to Congress issuing a gag rule in 1836, meaning that any future petitions on the issue would be automatically tabled, but also was a major factor in the city of Alexandria's successful drive for retrocession in 1848. Alexandria's return to the state of Virginia altered the Founding Fathers' original design of the federal city and, perhaps more importantly, made possible the Compromise of 1850. Among other things, the Compromise of 1850 ended the slave trade in the District of Columbia. Conveniently located, Alexandria picked up Washington's mantle as the leading slave depot, however, giving residents in the area the same easy access to the trade they had before the compromise.[33]

While Washington strove to be a place of compromise and unity, the fundamental contradictions and conflicts that characterized it during the first half of the nineteenth century were more pervasive. Embodied permanently in ink in the Constitution and in brick and stone in the most dominant architectural forms of the city, Washington was a city unsuccessfully negotiating the line between slave and free and between North and South. The historian Howard Gillette called it the "City of Failed Intentions" for just this reason.[34] Indeed, even the public buildings, which represented the republican values of justice and liberty, had been built using slave labor. Washington and the three-man board that supervised the building of the city viewed slaves as the salvation of the city's

Fig. 18. Slave coffles. Courtesy of Library of Congress

A Slave-Coffle passing the Capitol.

FIG. 19. *A Slave-Coffle Passing the Capitol.* From William Cullen Bryant and Sydney Howard Gay, *A Popular History of the United States* (London: Sampson Low, Marston, Searle & Rivington, 1876)

budget. By 1797 the government had hired 125 slaves at fifty-five dollars a year (payable to their masters) to work in city construction. The tension between Washington's neoclassical and Georgian architectural forms is highlighted further by the fact that many of the men building the Georgian mansions in the city were slave owners who hired out their chattel to the government for public buildings construction.[35]

Moreover, it is hardly coincidental that Greek-revival architecture, with its associations to classical democracy, was widely popular beginning in the 1820s and 1830s and yet was not popular for domestic architecture in Washington. This is perhaps even more significant because, as Washington's free black population grew by the 1830s, threatened white Washingtonians attempted to crack down on their freedom by passing Washington's most comprehensive and restrictive black code.

Nor is it coincidental that, within approximately one year of each other, slavery was abolished in the district, and the Capitol was finally completed, with its new tall dome visible for miles around. It is a myth that, in the midst of the war

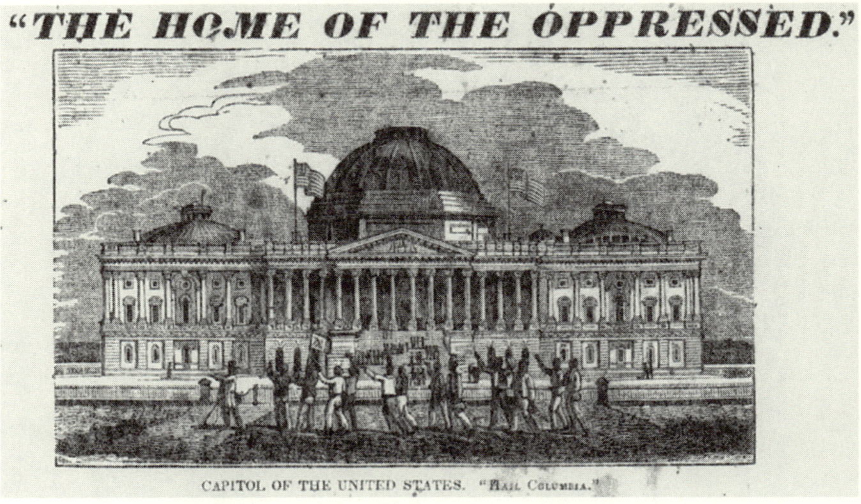

Fig. 20. An 1836 antislavery handbill. Courtesy of Library of Congress

to preserve the Union, Abraham Lincoln ensured that construction on the dome continued because he understood that the Capitol was the nation's most important symbol, both of its union and of its republican values. However, the myth embodies another truth, revealing the inherent tension in the United States between slavery and freedom. In addition, when the city implemented a major beautification and improvement program beginning in the 1870s, the architectural tradition most used, for public and commercial buildings, was beaux-arts, or classical-revival, which embodied the same values of Washington's earlier public architecture. This beautification was part of a broader Republican effort to reconstruct Washington after the Civil War.[36] However, the tension over race and freedom remained in postwar Washington. While much of the city's early domestic architecture, including many old urban plantations, met the wrecking ball to clear space for these new classical buildings, Washington's beautification campaign came at the expense of the city's brief civil rights agenda.[37] As a predominantly African American city without representation in Congress, Washington continues to deal with the tensions that originated during its founding.

Notes

1. Many scholars discuss these contradictions. See, for example, Howard Gillette, *Southern City, National Ambition: The Growth of Early Washington, D.C., 1800–1860* (Washington, D.C.: George Washington University Center for Washington Area Studies, 1996), iii–vi; Pamela Scott and Antoinette Lee, *Buildings of the District of Columbia* (New York: Oxford University Press, 1993), 13; James M. Banner Jr., "The Capital and the State:

Washington, D.C., and the Nature of American Government," in *A Republic for the Ages: The United States Capitol and the Political Culture of the Early Republic,* ed. Donald R. Kennon (Charlottesville: Published for the United States Capitol Historical Society by the University Press of Virginia, 1999), 80–81; Carl Abbott, *Political Terrain: Washington, D.C., from Tidewater Town to Global Metropolis* (Chapel Hill: University of North Carolina Press, 1999).

2. A brief background of the founding of the city is appropriate. Spurred by his desire to solidify national unity, President George Washington advocated and through a political compromise received permission to choose a location for a new federal city located midway between North and South and East and West. The Residence Act of 1790 called for a federal city near Georgetown, Maryland, to be carved out of lands donated by Maryland and Virginia. Within a year Washington hired the French-born Peter Charles L'Enfant to design the city as well as an array of public buildings. Because the city's opponents continued to work against removal of the Congress from Philadelphia, Washington was especially concerned that a house for the president and a hall for Congress be finished by the 1800 removal date to avoid the criticism that the city was unprepared to receive the government. Both buildings were completed to some degree in time for the government's arrival. See Pamela Scott, *Temple of Liberty: Building the Capitol for a New Nation* (New York: Oxford University Press, 1995), 3; Kenneth Bowling, *The Creation of Washington, D.C.* (Fairfax, Va.: George Mason University Press, 1993).

3. Scott, *Temple of Liberty,* 23; C. M. Harris, "Washington's Gamble, L'Enfant's Dream: Politics, Design, and the Founding of the National Capital," *William and Mary Quarterly,* 3d. ser., 56, no. 3 (July 1999): 529.

4. L'Enfant, as quoted in Gillette, ed., *Southern City,* iii.

5. Damie Stillman, "From the Ancient Roman Republic to the New American One: Architecture for a New Nation," in *Republic for the Ages,* ed. Kennon, 271–73; Len Travers, "'In the Greatest Solemn Dignity': The Capitol Cornerstone and Ceremony in the Early Republic," in *Republic for the Ages,* ed. Kennon, 160; Harris, "Washington's Gamble," 529; Scott, *Temple of Liberty,* passim.

6. *Daily Advertiser,* September 7–8, 1789, as quoted in Kenneth Bowling, "A Capital before a Capitol: Republican Visions," in *Republic for the Ages,* ed. Kennon, 45.

7. Scott, *Temple of Liberty,* 9–13, quote on 10; Stillman, "From the Ancient Roman Republic," 271–73. See also Pamela Scott, "Power, Civic Virtue, Wisdom, Liberty, and the Constitution: Early American Symbols and the United States Capitol," in *Republic for the Ages,* ed. Kennon, 402–47.

8. Scott, *Temple of Liberty,* vii.

9. Quote by Jefferson in Scott, *Temple of Liberty,* 23; first L'Enfant quote in ibid., 25; second L'Enfant quote in Scott and Lee, *Buildings,* 113.

10. Thomas Jefferson to Benjamin Henry Latrobe, October 10, 1809, as quoted in Stillman, "From the Ancient Roman Republic," 307–9.

11. Scott, *Temple of Liberty,* 44–59; Stillman, "From the Ancient Roman Republic," 305.

12. Scott and Lee, *Buildings,* 149.

13. William Seale, *The President's House: A History,* 2 vols. (Washington, D.C.: White House Historical Association, 1986), 1:4–30, 77.

14. Ibid., 1:89–93, 96 (quote). Hoban's inspiration for the White House was Leinster House (1745–51), the Dublin residence of the duke of Leinster; see Scott and Lee, *Buildings,* 152.

15. Scott and Lee, *Buildings,* 123–26.

16. Scott, *Temple of Liberty,* 6; Anthony Pitch, *The Burning of Washington: The British Invasion of 1814* (Annapolis, Md.: Naval Institute Press, 1998), 99–131.

17. Pitch, *Burning of Washington,* 223–24 (quotes).

18. Seale, *President's House,* 137–39 (quote); Pitch, *Burning of Washington,* 235.

19. Scott, *Temple of Liberty,* 6, 20, 62.

20. Seale, *President's House,* 146–56, 159, 163, 172 (quote).

21. Scott and Lee, *Buildings,* 19, 151, 154, 183.

22. Bernard Herman, "Southern City, National Ambition: Washington's Early Town Houses," in Gillette, ed., *Southern City,* 22–27. For a discussion of the origins and meaning of Georgian architecture, see Deetz, *In Small Things Forgotten,* 43, 92, 111–12.

23. Daniel D. Reiff, *Washington Architecture, 1791–1861: Problems in Development* (Washington, D.C.: U.S. Commission of Fine Arts, 1971), 49.

24. Until the 1870s there was a difference between the city of Washington and the District of Columbia. Washington City was the area planned by L'Enfant bounded by Boundary Street (now Florida Avenue) on the north and west and by the Anacostia River on the south. The District of Columbia was a ten-square-mile area that encompassed Washington City, as well as Georgetown, Alexandria, and Washington County (part of Maryland not in the city nor in Georgetown). After the collapse of the territorial government in 1874 (the city's brief experiment in self-governance), Congress consolidated these various jurisdictions under one governmental structure. The area outside of the city remained rural and agricultural until the 1870s and 1880s.

25. Herman, "Southern City, National Ambition," 27–28, 33.

26. James Goode, *Capital Losses: A Cultural History of Washington's Destroyed Buildings* (Washington, D.C.: Smithsonian Institution Press, 1979), 7. This was actually the second Duddington; the first one had been in the way of one of L'Enfant's proposed avenues, so he began tearing it down without giving notice or getting permission, creating one of the many headaches for George Washington that led to L'Enfant's dismissal.

27. Tudor Place History, http://tudorplace.org/about.html, accessed May 22, 2003.

28. Goode, *Capital Losses,* 9–10; Scott and Lee, *Buildings,* 160–61.

29. Scott and Lee, *Buildings,* 408 (Mason House); Goode, *Capital Losses,* 24–26 (Rodgers House); Herman "Southern City, National Ambition."

30. "An Account of the Octagon, Written by William Henry Tayloe, 1870," Tayloe Family Papers, Mss2T2117a1, Virginia Historical Society, Richmond. Much of this discussion of the Octagon is drawn from Laura Croghan Kamoie, "Between Two Worlds: Seasonal Moving and Slave Life in Rural Virginia and the City of Washington, 1799–1828" (paper presented at the American Historical Association Annual Meeting, Seattle, Wash., 1998). See also Laura Croghan Kamoie, *Irons in the Fire: The Business History of the Tayloe Family and Virginia Gentry, 1700–1860* (Charlottesville: University Press of Virginia, 2007), chaps. 4 and 5.

31. "Sale of Slaves Made by D.C. on a/c of Colo. John Tayloe to J. Bevan," Tayloe Family Papers, Virginia Historical Society, microfilmed as part of the series *Records of Ante-Bellum Southern Plantations,* series M, part 1: The Tayloe Family, reel 6, frames 115–16.

32. Mary Beth Corrigan, "Imaginary Cruelties? A History of the Slave Trade in Washington, D.C.," *Washington History* 13, no. 2 (2001): 4–27; Jesse Torrey, *A Portraiture of Domestic Slavery in the United States* (Philadelphia, 1817), 33–34, 41–42.

33. Corrigan, "Imaginary Cruelties?," 17–19, 25–27; Howard Gillette, *Between Justice and Beauty: Race, Planning, and the Failure of Urban Planning in Washington, D.C.* (Baltimore: Johns Hopkins University Press, 1995), 22–23, 31, 32 (quote).

34. Gillette, *Between Justice and Beauty,* chap. 1.

35. Bob Arnebeck, "Slaves at the Founding," 1–4, http://www.geocities.com/bobarnebeck/slaves.html, accessed January 21, 2003. Arnebeck also provides transcribed primary documents on slave hiring on that same site. See also "The 1790s," White House Historical Association, http://www.whitehousehistory.org/04_history/subs_timeline/c_africans/frame_c_1790.html, accessed June 3, 2002.

36. Kenneth Bowling, "From 'Federal Town' to 'National Capital': Ulysses S. Grant and the Reconstruction of Washington, D.C.," *Washington History* 14, no. 1 (2002), 9–25.

37. Gillette, *Between Justice and Beauty,* passim.

Contributors

Benjamin L. Carp is assistant professor of history at Tufts University, Medford, Massachusetts.

Emma Hart is lecturer in the school of history, University of St. Andrews, St. Andrews, Scotland.

Bernard L. Herman is Edward F. and Elizabeth Goodman Rosenberg Professor of Art History at the University of Delaware, Newark.

Paul E. Hoffman is Paul and Nancy W. Murrill Professor of History at Louisiana State University, Baton Rouge.

Laura Croghan Kamoie is assistant professor of history at the United States Naval Academy, Annapolis, Maryland.

Eric Klingelhofer is professor of history at Mercer University, Macon, Georgia.

Roger H. Leech is visiting professor of archaeology at the University of Southampton, England.

Carl R. Lounsbury is architectural historian at Colonial Williamsburg Foundation and lecturer in the department of history at the College of William and Mary, Williamsburg, Virginia.

Maurie D. McInnis is associate professor of American art and director of American Studies at the University of Virginia, Charlottesville.

Matthew Mulcahy is chair of the history department at Loyola College, Baltimore, Maryland.

R. C. Nash is senior lecturer in the department of history at the University of Manchester, England.

Louis P. Nelson is associate professor of architecture at the University of Virginia, Charlottesville.

Paula Stoner Reed is proprietor of Paula S. Reed and Associates, Inc., a cultural resource management company at Hagerstown, Maryland.

Jeffrey H. Richards is chair of the English department at Old Dominion University, Norfolk, Virginia.

David S. Shields is Mcclintock Professor of Southern Letters in the English department at the University of South Carolina, Columbia.

Natalie Zacek is lecturer in history and American studies at the University of Manchester, England.

Martha A. Zierden is curator of historical archaeology at the Charleston Museum, Charleston, South Carolina.

Index

aesthetics, 192–96
African Americans, 4–5, 7–8, 23, 33, 39–40, 45, 95, 156; in cities, 298–300, 345–48; Maroons, 108; pottery, 194–201, 273, 278–79; proportion to total population, 90–91; skilled artisans, 212–13
agriculture, 165–66
Alleynedale Hall, Speightstown, Barbados, 173, 181, 183
Alston, John A., 310–12, 314–17, 325n6
ambiguity, 192–93, 196
American Revolution, 9, 208, 285–309
Antigua, 35, 44, 116, 118
antislavery movement, 329. 345–47
archaeology (historical), 8–9, 159, 170–83, 194; Florida, 15–16, 20; Charleston, 267–84
architects, 58, 62, 67–69, 212–14
architecture, 29, 31–32, 58–73, 77–81; books, 58–59; classicism, 329–34, 347; French colonial, 148–53; Georginization, 81–82, 99n15, 109; Greek revival, 340, 347; impermanent, 31–33; plans 59–60, 62, 66, 70, 77–79, 147; slave dwellings, 39, 45, 47, 91, 146; Spanish, 33–34
artifacts, 270–82
"artisan mannerism," 175–77, 183–84
artisans, 206, 209–12, 301; builders, 58–59, 65, 68, 89, 207–9, 212–16; producers of consumer goods, 222–23
Atkins, Gov. John, 41
backcountry, 3, 287, 297, 301
Bacon's Castle, Virginia, 107, 176, 183
balls, 122, 314
barns, 133–34, 152
Beck, Monica, 158–59, 162, 166, 167n1
Bellumeau de la Vincendieres, Etienne, 127–29
Bermuda, 105–7
Bethesda Orphans' House, 64–65
Boazio, Baptista, 16, 19
Boston, Massachusetts, 106, 202, 302
brick construction, 32, 34, 37, 45–46, 61–62, 75, 77, 151, 159, 173, 175, 289; Flemish bond, 79; stucco, 88, 151
Bridenbaugh, Carl, 3–4
Brievengat House, Curaçao, 109–10
Bristol, England, 180, 182, 204
British empire, 5–6, 60, 103–5, 115–26, 302
Brown, David, 173, 183–184, 185n1
Bruton Parish Church, Williamsburg, Virginia, 74–75, 77–84
building, 8, 151–54; circular, 39–40; contracts, 213–15; cost, 84, 204; earth fast, 170–71; forms, 20, 29–30, 43, 74–79, 342; height, 36, 46; materials, 63, 68, 130, 133, 146, 267; ornamentation, 93, 151, 336; outbuildings, 342
Buildings of Charleston (Poston), 205
built environment, 30, 329–31
Bullman, John, 301

Campbell, Gov. Lord William, 303
Cann, Robert, 182–83
Cannon, Daniel, 205–6, 212, 214
Capitol, U.S., 332–33, 335–36
Caribbean, 1, 4–7, 22–23, 170–73
Carp, Benjamin L., 9, 285–309
carriages, 242–43, 248, 250, 252, 262n49
Carson, Cary, 172–73, 185n1, 233
Castillo de San Marcos, 15–16
Castle Island, Boston, Massachusetts, 106–7
castles, 102–14
Catesby, Mark, 46
ceramics, 22–24, 195, 230, 235, 268, 270–82, 320; Chinese export, 22, 24, 197, 276, 278–80, 317–18; colonoware, 194–201; creamware, 278; earthenware, 24, 197, 252, 270, 278; English, 270, 276, 278, 320; French, 271–73, 278, 280; majolica, 22, 24; Spanish, 271–72, 278, 280; stoneware, 271, 276, 280
Chappell, Ed, 173, 187n36
Charleston, South Carolina, 7–10, 44–45, 48, 64, 74, 84–89, 129, 157, 193–201, 202–20, 234, 248–50, 285–309, 311–12; archaeology, 267–84; Cannonborough, 205–6, 218n12; city grid plan, 84, 205; development of, 207–16; "Grand Modell," 202, 204; Hempstead, 205–7; occupations of landowners, 206; tenements, 209
Charleston Antebellum Architecture and Civic Destiny (Severens), 7
Charlestown, Nevis, 171–72
Chateau de Poincy, St. Kitts, 110–11
Chateau du Bois, St. Croix, 111–12
chimneys, 47, 146, 152
Christ Church, Lancaster County, Virginia, 82–83
Christ Church, Savannah, Georgia, 61–73
church buildings, 5, 41–42, 45, 61–71, 74–101, 116, 156, 213; Anglican 66–101; cruciform, 77–79, 89–92, 95, 100–101n35, 101n36; London, 86–87, 92; longitudinal, 77–79, 85–86; square, 159–61
Church of England, 74–101, 156; High Church, 92; Low Church, 79, 88
cities, 4, 7–8, 35–36, 47–49, 84–86; archaeology of, 267–84; development in, 208–16, 337–38; expansion, 202–3, 212, 337–38; land ownership in, 204–7, 328; mobs, 292, 300; plans, 84–85, 156, 161–63, 329; ugliness, 116. *See also* urbanism
Civil War, 3
class, 7, 91–93, 109, 184, 204, 232, 238, 242, 245–47, 255–56, 285–88, 290–96, 323
climate *See* environment
clothing, 9, 25, 93, 117–18, 232, 243, 250–57, 276, 280, 293; homespun, 252, 294
coins, 273–74
Coke, Thomas, 116
Colbeck Castle, Jamaica, 108–9
colonoware, 194–201, 273–74, 276, 278
comportment, 197
Confederacy, 3
Congregational Church, 155–69
Congress, U.S., 7, 328, 334–35, 348
Constitution, U.S., 329–30, 346
consumption, 4, 9, 118, 221–66, 276–80; consumer demand, 221–66; "consumer revolution," 221–22, 233–34; and nonimportation, 293–96; urbanity and, 244–65
courthouses, 5
Crane, Brian, 194
creolization, 4–6, 15–16, 19–24
Crèvecoeur, J. Hector St. John de, 8

Deagan, Kathleen, 19–20, 22–23, 26n3, 27n14, 28n25, 28n27, 283n14

Decatur House, Washington, D.C., 339, 342
Delaware, 2
District of Columbia, 2, 10
Dorchester, Massachusetts, 155–56
Dorchester, South Carolina, 6, 155–69
Drake, Sir Francis 16–17, 19–20
Drax Hall, Barbados, 32, 107
Dutch colonies in America, 6, 109–10, 170

earthquakes, 37–38, 42, 117
Elfe, Thomas, 210–11
Elliott, Barnard, 209–10, 219n21
English buildings, 58–63, 92; earth fast, 170–71
environment, 5, 29–57, 91–92, 216, 288
ethnicity, 6, 23, 134, 271
European building forms, 5, 30, 43, 58–63, 148
Exchange, Charleston, South Carolina, 203
exoticism, 196

Fairfax House, London, 176–77
family size, 225
farmers, 242–45
feudalism, 102
Flitcroft, Henry, 62, 70, 72n12
floor plans, 29, 147
Florida (La Florida), 4–5, 15–28
food, 9, 118, 194, 224, 232, 250–51, 253–54, 312–16, 322; grain production, 128–29, 137; wine and spirits, 250, 323
Ford, Timothy, 198
fortifications, 5, 15–16, 48, 61, 64, 102–14, 157
Forty Hall, Enfield, 178, 184
founders, 328–30
Francis I (France), 103
Franco-America, 6, 41, 110–13; refugees from, 138–39, 142–44, 146
Friends and Amateurs of Musick (Sargent), 322
frontier, 5
Froude, James Anthony, 115
furniture, 117, 210–11, 230, 242–43, 248, 263n55, 280, 288, 293

gables, 175–76
Gadsden, Christopher, 293–95, 299, 307n45
gardena, 112, 277, 289, 291–92, 302, 345
gentry, 117–19, 248, 286–303
Georgia, 2, 58–71, 156; trustees, 65–67, 69
German Americans, 135, 137
Girouard, Mark, 103
Glen, Gov. James, 45–46, 48, 293
Gothic revival, 103
Grady, Anne, 184, 185n1
Grimball, John Berkeley, 318–19, 324, 326n17
Guadeloupe (French), 33

Haiti, 6, 115, 127–29, 137
Hart, Emma, 8–9
Herman, Bernard, 4, 7–8, 191–201, 279, 342
Hermitage, l', Frederick County, Maryland, 128, 130–54
Hermitage House, Nevis, 171, 175
Heyward-Washington House, Charleston, South Carolina, 272–75, 282n6
hierarchy, 9–10, 92–94, 123, 238–40, 287–88, 329; segregation, 92–94
Hirsch, Edward, 191, 199
History of Jamaica (Long), 35
Hoffman, Paul, 4–5, 15–28
houses, 29, 103; castles, 108–10; diagrams of, 21–22; forms, 19–21, 34, 107, 108, 170, 183, 343; gentlemen's, 29, 107, 173–78, 203, 247, 293; manor, 103–5, 107; "single," 170, 197, 277; town, 213–14, 286, 289;

houses (*continued*)
urban country house, 289, 298, 328, 329, 340–44
household, 286–90, 300–3, 304n4
household goods, 224–57, 266–82, 293; amenities, 224, 228, 233–36, 239, 242; diversity, 228–29; necessities, 225, 236, 254; value of, 233–34, 240
hurricanes, 5, 29–57, 85, 90; houses, 39–41

identity, 1–11, 96, 119–20, 195–201, 287
imperialism, 102–3
indigenous materials, 6, 20, 30, 68–70, 183
Ireland, 103–5, 108
island culture, 5–6, 29–57, 117–24
Izard, Ralph, 213–14

Jamaica, 5, 31–33, 115–16; Spanish Town, 43, 74, 79–97
Jamestown, Virginia, 170, 183–84
Jefferson, Thomas, 330–34
Johnston, Rev. Gideon, 84–85, 88, 100n20
Jones, Inigo, 67
Joubert, Peter, 66–69

Kamoie, Laura Croghan, 10, 328–51
Kelso, William, 108
Kenilworth Castle, Warwickshire, 103
King, Julia, 173, 175, 185n1
Kingston, Jamaica, 49–50, 115–16
Klingelhofer, Eric, 5, 102–14

Laurens, Henry, 38, 46, 205–7, 285–309; household, 285–86
Labat, Jean-Baptiste, 121
Latrobe, Henry Benjamin, 331–32, 334, 342
leasehold, 204–5, 207–8
Leech, Roger H., 170–88
Leigh, Edgerton, 296
L'Enfant, Peter Charles, 328–29, 331
Leslie, Charles, 29, 33, 42, 44, 50
Lincoln, Abraham, 348
London, 84–87, 175–77, 184, 236–37, 248; land ownership in, 204
Long, Edward, 33, 35, 42–43, 53n14, 55n31, 101n38
Lord, Rev. Joseph, 155–56, 161, 168n11
Lounsbury, Carl R., 5, 45, 58–73, 97n1, 173
lowcountry, 1–2, 4, 7, 59, 155–69, 202–4
Lowe, Esther Winder Polk, 142–44
Lulworth Castle, Dorset, 103–4
lyricism, 192–93, 196

Madison, James, 335
Manigault, Charles Izard, 325, 327n40
Manigault, Peter, 213–14
manners, 247–48
maps, 16–18; St. Augustine, 16–18
Marshall, James, 137–38, 142
Marx, Karl, 3
Maryland, 2, 6, 127–54, 328–29; ethnic populations, 134–35
masonry construction, 20, 32, 37, 95, 115, 146, 151–53, 173, 183
Mattapany, Maryland, 173, 175
material culture studies, 1, 8, 164–65, 191–201, 233
Mauncy, Albert, 20
Maximus Poems (Olson), 191, 193
McInnis, Maurie D., 9, 310–27
merchants, 205–7, 238, 244–47, 249, 252, 254–55, 296
metropolitanism, 6–7, 19, 30, 43, 60, 85, 95–97, 116, 184–85, 236, 247–48, 293–95; in building practices, 202–3, 216
Middleton, Arthur, 315–16
Middleton, Thomas, 315–16, 322–23
Miles Brewton House, Charleston, South Carolina, 197, 212–13, 279, 303, 317–20

Mintz, Sidney, 119
Mr. Peter Manigault and His Friends (Roupell), 314–15
mobility, 6–7; forced (*see* Franco-American refugees)
Modyford, Gov. Thomas, 89–90
Mulcahy, Matthew, 5, 29–57
music, 322–23
Myths and Realities: Societies of the Colonial South (Bridenbaugh), 3

Nash, R. C., 9, 221–66
Native Americans, 15–16, 23; Carib, 30; Catawba, 195; pottery, 22–23, 194–201, 273, 276; women, 15, 23
natural history, 161–62
Nelson, Louis P., 5, 42, 74–101
New and Exact Account of Jamaica (Leslie), 29
New England, 155–59, 184; consumerism, 223–29, 233–34, 239, 244; township, 158
Newport Parish Church, Virginia, 77–78
Nicholas Abbey, Barbados, 32, 173, 183
Niemcewicz, Julian Ursyn, 135, 148, 151
North Carolina, 2–3

Octagon House, Washington, D.C., 341, 343–45
officials, 120–24, 175, 184, 238, 301
Ogelthorpe, James, 61–63, 65
Old Rectory, Dorset, 177
Oldendorp, C. G. A., 36, 53–54n18
Oldmixon, John, 34–35, 43
Olson, Charles, 191–93
Ordinance of Colonization (La Florida), 17

painting, 9, 310–27; portraits, 311–12
Parke, Daniel, 123
Peale, Charles Wilson, 311, 313–14
Peale, Raphaelle, 9, 310–27
Pepys, Samuel, 178–79
performance, 193, 324
piazza, 29, 292
Pickett, Dwayne, 173, 183–84
Pierce, Daniel, 184
Pinckney, Charles, 214–15, 279
planters, 207, 228, 238, 244
plantation economy, 234–36; dispersed location, 117, 121; French-Caribbean style, 130–54; houses, 32, 36, 45, 107–8, 112, 181–88; urban plantations, 289, 298, 328–29, 340
plaza, 16–18
poetics, 8, 191–201
politics, 5–6, 9, 48, 82–83, 88, 97, 119–26, 146, 287, 290–303; "country," 119; Stamp Act crisis, 290–96
poor people, 20, 61–62, 225–27, 238–39, 267
population, 36, 64, 88, 134–35, 222, 267, 281, 304n6; migration, 79, 84, 90, 155–56, 235; native born, 225–26; short-term residence of, 118
Port Royal, 49–50
post construction, 34, 39, 108, 171
Poston, Jonathan, 203, 205, 283n10
pottery. *See* ceramics
Poyas, James, 254–55, 265n81
Pratt, William, 162–63, 167
presence of place, 4, 7, 193
Pringle, Mary Mott Alston, 317–19
probate inventories, 222–24, 232, 234–38, 249–53
Program in the South Carolina Lowcountry and the Atlantic World, 1–2, 10n2
Projection, 192–93
Prown, Jules David, 164
public buildings, 5, 16–17, 32, 43, 45, 81, 116–17, 119, 202–3, 328, 330–32, 337
Puente, Elixia de la, 20
Puritans. *See* religion, dissenting

Raleigh, Sir Walter, 103
Rattray Green, Charleston, South Carolina, 289–90, 296
Reed, Paul Stoner, 127–54
regions, 1–11, 74–75; building patterns, 59, 74–77; consumption patterns in, 222–66; names of, 2
Regulators, 3, 9, 297
religion, 5–6, 74, 79, 300; denominational rivalry, 161; dissenting, 155–69; diversity, 92
renting, 209–10, 288
Reps, John, 10
Richards, Jeffrey, 6, 155–69
Robertson, Rev. Robert, 38–41, 44
Robinson, Billy, 198–99
Rochefort, Charles de, 33–34, 39
roofs, 20, 36, 39, 67, 159, 214; hipped, 133–34, 146
Roupell, George, 314–15
rural conditions, 4, 246–50, 297–98
Rutherford, George, 117
Rymer, James, 116

St. Augustine, Florida, 4–5, 15–28, 268, 271, 274
St. Catherine's Church, Spanish Town, 75–76, 89–97
St. Domingue. *See* Haiti
St. James Church, London, 86
St. Kitts (St. Christopher Island), 30–31, 40, 110–11, 116–17
St. Michael's Church, Charleston, South Carolina, 203, 213; rector John Bullman, 301
St. Nicholas Abbey, Barbados, 32, 173, 183
St. Paul's, London, 67
St. Philip's Church, Charleston, South Carolina, 75–76, 84–89, 300–301; Rev. Robert Smith, 300–301
Samuel Fortrey house, Kew, London, 176
Savannah, Georgia, 58–71
Seale, William, 334, 336
Second Meetinghouse (Old Ship), Hingham, Massachusetts, 159–60
Seloy, Cacique, 15
Senhouse, William, 36, 44, 47
sensus communis, 7
Severens, Kenneth, 7
Shammas, Carol, 235, 258n7, 260n17, 264n72
Shaw, Janet, 35, 44
Sherburne Castle, Dorset, 103
Shields, David, 1–11, 199
signature, 1–10, 267–84
silver, 117, 242–43, 250–52, 256, 293, 320
Simms, William Gilmore, 3
slaves, 121, 285, 298–300, 343, 345; house servants, 320–22; labor, 74–75, 143–44, 165–66, 298, 314, 345–48; liberation, 324–25, 347; mistreatment of, 144; revolt, 9, 90, 127–29, 142–43, 298–300, 302; trade, 329; value as property, 234–35, 241
Sloan, Hans, 32, 37–38
Smith, Capt. John, 30–31, 105–6
Smith, Rev. Robert, 300–301
society, 5, 88–95, 120, 242, 281–82, 303; patriarchal, 286–87; rituals of, 119–24, 242, 247–48, 314–16, 318–24
South, 2–4, 329
South Carolina, 3, 5–6, 30, 40–41, 44, 84–89; consumption in, 223, 234–66; exports, 235, 241; fluidity of city and country, 246–47; imports, 251–55, 271, 288
space, 7, 159; domestic, 195; interior, 7; urban, 8, 158, 191–201, 203–4
Spanish America, 6, 15–28, 102–3
Spencer-Pierce-Little House, Newburyport, Massachusetts, 182, 184
Spotswood, Gov. Alexander, 77–79
Stamp Act crisis, 290–96

status, 311; markers, 158, 255–56, 278, 287, 311–22
Stephens, Gov. William, 66–69, 73n43
Still Life with Oranges (Peale), 9, 310–27
Stoke Bishop House, Bristol, 178–80
style, 7; emulation of, 232–33; English, 43–45, 62, 233, 236; genteel, 117–19, 148, 175–82, 224, 236–37, 242, 246–48, 255–56, 267–69, 278, 286–87, 315–17; luxuriousness, 313–14; Palladian, 62, 67
Sully, Thomas, 312, 325
Summerson, John, 175–76
symbolic object, 122–24, 158, 255–56, 278, 287, 335

tableware, 230, 242, 249, 288, 320
Tayloe, John, III, 343–45
Taylor, John, 32–34, 50
taxation, 119, 133, 293
tea ware, 235–37, 249, 295
textiles, 250–57
Thistlewood, Thomas, 40–41
Thomas, Gov. George, 120–21
Thomas, Capt. John, 62–64, 68
Thornton, William, 334–35, 343
Tidewater, 1–3, 7, 59, 107–8; consumerism in, 223–32, 236–37, 239, 244, 257
Tidewater Towns (Reps), 10
Town House (Herman), 7
towns. *See* cities
trade, 6, 49, 88, 128–29, 162–65, 248–49; illicit, 271, 283n14
tradesmen, 238–39, 245
tradition, 193, 303
transatlantic conditions, 9, 88, 97; consumption, 221–22, 236, 248, 250–56, 268, 288; growth, 202–3, 216
trash, 197–98, 268, 279, 288
Turner, J. M. W., 183

Upton, Dell, 7, 11n4, 82, 99n9
urbanism, 6–11, 49–50, 119, 202, 232, 280–82; urbanity and, 244–50

vernacular architecture, 5–6, 133
Vesey, Denmark, 190
village, 158–59
Vincendieres, Etienne Bellumeau de la, 127–29
Vincendieres, Victoire de la, 129–30, 142–44
Virginia, 2–3, 5, 74–84, 89, 92, 107–8, 170–73, 175–76, 183–84, 328–29

walls, 34, 40, 43, 48–49, 75, 91, 183, 343; weatherboard, 69
War of Jenkins' Ear, 64
Washington, D.C., 328–51; destruction by British, 334–35
wealth, 8–9, 82, 88, 122, 223–27, 238–44, 248, 293–94, 296
Wesley, John, 64
West, Benjamin, 312
West Indies, 4–5, 29–57, 110, 115–26, 251; Barbados, 31, 36, 39, 41–42, 77, 84, 89–90, 107, 181–84; Cuba, 115; influence on South Carolina, 84–85; Jamaica, 31, 38–40, 42–43, 48, 77, 89–97, 108; Leeward Islands, 31, 35, 38, 44, 117, 120–121; Nevis, 31, 37, 39, 116; Monseratt, 37; Martinique, 41; St. Croix, 36, 110–11
White House, 332, 335–336
Whitefield, George, 64–65, 72n
Williamsburg, Virginia, 74–84
windows, 20–21, 38, 82, 91, 151, 214, 288; church 75–76, 79–80; sash, 69, 79, 82; shutters, 38–39
Winthrop, Gov. John, 106, 113n7
women, 122, 248, 294–96, 302
Wood, Joseph W., 158–59, 166
wood-frame construction, 37, 39, 64, 68, 77, 116–17, 289; log construction, 113, 146

Wormsley Manor, Georgia, 108
Wren, Christopher, 85–87

Zacek, Natalie, 5–6, 115–26, 257
Zierdan, Martha, 9, 197, 199, 267–84